Three Centuries of Scottish Posts

This book
is dedicated to
Jennifer and John

A.R.B.HALDANE D.LITT

Three Centuries of Scottish Posts

An Historical Survey to 1836

★

At the University Press
EDINBURGH

© A.R.B.Haldane 1971

EDINBURGH UNIVERSITY PRESS
22 George Square, Edinburgh
ISBN 0 85224 148 8

North America
Aldine Publishing Company
529 South Wabash Avenue, Chicago

Library of Congress
Catalog Card Number 70-106475

Printed in Great Britain by
R. & R. Clark Ltd, Edinburgh

Preface

★

Almost the whole of the research work undertaken in the preparation of this book has been done in Edinburgh and London. In Edinburgh the most important sources have consisted of manuscript letters, journals and family papers in the Scottish Record Office and the National Library of Scotland, to the staffs of which I am greatly indebted. In particular, I wish to thank most warmly Mr John Imrie, Keeper of the Records of Scotland. To Mr Imrie I am indebted in the first place for the suggestion that I should work on the history of Scotland's postal services, a task which over the past seven years has afforded me much interest and very great pleasure. Mr Imrie and Mr Ian D. Grant, an Assistant Keeper, read my manuscript and, besides directing me to additional material, devoted much time and labour to resolving problems which arose during preparation of the book for publication. For their help and kindness I am most grateful.

Research in London has been devoted almost entirely to the records at the Headquarters of the General Post Office. This body of material is by far the largest single source used in the preparation of the book. Indeed without it the book could certainly not have been written. The material in London is of very great bulk and complexity, and no-one attempting to make anything approaching full use of it could do so without expert guidance. In this I have been exceptionally fortunate in having the help of Mrs Jean Farrugia, the Departmental Record Officer at that time in charge of those records on which I have worked. Not only has Mrs Farrugia guided and advised me in my search for material, but she has read my manuscript and has made many helpful comments besides bringing to my notice further material for research. For her unfailing kindness and help over a long period I am very grateful.

I wish also to thank very warmly the following, some of whom have read my manuscript and have helped with comments and suggestions, while others have drawn my attention to valuable sources or other material: Mr J. J. Bonar, ws, Edinburgh, of whose wide knowledge and kindness I have frequently availed myself and who has generously allowed me to reproduce as illustrations certain items in his possession; Professor Howard Robinson, Oberlin, Ohio, whose own work on the British Post Office has proved most helpful; Mr James Mackay, Philatelic Department, British Museum, London; Mrs Gascoigne, Foulis Castle, Evanton, Ross-shire; Mr Eric Cregeen, School of Scottish Studies, Edinburgh; Mr P. W. Haberman, Junior, New York, who has kindly allowed me to reproduce part of a letter by Sir Walter Scott in his possession, and Mr G. D. Moir, Secretary of the Royal Scottish Geographical Society.

I owe a large debt of gratitude to Miss Winifred Ednie who has given up very many hours, most of them from her own spare time, in typing and re-typing parts of my manuscript, a task which has often entailed laborious deciphering of hardly legible handwriting.

I have again made full use of the great resources of the Signet Library, Edinburgh; and to the staff of that Library and also of Edinburgh Public Libraries I am much indebted.

I wish also to acknowledge generous grants from the Carnegie Trust for the Scottish Universities towards the cost of research and of reproduction of the maps.

As on previous occasions the help of my wife in the tedious work of comparing typescript, checking proofs and in very many other ways during the preparation of this book has been constant and invaluable.

A.R. B.H.

Foswell, Auchterarder, Perthshire, November, 1969

Contents

★

List of Illustrations

★

ACKNOWLEDGEMENTS
No. 1 of the illustrations is reproduced by courtesy of the
Trustees of the British Museum; the Map of 1813 is
reproduced by permission of the Controller of H.M.
Stationery Office; no. 17 of the illustrations is reproduced
by courtesy of the Trustees of the National Library of
Scotland, while nos. 5, 12, 14, 18, 19, 20 and 22 of the
illustrations and nos. 11 to XI inclusive of the Appendixes
are reproduced by courtesy of the Post Office.

Introduction

The story of the development of postal services in these Islands has, over the last hundred years, been the subject of numerous books. Very many of these, however, deal with special and often quite limited aspects of postal service. Comparatively few are devoted to the general history of Britain's Post Office, and of those few which do, nearly all deal primarily with the postal services established in England in Tudor and early Stuart times and later extended to cover the whole of the British Isles. So it has come about that the development of posts in Scotland as a distinctive part of the general postal service of Great Britain has been dealt with only incidentally and in no great detail. Except for one very short summary of the principal postal events up to the last years of the 18th century no history of posts in Scotland is in existence.

The only period during which postal development in Scotland was entirely independent of and uninfluenced by events in England was prior to the year 1603, at a time when such posts as existed were rudimentary in the extreme, used only for special purposes and in many cases for limited periods. Between 1603 and 1711 postal services in Scotland were under dual control, official communication between Scotland and England by the Edinburgh / Berwick road being maintained and largely controlled from London, while postal services in the rest of Scotland were controlled solely from Edinburgh. In 1711 the British Post Office came into existence and ultimate control of the postal service of the whole United Kingdom passed to London, the former Postmaster General for Scotland becoming Deputy Postmaster General. Since that time the chief administration of the Post Office has been exercised from Post Office Headquarters in London.

Such a situation, in which control of Scotland's postal affairs from Edinburgh gave way for a time to dual control from Edinburgh and London, and this in turn to ultimate control from London, necessarily presents problems for the historian. It may well be that the absence of a history devoted solely to the posts in Scotland has been due to the inherent difficulty of disentangling postal developments there from those in the United Kingdom as a whole, a difficulty which in the course of the last seven years the writer of this book has had ample occasion to appreciate.

None the less it was apparent that the absence of a postal history of Scotland left a serious gap which should if possible be filled. As an economic historian writing at the end of the 18th century has observed: 'The postage of a great trading nation's letters is undoubtedly in some degree a kind of political pulse whereby to judge of the increase or decrease of the public wealth or commerce.' Viewed in this light a postal history of Scotland may perhaps fairly be regarded as a contribution to the economic history of our country and as such the writing of a book of this kind seemed worth attempting. The pages which follow are the outcome of such an attempt.

The present work deals only with postal development affecting Scotland from the first emergence there of rudimentary posts in the 16th century up to the year 1836. To anyone making even a superficial study of the postal history of Great Britain it must be immediately apparent what great changes came with the reforms of the Post Office which took place in the years immediately after 1836 and particularly with the introduction in 1840 of uniform Penny Postage. Up till 1836 the Post Office in this country contained many of the same features, many of the same weaknesses and not a few of the same anomalies as had characterised it for more than a century. For almost forty years from 1797 control of the British Post Office was virtually in the hands of Francis Freeling, an able administrator whose loyalty and ability for long far outweighed a conservatism, a passion for economy and an eagerness for postal revenue which became more marked with the passing years. These characteristics, and the postal policy which resulted from them, had been accepted, while the French wars lasted, as justifiable if burdensome consequences of the wars; but in the third decade of last century agitation for a more liberal policy in postal as in other matters became increasingly clamant. After Freeling's death in 1836 the floodgates, already starting to yield to the weight of growing criticism, were burst wide open. From now on the Post Office ceased to be accepted by the public largely as an instrument of taxation and came to be looked on primarily as a public service. Within the next few years the Post Office underwent a series of changes from which it was to emerge fundamentally altered in character and soon also in size, and almost unrecognizable as the same department as that which had been largely the creation and wholly the pride of Francis Freeling.

The year 1836 was, then, in postal history a real landmark; the end of an epoch. But there were other considerations, too, which pointed in the same direction. During the whole of the forty years during which Francis Freeling held the post of Secretary to the Post Office there was maintained at the Post Office Headquarters in London a very complete series of records covering every aspect of postal activity and administration. These records comprise in the first place Minutes passing between the Secretary and the Postmaster General on a wide range of postal matters, and notes of the decisions reached. In addition there was preserved a great body of original papers in the form of correspondence, memoranda, reports and sketch maps emanating from landed proprietors, local postal officials, postal surveyors and many others, bearing directly on existing postal services and plans for their improvement. The period to which these records apply covers the introduction, growth, and final decline of the mail coach, development of posts in cities and towns, a wide extension of rural posts and finally the beginning of the great changes which came about for the Post Office by the application of steam to land and sea transport. These records accurately, vividly and almost completely reflect the state and extent of Post Office activity in progress during a period of prime importance in its history. This great body of material refers of course to the whole of the United Kingdom with the exception of Ireland, but no small part of it refers to Scotland, where problems of social economy, geography and to some extent personality greatly complicated the administration and development of postal services.

Of the records created after Freeling's death, few of the type of those for the keeping of which he had been so largely responsible have survived. Moreover, while the Post Office enormously extended in both size and scope, the records of its growth came to be predominantly statistical and factual in character. Subsequent records often lack the original documents of the type which have been preserved almost intact for Freeling's time and which, for the historian, constitute the unique value of the records up to 1836. To suggest that after Freeling's death and the introduction four years later of uniform Penny Postage the history of the Post Office ceases to have interest would of course be grossly unfair and quite untrue; but perhaps it would not be entirely untrue to suggest that from these dates the story of the Post Office, shorn of many of its old features, good and bad, and perhaps, too, of some of its more vivid personalities, lacks the colour of the records of former days.

If the records for a crucial part of the period before 1836 are almost unique in character and value, and if the reasons for ending the present work at that date may seem at least logical, it cannot be inferred that research even up to that date has been exhaustive, and no claim is made that this book can be regarded as a definitive history of the Scottish Post Office. Very great use has been made of local records, both manuscript and printed, in Edinburgh, and particularly of the rich store-house of records at the Post Office Headquarters in London. The broad picture which has emerged is, at least for much of the period, clear in outline and it may be felt that detail and colour is not altogether lacking; however, it is certain that with still further research much could be added. In particular, an extended study of local records and family papers would almost surely yield much of interest, if perhaps little to modify or alter the main outline. Here, as in so much other research work, there can hardly be an end. Completeness and finality is beyond the reach, and should perhaps be beyond the proper ambition, of any historical writer. However this may be, it is the hope of the author that within these limitations the present work may be of interest and perhaps of some value as a contribution to the social and economic history of Scotland.

A.R.B.H.

Principal Abbreviations used in Notes and References

★

A.P.S.	Acts of the Parliament of Scotland
H. R. & B.	Reports of the Commissioners for Highland Roads & Bridges 1804/60
N.L.S.	National Library of Scotland, Edinburgh
N.S.A.	The New Statistical Account of Scotland 1845
O.S.A.	The Statistical Account of Scotland 1791/99
Post 40 &c.	Post Office Records, St Martins-le-Grand, London
R.P.C.	Register of the Privy Council
S.R.O.	Scottish Record Office, Edinburgh

One

Scotland's First Posts

The story of the development of the Post in Scotland as a public service for the regular conveyance of letters begins little earlier than the opening years of the 17th century. In England, however, the rudiments of a postal service had then been in existence for nearly 100 years; and since much of what came at last to be the postal system of Scotland is linked, at least in its later development if not in its actual origin, with developments in England, the story of Scotland's posts must inevitably be prefaced by some account of events south of the Border.

The history of posts in every civilized country is, in its opening chapters, the history of travel and communication and can thus be traced back almost to the earliest days of man's emergence as a civilized being. In Europe, signs of well-developed systems of communication are to this day clearly to be seen in every country where Rome gained more than the most tenuous hold, and in England the roads made by the Romans were among the most prominent of the works which endured through the centuries which followed the final decay of their Empire. The quality of the work done by the Roman road-builders, and the careful routing of the roads they made, ensured their survival and continued use for centuries to come, and when in the course of the Norman and Plantagenet dynasties England developed as a united and firmly governed kingdom, the Roman roads formed the basis of the network of roads and tracks which gradually spread out to cover the land. Over these roads of medieval England passed a growing stream of travellers, a very few in cumbrous wagons or carts, many on horseback, but by far the greatest number on foot. By no means the least frequent traveller was the king himself. The Court moved constantly, its progress throughout the country dictated by the need for the king to show the length and strength of his arm, and no less by the more practical desire on his part to live at the expense of rich and powerful subjects for whom a royal visit was perhaps salutary and certainly costly. Nobles and rich merchants rode on horseback, sometimes accompanied by their womenfolk conveyed in heavy and elaborate wagons. For the rest, the roads, tracks and footpaths of medieval England gave passage to the wide miscellany of travellers which Chaucer knew. There were wandering musicians, travelling shoemakers and pedlars laden with petty wares, quack doctors, labourers who had broken their bonds and fugitive criminals lurking in byways and coppices, every man's hand against them. There were mendicant friars, too, professional pilgrims living by alms, and pardoners, 'strange nomads who sold to the common people the merits of the Saints in Paradise'; and many another.[1] With all their diversity of calling and character all these had one thing in common. They served as links between different and often widely separated sections of the community. They brought tidings of the outside world and transmitted by word of mouth, or much more rarely by letter, news or ideas for which they were the only vehicle. For the rich there was always the possibility of sending special messengers. These were regularly employed in the service of high Church dignitaries, of nobles and Sheriffs, of merchants and Bankers, for it was not, it seems, till Tudor times that the use of private messengers was jealously watched and closely restricted lest plots against the crown should be facilitated. As for the king himself, royal messengers were a regular and important part of the Court establishment, accompanying it everywhere in constant readiness to bear royal proclamations, summonses to parliament or other messages to every part of the land, or even to carry letters to the Papal Court and to the kings of France or

Scotland. In the 14th century these men were paid at the rate of 3d a day while on the road and had 4/8d a year to buy shoes. Their royal duties gave them special privileges and authority, and big fines were levied on any who attempted to stop them on the road.

Such was the system, if system it can be called, for transmission of news or letters in England up till the end of the 15th century; but as time passed the movements of the king and his Court became less frequent, the destination of royal despatches tended to become less diverse and the need for arrangements for regular transmission of these over fixed routes began to make itself apparent. As yet nothing approaching the establishment of regular routes with facilities for travel or transmission of messages had been achieved, but on certain roads such as those from London to Dover and Plymouth a growing traffic of officials on king's business or carrying royal despatches was on the move, while even on the road north to York and the Scottish border traffic was growing.

Early in the reign of Henry VIII one Brian Tuke was appointed as the first Master of the Posts of England, with responsibility for seeing that horses were available at fixed points for the use of those carrying the king's despatches. It had been the original intention that the provision of horses for the king's service should be the obligation of towns and villages on or near the chosen routes. Such an arrangement proved neither popular nor satisfactory, and though for many years to come those riding for the king retained the right of requisition, the responsibility for providing horses soon came to be placed primarily on the shoulders of those – generally innkeepers – who had been appointed by Tuke at fixed points for the purpose. These early postmasters received 12d a day to keep horses in readiness and 1d a mile for their use.

During the reign of Elizabeth no real development appears to have taken place in this system of posts, though from her time date the earliest known instructions to postmasters – that two horses were to be kept always in readiness and that those carrying royal despatches must be equipped with a bag for their conveyance and a horn to blow periodically on the road. By the end of the 16th century the payment for horses had risen to 2d a mile and the speed expected of messengers to 7 miles per hour in summer and 5 in winter. Public use of the posting system was

[3]

as yet hardly recognized, but at least it does not seem to have been entirely excluded. Almost certainly the first use by the public of the system of posts on the roads of England was purely for travelling. Few could write but many had to travel, and since royal messengers had preference in the use of horses it is probable that these were used by many who pretended to be on the king's service.

The first half of the 17th century saw the first real development of the posting system of England. Though the system of posts on the main routes continued to be primarily for the conveyance of royal messages, public use of it was coming to be increasingly recognized. The main routes on which men and horses were stationed were now those to Scotland, Ireland, Dover and Plymouth. Some places off but adjacent to these routes were now being served, while in Scotland itself James vi had set up a series of posting stations, of which more will appear. With a view to improving the service, increased payments had been fixed both for the use of horses and for the services of a guide to the next stage on the journey which the state of contemporary roads entailed, while the postmasters at each stage were given the monopoly of hiring out horses and the collection or delivery of letters. These monopolies were in-intended not only to improve the standard of the service but to concentrate all carriage of letters or messages into the hands and under the eye of the Crown.*

The first great step towards the transformation of the arrangements for royal despatches into a public letter service came in the reign of Charles I. By a proclamation dated from his Court at Bagshot in Surrey on 31 July 1635 the king appointed Thomas Witherings to be the first Postmaster General of England. Witherings had prepared a comprehensive plan to cover the country with a postal network. A central letter office was to be established in London through which all mail was to be routed, and fixed postal charges were to be levied. The lowest rate was fixed at 2d up to 80 miles and the charge for a letter to Scotland was to be 8d.[2] For many of the postal routes, how-

---

* In 1633 Charles I intimated to all His Majesty's Posts or their deputies from Bishopsgate to Berwick that Lord Traquair had power to sign all packets from the Court or from London to Scotland and from thence to the Court and ordered all despatch to be used in forwarding such packets. (*Historical Manuscripts Commission*, 9th Rep. App. p. 244. No. 31.)

ever, the real charge was increased by the fact that all letters went in theory at least if not always in practice through London. Hitherto the cost of maintaining horses and riders had been a heavy burden on the Crown. In 1609 the cost was estimated at £3,400 per annum,[3] but now the aim was to make the service self-supporting. Public use of it was for the first time welcomed, though even now emphasis continued to be placed on state security rather than on revenue. Witherings was to have a monopoly of letter-carrying and horse-hiring and was to be allowed to retain any surplus after paying the wages of postmasters, letter carriers and all other charges.

The Civil War prevented Witherings' plan from coming into full operation, and during a large part of the period of the Commonwealth postal affairs in England remained in a confused state, into the details of which it is happily, for the present purpose, unnecessary to enter. It is, however, clear that it was about this time that the posts of England first came to be 'farmed out' or let to tenants who paid fixed rents – rents which constituted the earliest revenue of the Post Office in the British Isles. By 1657 this rent had increased to £10,000 per annum and in that year Cromwell's second parliament passed an Act 'for settling the Postage of England, Scotland and Ireland', the first regulation by Act of Parliament for the establishment of a Post Office for the British Isles as a whole.[4]

The attempt which has been made in the earlier pages to trace the history of the postal service in England up to the Restoration has carried the story some way beyond the date when a similar service first made its appearance in Scotland. Before the Union of the Crowns in 1603 events south of the border made little real impact on the northern country. Until that date such primitive developments in communication as can be traced in Scotland owed their origin less to events in England than to a growing need for some means of transmitting news felt by, and common to, all the countries of Western Europe. It is indeed symptomatic of the relations between Scotland and England that until the end of the 16th century not a few of the earliest examples of transmission of news in either country had related to war or threat of war between the two. In 1481, when Edward IV was at war with Scotland, a system of posts was set up by the English king for the relaying of despatches to and from the North. In the spring of 1515, during a later invasion of Scotland, the English Envoy in Stirling wrote to Henry VIII acknowledging a letter brought north by relays of horsemen which the king had despatched to him from Greenwich considerably less than a week before, while the obvious importance attached to the Great North Road from London through York to Berwick during the reigns of both Henry VIII and Elizabeth is almost certainly to be attributed at least partly to English fears of troubles on the Border.

In Scotland itself one of the earliest references to a system of communication would seem to be a record of the Privy Council in the spring of 1547 when a further invasion, this time by sea, from the South threatened. In that year the Council recorded that a line of 'bailes' or beacons had been established between St Abb's Head in Berwickshire and Arthur's Seat at Edinburgh, with horses stationed at each to post from one to the next carrying the news,[5] so anticipating by forty years the July night of 1588 when beacons flaming from the South Coast to Cumberland told England that the Spaniards were in the Channel, till 'the red glare on Skiddaw roused the burghers of Carlisle'. These early posts, if posts they can be called, were all of the nature of temporary expedients adopted for special purposes and abandoned when the particular need had passed. The future growth of a regular system of communication in Scotland is more clearly foreshadowed by the appearance in the Accounts of the Lord High Treasurer of Scotland between 1531 and 1541 of frequent references to payments to messengers 'to pass at the post', 'to ryn the post', 'to pass at the post all Nycht', or in one case 'to ane boy to rynn to Newbottil with ane writing'.[6] Before the close of the 16th century John Finlayson 'callit the post' figures in the records of the town of Dumfries,[7] and Aberdeen had a common post in the person of Alexander Taylor for whom in September 1595 the town ordered a livery of blue cloth with the city's arms emblazoned on the left sleeve.

If the records of the 16th century in Scotland yield little of interest to the postal historian, the end of the century saw the country on the threshold of its real postal history. In England the reign of Elizabeth had seen no important development of the system of posts and postal routes which had been set up by Brian Tuke under Henry VIII, but despite the continuing fear of rebellion or unrest which had largely limited the use of posts to the state, some private letters had, as time passed, come to be grudgingly admitted. In particular the Great North Road through York to Berwick was attaining growing importance in the postal organization, and the growing frequency of references to Edinburgh as the northern terminus showed that times were changing. With this had come complaints of the slowness and inefficiency of the carriage of mail, private and royal alike, and some attempts to meet these. New regulations made in the latter part of the 16th century aimed at accelerating the post through a better supply of horses, while the time allowed at the stages where horses were changed was cut to a quarter of an hour. Despite all this, the actual improvement in the performance of men and horses on the road was small. On the North road from London to Berwick, with its 20 stages, the time officially allowed for the transport of the mail was 40 hours in summer and 60 in winter. In fact, this proved quite unrealistic, the time taken even for urgent messages being often as much as 8 days. The speed on the northern stages seems to have been particularly slow, that between Berwick and Alnwick sometimes taking 17 hours. Still, the mail, royal and private alike, was on the move and if regulations made in London showed little knowledge of practical difficulties, they and the complaints which gave rise to them at least showed that men's minds were turning more and more to the need for better communications.

While Scotland could as yet boast of little comparable development, it is certain that events south of the border were in the closing years of Elizabeth's reign being followed by watchful eyes in Edinburgh. On 5 April 1603 James VI of Scotland left Edinburgh for the South, and two days before he reached London the Privy Council of Scotland had taken the first step towards the establishment of an official postal system north of the border, a step which it can hardly be doubted, had been in contemplation for some time before the Union of the Crowns. An Order of 5 May of that year narrates the establishment by the king of postmasters at stated points between Edinburgh and Berwick, with certain allowances and fees for keeping horses for the service of the post by day and night 'as has been done in England for many years'.[8] The points chosen for the establishment of these posts were Cockburnspath,

Haddington and the foot of the Canongate. In those days Cockburnspath (or 'Colpranspath' as it was then more commonly called) was clearly a place of some importance, for the postmaster there had, besides his pay, a gift of fishings and certain Customs dues on goods coming by land or sea for the upkeep of the harbour at Cove,[9] and all through the 17th century, when the road from Edinburgh to Berwick was the chief and almost the sole artery of postal traffic in Scotland, Cockburnspath remained a key point.

The duties of these early postmasters on the road to Berwick were not light. On 17 May 1603 William Arnot, the postmaster at Cockburnspath, entered into an 'undertaking' in which his duties were narrated in some detail, and these were repeated in the undertakings of his colleagues John Kinloch at the Canongate and Alexander Simsoun at Haddington. The duties of the postmaster were to keep in his stables three 'habill and sufficient' post horses with 'furniture' suitable for the service of His Majesty's packets by day and night, 'ane fair peper buik' in which to enter month, day and hour when packets were delivered to him, 'twa baggis of ledder weil lynit' to carry the packets and two horns to sound on the road when other travellers were met with and at least three times in every mile. He further undertook to receive and send away at all times packets and letters of His Majesty and, within a quarter of an hour of receiving such packets or letters, to 'ryn' with them to the next post at a speed of 6 miles per hour from 1 April to 30 September and at 5 miles per hour during the rest of the year. Kinloch undertook also to provide good and sufficient horses to all who appeared to hold a commission from the king, and if no post horses of his own were available, to do his best to procure them. While these early postal arrangements were primarily for the conveyance of the King's Mail, the possibility that they might be used by members of the public would appear to be implicit in the further instruction that no other letters were to be delivered till those of the king had been handed over to the next post. John Naysmith, a merchant and burgess of Edinburgh, became surety for Kinloch's due performance of his duties on pain of £1,000(s) should he fail.[10]

Since this early postal service on the Berwick road was instituted and kept up primarily if not solely for the conveyance

of the King's Mails, the salaries of the postmasters were
initially paid from the Treasury. The salaries paid to these men
in the early days were low. In 1603 the postmasters at the foot
of the Canongate and at Haddington are reported to have received £150(s) and £250(s) respectively, while at Cockburnspath, which from the start appears to have been regarded
as a busy point on the postal route, the salary was £300(s).
Later in the century these rates of pay appear to have been increased to £600(s) at the Canongate and Haddington, and
£800(s) at Cockburnspath.[11] In addition the postmasters received a weekly payment for the keep of horses, while those
hiring horses from them were to be charged so much a mile. As
time passed the rate for horse-hiring increased. At the start of
the service the charge appears to have amounted to 2/-(s) a
mile for those riding with the king's commission and 2/6d(s)
for others, but before long, in the South at least, a charge of 3d
sterling a mile was allowed.

These early postmasters had a monopoly of hiring out
horses. Though this monopoly was jealously guarded it seems
doubtful whether it was in fact of much value. Those hiring
horses, whether for conveyance of royal despatches or for
private use, rode hard without much heed for the horses or their
owners. Claims for horses damaged or destroyed were common,
but such claims, and even the hiring charges, often went unpaid. Despite their annual salaries and such profits as they
could make from hiring, the records of the early years of the
17th century show that the postmasters fared but poorly, while
the standard of service at least to the general public suffered.
Soon complaints were reaching the Privy Council against all
three postmasters on the Berwick road that not enough horses
were being kept to serve the Royal Mail, that the 'peper
buiks' showing the times of receipt of packages were not being
regularly kept and that the postmasters were showing indis-
cretion in taking their neighbours' horses.[12] The last complaint
seems to have been directed against Kinloch, the Canongate postmaster who, presumably relying on the original instruction to obtain horses if none were readily available, had
requisitioned a horse belonging to one Andrew Abernethy at
Holyrood. The Privy Council rejected Kinloch's plea that his
office entitled him to take Abernethy's beast and ordered him
to restore it or pay £50(s)[13]. References to carelessness and

delay in transmission of letters and of loss of packages in transit
are frequent. In 1631 the postmaster at the Canongate was in
trouble for carelessness in the delivery of a postal packet. The
Privy Council ordered his punishment by the Postmaster
General, while the post-boy concerned was committed to the
Tolbooth.[14] In the same year an important packet received by
the postmaster at Haddington failed to reach the next post. On
enquiry it transpired that a 'foote boy' to whom the postmaster
had given it had lost it on the road where it was later found
and that the postmaster had made no enquiry as to its fate.[15]
If such complaints – and they are many – make it plain that
all was not well with the new service, they make it equally
clear that at least so far as the Royal Mail was concerned
high standards were expected and demanded of those operating it.

In 1616 Sir William Seton was appointed to supervise the
postal services in Scotland, and stricter regulations as to the
provision of horses for the service and better timekeeping
marked his advent.[16] Shortly after his appointment the Privy
Council, in the course of enquiry into complaints against the
three postmasters, ordered that in future their fees should be
paid to Seton so that he could pay them according to the
efficiency of their service. The enquiry showed that the postmasters were so hard pressed for money that their fees were
often assigned to their creditors, or arrested, so that they were
not able to keep horses.[17] Despite the agreement of the Privy
Council that the salaries of the postmasters should be paid
through Seton, these continued in fact to be paid with considerable regularity through the Treasurer and Comptroller,
but the postmasters remained in financial difficulties.* Some
twenty years later all three postmasters on the Edinburgh/
Berwick Road petitioned Parliament for payment of no less
than six years' arrears of salary, while they complained that
'our burthings be great in menteaneing of men and horss
daylie whither wee be imployed or not. . . .'[18] They pointed out
that in England the postmasters had relieved the Exchequer of
their fees in return for permission to retain postal dues on
letters carried by them and asked that they should either have

---

* Entries in the accounts of the Treasurer and Comptroller for the years
1603/25 show that during this period the payments for maintenance and operation of the postal services between Edinburgh and Berwick totalled £42,000 stg.

the same privilege or that their salary should be paid by the Master of the Letter Office in England.* How Parliament dealt with the matter of the arrears is not recorded, but so far as the future payment of salaries on the road between Edinburgh and Berwick is concerned, it seems probable that through whatever channels these postmasters' salaries reached them, during the 17th century this was seldom if ever by re-tention of postal revenue. It seems equally probable that those who held the appointments continued to find them of small profit. On 10 August 1669 James Arnot, the postmaster of Cockburnspath, acknowledged receipt of a payment from the Scottish Treasury of £10 sterling, 'in consideration of his low condition',[19] but by March 1671, despite any help or per-quisites he may have enjoyed, Arnot was again forced to petition the Council for arrears of salary to enable him to ward off creditors who were pressing him and threatening to poind (arrest) his horses.[20] In 1685 the widow of the postmaster at Haddington petitioned the Privy Council for help owing to the scarcity of horses and their poor condition through lack of fodder. The Council dealt with the matter by the expedient of ordering the magistrates of Haddington to aid the widow.[21]

While the postal records of the early part of the 17th century refer mainly to the establishment and upkeep of the postal route between Edinburgh and Berwick, there is evidence that plans were at this time also in hand to extend facilities for travellers either on private business or carrying messages over a wider area. As early as the summer of 1615 the Privy Council had before it a proposal by Sir William Seton to establish post horses 'as in France' at convenient places for the transmission of urgent despatches and 'for the ease of ordinary travellers', where those making journeys could be sure of getting adequate horses at fixed charges. Some such reform was clearly overdue, for at a meeting of the Convention of Royal Burghs at Stirling in July 1611 complaint had been made of the poor quality of horses and gear provided by 'the staiblers and sick as settis

---

* Despite the fact that the Scottish postmasters considered the arrangements in England for payment of salaries better than those in Scotland, there is evidence that in England too complaints about arrears were no less common. In 1628 the whole of the 99 Postmasters in England presented a collective petition in which they claimed to have been unpaid since 1621, the total sum due to them being over £22,000. (Howard Robinson, *The British Post Office*, 35.)

thair hors in heyr' within certain burghs, of difficulty and delay in getting horses, and of exorbitant charges.[22] Seton asked that he be given a yearly fee as Master of the Posts, and as has been seen this led in fact to his appointment in the following year to supervise the whole postal service in Scotland. His detailed proposals are contained in a long and complex document preserved in the Records of the Privy Council.[23] This system of 'posts' — using the word as denoting provision for travel rather than for postal service in the modern sense — was described as intended to cover the country to Berwick in the South-east, to Kelso, Morpeth and Alnwick in the South, and in the West to points described as 'the furthest western parts of common resort'. How far north the system was to extend was left open for consideration. It may well have extended at least across the Firth of Forth, for there is some evidence that in the event Burntisland and Kinghorn were specifically excluded from Seton's jurisdiction. Seton's application for appointment as Master of the Posts was granted, and subsequent references to his activities in relation to the Berwick Road make it clear that over this road at least he had general supervision. How far his more ambitious plans were adopted is not known. It is, however, on record that at a meeting of the Convention of Royal Burghs in Perth in July 1616 it was remitted to certain of the burghs 'to treitt ressone and conclud' with Seton as to his proposals.[24] Perhaps the burghs felt some doubts about a plan which threatened to place unwelcome burdens on them, for a few days later a further meeting of the Convention postponed the matter for further consideration, and in the meantime promised 'for furnising and serving of his Maiestie (quhen) it sall pleis God that he repair to this his Kingdome . . . to advertes the said Sir William be writt what nummer of horses everie burgh sall intertein for the said service, everie horse with fourtie punds money well furnisit with ryding graith for auchtein pennies ilk mylle. . . .'[25]

During nearly the whole of the first half of the 17th century the road to Berwick and the South remained the chief, and virtually the sole, artery of postal traffic in Scotland. In a letter from Lord Broghill to Secretary Thurloe in November 1655 reference is made to a conference over the postal arrangements in Scotland when it appears to have been agreed that except for the road between Edinburgh and Berwick no part of Scotland required or could support a horse post.[26] The strained relations between Cromwell and the Scots at this time is shown by the provision that no Scotsman should be a postmaster between Edinburgh and Berwick or act as post-rider on this route. Shortly before the middle of the century, however, there began to come into prominence another road which was for long to occupy an important place in the postal history of the British Isles. During the latter years of Elizabeth's reign military settlements and subsequent rebellions in Ireland had made vital the maintenance of communications across the Irish Sea. To Southern Ireland the route was by Bath and Bristol to Milford Haven, while despatches to Dublin went by Chester and Holyhead. For Northern Ireland, however, the crossing from Portpatrick to Donaghadee was much the shortest, and despite its remoteness and poor harbour Portpatrick came to be chosen as the point of departure for boats from the Scottish coast. For communications from England this involved a tedious ride from Carlisle along the north side of the Solway Firth ; but there was also the route south-west from Edinburgh, and from 1642, when a rising in Ireland led to the sending of forces from Scotland, this route came to be increasingly used first for military despatches but later for civilian communication. In that year the Privy Council commissioned the Earl of Cassillis, Lord Angus, the Justice Clerk and the Sheriff of Teviotdale 'to thinke upon the best wayes and meanes for establisheing of posts betwix Portpatrick and Carleil and to call before theme suche persons as knaw the bounds and to try the most commodious places quhair the post stages may be established and to report'. The points chosen included 'Blaickburne', Hamilton, Ayr, Girvan and Ballantrae on the road from Edinburgh to Portpatrick, and Annan, Dumfries, Gatehouse-of-Fleet and Glenluce on the road from Carlisle. The postmasters on the road from Edinburgh were to keep three horses in readiness and to have £50 sterling each, half of which was to be paid in advance. John McCaig, postmaster at Portpatrick, was to keep 'ane post bark'.[27]

If military requirements had led to the establishment of the route by Portpatrick, it seems clear that civilian use of it as a postal route was not sufficient to make it an economic proposition or attractive to those in charge of the postal stages, while it is hardly surprising that the maintenance of a packet boat proved a constant problem. In 1662 Parliament found it necessary to legislate anew for the establishment of posts between Scotland and Ireland, the route this time passing through Glasgow and Kilmarnock, while Robert Mein, then in charge of the Post Office in Edinburgh, was paid £200 sterling to establish the posts and build a boat.[28] By that time the first postal rates for Scotland had been fixed and Mein was allowed to charge and retain 6/–(s) for letters to Ireland. Mein was given a monopoly of letter carriage and almost immediately after his appointment complaints of infringements of the monopoly led to a Proclamation by the Privy Council prohibiting the carriage of letters between Scotland and Ireland without Public Warrant 'whereby seditious designs may be keipt on foot to the disturbance of the peace'.[29] Only five years later Portpatrick figures once more on the agenda, and in 1677 Parliament legislated anew for posts on the Glasgow–Kilmarnock route, the postmaster at Portpatrick to make the crossing to Donaghadee twice a week and to have £150 for the making of a boat, £100 to be paid at once and £50 as progress warranted;[30] but even this did not end the matter, for three years later John Grahame, then Postmaster General for Scotland, received from the Treasury £1,866.13.4d(s) for establishing horse posts between Edinburgh and Portpatrick.[31] One can only guess at the delays, annoyances and frustrations which lie behind these recurrent 17th-century references, but that these existed can hardly be doubted. That they continued in the 18th century will later appear, and well into the 19th century when the organization of the postal services of Scotland was far advanced, the route to Ireland by Portpatrick continued to present its own peculiar problems.

The extension of these early arrangements for the conveyance of Royal Mail or military despatches into a public service, was both in England and in Scotland long delayed and grudgingly conceded. The fear of civil unrest, facilitated and stimulated by growing ease of communication, was a very real one in Tudor, Stuart and Commonwealth times alike – a fear which gave way only slowly to the gradual conception of a postal service which would serve a useful rather than a dangerous purpose, while bringing in welcome revenue to the Crown. It was not till 1657 that the Act of Parliament passed under the Commonwealth made effective provision for postal rates. On the Restoration this enactment was confirmed with little change by Charles 11 in 1660, and these dates can be regarded as marking for England, at least, the birth of the Post Office as a public service. About this time further efforts were made to speed up the mail. Among the devices used was the earliest form of postmark on letters shewing the date of posting and 'labels' accompanying mail to be signed by each postmaster to show the hour of receipt and despatch. At this time and for very many years to come the great majority of letters were not pre-paid, but it was in the option of the sender to pay the postage; and, to ensure that the proper charges were made and unreasonable delay in transit detected, a list of distances between the various postal stages was prepared in 1669.[32] The rates fixed by the Act of 1657 had applied mainly to England except for a charge of 5d for letters from London to Edinburgh,[33] but five years later an Act of the Scots Parliament, which provided for the establishment of a post road to Portpatrick, fixed letter rates at 2d from Edinburgh to Glasgow, 3d to every other part of Scotland, and 6d for letters to Ireland.[34]

The emergence of postal rates and postal revenue brought with it a growing emphasis on the state's monopoly of letter carriage, and from this time on attempts on one side to guard, and on the other to attack, the monopoly play a prominent part in postal history. But almost from the first, when the idea of monopoly and royal or state control of posts was predominant, there was at least tacit if not express recognition of the continued existence of, and indeed the need for, some communication through unofficial channels. Not a few of the early postal enactments exclude from the monopoly the carriage of messages sent by nobles and persons of consequence and by merchants, or even private messages passing between persons of lower degree purely on their own personal affairs. In addition to private communication between individuals, public bodies and certain towns had for many years past employed their own messengers. In Scotland the meetings of the Convention of Royal Burghs, such as those which considered Sir William Seton's proposals in 1616, were almost certainly convened by the Convention's own messengers appointed for the purpose, and long before the middle of the 17th century the Convention was making quite regular payments to their 'common post'. Glasgow appointed its own Burgh post in 1630, 'ane trustie youthe' to hold the office for one year. By 1645 the position of burgh post in Glasgow seems to have become more permanent, for in December of that year Donald Clarke, their post, had a wage of 6/8d together with clothes and shoes. Shortly after the Restoration Glasgow's postal service was still further developed when a loan of £42 (s) to Johne Fergusone was recorded to enable him to buy 'ane sufficient hors' for the service of the town, while in the autumn of 1663 Fergusone was getting a salary of £3 a year and 1d (stg) for each letter taken by him – probably to Edinburgh.[35] In Dumfries the records show that the town had its posts before the end of the 16th century. This latter was a private service which continued at least till the last quarter of the 17th century. At that time regular annual payments were being made to one of the baillies 'for his incurragment to mantean ane post from this burgh to Edinburgh weekly', while the constant fear of pestilence at this time is shown by a payment in 1651 of 12/–(s) to William Carruthers 'for carring of ane letter to Saunt Moungo to try about the sikness'.[36] In 1680 the Burgh of Irvine was paying to Alexander Winton a yearly salary of £3 sterling to carry letters to and from Edinburgh with an additional fee of 2d for each letter sent by burgesses of the burgh and 4d for letters sent by others.[37] The Burgh Records of Edinburgh show a payment as early as the autumn of 1556 to John Sym for taking messages to St Andrews and to the Borders.[38] It seems, too, that Edinburgh had in the early 17th century some form of local communication service, for in the summer of 1632 James Ord of Leith was appointed postmaster at Leith to furnish horses between that port and Edinburgh for 2/–(s).[39] Edinburgh, and probably also Glasgow and Aberdeen, appear to have regarded themselves as having acquired at least by use and custom some rights to messenger services, for in 1633 the City of Edinburgh asked their Town Clerk to try to arrange with King Charles I to prevent Sir William Seton 'frome incrotching upone the liberties of this Burgh be ane pretendit gift of postmaistership . . .'.[40]

The provision by the City of Aberdeen of livery for their common post in 1595 would seem to show that by that date the city had a regular messenger in fairly constant employment, and from now on references to payments to the common post

appear with some regularity in the city's accounts. As early as
1612 the accounts contained the following entry: 'Item, to
Patrick Leslie for careing a letter to Auford [Alford] to know
if ther wes any infectione of the pest as was bruited 1 lb' [*sic*].
Whether these early messengers were purely local or for longer
journeys is not apparent, but shortly after the middle of the
17th century the transmission of letters between Aberdeen and
Edinburgh had become so frequent as to have acquired almost
the dignity of a postal service. In 1667 the magistrates of
Aberdeen represented to the Privy Council that 'several considerable persons' and even members of the College of Justice
had complained of miscarriage of letters and delay in transmission.[41] The city, it was reported, had 'long experience of the
prejudice sustained, not only by the said burgh of Aberdeen,
but by nobility and gentry and others of the North country by
the mis-carriage of missive letters and by the not timeous
delivery and receiving of the same'.[42] Patrick Grahame of
Inchbrakie in Perthshire had been appointed Postmaster
General for Scotland a few years earlier,* and following their
complaint before the Privy Council the magistrates of Aberdeen obtained from Grahame authority to set up a regular post
to Edinburgh. In January 1667 the magistrates entered into a
contract with John Wells for a regular postal service between
the cities twice a week. Wells was to be allowed to charge
those using this post at the rate of 2/–(s) for a single letter,
4/–(s) for a double letter and 5/–(s) an ounce for packets.[43]
Wells was also 'to export and delyver at Edenburghe' all
letters and papers for the magistrates of Aberdeen besides
supplying them regularly with weekly and daily papers and
newsletters from the South. For this service Wells was to have
£5 sterling per annum, to be free from any 'cess and taxatione'
on the profits,† and from all quartering of soldiers on him, a
burden which both in Scotland and England was at one time
apt to be placed on postmasters. He was to have a monopoly of
this postal traffic but, as was usual in early postal arrangements,
this was to be 'without prejudice to noblemen, gentlemen

---

* Patrick Grahame was a staunch supporter of Montrose, whose standard had
been raised at Inchbrakie in 1644. His appointment as Postmaster General at
the Restoration appears to have been a reward for his services. (Chambers, *Domestic Annals of Scotland*, vol. 11, 315/16.) † Surely this must be one of the earliest references to what later generations were to know as Schedule D Income Tax.

and all other persons to send post express about their own affairs' — an ill-defined qualification which was later to cause trouble on the Aberdeen route. The contract was to last for seven years and as it was to be registered in the Books of Council and Session it was clearly regarded as a document of some importance.[44] So Aberdeen acquired an early prominence in Scotland's postal system, and the establishment of a weekly post from Edinburgh to Inverness *via* Aberdeen in 1669 following a formal proclamation by the Privy Council still further strengthens the claim of that city to be considered a key point in early Scottish postal development.

John Wells did not live to see his contract out, for in 1672 the Privy Council had before it a petition by his widow that she be allowed to retain the Aberdeen postmastership for the two unexpired years of her late husband's contract.[45] Powerful interests ranged themselves on either side, but the widow prevailed and held the office till 1674 when, despite much opposition by Aberdeen, John Grahame, who had in that year succeeded his father as Postmaster General, took over the Aberdeen postal service as part of the growing postal system of Scotland.[46]

The incorporation of Aberdeen's postal arrangements into an official postal system does not appear to have had happy results, and complaints were frequent. In December 1677 the Provost and Council wrote to the Aberdeen Dean of Guild, then in Edinburgh on business, asking him to bring the postal grievances of Aberdeen before the Privy Council.

'Ye know', they wrote, 'what great prejudice the merchants and inhabitants of this burghe and countrie sustaines by the abusses off the Post Office heir in ther exorbitant pryces of forrayne letters and in miscarriage of letters and other papers entrusted to them and not duelie delivered. We remit the enlargement of the particulars to your selfe as being sufficientlie knowin thereunto. And we desyre ye by advyce endeavour the rectification thereof aither by ane sumonds before the privie counsell or by ane petitione as shall be fund most convenient.'[47]

A short time later the Aberdeen magistrates wrote to Alexander Bruce, one of their bailies, then in Edinburgh :

'We desyre ye meit with the Generall Post Master and remynd him that sieing this brughe dispensit with their gift from his father in his favors that we may have the news leters and gazet and our letters frie and that he promisit at his last being heir that we should meit with favor and courtesie in that affair. . . . Ye may appologise with Provost Mill that ye being in Edinburgh the town's letters came to your hands least it be thought ye came express for that affair.'[48]

Despite the complaints of Aberdeen, whether made to the Postmaster General or to the Privy Council, the postal arrangements of Aberdeen remained unsatisfactory, for on 8 December 1680 David Aidie, an Aberdeen baillie, wrote from Edinburgh to the Provost in Aberdeen complaining that letters were going astray.

'. . .ye say ye have receaved bot one from me since I cam heir. Pray inquire at the post if they miscarie not for I have written with everie post since I came heir besydes on Friday last with Mr Scrimger cuper. It is verie unfitt my letters should fall in other hands.'[49]

A few weeks later Aidie is again complaining of miscarriage of mail at both ends.

'I have been inquiring', he writes on New Year's Day 1681, 'at the Post Office heir but they keep no register of letters to quhom directed only in the generall so mannie att such and such reats. . . . Therefore cause Mr Farquhar's [the Aberdeen postmaster] books quhat letters came to his hands that day for if they snap up letters ther is no doing business and we must know what is become of that letter.'[50]

Alexander Farquhar, who is referred to in Aidie's letter of 1 January 1681, was one of the candidates for the postmastership of Aberdeen in opposition to Wells' widow in 1672, and two years later, when the Aberdeen post had come under the control of John Grahame the Postmaster General, Farquhar was in charge at the Aberdeen office. The correspondence between the Aberdeen magistrates and their colleagues in Edinburgh suggests, even then, some doubt as to Farquhar's integrity; but, however this may be, a few years later he became involved in a violent dispute with John Grahame. The trouble started when in the summer of 1686 a letter, written by one George Lesly in Banffshire and sent by way of Aberdeen to Edinburgh, was intercepted by the Letter Office in the capital. Lesly had claimed that his letter was in connection with official business and that in the circumstances it should not have been held up by postal officials in Edinburgh and that he was not liable for postal dues. '. . .for ye know', he had written to the Aberdeen postmaster, 'I am not wanting to pey postage of them. . . . I supose it may be found kitle to intercept ane Publict persons letters unles payment were refused.'[51] The interception of Lesley's letter led to the discovery that Farquhar, besides despatching the official bag with letters to Edinburgh, was conducting a regular unofficial post between the cities, the profits of which no doubt went to Farquhar himself. The matter came before the Privy Council. Summonses and counter-summonses, claims and counter-claims passed between the postmaster of Aberdeen and the Postmaster General, and before the matter ended a lurid light, not untouched with humour, had been cast on at least one branch of contemporary postal arrangements. Letter carriers between Edinburgh and Aberdeen told in evidence of conveying to Edinburgh private packets containing cloth, stockings and even 'Findhorn haddocks' with letters concealed in them. These packets were to be delivered to Farquhar's correspondents in Edinburgh or to his wife who was then in the city on private legal business. One such packet was alleged to have contained twenty letters for delivery to James Baird, an Edinburgh Writer.[52] Mrs Farquhar seems to have been a woman of spirit, for on learning that John Milne, a letter carrier, had allowed one of the unofficial packages to get into the hands of the Edinburgh Post Office she expressed the wish that the witness 'might break his neck if he did the lyke again'.[53]

These letters did not of course appear in the Register of Letters kept either in Aberdeen or Edinburgh and paid no official postage. In the light of this evidence John Grahame, who clearly believed in calling a spade a spade, claimed that Farquhar had

'keept a close and only trade of a private correspondence and practiced corrupted and debauched the foot posts for carrying on his villainous and detestable designes and wherein he at length arrived to that height of insolence and roguery that he was in use to send the third, halfe or sometimes the two parts of the letters delivered in to his office at Aberdeen to his private confidants at Edinburgh . . . intending by this means to enhance the greatest part of the revenue and emoluments of the office to himself to the defrauding of the complainer his master and to the public prejudice.'[54]

In reply Farquhar blamed the letter carriers and attacked their credibility as witnesses on the grounds that they were the servants of Grahame, the complainer. A few letters had, he admitted, been sent as private packages, but these often contained money not suitable for the Public Letter Office. In any event the loss, he claimed, was small and would be made good to Grahame through whose personal animosity, he averred, the action had been brought. Finally he explained that he was involved in a long law suit in Edinburgh, that owing to poverty he was unable to pay those acting for him, and that for this reason he did not want to put them to the additional expense of paying postage on letters. It would be hard, he added, if a poor man should be charged with postage on letters about his own private concerns.[55]

John Grahame, the Postmaster General, had at the outset not unnaturally dismissed Farquhar from the Aberdeen office, and on the evidence the Privy Council upheld his dismissal 'since if he [Farquhar] had continued in that intercourse begune he might not only have prejudged privat interests but even the publict concerne by such a clandestine convoyance'.[56] Farquhar, the Council observed, had carried his 'malversations' to such a pitch that 'the postadge upon the road from Aberdeen to Edinburgh was very near given over and slighted'. Meantime Farquhar's fortunes had not prospered, for in December 1686 he was referred to as 'hunted with captions for his owne personal debts and now residing in the Abbey'.* With the Privy Council, the weight of evidence and his own creditors against him, it might reasonably have been concluded that Farquhar was a broken man, but he appears somehow to have extricated himself from his troubles, for in 1690 John Blair, then Postmaster General for Scotland, entered into a contract with Farquhar and his wife appointing them Keepers of the Letter Office in Aberdeen,[57] a post which they held till February

---

* The right of sanctuary for debtors at Holyrood Abbey probably dates from a Charter of David 1 and continued in existence far into the 19th century. Indeed the privilege of sanctuary has never been repealed by Act of Parliament. Alexander Farquhar 'ale Seller' appears in a list of lodgers in the Abbey at Whitsunday 1686 who were to be protected by the Baillie of Holyrood. The word 'gone' is marked against the entry. (Register of Protections of the Sanctuary of Holyroodhouse, vol. 1, 1686 –1712. S.R.O. RH. 2/8/17.)

1693. On that date Mrs Farquhar, acting as 'factrix of Alexander Farquhar Postmaster', finally renounced all benefits she or her husband might have in the Aberdeen postmastership, Farquhar being away from Scotland and his wife being too much occupied on her own affairs to attend to the business of the Post Office.[58] Perhaps the law-suit in Edinburgh had not yet been concluded, despite the efforts of the unpaid legal advisers.

The years which witnessed the establishment of posts on the roads from Edinburgh to Berwick, Portpatrick and Aberdeen saw many changes in the administration of the growing postal service, centred in Edinburgh but partially controlled from London. Exactly how long Sir William Seton remained Master of the Posts after his appointment in 1616 is not clear. The Privy Council records make reference to him at least as late as 1631. Edinburgh was complaining of his activities in 1633, and in 1641 an Act of the Scottish Parliament ratified his appointment for life as 'His Majesty's first and cheefe postmaister of all his Hienes postmaisteres and of all postmaisteres jornay maisteres and keepers of jornay horses' at a salary of £500(s) per annum, but without prejudice to the privilege of Burntisland and Kinghorn as to journey masters and keepers of journey horses.[59] No reference to any new appointment appears till 1649 when the Commonwealth took over more complete control of the posts in Scotland and removed most of the officials. On the Restoration Charles II made certain re-appointments including that of Robert Mein as Keeper of the Letter Office at Edinburgh through which the whole of Scotland's letters then passed.

When Patrick Grahame was appointed Postmaster General for Scotland in the autumn of 1662 his salary was £500(s) per annum. The payment seems a modest one, but Grahame as Postmaster General was entitled to retain postal charges for the conveyance of all private mail, of which he had a monopoly. He and his successors for many years had also the appointment of local postmasters with horse-hiring rights, though judging by the experience of the postmasters themselves, at least on the Berwick road, these would not seem to have been of much value. In 1674 on the death of his father, John Grahame, the opponent of Farquhar in the dispute over the Aberdeen post, succeeded to the office which he held till 1689 at a salary which had been increased to £1,000(s). To what extent the office of Postmaster General was at this time in fact profitable must be a matter of conjecture, but there is evidence that by John Grahame's time it had become of some value. It will be recalled that some thirty-six years previously the Commonwealth Parliament had decided to let out the office of Postmaster General in England for an annual rent, and on John Grahame's death in 1689 it was decided to make similar arrangements in Scotland. The office was accordingly auctioned (or 'rouped' as we say in Scotland) and John Blair, an apothecary in Edinburgh, made a successful bid of 5,100 merks (£283.6.8d sterling) per annum. Meanwhile John Grahame's widow, Alison, was petitioning the Privy Council for payment to her of part of the rent to be paid by the new Postmaster General. The cost of the establishment of posts had, she claimed, swallowed up much of her own marriage portion, had involved her husband in other debts and had reduced the family to straits. The early years of her husband's appointment had yielded no profit and he had died just when his office was becoming profitable. Alison's petition was favourably received. No direct mention is made of any payments to her from the rent of the new Postmaster General, but the Privy Council allowed the widow till Martinmas 1689 to recover all money payable to her husband.[60]

Among the items which the Privy Council had authorized Alison Grahame to collect in 1688/9, the most important appears to have consisted of balances due to her late husband by Robert Mein, Keeper of the Letter Office at Edinburgh. Mein had at that time been for at least sixteen years in charge of the Edinburgh office, and the nature of his dealings with Colonel Roger Whitley, who then 'farmed' the office of Deputy Postmaster General in England, as recorded in Whitley's letterbooks* for 1672–7, show only too clearly that Grahame had

---

* These letter-books, commonly known as the 'Peover Papers', at one time in Peover Hall, Cheshire, and now held in the Record Office of the G.P.O. in London, were written in the reign of Charles II and are copies of letters sent by Colonel Roger Whitley, the Deputy Postmaster General between the years 1672 – 1677 to postmasters and others in England, Wales and Scotland. No incoming letters have survived. The Peover Papers are the earliest records in the possession of the Post Office and there are no other records to equal their value to the postal historian until the start of the records kept, mainly by Francis Freeling, between 1790 and 1836.

not been alone in experiencing trouble in dealing with the Edinburgh official.

Besides showing the ability and the stubbornness of Mein, Whitley's letters illustrate the difficulties only to be expected from an arrangement whereby an official in Edinburgh was responsible to and paid by the postal authorities in London for letters passing between the capitals, while responsible only to the Deputy Postmaster General of Scotland for all purely Scottish correspondence. Whitley's position was constantly weakened by the knowledge of his dependence on the experience and ability of his Scottish colleague and by the care which he himself took throughout to avoid anything which might seem to trespass on the independence of Scotland in postal matters. Writing to Mein in September 1673 in criticism of the latter's accounting, he refers to the need for making new arrangements 'without invading or shocking the Rights of that Kingdom (Scotland) which I acknowledge have noe dependence on this; But I desire . . . that they may both Continue in brotherly Amity and Unity'. Again in November 1674 he wrote, 'I pretend not to your Postery in Scotland, only what concerns England', and these references are typical of many in the correspondence.

Difficulties in accounting between the two men for balances due to or by one or the other in respect of postal charges on letters passing between the capitals were constant. Mein claimed one-eighth of the postage of all letters from London, besides 1d for delivery, and this Whitley would not concede. Too many letters and packages to Scotland, he further complained, were undelivered or unaccepted. Whitley blamed the carelessness of the letter-carriers in Scotland and, suspecting that certain packages contained enclosures for distribution by the recipient, urged that these be opened and the contents delivered and charged. Mein on his part complained of mail bags for Scotland being opened and letters abstracted. Whitley retorted that this was likely to have happened 'behind Berwick' rather than south of it, since Scottish postmasters had more to gain from taking letters from the bag and more facilities for dealing with them. The bags from Scotland, too, he complained, were often in a shocking state and full of holes. But of all the difficulties the most constant and the most troublesome lay in the transfer between the capitals of balances between the two officers. In those days when currency was hard to come by, Bills drawn by one on the other or much more frequently on private individuals or merchants, were constantly used, their acceptance by him on whom they were drawn as constantly delayed or refused. Gold, too, 'in Signetts or otherwise' was often sent by Mein, and Whitley was at pains to point out on such occasions that Mein would only be credited with what it would fetch. Time and again Whitley enquired as to the nature, the sufficiency and even the existence of the guarantees which, in common with all postmasters, Mein was under obligation to provide in respect of money due by him. On this subject Mein's replies were so evasive and so unsatisfactory that it is hard to avoid the conclusion that no such guarantees in fact existed. Whitley, it is certain, had a hard row to hoe, in dealing with a shrewd and perhaps not over-scrupulous colleague. In the summer of 1677, with Whitley's 'farm' of the Scottish posts in London drawing to a close, accounts between him and Mein were still unsettled, the advantage, as one might conjecture, in Mein's favour.[61]

The contract between the Privy Council and John Blair, the new Postmaster General, in August 1689 which conferred on him the whole 'privileges, immunities, casualties, dignities, profits and duties' of the office narrates in some detail the terms of his appointment.[62] The postal rates for single letters from Edinburgh to Dumfries, Glasgow, Ayr, Dundee, Kelso, Jedburgh, Perth, Stirling and Hamilton were fixed at 2/-(s); for those to Carlisle, Portpatrick, Aberdeen and Dunkeld at 3/-(s); and to Kirkcudbright, Inverness and beyond Aberdeen at 4/-(s). Blair's contract empowered him to establish a general letter office at Edinburgh, together with local offices in such places as he might choose and to provide horses for those riding post or on ordinary journeys, which were to be exempt from being pressed for service by others. The postal rates quoted were for letters consisting of one sheet, with double or treble charges for those with two or more sheets. This regulation was at this time and for long after literally and strictly interpreted, and far into the 19th century when the provision was still in force, the critics of postal regulations were pointing out the absurdity of a rule by which a large and perhaps heavy letter, so long as it consisted of one sheet, paid only the charge applicable to a single letter, while a much smaller and lighter letter written on two sheets or with the least enclosure paid double.* The list of towns mentioned in John Blair's contract of 1689 shows that, though Scotland was still very far from having anything approaching a satisfactory postal system, postal facilities of some sort were in fact gradually extending, at least south of the Forth and up the east coast to Aberdeen, while the future provision of a postal service for rural areas was faintly foreshadowed by an allowance of 1/–(s) a letter to be paid to all appointed persons bringing letters from towns and villages to the nearest post-town. The fact, too, that Blair was prepared to offer for seven years a payment of 5100 merks per annum in return for what he could make from private postal dues collected tells its own tale. On the road from London to Edinburgh by Berwick reasonable speed and fair regularity had at last been achieved by the horse post and it was claimed that at or about this period the proceedings of the English parliament on Saturday were in the hands of the Edinburgh public by the following Thursday.

John Blair completed his seven years' contract on 1 November 1696. The exact financial outcome of his venture is not apparent, but from an account covering the whole period of his tenancy made up by William Menzies his cautioner, it would seem that after crediting against rent due by Blair various items paid by him in respect of official postal services on the Berwick, Portpatrick and Aberdeen roads there remained due by him a balance of £3368(s). For a short time after Blair's contract ended the office of Postmaster General in Scotland was held by Sir Robert Sinclair of Stevenson near Haddington, but despite the fact that he appears to have paid no rent and received, in addition to the whole revenue from private letters, an annual sum of £300(s), Sinclair soon relinquished the office as unprofitable. Sinclair must have been a singularly bad manager, and his failure to show a profit is the more surprising because when in

---

* To this regulation was due the almost invariable custom of sending letters in the form of one sheet, often nearly illegible from the amount of writing crammed onto it and often cross-wise, folded and sealed with the address written on the back. An envelope of any sort would have made it chargeable as a two-sheet letter. As late as 1796 Parson Woodforde in Norfolk recorded in his diary that in a letter reaching his household from Somerset 'compliments' which had been omitted from the body of the letter had been added on a very small strip of paper inserted by the sender between the seal and the letter itself, thus making it chargeable as a double letter. 'Very expensive compliments', he sourly commented.

the autumn of 1701 the office of Postmaster General was again let, this time to George Main, an Edinburgh jeweller, the annual rent had been increased to 21,500 merks (£1194.8.od sterling), more than four times what Blair had paid twelve years earlier.[63]

Main held the office till 1707, and an account which was made up between him and the Receiver General in London for the period from Martinmas 1704 till Whitsunday 1707 gives much detail as to the complex method of accounting, all items being noted in sterling. The salaries of the postmasters on the Berwick road and the expenses of maintaining the postal route to Port-patrick with the packet boat to Ireland, though now paid by the Postmaster General in Scotland, had long been regarded as a charge against the General Post Office in London. Over the two and a half years covered by the account these payments amounted to £550, and, as in the case of Blair, these outlays were allowed against the rent. Main was also credited with the cost incurred by him in forwarding all official letters and pack-ages north or south along the Berwick road and certain in-cidental expenses, amounting over the period to the formidable total of over £2680. During the period of the Account, Main had also made periodical remittances to the Receiver General in London amounting to £260, and these were of course also entered on the credit side, making a total in all of £3490 paid out, more than cancelling the rent of approximately £3000 due by him over the period.[64] It would therefore appear that on these transactions Main was, like Blair, substantially out of pocket; but in the case of neither tenant does the statement take account of receipts or payments in respect of other postal traffic in Scot-land. Among the records which have survived is a statement showing the number of letters passing north and south on the Berwick road during the year from May 1693 to April 1694 when John Blair was Postmaster General. This shows the sur-prising total of 67,033 letters for the year in question, and it is certain that as the years passed the amount of postal traffic was growing. Indeed the large increase in rent between Blair's time and that of Main can be explained on no other assumption. Much the greater part of these letters would be official* but

---

* One of the most authoritative writers on British postal history has stated that during the three years to March 1693 the amount due for postage on letters from London to Edinburgh was at the rate of £500 p.a., but that official correspond-

there would be some private mail also, paying postage.[65] It seems therefore a fair assumption that, despite the experience of Sir Robert Sinclair, the office of Postmaster General for Scotland had, by the end of the 17th century become one of some, though uncertain, profit.*

The Postal Act of 1660, which largely repeated the provisions of the Commonwealth Act of 1657, was intended to apply to the whole of the United Kingdom, but in postal as in other matters, Scotland still looked on herself as largely independent of her southern neighbour. Only on the road from Edinburgh to Berwick and to a smaller degree on the route to Ireland by Portpatrick was control from London apparent. Postal charges fixed in Scotland in the latter part of the 17th century were fixed with little reference to those ruling south of the Border, an absence of uniformity which was all the more apparent from the use in Scotland of the Scots mile and Scots money. The independence of Scotland in postal matters was emphasized in 1695 by the passing of an Act of the Scots parliament which had established for Scotland a General Post Office in Edinburgh through which all letters would pass. As in previous enactments the Postmaster General, whether holding the office by appointment or as tenant, was given the monopoly of carrying letters except such as were sent privately by servants or by express, or letters accompanying goods sent by common carrier. The rates of postage then laid down were 2/–(s) for a single letter to Berwick or to any place within 50 miles of Edinburgh, 3/–(s) for distances between 50 and 100 miles, and 4/–(s) for dis-

---

ence would probably account for nearly the whole. In 1707, the year of the Union, when official correspondence would presumably be at its height, the postage dues on such correspondence averaged £66 a month. (Joyce, *History of the Post Office*, 53.)

* While there is no means of ascertaining the exact amount of any profit made by the tenants of the Post Office in Scotland in the last years of the 17th and early years of the 18th centuries, some light is thrown on the problem by the fact that when, after the Union of 1707, George Main became Deputy Postmaster for Scotland, his salary of £200 per annum is believed to have been based on the average amount which he made from the postal business during his years as tenant. (Joyce, op. cit., 117.)

The amounts due by the Treasury for official correspondence between England and Scotland must have grown rapidly, for a letter to the Treasury dated 25 March 1716 refers to expenses due to George Main for the quarter ending 24 June 1715 being £885. 19. 8, while similar payments due to Main's successor James Anderson for the period 24 June 1715 to 25 March 1717 amounted to £5699. 0. 8d. (Post 3/5.)

tances over 100 miles. The Privy Council were to establish post offices at convenient places, and it was once again provided that packet boats were to carry the post weekly from Portpatrick to Donaghadee. The significance of the Act of 1695 in Scottish postal history lies partly in the fact that the fixing of postal rates up to and over 100 miles shows that the radius of actual or at least potential postal services reaching out from Edinburgh was increasing. For the rest, its provisions would seem to have been largely a repetition of those which had already found a place in earlier orders or enactments, and it is hard to avoid the conclusion that the purpose of the Act was at least in part to stress the independence of the northern country.

Looking back on the postal history of Scotland in the 17th century, it must be acknowledged that clarity, at least in detail, is to some extent lacking. The Acts and Orders of the Scots Parliament and Privy Council are often repetitive, sometimes confusing and at times apparently contradictory, while references to both Scots and English mileage and money do nothing to help. Despite the Union of the Crowns, lack of any real unison between Scotland and England was all too evident, a lack which was nowhere more apparent than in postal arrangements, where from Edinburgh to the Border the interests of the two countries overlapped, while north of Edinburgh those of Scotland were almost alone concerned; but changing times were soon to come, and within four years of the legislative Union of 1707 an Act of the British Parliament was at length to bring order and uniformity where confusion had reigned and was to open the way for the ultimate development of the postal arrangements of Great Britain into a vital and well-ordered public service.

REFERENCES

1. Jusserand, *English wayfaring Life in the middle Ages, passim.*
2. Joyce, *History of the Post Office,* 18.
3. Ibid., 7.
4. Howard Robinson, *The British Post Office,* ch. iv.
5. R.P.C., First Series, vol. I, 73/4. Other beacons were sited at Fast Castle near Cockburnspath, at Dounlaw above Spott, on North Berwick Law and also on 'Bynnyngiscrage above Linlithgow'. A rather similar system of beacons was established up the south-east coast of Scotland between 1803 and 1805, when the fear of French invasion was at its height.
6. *Accounts of the Lord High Treasurer of Scotland.* vol. vi, 1531/38.

7. John M. Corrie, *The Dumfries Post Office 1642–910*.
8. R.P.C., First Series, vol. vi, 567/8.
9. S.R.O. PS. 1/75, fol. 227/8.
10. R.P.C., First Series, vol. vi, 566/8, 570/1.
11. Taylor, 'The King's Mails 1603–1625', in *Scott. Hist. Rev.* xlii. During much of the 17th century salaries and other payments in Scotland continued in many cases to be quoted in Scots (s) money rather than sterling. It should, therefore, be noted that at this period the relation of Scots money to English was as follows: 12d Scots = 1d sterling; 1 merk Scots = 1/1⅓d sterling; £12 Scots = £1 sterling.
12. R.P.C., First Series, vol. xii, 69, 82.
13. Ibid., vol. xi, 181.
14. R.P.C., Second Series, vol. iv, 349.
15. Ibid., 182.
16. R.P.C., First Series, vol. x, 832.
17. Ibid., vol. xii, 365.
18. A.P.S., vol. vi (1), 373. The Inventory of the estate of George Forrest, Postmaster at Haddington who died in March 1637 included a sum of £2100 Scots owed to him by the Treasurer for 7 terms of his 'post fie'. (S.R.O., Com. Edinburgh Tests, 12th Jan. 1638.)
19. S.R.O. E.28/71/34.
20. R.P.C., Third Series, vol. iii, 305/6.
21. Ibid., vol. x, 207.
22. *Records of Convention of Royal Burghs*, vol. ii, 317.
23. R.P.C., First Series, vol. x, 832/9.
24. *Records of Convention of Royal Burghs*, vol. iii, 29.
25. Ibid., 31/2. In February 1638 Charles i ordered that the Council and Session were to meet at the Castle of Stirling, a post should be established at Linlithgow and another at Stirling. (h.m.c.8: 9th r 11. p. 248. No. 107.)
26. A.P.S., vol. vi, (2), 893.
27. R.P.C., Second Series, vol. vii, 202, 228, 327.
28. R.P.C., Third Series, vol. i, 263.
29. Ibid., 309.
30. Ibid. vol. v, 285/6.
31. S.R.O. E. 26/11, p. 309, 20 Jan. 1680.
32. Howard Robinson, op. cit., 58/9.
33. Ibid., 46.
34. R.P.C., Third Series, vol. i, 263.
35. Braid, *Postal History of Old Glasgow, passim*.
36. Corrie, op. cit., *passim*.
37. Welsh, *Ayrshire Postal History, Postal History Society Bulletin*, No. 106.
38. *Extracts from Records of Burgh of Edinburgh, 1528/57*.
39. Ibid., *1626/41*, 110.
40. Ibid., 120.
41. R.P.C., Third Series, vol. ii, 252.
42. Chambers, *Domestic Annals of Scotland*, vol. ii, 315/16.
43. *Aberdeen Council Letters*, vol. iv, 297.
44. Ibid.
45. Ibid., vol. v, 171.
46. Kennedy, *Annals of Aberdeen*, vol. i, 262.
47. *Aberdeen Council Letters*, vol. vi, 119.
48. Ibid., 127.

49. Ibid., 246.
50. Ibid., 270.
51. R.P.C., Third Series, vol. XII, 404.
52. Ibid., 568/70.
53. Ibid.
54. Ibid., vol. XIII, 24 et seq.
55. Ibid., 3 et seq.
56. Ibid., 24 et seq.
57. S.R.O. E.89/1/13.
58. S.R.O. E.89/5.
59. A.P.S., vol. V, 548.
60. R.P.C., Third Series, vol. XIII, 548, 554, 564.
61. G.P.O. Peover Papers. Letter and Account books of Col. Roger Whitley, Deputy P.M.G., 1672–1677.
62. R.P.C., Third Series, vol. XIV, 38 et seq. See Appendix I.
63. S.R.O. E.89/5/1–2.
64. S.R.O. E.208/2/1.
65. S.R.O. E.89/1/4(12).

Two

The Scottish Postal System of the Early 18th century

The circumstances which led up to the passing of the Post Office Act of 1711 bear more than a little resemblance to those which had brought about the Union of the Parliaments four years earlier. The Union of 1707 was based not on mutual friendship nor on any widespread desire on either side for closer human ties, but rather on recognition on both sides of the Border of a need rapidly becoming imperative. It was an act of expediency rather than of sentiment, dictated by the head rather than by the heart. For England, impoverished by years of Continental war, stable and peaceful relations with Scotland had come to be essential. For Scotland, naturally poor and with only a small Continental trade, the prospect of a growing market in England and of a share in the vast markets and resources of the extending Empire had come to outweigh considerations of sentiment and prejudice and the fear of involvement in England's wars. So in 1711 considerations of financial need, of expediency and hard common sense, dictated for the postal services of the two countries the provisions of another Act of Union.

The existence of separate postal administrations and of differing rates of postage in a kingdom now united rendered it in the words of the preamble to the Act 'most likely that a correspondence by posts will be best managed and ordered for the public good by uniting the said two Post Offices under one Postmaster General'. But the financial needs were not disguised. The seemingly endless war had taken its toll of the financial strength of England. Annual expenditure had risen to £13,000,000. In the winter of 1709–10, the Commons, in addition to the ordinary revenue expenditure, had voted over £6,000,000 for war needs, raised by means of the unpopular Land Tax, increased taxes on candles, beer and coal and extensive use of State Lotteries. So the preamble of the Act of 1711 foreshadowed new and increased postal rates which '... may in some measure enable Your Majesty to carry on and finish the present War ...'. To this end '... in order to raise a present supply of money for carrying on the War ...' a sum of £700 was to be paid into the Exchequer each week by the Postmaster General. This provision, together with the increased postal rates now introduced, was in terms of the Act to continue for three years. In the event, they marked the commencement of an almost continuous rise in postal rates over more than 100 years to come.

The Act of 1711 was to remain the basic legislative provision for the British Post Office for over a century. Its passing opened the way for a real development of the post throughout the United Kingdom, but the circumstances in which it was passed identified the Post Office then, and for long after, as a means of taxation almost more than as a public service. So far as concerns Scotland the new postal rates introduced in 1711, all now stated in sterling, were substantially higher than those under the Scots Act of 1695. The postage rate between London and Edinburgh was fixed at 6d for a single letter, while in Scotland itself the rates were now 2d for the first 50 miles, 3d between 50 and 80 miles and 4d over 80 miles. The rate for the hiring of horses of which postmasters retained the monopoly was fixed at 3d per mile, while of special importance for the future development of rural posts in both England and Scotland was the provision that the Postmaster General could set up cross-posts as and where required. The increase in rates was in fact higher than the figures showed, because now for the first time the English mile was used in reckoning distances in Scotland. Nearly forty years earlier it had been discovered that the estimated distances on which postal rates in England had been based were inaccurate. The discrepancy had come to light following the establishment in 1663 on part of the Great North Road near London of the first of the countless Turn-pike Trusts which over the next two centuries were to carry the main responsibility for the maintenance of the roads of Britain. These Trusts were compelled to erect milestones showing the measured mileage, and in 1674 the task of making a detailed survey of English roads had been undertaken by John Ogilby. His measurements, which were of considerable accuracy, showed that the estimates of distance hitherto used by the Post Office were in very many cases far short of the actual mileage, the distance from London to York for instance having hitherto been estimated at 150 miles compared with the real distance of 192 miles as now measured. Ogilby's distances were from now on adopted by the Post Office as standard. This was on the basis of the English mile of 1760 yards which compared with the old Scots mile of approximately 1934 yards.

George Main, the Edinburgh jeweller, who had held the office of Postmaster General for Scotland on lease from 1701, continued as tenant till 1707, but following the Union his position became first Post Office Manager for Scotland and then Deputy Postmaster General.* In this capacity he appears to have continued till 1715, to be succeeded by James Anderson, a Writer to the Signet in Edinburgh, who held the office till the autumn of 1717. If Anderson's term of office as Deputy Postmaster General was short, it was of no little importance in the postal history of Scotland, while some of his copy letters which, along with other contemporary documents, are preserved in the National Library of Scotland in Edinburgh, show Anderson himself to have been a man of strong character and possessed of a certain sense of humour. He was to need both in his two years at the Post Office.

When James Anderson took up the duties of his office in the

---

* A letter to the Treasury dated 10 July 1711 refers to George Main, Deputy Postmaster General of North Britain at a salary of £200. (Post 1/4.)

Four years later Main appears to have fallen out of favour, for letters to the Treasury of 14th June 1715 refer to several applications by 'Mr George Maine to have his Deputation renewed as Postmar. of North Britain, in which Station he has served for about 14 years before and since the Union. . . . We are of opinion that it is for His Majesty's Service that Mr Maine should be removed from his office of Deputy Postmar. of Scotland and that Mr James Anderson be appointed to supply that place.' (Post 1/6, pp. 11/12.)

Number 5.

15

LONDON POST

Communicating the High Counfels of both Parliaments in *England* and *Scotland*, and all other
Remarkable paffages, both Civill and Martiall in
his Weekly Travells through the three Kingdoms.

Printed and entred according to order.

From Thurfday February the 4 to Thurfday February 11. 1646

THe Feare we had of the fcarcity of Bread, is by the mercy of God
prevented; for (to adde to the number we had before) there are
of late many Ships come in laden with Corne in great abundance.

E   Ia

1. A news-sheet of 1647.

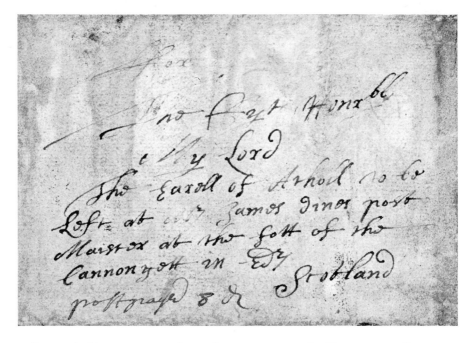

2. Letter (1664) sent care of an early postmaster at the Canongate, *p.* 8.

summer of 1715 the Scottish Office was beset with difficulties and problems – problems which the political events of the time were soon to accentuate. With the passing of the Act of 1711 ultimate control of the Post Office in Scotland had passed from Edinburgh where it had hitherto rested, to London. The office of Postmaster General in London was then and for long after a joint appointment, the holders in 1715 being Lord Cornwallis and Mr James Craggs. In the spring of that year a letter addressed by them to Scottish postal officials had demanded, no doubt with the terms of the Act of 1711 in mind, that postal revenue from Scotland be transmitted to them in good bills or money with such accounts as might be necessary in the interests of the service. The fact that the joint Postmasters General subscribed themselves as 'your loving friends' did little to temper the curt and peremptory nature of the order.[1] On his appointment Anderson himself was called on to swear a comprehensive oath that he would not

'wittingly, willingly or knowingly Open Detain or Delay or Cause, Procure, Permit or suffer to be open'd, Detained or Delayed any letter or letters pacquet or pacquets which shall come into my hands, power or custody by reason of my employment in or relating to the Post Office except by the consent of the person or persons to whom the same is or shall be directed or by an Express Warrant in writing under the hand of one of the Principal Secretaries of State for that purpose or except in such cases where the party or parties to whom such letter or letters pacquet or pacquets shall be directed or who is or are hereby chargeable with the payment of the Post or Posts thereof shall refuse or neglect to pay the same and except such letters or pacquets as shall be returned for want of true directions or when the party or parties to whom the same is or shall be directed cannot be found; And I will not any way embezzle any such letter or letters pacquet or pacquets as aforesaid.'[2]

An oath in similar terms was, it seems, demanded from all sub-postmasters or 'Deputies' as they were called in Scotland, to be re-sworn by each immediately after the death of Queen Anne in 1714.

While the exact nature of the arrangements hitherto in force for collection by the Edinburgh office of local postal revenue are somewhat obscure, these had certainly been complex and almost

as certainly unsatisfactory. At the date of the passing of the Post
Office Act of 1711 the net post office revenue of Scotland was
believed to be only about £2000 per annum.[3] The weekly payments to the Exchequer required under the Act meant pressure
on the Postmaster General who in turn must press the Edinburgh office, forcing the latter to bring pressure on local
postmasters. It is probable that these local officers were often
placed in an embarrassing position, for it seems that public
bodies such as Town Councils were, in common with not a few
private individuals, in the habit of settling their postage bills
only periodically. Thus in July 1709 Dumfries Town Council
paid a bill of £3.14/− for postage covering the period 1 April to
4 July and again on 8 September 1711 John Johnstone, the
postmaster, received from the town £3.15/− for the cost of
letters from 1 December 1710 to 22 August 1711.[4] During the
next century with the spread of postal services to rural districts
the delay in settlement of postage accounts was to become increasingly apparent and progressively more serious.

On top of these problems came the Rising of 1715; so when
James Anderson took up office his satisfaction at the appointment must have been tempered by the knowledge that his was
to be no easy task. His letters are eloquent of troubles and
frustrations on every side. To the postmaster of Perth, he
writes soon after his appointment, complaining of delay in
settling accounts 'for I am in pain to have the accounts of this
office made up ...'. The postmaster at Minigaff was badly in
arrears and soon Anderson is writing to the postmaster of
Wigtown asking whether he can recommend a reliable replacement.[5] Even the end of the Rising brought little relief. The
accounts of the postmaster of Montrose were in confusion, and
in July 1716 Anderson writes to him as to the proper method of
straightening them '... while the Rebellion lasted and the
Horse Post, there was unusual deductions, but now things
being brought to their wonted channells we goe into the
common road again'.[6] Officials in London were pressing him.
In September 1717 he writes to the London office referring to
the accounts for the last seven quarters having been brought up
to date by the accountant, but within a week he refers again to
efforts to bring the accounts up to date: 'The Arrears were
great in the Rebellion and even last Winter when I drew out
matters they were considerable, but are now brought to a

small compass.'[7] Clearly his philosophy and with it perhaps also his digestion were being strained, for on the same day he writes to an unspecified correspondent referring to efforts to clear up the confusion caused by the Rising : 'This is a good season for pills whereof enclosed is two small boxes which I heartily wish may do you much good.'[8]

Worries over the Portpatrick packet boat persisted. In the summer of 1716, when writing to the postmaster of Aberdeen, he refers to a forthcoming visit to Portpatrick to settle the matter, though it seems that even the most suitable port on the Scottish side for the packet boat to land was then in doubt. By the late summer, however, Portpatrick had evidently been decided on, for a document dated 18 August narrates that John Blair of Dunskey and Sir Charles Hay of Park had entered into a contract with Anderson to extend the quay, the water within the quay to be sufficient to take three packet boats of 14 tons each.[9] Anderson's visit to Portpatrick must have been so far successful, for in the autumn of the following year he writes to the postmaster of Stranraer referring to delay despite the virtual completion of a contract regarding the boats. Well might he complain, for two months later he writes again at great length to the Stranraer postmaster referring to further trouble over the packet service : 'I wish the true good of the Service were considered and less humour, and if things had been done as they ought there had been less noise and I had been free of a great deal of trouble,'[10]

The Post Office Act of 1711 had meant the end of the system, long in force, whereby the Postmaster General for Scotland took for himself the revenue of the Post Office. From then on the postal revenue fell to the Crown or the Treasury, the Postmaster General in England and the Deputy Postmaster General in Scotland being paid officials. There appears to be no record of what salary was paid to James Anderson, but at this period and for very many years to come one of the privileges of the office was the receipt free of charge or at least on highly advantageous terms of newspapers for long referred to as *Gazettes*, newsletters and Reports of parliamentary proceedings. In the latter part of the 18th century and all through the war with France, when public interest in political and foreign affairs was intense, the receipt and circulation of such publications was to be a valuable source of profit to postal officials; but even in the early years of the century it was a perquisite of office by no means to be despised, particularly in England but also to some extent in Scotland. In the late autumn of 1717 James Anderson wrote to the Principal of Glasgow University enclosing an account for £11.5/– for supplying newsletters, including the *London Gazette*, to the university from 1 August 1715 to 1 November 1717 at a cost of £5 per annum, and a few days later he was in correspondence with Mrs Shiells of the Coffee House of Glasgow over payment of her account for papers.

'I can assure you', he wrote, 'that it was given up to me that you paid yearly £14 for the Gazett, Evening Post, Flying Post, Postman and copy of the written letters besides the votes, and because you had laid down the Postman you was rebate 40/–, since one pacquet would enclose all and I can also assure you there is so very little gain that they are furnished so rather to oblidge than make a proffit, and if you think 40/– p.a. too small a deduction for the Postman make what you please in reason for I love no debates in any case, far less in such very small matters, but am surprised with your suggestion in having the speeches and votes in recompense for a pretence that your news sometimes miscarry which I scarce imagine can be, they being carefully laid up and indexed to you by every post.'

The postmaster of Glasgow had, it seems, been successful in settling his accounts with the lady and also with the University of Glasgow, for on the same day Anderson wrote to him enclosing a copy of his letter to Mrs Shiells and referring to the small profit on newspapers and the difficulty of pleasing everyone. 'You did well in drinking a bottle of wine which I find is cheaper with you than with us.'[11] But Glasgow was not alone in receiving through the Edinburgh post office newsletters and other publications from the South. It will be recalled that such items figured in the complex negotiations with regard to the post to Aberdeen in the latter part of the 17th century, and about that time further references appear in the Town Council Minutes of Dumfries to arrangements for the transmission of newsletters to the Dumfries postmaster from Carlisle, and particularly from Edinburgh.

It has been generally accepted by postal historians that except for the horse post to and from England on the road between

Edinburgh and Berwick, Scotland's mail, up till 1715, was everywhere carried on foot.* Five years earlier Glasgow had asked for a horse post to Edinburgh at an estimated cost of £200 p.a., but this had been refused by the Treasury. On 29 November 1715 Anderson made it known that 'for the conveniency of the noblemen and gentlemen at Stirling that they may not loose [*sic*] so much as one post for correspondence with London or any part of that road' a horse-post would go three times a week from there to Edinburgh, taking back to Stirling any letters which had come in by the London mail. The instructions given by Anderson to the postmasters on the Stirling road in this connection were curt and hardly encouraging, perhaps reflecting the peremptory terms in which the Postmasters General were in the habit of addressing him. The instructions read :

> 'For His Majesty's Special Service. Whereas the management of the postage of letters in Scotland is committed to my care and conduct. These are therefore in His Majesty's name to require you in your respective stages to use all diligence and expedition in the same and speedy conveyance of this pacquet from Stirling to Edinburgh and thereof you are not to fail as you will answer the contrary at your peril.
>
> Ja. Anderson
>
> To the several Postmasters betwixt Edinburgh and Stirling. Haste, Haste, Post Haste.'[12]

The new horse post between Edinburgh and Stirling marked a great step forward. In the following summer Anderson wrote to the postmaster in Glasgow referring to the approval by the Postmaster General of his decision to defer for a little a proposed horse post between Edinburgh and Glasgow.[13] Up to this time the post between the cities had been carried three times a week each way by foot posts, who covered the 36 miles in two days, calling at Linlithgow and Falkirk. For this they were paid £40 per annum compared with £32.10/– per annum paid to the foot posts who went between Glasgow and Ayr with equal frequency, and just over £43 per annum paid to

---

* While this has been generally understood to have been the position prior to 1715 it has been noted in an account of the Dumfries Post Office that in a Petition to Dumfries Town Council in 1690 reference is made to an attack on 'the London post's horses that was coming ryding through the town with the packit. . . .' (Corrie, op cit., 10.)

those going twice a week between Ayr and Portpatrick. In a Memorial submitted to the Postmasters General, undated but almost certainly written in 1716 or early 1717, Anderson proposed that the foot posts between Edinburgh and Glasgow be replaced by horse posts to do the journey in ten hours in summer, or twelve hours in winter, with only one change of horses at Falkirk.[14] Whether this plan was immediately accepted is not clear, but in the spring of 1717 Anderson was able to announce the start of a horse post between the cities.

On the Aberdeen road, where perhaps the memory of Farquhar lingered, smuggling of letters still went on. In the summer of 1716 the Aberdeen postmaster had written to Anderson suggesting that some small extra payment to the runners would make for better speed and less smuggling. Anderson turned the proposal down on the ground of cost, and in the following year found it necessary to warn the runners against carrying anything 'to the prejudice of the service'.[15] The suggestion had even been put forward that a horse post should be put on the Edinburgh to Aberdeen road, and Anderson was at some pains to show that the extra cost as compared to the foot post would only be some £50 per annum. This however was considered excessive and the scheme was abandoned.

In the early spring of 1716, at the request of the Duke of Argyll and of General Cadogan, then in charge of the Government troops in Scotland, a horse post was established by way of Dunkeld, Blair Atholl and Kingussie to Inverness, to convey military despatches. On the postmaster at Perth fell the responsibility of providing horses at Dunkeld and Blair Atholl, and of sending letters south as far as Kinross, while the magistrates at South Queensferry were directed to provide boats across the ferry and horses on to Edinburgh.[16] This post was a purely temporary one to meet the military needs of the moment and was withdrawn in 1718 despite the plea of the magistrates of Inverness for its continuance. In June 1719 Inverness Town Council wrote to Sir John Inglis, then in command at Edinburgh:

'Gentle Sir, We hade a letter from Commissionaire Munro last week anent a project of settleing three maills a week all the year over by post horses from Edinburgh to this [by] the Laigh Road [via Aberdeen]. We do indeed think the project verie good & that in a short time it will prove to the advantage of the Revenue. But if it could be thought advisable to settle only 2 post horses Weekly & to continue one foot-post [by] the Highland Road the Summer Season at least, it would be of very good use to this town because of the monie that is frequently sent by the Highland post that cannot be sent in the Bagg [by] the Laigh Road & for several other reasons that Mr Munro can inform you, whom we have written to by this post.'

The application for a continued post-service by the Highland Road was, however, unsuccessful. The post to Inverness reverted to the old route by Aberdeen which had been established in 1669, and many a long day was to pass before Inverness got a direct post to the south by the Highland Road.*

Anderson's days as Deputy Postmaster General were drawing to a close, and on 26 November 1717 his 'loving friends' Lord Cornwallis and James Craggs wrote to him intimating the appointment in his place of Sir John Inglis, lately Commander of the King's Forces in Scotland. Anderson's time as Deputy Postmaster General had been short, but in two and a half years not a little had been accomplished. In particular the establishment of permanent horse posts from Edinburgh, first to Stirling and then to Glasgow, was the first real step on the road which was to lead to horse or horse-drawn posts throughout much of Scotland. It had been for the Scottish Post Office a time of difficulty both in finance and administration, made more difficult by the events of 1715, and perhaps it was with a sense of relief that Anderson laid down the reins of postal administration and turned again to the more familiar problems of the wills, settlements and litigation of his legal practice.

The monopoly of letter-carrying had, as has been seen, been claimed by the Crown from very early days, first as a precaution against civil unrest and treason and later as protection of what was coming to be a source of profit; but almost from the

---

* Perth had evidently become a postal centre of some importance a considerable time earlier, for the Burgh records contain a letter dated 7 November 1689 from John Blair to the Provost and Town Council which states 'There is designed ane letter office at Perth together with ane foot post who is to travell by Kinross and Queensferry to Edinburgh; also he is to travell up to Dunkeld', and on 19 December 1689 Robert Anderson, Glover, Burgess of Perth, was appointed with power to 'erect and set up ane post and letter office at the Burgh of Perth and to exact the dues of whatsoever letters shall be given in there.' (S.R.O., Perth Burgh Records (B.59.), document No. 1492 (temporary reference).)

first some exceptions to this monopoly had been recognized mainly in favour of the rich and powerful. The Act of 1711 continued these exceptions including specifically the existing privilege of letter-carrying claimed by the universities of Oxford and Cambridge. None of the early Scottish Statutes affecting the Post Office mention University posts, but in fact the oldest Scottish foundation, St Andrews, claimed and exercised rights of sending letters by its own post at least as early as the beginning of the 18th century. At that time the University post had a 'blazone' or badge of office and the University accounts of that period show the cost of sending letters by it, 1/−(s) for a letter from St Andrews to Perth or 2/−(s) for one to Edinburgh.[17] The University post went to Edinburgh once a week, leaving St Andrews on a different day from the Town post so that the university had in effect two posts a week to Edinburgh. On 14 November 1715 James Morice wrote from St Andrews to John Mackenzie of Delvine then at Edinburgh 'we have a Post that goes weekly from this to Dundee from quhence an open line may be easily sent to Delvin by the people about Couper Angus who have very frequent occasions to be there'.[18] A month later Morice writes again to Mackenzie at Edinburgh advising the employment of 'Jo. Robertson our Town Post, bearer hereof because he is not obnoxious to them that guard the passes, but J. Smart is by reason of his rash unadvised talk, which caused some things he was carrying to be taken from him'.[19] Smart's 'rash talk' may have cost him his job, for a later entry in the University records mentions what was apparently a fresh appointment of a University post 'betwixt this and Dundee . . . to carry letters and others for the Masters and Students and all belonging to the University'.

The postal network was spreading out. At a time when men 'wrote with difficulty and spelt by chance' rapid extension was hardly needed, nor indeed would it have been possible. In 1708 when George Main was Manager for Scotland, the Edinburgh office with a total staff of seven, including three letter-carriers for the city, controlled a total of 34 Post Towns throughout the country, a total which by 1715 had grown to close on 60. Anderson's letters show him in communication with offices stretching to Berwick, Dumfries and Portpatrick in the south, and to Perth, Dundee, Aberdeen and Inverness in the north and north-east in addition to the temporary Military Post by Blair Atholl and Kingussie to Inverness. To the west, Stirling and Glasgow were now linked to Edinburgh by the newly established horse posts, and from Glasgow postal links were being opened up to Dumbarton and on into Argyllshire. In the summer of 1717 Anderson was in communication with Inveraray, and since a letter to him from that town dated 4 July refers to lack of opportunity to forward a packet to Islay, it seems probable that the correspondent was the Inveraray postmaster.*

Inveraray in the first half of the 18th century was, as the ancestral home of the Dukes of Argyll, the unchallenged focal point of Argyllshire and the centre of an administrative activity without parallel in any part of western Scotland. From Inveraray the vast Argyll estates stretching down Loch Fyne to Knapdale and Kintyre in the south, to Morvern in the north and including much of Mull, Coll and Tiree, were administered. Between 1703 and 1743 the second duke, by the removal of many tacksmen and the increase in rents, opened the way for the widespread development and improvement of the Argyll estates which, after some initial dislocation, took place under his immediate successors. It may readily be supposed that close and detailed administrative control over such wide areas could not be achieved or maintained without frequent and sustained communication, a supposition which is amply confirmed by contemporary record.

Besides being the centre of the Argyll estates, Inveraray was the principal centre of the judicature in the West Highlands, and this, with the consequent presence in the town of both court officials and lawyers, would certainly entail much correspondence with the south and particularly with Edinburgh. Close connections with the South, too, were maintained by local gentry who were merchants as well as lairds, like Campbell of Knockbuy who had mercantile ties with Glasgow and who, about 1740, in a droving partnership with Campbell of Inverawe, used to send several thousand cattle south each year.

---

* N.L.S. Ibid., 82. The supposition that Inveraray had a postmaster by this time is confirmed by the fact that Neil Duncanson, postmaster at Inveraray, appears on the assize of the Justiciary Court of Argyll in 1718 and 1720, as does his successor Alexander Shearer in 1729, 1731 and 1732. (*Justiciary Records of Argyll and the Isles* ii, 350, 358, 402, 447 and 459. Stair Society, 1969.)

Apart from all this, the supplying of the everyday needs of the well-to-do must have called for no small amount of letter-writing. Letters of James Campbell of Stonefield, Chamberlain of Argyll in 1728 and 1729, show him in correspondence with merchants in Glasgow and Greenock for the supply of butcher meat, tea, flour, bread and lemons in addition to coal and wine, the latter in large quantities.

Among papers preserved in the Scottish Record Office in Edinburgh is a manuscript notebook of Archibald Campbell, innkeeper and postmaster at Inveraray, covering the period 1734/5. Here Campbell, in his capacity as postmaster, has recorded the letters received and despatched at Inveraray week by week.[20] The record shows that during the period 27 April to 31 December 1734 a total of over 2450 letters passed through the hands of the Inveraray postmaster. With the exception of a very small number to and from Campbeltown, all these letters are noted as having been despatched to or received from Edinburgh and Glasgow, the letters received from the South substantially exceeding those despatched from Inveraray. The writer of the account of Inveraray in the first *Statistical Account of Scotland* observed that before 1745 Inveraray was served by one weekly runner from Dumbarton. This is borne out by the entries in Campbell's notebook, the incoming letters being entered at approximately weekly intervals, the southbound ones leaving Inveraray each week about three or four days after the letters from the South had come in. Campbell's notebook shows a steady flow of correspondence all through the period, with an average of 30 to 40 letters received and despatched each week, rising to between 50 and 60 on occasions.

Besides noting the number of letters passing through his hands, Campbell has noted the amount of postage on these letters, 2d and 4d on those to and from Glasgow and 4d, 6d, 8d or even 10d on those to or from Edinburgh. It is known that at this date and for a long time after, detailed Reports were being rendered by the Chamberlains on the Argyll estates on the mainland and in the islands and very full instructions sent to them, and it seems probable that this accounted for some of the higher priced letters at least to and from Edinburgh. Campbell has also noted the number of letters on which the postage had been paid in advance. This shows that while a considerable proportion of the letters received from the South including, no doubt, those from the Duke or his secretary, had been paid for on despatch, very few of those sent south were prepaid. All through the 18th and well into the 19th centuries it was the common practice for letters to be paid for by the recipient. This practice seems to have been based on the supposition that postal officials would take more care of letters in the knowledge that payment depended on their safe delivery. It appears, however, to have been the generally accepted rule that when letters were despatched to persons inferior in rank or in poorer circumstances the postage was paid by the sender. In the case of the Inveraray letters, it may well be that many of these were addressed to small tenants and others in poor circumstances on the Argyll estates which would account for the fact that many of the letters from the South were prepaid.

Besides being postmaster at Inveraray, Campbell was also the innkeeper, a combination of functions which is apparent from an entry in one of his notebooks of items recording purchases for the inn as well as the records of his postal activities. He was evidently a farmer as well, and in one book occurs a note of payments made to those who helped him with his hay-making. To what extent his farming and innkeeping activities proved profitable cannot be known, but the writer of the statistical account of Inverary in 1792 has recorded[21] that despite the fact that prior to 1745 the Inveraray postmasters were allowed to retain the whole of the postage collected by them all went bankrupt.*

While the administration of the great Argyll estates must surely have accounted for much of the correspondence passing through Inveraray at this time, there is contemporary evidence of another busy enterprise some twenty miles to the north, which may well have added to Archibald Campbell's labours, if not to his income. On the north-west shore of Loch Etive close to the foot of Glen Esragan lies the small cluster of houses known as Inveresragan. Here for at least eleven years

---

* If as suggested in the Statistical Account the remuneration of the Inveraray postmasters depended on the postal charges collected by them, the fact that many of the higher charged letters from the South as recorded by Campbell had been prepaid would seem to go some way to explain their financial straits. The Inventory of the estate of Neil Duncanson, postmaster at Inveraray in 1725. contains assets amounting to only about £30 (Scots). (S.R.O. Com. Argyll Tests. 7 December 1725.)

between March 1733 and June 1744 Colin Campbell carried on a trading business known as the Loch Etive Trading Company. The full details of this concern are not known, but the papers which have survived give a vivid if incomplete picture of early 18th century trading on the west coast.[22] Here at Inveresragan Campbell appears to have established a general store supplied with goods of all sorts by coastal shipping. From Inveresragan he was in correspondence with customers and colleagues in the surrounding districts of Lorn and Appin and as far afield as Glasgow and Leith over the purchase and subsequent sale of a miscellany of goods as bewildering in its variety as it is fascinating in its composition. Leith and Glasgow supplied him with meal, wine, tobacco and cheese which he supplied to his Argyllshire customers, together with other goods varying from candy, soap, sugar and spices to nails for horseshoes and coffins, tar, door-locks and linen. To his more fashionable customers he sent silk and ribbon, coloured thread and wig powder, while those inclined to reading sent to him for volumes of Tacitus and Homer or popular plays. At a time when high finance was in its infancy Campbell acted to some degree as banker for his customers, and some of the letters show him involved in intricate financial transactions, drawing and accepting bills and dealing as best he could with clients who wrote of being 'vastly pinched for money'.

It is clear that not all this correspondence passed through the post. Many of Campbell's customers ask that goods be sent 'by the bearer' but there is a note of postage due for the period 21 February to 20 June 1738 showing a total of £1.8.1d and, as Inveraray was at this time by far the nearest post town to Inveresragan, Campbell's letters outward and inward bound must have passed through it. Many of these letters would no doubt be charged at 2d or at most 4d, but even taking the higher figure this would appear to mean eighty-four incoming letters over the period. The records of an obscure and little known enterprise on Loch Etive deserve perhaps only a small place in the history of Scotland's post, but they go at least to show another source from which letters reached the office at Inveraray, to add to the problems of Archibald Campbell struggling with his postal duties, his wine casks and perhaps his hay.

While these gradual developments in the Scottish postal

3. Letter opened by the rebels, 1745.

4. The Royal Mail Coach, *p.* 74.

system were taking place, events in relation to postal affairs south of the Border had been moving forward with some rapidity. Ralph Allen, the son of a Cornish innkeeper had, during his early days at the Bath post office, conceived the idea of organizing Cross Posts connecting the main postal roads which radiated out from London. The lack of properly organized Cross Posts had hitherto been a serious weakness in the English postal system. Letters between places nearly adjacent but on different postal routes required to go via London. This might mean a long and circuitous journey for a letter addressed to a person living within a few miles of the sender, and as letters were charged strictly by distance the absence of Cross Posts inevitably led to much illegal carriage of letters and loss to the Post Office. In 1720 Allen undertook, as 'farmer' or tenant, the organization of Cross Posts and also of those letters between points on the same postal route which for this reason did not go through London. In the course of over forty years as tenant Allen acted as both the architect and the organizing genius of a great network of postal roads bringing service to the public and growing profit, incidentally to himself, but primarily and permanently to the Post Office.

In Scotland very many years were to pass before anything approaching a similar system of Cross Posts came into existence, and at least until well into the second half of the 18th century the handful of main routes which linked the chief centres of population appear to have continued to serve with reasonable adequacy the postal needs of the country. Though the Act of 1711 had authorized the Postmasters General to set up Cross Posts as required to link the main postal routes and serve towns not on these routes, this authority was in Scotland little used. Those towns whose names figure in the postal records of the time were all on established postal routes and even Dunbar, so near the main post road to England, was for long without a post. Edinburgh, and to a smaller but growing extent Glasgow, were the hubs, themselves linked by way of Linlithgow and Falkirk, and from them radiated postal routes to Berwick, Dumfries, Ayr and Portpatrick in the south and south-west, to Dumbarton and Inveraray, Stirling and Perth in Central and western Scotland, while the old and important route still led through Fife by Dundee to Montrose, Aberdeen and Inverness and soon on to Thurso. Till past the turn of the century the great mass of the Scottish Highlands outside these routes was virtually without organized postal facilities of any sort, though contemporary records contain more than a suggestion that a foot post up the north-east coast from Inverness had been started some time in the second quarter of the century.

On the postal route between Edinburgh and Aberdeen, which had caused so much worry to the two Grahames of Inchbrakie and later to James Anderson, troubles persisted. The route from Edinburgh was through Fife by the Tay ferry to Dundee. Carriage of mails over successive stages by relays of carriers had not yet been instituted, the same carrier taking the mail to Dundee, Montrose and finally on to Aberdeen which was reached on the third or sometimes the fourth day. The despatch of the mails three times a week from Edinburgh was not well co-ordinated with the arrival of mails from the South, the merchants of Aberdeen and intervening towns on the route complaining bitterly of the delays which affected their business. Part of the blame seems to have been laid on the carriers, and they in their turn grumbled about the delays at the ferries. In July 1729 the Convention of Royal Burghs had the matter before them at their meeting in Edinburgh and the representatives for Edinburgh, Kinghorn and Dundee were instructed to ask the magistrates of these Burghs to give order to 'their shoar masters or others concerned in the passage of boats to give the said runners as ready passage and at as easy a rate as possible'.[23] The matter of ferry charges was of some importance to the mail carriers whose payment about this time amounted only to 6/8d for the return journey to and from Aberdeen and 1/6d for the ferries. The low pay for letter-carriers inevitably resulted in unofficial carrying of letters and parcels at lower rates 'without which it is understood they could not live'; but it seems that this was a problem not only on the Aberdeen road, for in 1738, when Archibald Douglas was Deputy Postmaster General for Scotland, the staff at the Edinburgh office included an 'Apprehender of private letter carriers'. Carriage of mail by unofficial methods was at this time and for many years to come symptomatic of a growing need ill-supplied by a lagging service. Even at a later date, when demand and supply in terms of postal facilities had come to be more closely matched, the use by the State of the post as an instrument of taxation resulted, as will be seen, in the long continuance of methods of evasion – a period which was not to reach its termination until the great postal reforms of the second quarter of the 19th century.

REFERENCES

1. N.L.S., Anderson MS, 3.
2. Ibid., 4.
3. Macpherson, *Annals of Commerce.*
4. Corrie, op. cit., 61 et seq.
5. N.L.S., Anderson MS, 67, 109/10.
6. Ibid., 67.
7. Ibid., 106.
8. Ibid.
9. S.R.O. GD. 72. No. 632.
10. N.L.S., Anderson MS, 110.
11. Ibid., 120/1.
12. Ibid., 143.
13. Ibid., 69.
14. Ibid., 132.
15. Ibid., 66, 111.
16. Ibid., 15, 19/20.
17. Dickinson, *Two students at St Andrews, passim.*
18. Ibid., 62.
19. Ibid.
20. S.R.O. GD. 1/2/11/1-7.
21. *O.S.A.,* v, 304.
22. S.R.O. GD. 1/2/15/1–205.
23. *Records of Convention of Royal Burghs,* v, 499.

Three

Postal Development in Scotland in the Late 18th century

The contemporary sources which have been used in attempting to reconstruct the postal history of Scotland in the first half of the 18th century are, as has been seen, both numerous and varied. In contrast, those available for the thirty years which followed the turn of the century are relatively few in number. The beneficial effects which had been looked for from the legislative Union of 1707 had been retarded by the political events of 1715 and 1745 and, in the Highlands at least, by the great social and economic changes which had been set on foot in 1748. In that year the wide powers of jurisdiction which many landed proprietors in both the Highlands and the Lowlands had for generations exercised over those living within their lands, were at a stroke swept away by a government which had good reason to fear the divided loyalty which these rights and duties created. The bewilderment and confusion caused by this sudden breaking of old ties and by the economic changes which both preceded and followed it were intense, and for many years to come much of Scotland, at least north of the Forth, was a distressed area. The relative scarcity of contemporary record during much of this period may perhaps be attributed in part to a decrease in national pride following the Union and the subsequent failure of the two Risings, and to delay in the emergence of the new pride and the new prosperity which were to come. So far as postal affairs during this period are concerned, the absence of contemporary record such as James Anderson's papers or Archibald Campbell's *Notebook* may be purely accidental and does not in fact indicate any real absence of postal development between 1750 and 1780; but that development is to be deduced from statistical evidence rather than from the more dramatic and colourful happenings of the first half of the century.

The great forward surge in the development and fortunes of the Post Office in England which took place as a result of Ralph Allen's organization of Cross Posts between 1720 and 1764 was matched by no such dramatic growth in Scotland. Save in parts of the Lowlands the geography of Scotland did not readily lend itself to the development of Cross Posts, while the relative absence of considerable centres of population outside the main towns made a system of Cross Posts far less necessary than in England. Furthermore, at this time and for many years to come, postage rates were fixed with reference to the distances over which letters were carried, and so from the point of view of postal revenue Cross Posts or short cuts of any sort were, at least in Scotland where postal traffic was relatively small, not attractive. The roads of Scotland, too, were in the middle years of the 18th century far from suited to any rapid or extensive growth of the postal system. Only between the main cities were they passable and even there only with difficulty. For the rest, roads were still, over much of the country, almost non-existent. The work of General Wade had been largely confined to the making of some 250 miles of road between Crieff, Inverness and Fort William, and these, with the additional roads built by the Army after Wade's death in 1748, were neither intended nor suited for civilian use. More than half a century was to pass before the task of building roads and bridges in the Highlands for civilian use was seriously put in hand. Outside the Highlands the construction and maintenance of public roads had long been a task utterly beyond the powers of those responsible for directing the old system of statute labour, and the system of Turnpike Trusts which eventually took its place was still very much in its infancy.

With all this it is perhaps hardly surprising that in the middle decades of the century postal development in Scotland was still largely confined to the main lines of communication and that even there it was at best gradual. The road between Berwick and Edinburgh had long been regarded as little more than an extension of the great road from London to the North. The post on this road had, of course, from the first been a horse post. Even so the time taken by the mail on the journey from London to Edinburgh up to the middle of the century was 85 hours while the return journey rather inexplicably took 131 hours. The slowness of the journey was at the time explained by lack of organization or sense of urgency at the various stages. Sir Robert Carey had easily bettered this speed on his ride north in 1603 with the news of the death of Queen Elizabeth; but then he was the bearer of urgent tidings of supreme national importance, whereas it is on record that during the first half of the 18th century there were frequent occasions when even Provost Alexander, the sole banker in Edinburgh at the beginning of that century, received by the London mail only one solitary letter.[1] In April 1758 a Memorial setting out a plan for speeding the London mail was presented to the Postmasters General at the instance of George Chalmers, an Edinburgh Merchant. Delays in the post, maintained Chalmers, were due to the unnecessary deviation of the mail route to York. A more direct route from Ferrybridge, by Wetherby to Boroughbridge was proposed. This route appears to have been adopted in 1760, and many years later Chalmers was still vainly petitioning the Government for some financial recognition of a plan which had, it was claimed, almost doubled the net revenue of the Post Office in Scotland between 1758 and 1772.

Despite the adoption of the improved route, however, weaknesses in the postal arrangements between London and Scotland continued to be cause of grievance. These were fully set out in a Memorial prepared by the Annual General Convention of Royal Burghs in Scotland in February 1762 asking for the extension of a daily post from Newcastle *via* Edinburgh to Aberdeen, Glasgow and Greenock and also from Carlisle to Dumfries. Those concerned in the conveying and despatching of mails, it was complained, were 'apt to relax and fall back in their duty' with the result that letters arrived too late to be answered by the next post leaving Edinburgh, where four hours were needed for their distribution 'even within the walls, by carrier'.

'It is well known at present,' continued the Memorialists, 'what shameful delays are made by most of the Postmasters in dispatching the mail, the bad and lame horses employed by many of the contractors for conveying it, some of which may not be worth 10/– or 20/– apiece, so that they scarcely go at a trot and every common traveller passes the King's mail on the first road in the Kingdom.'

Instead of being ready to take the mail at the various stages, the horses were often at work in the fields and the mail had sometimes to be conveyed in chaises hired by ordinary travellers. Stages of as much as 30 to 50 miles were believed to be part of the trouble, as well as negligence at the Queensferry crossing of the Forth on the road to Aberdeen. To ensure better time-keeping, one way-bill for the whole journey between north and south should be used – and this to be on parchment. To complete the indictment, both postmasters and contractors were underpaid, while the new arrangements whereby the revenue from by-letters (*i.e.* local letters) was now taken by the Post Office instead of being treated as the perquisite of postmasters had so much reduced the remuneration of the latter that some had thrown up their jobs and others were likely to follow suit. It was a sorry picture indeed, but all the contemporary evidence suggests that it was little, if at all, overpainted.

On the further extension of the east coast road from Edinburgh to Aberdeen, the middle of the century witnessed a change to horse posts carrying the mail in relays from stage to stage, replacing the slow foot posts who had eked out their miserable pay at the expense of the Post Office. Hitherto only three posts a week had passed between Edinburgh and Aberdeen, but about 1763 this was increased to five a week. London letters for Aberdeen were, however, still held up for two days or longer in Edinburgh, a delay which was to be a continuous source of grievance till almost the end of the century. Beyond Aberdeen, Inverness was still served by a post three days a week. In the summer of 1755 a gentleman in Morayshire complained that no news had come from Edinburgh, a circumstance which was understandable since the southbound mail had by mistake been returned in place of that which was northbound from London.[2] If this reflected little credit on the standard of postal service it did at least indicate the existence of a regular correspondence with London. As to the service north and west from Inverness itself, there is some evidence that at or shortly after the middle of the century branches of the postal route led to Fort Augustus and Fort William; to Wick, Thurso and Kirkwall; to Cromarty and Fortrose; to Loch Carron and Skye; and to Ruthven in Badenoch. How frequent or efficient these services were may, however, be doubted, and it will be recalled that in 1773 Samuel Johnson and James Boswell received no mail between leaving Aberdeen on 24 August and reaching Glasgow on 28 October. The lowest postal rate in Scotland fixed by the Act of 1711 had been 2d up to 50 miles. In 1765 the rate for one stage was reduced to a penny, though the exact distance constituting a stage must have varied on different routes. The reduced rates remained in force till 1784, and over half a century was to pass from then before one penny was again to be the charge for ordinary postage over even the shortest distance in the United Kingdom.

All through the 18th century Edinburgh continued to be the central point in Scotland for postal administration. Edinburgh, too, was the main collecting point for Scottish postal revenue, and the growth of the Edinburgh office over the period can be looked on as a fair reflection of the growth of Scotland's postal service. In 1741 when the post of Deputy Postmaster General in Scotland was held by Alexander Hamilton, the Edinburgh staff consisted of the Deputy himself and eight others as well as three carriers for the Edinburgh area, and thirty years later the staff was still only 10 besides letter-carriers.[3] As the century wore on the work of the office grew at increasing speed and by 1788 the Edinburgh staff had risen to 31. With the increase in staff had gone a corresponding increase in postal revenue collected by the Edinburgh office. At the time of the Union in 1707 the nominal revenue of Scotland's Post Office consisted solely of the yearly rent of £1194 paid by George Main, and as has been seen this was largely cancelled out by outlays made on behalf of the Crown. By the middle of the century the total revenue of the Scottish Office had climbed slowly to not far short of £10,000, but the rate of growth was increasing and by 1783 the Edinburgh office was collecting over £40,000 per annum.[4] The increasing staff and the growing revenue were a direct reflection of a widening service. In Alexander Hamilton's time the number of post offices controlled by and accounting to the Edinburgh office was reported as 106, a figure which had risen by 1781 to 140 and by 1791 to 164.[5]

If the evidence and sources for tracing the history of the Post Office in Scotland during the middle years of the 18th century are, as has been suggested, somewhat dry, factual and lacking in human interest, a marked change was in fact about to take place. The great political and social changes of the half-century following the Union had brought to Scotland and particularly to the Highlands a degree of confusion and distress which could hardly be, and was not in fact, ignored. As memories of 1745 receded, though military surveillance of the Highlands continued, it became increasingly clear that the failure of the rising, and the events which immediately followed, had left in their wake a poor and distressed but peaceful country. Growing interest in Scottish affairs and Scottish problems brought to Scotland writers and economists, farmers and social workers. The enlightened policy of the Commissioners charged with the management of estates forfeited after the two risings led to improved standards of farming and estate management over wide areas and even to some measure of industrial development. The new interest in Scotland and Scottish affairs led to comprehensive surveys of the country, the results of which, in the closing years of the century, were embodied by Sir John Sinclair in the *Statistical Account of Scotland*, and by other writers in detailed reports on the way of life and the agricultural development of nearly every Scottish county. Finally the great engineer Thomas Telford and his colleagues, working for the Commissioners for Highland Roads and Bridges, brought about in the early years of the 19th century a great opening up of Highland communications. All these developments in Scotland and particularly in the Highlands led naturally to increased need for, and use of, postal facilities and it was fortunate indeed for the Post Office, and no less for the postal historian, that these events coincided with the appearance on the scene of one of the great figures in postal history.

When John Palmer persuaded the younger Pitt in 1784 to allow him to try the experiment of introducing mail coaches on the postal roads of England, he chose as his Chief Assistant an active young man named Francis Freeling who over the next few years acted as Palmer's surveyor on many of the new mail coach routes. At the time of Palmer's dismissal from the Post Office service in 1793, Freeling held the position of Resident Surveyor at the Headquarters of the Post Office in London. In

1797 he became Joint Secretary of the Post Office and almost immediately after sole Secretary, a post which he was to hold for nearly forty years. During his long tenure of office this loyal and active servant of the Post Office occupied a position of unique importance and authority. The office of Postmaster General was a joint appointment frequently held by two members of the House of Lords. Though the Postmasters General took a considerable interest in postal affairs they were in most cases largely ignorant of the details of the work, and as time went on Francis Freeling's became increasingly the guiding hand at the Post Office Headquarters. Neither the Postmasters General nor Freeling himself possessed any extensive knowledge of Scotland, and much guidance and advice was sought and received from the post office staff in Edinburgh and from the two surveyors who covered the Scottish area. Extensive correspondence between London and Scotland and the huge accumulation of collected papers which resulted has been carefully preserved in the Record Office of the Post Office Headquarters in St Martins-le-Grand, and from this emerges over a period of forty years a vivid and detailed picture of Scotland's postal services.

It has been seen that from a very early stage the extension to Aberdeen of the main postal artery from London to the North occupied an important place in Scotland's postal system, and in the closing years of the 18th century this route continued to occupy a prominent place in the developments then taking place. In 1790 Freeling, in his capacity of Surveyor of Mail Coach routes, paid one of his few visits to Edinburgh. His visit was mainly in connection with a plan which led to important developments for extension of postal services in the Edinburgh area of which more will appear, but there can be little doubt that on that visit he would hear much of a problem which was shortly to become acute.

The post from Edinburgh to Aberdeen had, shortly after the middle of the century, been so far improved that it was now conveyed by relays of horse posts carrying the mails in three stages. This was a vast improvement on the old system whereby a foot post carried them all the way; but even this improved service was liable at times to serious interruption such as that which occurred in the spring of 1793 when Francis Freeling had to take urgent steps to prevent the 12 men engaged on the vital

Queensferry Passage from being pressed for service in the Navy.[6] While the actual transit of the mail had been quickened, however, the main grievance of Aberdeen and the intervening towns remained — that the northern mail often did not leave Edinburgh for two or sometimes three days after the arrival of the mail from London.

> 'The institution of Posts', stated a Memorial by the Northern Towns about this time, 'was in the first place to facilitate commerce by the conveyance of letters with the quickest possible despatch from one end of the Kingdom to the other, and in the next place to raise a Revenue for the Government; and they [the Memorialists] cannot conceive that either of these ends will be prompted by the letters of two-thirds of the Kingdom of Scotland lying dormant for many hours at Edinburgh.'[7]

Persistent pressure by the northern towns resulted in reducing to some twelve hours the delay of the London mail in Edinburgh, and in 1794 and 1795 the controversy centred on further reduction. The Aberdeen merchants argued with some force that merchants in Edinburgh, speculating for example on the price of corn, could on receipt of early morning news from the South despatch an express rider to the North and so forestall those in Aberdeen waiting for the later arrival of the mail from Edinburgh. Those in Edinburgh argued that delay was necessary to facilitate Court and other official business, and particularly to allow Edinburgh newspapers to print news from London in papers for sale in the North. Considerations of prestige seem to have been by no means absent from the minds of those in the capital, and it was even argued that some Aberdeen people would not be sorry of an excuse for delay in answering letters, particularly those of a financial character. Secretary Dundas, the Lord Provost of Edinburgh, the Chamber of Commerce under their Chairman Sir William Forbes, the Law Societies of Edinburgh and many another were drawn into the argument, while the hour of despatch from Edinburgh was slowly advanced from 9 p.m. on the day of arrival of the mail from London to 3 p.m., a compromise suggested by Sir William Forbes as 'calculated to obviate all difficulties, to preserve to the Capital of Scotland its just distinction and convenience and to afford great accommodation to the Northern towns, tho' not to the extent solicited . . .',[8] then to 1 p.m.; and finally to 9 a.m.

The Surveyors and other postal officials did not speak with one voice, and long before the battle ended Francis Freeling and the Postmasters General must have wearied of the subject.[9] For the Surveyors, indeed, such changes as were taking place on the mail route to Aberdeen meant much work and worry. In 1798 when the hour of departure from Edinburgh was finally advanced to 9 a.m. no fewer than nineteen Post Towns in Fife and Kinross-shire were affected. For these, the postal service had hitherto been maintained partly by horse posts and partly by foot carriers. Now the whole service was to be by horse post and it was expected that the existing Revenue of £6000 per annum would be increased by one-sixth. As the century drew to a close the weight of mail, loaded with newspapers, Army Reports, and Reports of parliamentary proceedings, grew to as much as 20 stone, and it became clear that only horsedrawn vehicles could finally solve the problem of an accelerated mail service to the North. Soon after the establishment of the mail coach from London to Edinburgh in 1785, Palmer had proposed to continue the coach service to Aberdeen. Indeed in August 1788 the Freedom of the city of Aberdeen was conferred on Palmer 'to whom the commerce of the Nation is so highly indebted for the regulations and improvements in correspondence and for the establishment of a safe and expeditious mode of conveyance by mail coaches'.[10] So far as the city of Aberdeen was concerned, this honour was somewhat premature, for the state of the road between Perth and Aberdeen made the introduction of a mail coach on it at that time impossible. Successive reports on the state of the road up the east coast showed that though parts of it had been greatly improved under the care of Turnpike Trusts, much was still unfitted for rapid wheel traffic, and it was not till 1798 that the establishment of a mail coach at length brought with it the prospect of a final solution of the problem.*

While the controversy over the post to Aberdeen was raging, a development took place in the post from that city to Inverness.

---

* The introduction of mail coaches on the Aberdeen road did not in fact result in an immediate end of the controversy. As late as March 1816 merchants in Dundee, Perth and Inverness were still complaining of the delay, by then reduced to three hours, in sending on the London letters from Edinburgh. Dundee merchants in particular complained that they did not receive these till 8 p.m. and so were frequently doing business in the coffee houses or the Exchange at midnight.

For many years past this post had been only three times a week, but in the early months of 1793 Robert Oliphant the Deputy Postmaster General in Edinburgh sent on to Freeling a Petition in the form of a Memorial by local proprietors and others that a daily post should be established. The Memorial bore an impressive list of names including that of Lord Adam Gordon Commander in Chief of the Forces in North Britain who urged the military advantage of a daily post. The gross annual revenue to the Post Office from the towns between Aberdeen and Inverness was stated to be over £2600 of which Banff contributed £422, Elgin £368, and Inverness itself £700. The increased revenue from a daily post would, it was thought, more than offset the increased cost of the service based on a figure of 3d per mile or £4.13.4d per mile per annum, at that time considered to be the standard cost of a horse post.[11] Freeling recommended to the Postmasters General that a daily post be tried, and in the spring of 1794 he was able to report that the change had proved highly profitable, and should be made permanent.

North of Inverness a post to Thurso, which went three days a week, had for some years been in existence. The writer of the account of the Parish of Kilmorack in the *Statistical Account of Scotland* notes that at one time the local proprietors had themselves employed a runner to bring their mail from Inverness, but later a post office was successfully established at Beauly through the efforts of Colonel Fraser of Belladrum, who became surety for the postmaster.[12] Offices were also established about this time at Tain and Dornoch, and in the last years of the century Freeling was in correspondence over Petitions that a daily post be established, in the first place to them, and soon after all the way to Thurso. The outcome of an experimental extension of a daily post to Tain had not been encouraging, an actual decrease in postal revenue having resulted. Ronaldson, the postal surveyor, had reported in September 1798 that this was partly due to so many 'respectable inhabitants' being away on service and partly to 'the lower classes now receiving and sending their letters under their privilege as soldiers and which there is much reason to believe is not confined to those only who are strictly entitled to it'.[13] The exact nature of the postal services about this time is not always easy to determine, contemporary records mentioning rather indiscriminately 'runners' and 'riding work'. In the autumn of 1802 Freeling supported a request by the local people that the existing post between Dornoch and Wick should be changed from 3 days a week to a daily service, the additional cost including the ferries at Helmsdale and at the Little Ferry across the mouth of Loch Fleet being estimated at only £80 per annum while the postal revenue was believed to amount to £1000 per annum. William Kerr, the Secretary at the Edinburgh office, had supported the application, but in answer to complaints of delays in the post had written '. . . the riding work is in general performed in the time stipulated except during snowstorms, and when the runners are detained I believe it is by some of the gentlemen of Caithness themselves'.[14] Further major improvement on this coastal road was to come only with the completion of Telford's road and bridge work in the north-east in the second decade of the 19th century.

Of the many Scottish problems which faced the postal authorities in the last years of the 18th century, one of the most urgent concerned the closing of a postal gap on the southern edge of the Highlands. Up till the year 1793 no postal service directly connected Stirling with Perth. From Stirling a daily post went to Crieff and another, on 3 days a week, to Auchterarder, but neither continued to Perth, and in the spring of that year Freeling and his colleagues had before them a Memorial which pointed out the obvious weakness of an arrangement whereby letters between Perth and Stirling must go round by Edinburgh. It seems that in this instance the benefits from the proposed postal link were so patent as to offset in the minds of the Post Office any reduction in revenue which might result from letters being carried over a shorter distance. George Haldane, the Laird of Gleneagles Estate on the Ochils, had taken up the matter with vigour arguing with much apparent reason that the best line between Stirling and Perth went through Auchterarder.[15] Certain of the officials at the Edinburgh office and Freeling himself supported this view which seems to have been virtually accepted when Mr Smythe of Methven entered the lists with equal vigour in support of a line through Crieff. From the contemporary documents it is easy to see that feelings and tempers ran high in Strathearn while the battle raged. Haldane as 'Preces' of the County had local authority and not a little postal opinion on his side, but Smythe proved a tactician of no mean order. At a meeting held in Perth at the beginning of September 1793 the voting in favour of the Crieff route was overwhelming, and Haldane's contention that the meeting had been arranged for a time when his supporters were kept away by the calls of the harvest seems not to have been accepted.[16] Freeling himself felt that too much consideration had been given to the convenience of the people of Crieff, and in a letter to the Postmasters General expressed his personal view that there was no comparison between the two routes, that by Auchterarder being obviously the better.[17] The voting for Crieff, however, was held to be conclusive of local opinion and at the end of September Francis Ronaldson, the Postal Surveyor for the area, reported the establishment of a daily post from Stirling to Perth by way of Crieff, a change which involved him in a long journey 'regulating the offices at Perth, Crieff, Auchterarder, Dunblane and Stirling in consequence of this Establishment'. Auchterarder got a branch service from Crieff while another branch went from Stirling by Dunblane and Doune to Callander.[18]

If the exact line of the new postal route between Perth and Stirling was the subject of doubt and controversy, the general desirability of establishing a postal link between the towns seems not to have been questioned; but hardly had the new route been established when questions of a more fundamental nature arose. In October 1793 Edwards, one of the officials of the Edinburgh office who had been closely concerned in the matter, wrote to Freeling raising the whole question of the implications of this postal link across Central Scotland. It now appeared, wrote Edwards, that the real intention, at least in the minds of some of those who had put forward the plan for the new route, was not merely an improvement in the local posts but the diversion through Perth to Stirling of all correspondence for South and West Scotland reaching Perth from the North. These letters at present went *via* Edinburgh, an arrangement which, while no doubt facilitating the correct charging of these letters, added to the postal dues, since letters were still charged strictly on the distances over which they were carried. Edwards estimated that the proposed diversion would cost the Post Office £1000 to £1500 per annum, while he claimed somewhat inexplicably that it would not in fact improve the postal service to the South and West. Oliphant, the Deputy Postmaster General in Edinburgh, argued that 'the cheaper letters are the greater will be the number written' and had in fact ordered the new plan to be put into effect.[19] The immediate outcome of the matter is not apparent from the correspondence, but it is clear that the financial argument was in Freeling's mind of prime importance, and it is probable that in this as in many other matters Oliphant was over-ruled. During the 17th and part of the 18th centuries when postal revenue went to the crown, any change in postal routes likely to affect post office revenue needed royal assent. At a later stage when the revenue of the Post Office had ceased to be the property of the crown this difficulty could not be pleaded as an obstacle to changes in the routing of posts. By then, however, the Treasury was becoming increasingly jealous of any changes likely to decrease postal revenue, and throughout all his years at the Post Office Freeling was to remain highly sensitive to any criticism of the routing of letters.

While the battle in Strathearn swung to and fro, three other matters on the borders of Perthshire claimed the attention of the London office. Happily these were smaller in scale and less controversial in character. The village of Newburgh in Fife on the southern shores of the Tay estuary had hitherto received its letters through the Perth office. Trade and industry in Newburgh were on the increase. Ships carrying salmon in season and brown linen left the port each week for London, and Newburgh with deeper water than Perth was to some extent the port for the county town, which meant frequent and urgent communication between the two on Customs and other matters. In the spring of 1793 the bailies of Newburgh, enlisting the support of the merchants, the tanner, the schoolmaster and the local lawyer, petitioned for a post office in the town with a runner to collect the postal bag at Crossgates on the road from Edinburgh to Perth.* It must have been with some relief that Freeling, supported by the view of his Scottish officials, agreed to this modest and simple proposal.[20]

On the south side of Strathearn a further small improvement in the postal service took place just after the turn of the century.

---

* It is unlikely that the collection point suggested for the Newburgh letters can have been Crossgates in Fife over fifteen miles off. It is much more probable that the 'Crossgates' then referred to was some nearer point on the Perth road no longer so named. This supposition would seem to be confirmed by the marking of 'Crossgates' only a few miles from Newburgh in the map of 1813 (at end).

Up till 1803 letters for the village of Dunning had reached it by way of Perth. In that year Freeling approved an application by the Dunning people for a daily post branching off at Bridge of Earn from the main postal road between Edinburgh and Perth. The new mail service to Dunning which was to be operated by runner at a cost of 1/– a day would be shorter than that by Perth, and by keeping to the south bank of the River Earn would avoid a crossing of the river 'by ford or boat'. Dunning, the surveyor had reported, had a close connection with Perth 'in several branches of manufactures' while the district was 'abounding with Noblemen's and Gentlemen's seats'.* South of the Ochil Hills the small village of Blairingone also sought postal facilities. In the absence of special claims the size of the Blairingone community would hardly have justified a postal service, but in a Petition of March 1796 the local inhabitants based their claim largely on the existence of a coal mine, the property of the Duke of Athol, which supplied Crieff, Comrie and much of Strathearn, a bleachfield at nearby Dollar and the important linen industry of Dunfermline partially dependent on flax grown on the farms of Fife and southern Perthshire. Here too the Petitioners prevailed and a post office with a runner to Dunfermline was set up at a cost of £18 per annum.[21]

While the more liberal policy of the Post Office in the last years of the 18th century was thus showing itself in the extension of postal services and the establishment of offices in places where their profitability must have been marginal, applications for services were still scrutinized with critical eyes both in London and in Edinburgh. In the summer of 1793 William Kerr, the Secretary of the Scottish Office, advised against the establishment of offices at Tranent, East Linton or Cockburnspath. Of the latter, once a key point on the old postal road between Berwick and Edinburgh, he wrote that it consisted of 'a single house or a few scattered cottages', but an office at Ayton in Berwickshire might, he thought, be justified owing to the proximity of the 'sea-port' at Eymouth.

In west Perthshire at the close of the century another problem

---

* Post 40/64M/1803. The reference to avoidance of a crossing of the River Earn 'by ford or boat' in 1803 seems obscure. The Rev. Neil Meldrum in his *Forteviot. The History of Strathearn Parish,* has recorded that Forteviot Bridge was built about 1766, and James Stobie's map of Perthshire (1783) indicates a bridge at Dalreoch, though the present bridge at that point appears to have been built in 1811.

loomed. The Earl of Breadalbane, who was to prove an ardent if uncompromising advocate of postal extension, had complained to Ronaldson, the Surveyor, of the bad postal facilities in the wide tract of country lying between Balquhidder, Loch earnhead, Killin and Tyndrum; and well he might. The nearest post offices were at Callander and Crieff to the south and east, while to the west there appears at this time to have been no postal connection between Perthshire and the post route from Dumbarton to Inveraray, which was soon to stretch north to Appin and Fort William. In this area, where particularly around Loch Tay many of the farms on the Breadalbane property were benefiting from 'the late improvements in the rearing of cattle and other Agricultural concerns in that Country', very many people were thus without postal facilities within 20, 30 or even 40 miles. Urged on by Lord Breadalbane, Ronaldson now proposed foot posts from Callander to Lochearnhead and Killin 3 days a week with an extension to Luib once a week. Ronaldson proposed for the postmasters at Killin and Luib the modest salaries of £5 and £4 per annum respectively, while the foot posts from Callander to Lochearnhead and from there on to Killin were to get only 6/– and 3/– a week respectively for their thrice-weekly tramp. For the five-mile walk from Lix road junction to Luib the letter-carrier was to be rewarded with 1/6d each week for the return journey.[22] The local people in the Breadalbane country had collected £54 to make good any loss to the Post Office, but the surveyor advised against its acceptance in accordance with the usual post office policy at this time that the establishment and continuance of new services must be judged purely on their own merits and performance. Freeling advised that the plan be tried, and Lord Auckland, who with Lord Gower at this time held the post of Postmaster General, concurred in an experiment in 'a district so totally unknown to me'. Two years later Ronaldson recommended that the new post offices, now including one at Dalmally, should be made permanent in view of 'the now improving state of this part of the Highlands of Scotland and the prospects of further advantage from the Peace and the return of the Proprietors and many of the inhabitants of it from the service of their Country'.[23] The postal authorities were not alone in premature rejoicing over the Peace of Amiens.

Since the abandonment in 1718 of the direct horse post

between Perth and Inverness which had been set up for Army purposes at the time of the Rising of 1715, postal facilities on this road north of Dunkeld had been virtually non-existent. Even for Pitlochry and Blair Atholl the nearest post office was at Dunkeld. In the spring of 1799 the Duchess of Gordon applied to the Post Office for a horse post to Blair Atholl three times a week with a foot post on from there to Pitmain in Badenoch. She pointed out that at present the post from Edinburgh to Pitmain by Aberdeen travelled 259 miles and took three days, whereas by what was then known as the Highland Road by Dunkeld and Blair Atholl the distance would be only 112 miles. The duchess admitted to some doubts as to whether the revenue would justify the cost but added

'... in an age of Liberal Improvement an accommodation tending to the general advantage of a State by circulating Intelligence more rapidly through all its parts will not, it is hoped, be weighed altogether in the Scale of common interest nor refused merely on the ground of its not being a profitable bargain.'*

Ronaldson, the Surveyor, to whom the application had been submitted, wrote:

'At a very early period when Posts were in their infancy in Scotland the communication with Inverness was through this country [Badenoch] once a week or once a fortnight, and as I have been informed it was then very usual to lose all communication in Winter for a month or two altogether – and as soon as correspondence began to improve and regular posts became of importance to the Country and to Inverness this course was totally abandoned and the circuitous route by the East Coast adopted as the best and surest.'

On the whole matter the Surveyor had no hesitation in ranking himself with those who, if not set on a profitable bargain, were at least averse to a ruinous loss and the plan was summarily turned down.[24]

While these events had been taking place on the postal routes up the east coast and on the southern edge of the Highlands, important developments had occurred on the roads leading to the Atlantic seaboard. Until the middle of the 18th century it seems virtually certain that Inveraray was the most northerly post office on the road from Dumbarton, dealing with

* See Appendix VI.

all postal communications with the South together with the postal needs of Argyllshire north and west of Loch Fyne. During the second half of the century these needs had been growing. On the Argyll estates successive dukes, profiting by the estate reorganization and the increase in rents set on foot by the second duke, had pressed forward with large and ambitious projects, including the planning and building of the new castle and the new town of Inveraray together with large-scale improvements in agriculture and forestry on both the mainland and island properties. In particular, John, the fifth Duke, acting through his various estate chamberlains and James Ferrier, w.s., his Edinburgh agent, showed himself to be 'one of the most able and energetic landlords of his day going about his business, changing the face of the land, moving populations, setting down towns and villages, founding industries, meticulously controlling the life of the inhabitants of his estate'.[25] Besides his great activity on his own estates, John Campbell was one of the chief promoters of the Crinan Canal, the construction of which was in active progress between 1793 and 1801.

Exactly at what date post offices immediately north of Inveraray were established is not clear. In October 1760, Archibald Campbell, postmaster at Inveraray, in a Memorial to the Justices of the Peace and the Commissioners of Supply of Argyllshire, complained that his salary was only £15 per annum though he had been postmaster for fourteen years. 'Every week', his Memorial stated, 'three runners are dispatched to and arrive from Dumbarton, as many to Campbeltown, two to Cowall, one to Islay, two to Argyll and four to Lorn.'[26] At the time of the *Statistical Account of Scotland* (1791/9) it was reported that Argyllshire had a total of ten post offices. Six years later the people of Campbeltown asked for a daily post, the net cost to be guaranteed by the Duke of Argyll. In ordinary circumstances Freeling would have turned this down, but in view of the Duke's great local interest it was decided to make an exception in this instance and a daily post was granted.[27]

The weekly post from Dumbarton to Inveraray in the middle years of the century had already been increased to a thrice-weekly service with 'Receiving Houses' for the deposit and receipt of mail at Luss, Arrochar and Cairndow, and this in turn was soon to grow to a six-day service, adding to the problems of the surveyor and local officials to whom fell the task of maintaining the regular carriage of growing loads over the steep gradients between Arrochar and Cairndow. Until at least the end of the year 1771 the post between Dumbarton and Inveraray had been a foot post, but in December of that year the duke wrote to Donald Campbell the chamberlain of Argyll, and to the chamberlain of Kintyre, who between them looked after estate matters at Inveraray, the central districts of the estate and Kintyre:

> 'Consider in what manner a Horse Post may be established between Dumbarton and Inveraray or whether an equal dispatch might not be had by three foot runners which would be a great saving of expense, and send me a state of that matter in writing as soon as you can.'

With all this activity Ronaldson, the surveyor of the Western area, was justified in referring to Inveraray in 1799 as a key point where the postal receipts a few years earlier had been reported as bringing in a net profit of £319 sterling and where the postmaster's salary was noted as £32 per annum.[28] The amount of the salary may seem modest but it compared well with that for many an office in larger towns elsewhere in Scotland.

It will be recalled that the improvements carried out in the Breadalbane country between 1800 and 1802 included the establishment of a post office at Dalmally, and there seems little doubt that well before that time the post was continuing north from Inveraray by Bonawe through Appin to Ballachullish and Fort William. In the summer of 1800 Ronaldson, the surveyor, had gone to Argyllshire to investigate complaints of delay in the posts on this route. The surveyor's report shows that at this time the route of the post north of Inveraray crossed Loch Awe at Port Sonachan and continued down Glen Nant to the Bonawe Ferry over Loch Etive. From Bonawe the route led through Glen Salach and so down to the shores of Loch Creran which was crossed at Shian Ferry. Ronaldson found that part of the cause of complaint lay in delays at the ferries. He proposed to cut out the crossing of Loch Awe by arranging for the post to make a detour from Cladich on the south side of Loch Awe to Dalmally, and so on through the Pass of Brander to Bonawe. To speed the crossing of Loch Creran he proposed that this be made at Creagan where the loch is narrower and less exposed than at Shian.

But there seems to have been human failings in this North Argyllshire post to add to the physical difficulties:

'I found', wrote the surveyor in his report, 'it had been the general practice for the post from Bonawe to Appin to lodge regularly at night in or near the house of Ardchattan, and did not cross Shian till the following morning, losing 12 hours to the Appin, Strontian and Fort William districts of country; and I consider it an improvement of itself to remove such private lodgings or accommodation out of the way of posts, which, as I have been informed, is sometimes done for the sake of perusing newspapers as well as answering or writing letters.'[29]

Ronaldson during his long service as surveyor was to prove himself a just and kindly man,[30] but a reader of today may well feel some doubt as to how far the postal problems between Dumbarton and Fort William were in fact resolved by depriving the post carrier, with a long walk already behind him, of a comfortable night's rest at Ardchattan. Later, after pony posts had taken the place of foot posts the case may have been different, but until that time came the road from Dumbarton to the north-west was to remain one of the hardest in all Scotland. Only five years after his adverse comments on the Ardchattan postmen Ronaldson wrote of the foot carrier's work:

'I have sometimes observed these mails at leaving Dumbarton about 3 stone or 48 lbs weight and they were generally over 2 stones.* During the course of last winter horses were obliged to be occasionally employed; and it is often the case that a strong Highlander with so great a weight on him cannot travel more than 2 miles an hour, which greatly retards the general correspondence of this extensive district of country.'[31]

While the postal network spreading north-westward from Glasgow had reached the seaboard of Argyllshire on Loch Fyne, Loch Etive and Loch Leven, other post roads were being opened up to the Atlantic coast. At some date in the third quarter of the 18th century Inverness had been linked with Fort William by a post route through the Great Glen by Fort Augustus. Fort William at the end of the 18th century was already a

* The Dutch stone of 16 lb was in use at this time.

centre of considerable importance for the Western Highlands, a large part of its trade passing up and down Loch Linnhe. Shipping inward bound brought meal, coal and general supplies, to take back slates and wool, for Fort William was at that time the main wool market of the West. The time was very near when in addition Fort William was to become, and to remain for upwards of twenty years, the scene of great activity during the building of the Caledonian Canal. Postal routes were soon to lead from Fort William across Corran Ferry to the old lead and silver mines at Strontian on Loch Sunart, still in spasmodic though not continuous operation, and by Lochiel and Glenfinnan to Arisaig to serve the needs of the growing fishing industry of which so much was hoped.

Northward again a postal route from Inverness had been opened to the Kyle of Lochalsh with a branch by way of Loch Maree to Poolewe, while Ullapool on Loch Broom was soon to get the most northerly of the postal links between the Atlantic coast and Inverness. Here at Ullapool the British Fishery Society had in the closing years of the 18th century established one of the most important of the several fishing stations built by them on the west coast and among the Islands. The station at Ullapool, in common with much of the work of the society, was ultimately to fail in its purpose, but for over fifty years the Ullapool station was to be the centre of much varied and hopeful activity. Ullapool in 1802 had no regular postal link with the east coast. In the summer of that year John Maloney, the agent for the British Fishery Society there, applied to the Post Office for a weekly post to Dingwall. The amount of necessary correspondence during the herring fishing season was, he claimed, astonishing. The society employed a runner to take letters to Dingwall, but he could not bring back incoming mail since the Dingwall post office would not part with letters till the postage had been paid. Lists of the addresses on letters lying at Dingwall – often 60 to 100 at a time – were posted up at Ullapool Church, but before payment for these could be sent by runner the news of herring shoals on another part of the coast might reach the fishing fleet, which thus sailed in ignorance of news or orders which might be awaiting them. At best, argued Maloney with some force, the inducements for 60 to 100 people to entrust money to ignorant and illiterate runners were not apparent. It happened that William Kerr,

Secretary at the Edinburgh post office, was himself a share-holder in the British Fishery Society, an interest which he felt called on to disclose in supporting Maloney's Petition. James Shearer, the postal surveyor for the North, was authorized if, on his next visit he thought it justified, to establish experimentally a runner for one year between Ullapool and Dingwall at a salary of £30 to £35 a year. This was done, and two years later the surveyor was able to report favourably on the Ullapool post which was made a permanency.[32]

The growing importance of Ullapool as a fishing port and the hope of getting a regular postal service established between it and Dingwall had evidently raised in the minds of some people a doubt as to whether Ullapool might be substituted for Poolewe as the mainland terminal of the post to Stornoway, and in the spring of 1803 James Chapman, chamberlain of Lewis, wrote from Seaforth Lodge to Colin Mackenzie, Writer to the Signet in Edinburgh, on the subject. Chapman reported that he had discussed the matter with those in Stornoway who had been unanimous in their view that even with a much better boat than the existing one fewer passages would be possible to Ullapool than to Poolewe, the prevailing winds favouring Poolewe. Ullapool was so far up Loch Broom that with a contrary wind a boat might take a whole day to reach it from the entrance to the Loch.[33]

So, on the north and west coasts of Scotland the postal routes had at various points reached the Atlantic seaboard. The claims of the Islands were already becoming urgent, and long before the 18th century reached its close the post was to overleap the Pentland Firth and the Minch, to link with the mainland the Northern Isles, Skye and the Outer Hebrides.

In the Lowlands of Scotland, too, the closing years of the 18th century brought changes in the postal service linking Edinburgh through the Southern Uplands with Carlisle and the South. Writing of the postal arrangements in Roxburgh-shire in the second half of the 18th century, Dr Thomas Somerville of Jedburgh gave the following description of the position as it existed about 1766:

'So late as the year 1766, the town of Hawick had not obtained the accommodation of a post office, though it had made a considerable progress in different branches of manufacture, particularly of carpets. Sir Gilbert Elliot, grandfather of

Lord Minto, found it necessary, in 1767, to exert his utmost interest for permission to make the experiment of a Hawick post thrice in the week, to and from Edinburgh and Berwick, on the condition of securing Government against loss. Mr John Elliot, one of the trading burgesses, tendered his gratuitous service as post-master to the town for the first year; and it was found upon trial, after deduction of all the necessary expenses for salaries of post-boys etc. a clear profit of £40 per annum would have accrued to Government. The profit for several years past has exceeded £1000. To remedy the difficulty of conveying epistolary correspondence, and a tardy circulation of public intelligence, one of the carriers in every market town received a salary of a few pounds yearly, on condition of his returning in the course of the week from Edinburgh, and being the bearer of all the letters and newspapers. He was distinguished by the name of "the Post". The salary paid out of the funds of the town of Jedburgh for this purpose was £4 per annum.'[34]

By the last quarter of the century the post linking certain of the Border towns with Edinburgh had been put on an official basis, but here, too, changes were soon to come. The introduction in 1786 of mail coaches on the main coastal route by Berwick had brought into still greater prominence the Great North Road, from early times the main postal artery for communication between North and South. Two years later, mail coaches running between Carlisle and Glasgow added a parallel route of growing importance for traffic from north-west England to the Clyde basin. Between these two, a postal route served by riders had for some years carried mail three times a week from Carlisle by Langholm, Hawick and Selkirk to reach Edinburgh by the valley of the Gala Water. By 1795 the postal traffic from Carlisle to Edinburgh by this route had, it seems, dwindled. The route now did little more than serve for communications between Hawick and Selkirk with connections to Jedburgh and Kelso, and the Post Office grudged the long rides from Langholm to Hawick and through the 'dreary and uninhabited country' between Selkirk and Edinburgh.

Under the new plan the Carlisle to Edinburgh ride was to be discontinued, to be replaced by a daily post from Berwick to Kelso with connections four times a week from there by Jedburgh to Hawick, and by Melrose to Selkirk. The people of Selkirk reacted strongly to the prospect of losing their direct post to Hawick, Carlisle and the South. The Duke of Buccleuch, drawn reluctantly into the controversy, forwarded letters of protest from Mr Plummer at Sunderland Hall and Mr Pringle the local Member of Parliament. Other local interests joined in the argument, urging the disadvantage of a plan which would take letters from the Selkirk district for Dumfriesshire and Carlisle on a long, circuitous and costly route by Kelso, Berwick, Edinburgh and Moffat. The Postmasters General, Lords Leicester and Chesterfield, called on for a decision, fell back on their usual device in time of perplexity. 'Try the experiment for one year,' they ordered, 'and then report.' In face of continued criticism the trial period was reduced to three months, the final entry in the correspondence being a plaintive minute from Thomas Elder the Post Office Secretary in Edinburgh, to be echoed through the coming years by many a postal official, 'It is impossible to please everyone.'[35]

REFERENCES

1. Thomas Somerville, D.D., *My own life and times 1741–1814*, 354.
2. Dunbar, *Social Life in Former Days*.
3. Lang, *Historical Summary of the Post Office in Scotland*.
4. *N.S.A.*, 11, 750.
5. Lang, op. cit.
6. Post 40/115B/1793.
7. Quoted by J. W. Hyde, *The Royal Mail*, 3rd ed., 128.
8. Post 40/142B/1794.
9. For details of the work of Postal Surveyors see Chapter Ten.
10. *Aberdeen Journal*, 5 August 1788.
11. Post 40/94A/1792.
12. *O.S.A.*, xx, 408.
13. Post 40/112T/1798.
14. Ibid./15L/1802.
15. Ibid./106B/1793.
16. Ibid./176C/1793.
17. Post 42/176C/1793, vol v.
18. N.L.S., Journal of Francis Ronaldson, 26 Sept./7 Oct. 1793.
19. Post 40/7D/1793.
20. Ibid./196A/1793.
21. Ibid./97.1/1796.
22. Ibid./66B/1800.
23. Ibid./72G/1802.
24. Ibid./8W/1799.
25. *Argyll Estate Instructions 1771/1805*. Cregeen, Scott. Hist. Socy., *passim*.

26. N.L.S., Saltoun Collection, Box 420. It seems probable that by 'Argyll'
    Campbell meant that part of the country lying between Lorn and Kintyre
    and including the country on the north-west side of Loch Fyne.
27. Post 40/77s/1798.
28. Post 14/337/1799.
29. Post 40/66B/1800. See Appendix VII.
30. See Chapter Ten.
31. Hyde, op. cit., 63/4.
32. Post 40/60.1/1802.
33. S.R.O. GD. 46/17, vol. 24, 98/101.
34. Thomas Somerville, D.D., op cit., 354/5.
35. Post 40/20H/1795.
36. Ibid./79H/1795.

ℱour

The Era of the Mail Coach

When in the late summer of 1784 the first mail coach to run in these Islands left Bath for London, nearly three centuries of postal history lay behind. The story of these intervening years is the story of foot and horse posts, their speed, their safety and their success largely conditioned by the state of the ways along which they struggled to their destinations. In England and in Scotland alike the development of roads outside the immediate proximity of towns came slowly. In England little attention had been paid to road-making or road repair before the end of the 17th century, and though the Turnpike legislation which was later to bring such a transformation dated from 1663, little use of it had in fact been made before 1700. From that date conditions started slowly to improve, and on some of the main routes wheel traffic became possible; but even on routes like those from London to York, Exeter or Oxford a day's journey was little more than thirty miles, while the type of cumbrous unsprung vehicles in use was such that the few hardy travellers who ventured on long journeys had reason to be thankful that they and their horses could rest overnight before facing the ordeal of another day on the road. After the middle of the century conditions started to improve more rapidly. Metcalfe and McAdam, the pioneers of scientific road construction, were soon to be at work, but as late as 1754 the stage coach between London and Edinburgh took ten days for the journey in summer and twelve in winter.

In Scotland progress in road-making was equally slow. Until the beginning of the 17th century almost the only means of travelling was on foot or on horseback and a journey of any length by either method was a hazardous undertaking. It was not until 1661 that the Justices of the Peace, on whom responsibility for road-making and maintenance rested, were armed with any powers to make the performance of their duties possible. In that year a system of Statute labour was introduced, but the six days' labour in each year imposed by the new legislation on tenants and smallholders of land was far too little to make any real impact on the problem, and when opposition to the provision of labour led increasingly to commutation of this into money payments, the value of a day's work was at first assessed at only 3d. It is easy to appreciate that this was little more than a token payment, wholly inadequate for its purpose even in days when labour was cheap. The bare existence and still more the quality of roads beyond the immediate proximity of towns still depended almost solely on the efforts and initiative of local officials or landowners. As late as 1740 it was reported that in the whole county of Aberdeen there was no road fit for wheel traffic, and throughout Scotland in the first half of the century there were vast rural areas where at best the only vestiges of roads were the tracks of foot passengers and livestock.

In Scotland as in England the provision for the setting up of Turnpike Trusts initiated under Charles 11 remained for long unused and almost unnoticed. The system of levying tolls for the maintenance of roads had been in operation in Scotland before 1707, but it was not till 1714 that the first Turnpike Trust of the type so widely used in the years to come was set up in Midlothian, and many more years were to pass before this method of providing for road construction and repair became widely used.[1] But if the Turnpike came slowly, its use and popularity were to grow with increasing speed, and between 1750 and 1844 no fewer than 350 local Turnpike Acts were passed throughout Scotland.

Statute labour and Turnpike Trusts could be effective only in those parts of the country where population and traffic could provide either manpower or revenue. They could be of no avail in sparsely populated districts and especially in the Highland areas. Here in the Highlands the work of Wade and the military road-makers who followed him resulted, over a space of about fifty years, in the construction of close on 1,000 miles of road and nearly as many bridges at a total cost to the Government of over £300,000. Built for military use, rapidly and with little engineering skill, these roads quickly fell into disrepair. Travellers like Dorothy Wordsworth, Mrs Grant of Laggan and Thomas Newte who toured the Highlands at the end of the 18th century have left varying accounts of their experiences, but nearly all agreed that despite all that had been spent on them a large part of the roads of the Highlands were then rapidly becoming almost impassable. By the end of the 18th century little more than half the total mileage of roads constructed by the Army was being maintained in any usable condition. Even this was being steadily reduced, and in 1814 a residue of only some 300 miles was handed over to the care and maintenance of the Commissioners for Highland Roads and Bridges who were then engaged on the first major work of Highland road and bridge building for civilian use.[2]

While the construction of roads for civilian use made no real progress in the Highlands and little even in the rural areas of the Lowlands before the end of the 18th century, contemporary records show that in and around the towns some wheel traffic was already on the move, while between Edinburgh and Glasgow and on the main road leading from Edinburgh to Berwick and the South the first steps towards a regular transport service had already been taken. As early as 1678 William Hume had tried the experiment of establishing a service between Edinburgh and Glasgow, the return journey by coach drawn by six horses to be done in six days. Hume was to be allowed to charge passengers fares of £4.16/–(s) in summer and £5.8/–(s) in winter, but despite this and an annual subsidy of 200 merks (£11.2.6d sterling) the experiment was soon abandoned, and it was not until 1749 that a regular wheel service between the cities came into being.[3] The vehicle which then made the journey twice a week, taking two days each way, is described as 'a caravan', which suggests that it may have been for the carriage of both goods and passengers. On the road to London at the beginning of the century there appears to have been no regular service, and those wishing to make the journey had to combine to hire a coach. At this period it was the custom to advertise well in advance of the departure of coaches, and the *Caledonian Mercury* for 9 May 1734 carried the announcement that

'a coach will set out towards the end of this week for London or any place on the road; to be performed in nine days or three days sooner than any other coach that travels the road. For which purpose 80 stout horses are stationed at proper distances, or you may have a by-coach at any time upon acquainting Alexander Forsyth opposite to the Duke of Queensberry's lodging in the Canongate. Gentlemen and ladies will be carried to their entire satisfaction.'[4]

The cost of the journey is not mentioned, but this is likely to have been considerable, while the satisfaction of the gentlemen and ladies after nine days behind the stout horses may well have been somewhat qualified. Certainly Lord Lovat and his two daughters, who took eleven days to go in their own coach from Inverness to Edinburgh in 1740, using parts of the military roads made by Wade and his successors, found such a journey no child's play. By 1763 a stage coach was running with some regularity to London once a month, and four years later coaches were going from Edinburgh twice a week to Stirling, and three times a week to Perth.

While long cross-country journeys were thus slowly graduating from bare possibility to fair regularity, if not to comfort, travel by carriages and coaches, public and private, in and around the main cities of Scotland was becoming more popular. Hackney coaches had been established in Edinburgh as early as 1673, and a post chaise service between Edinburgh and Leith was in existence in 1702. Neither of these facilities appears to have been popular, but the number of people owning private vehicles was on the increase, the total of four-wheeled carriages on which duty was paid rising to 396 in 1763 and to 1427 in 1790.[5] Outside Edinburgh wheel vehicles increased more slowly. Private carriages had made their appearance in Glasgow, Aberdeen and Inverness by the middle of the century, while in 1773 Dr Johnson was able to hire a good chaise and horse in Banff.

By the last quarter of the 18th century many of the roads of England and at least some of the main roads in Scotland had, whether by Statute labour, by the work of Turnpike Trusts or by the enterprise of private individuals, been so far improved that wheel traffic could pass over them with lessening hazard and increasing speed. With the possibility of greater speed in communication had come growing demand for that speed in the conveyance of passengers, goods and mail. Stage coaches were already carrying letters officially and unofficially on the cross roads of England, but on the main roads radiating from London the mail was still carried by post boys on horseback. The time was ripe for a revolution which was to bring to the postal services of the United Kingdom the greatest change which they were to undergo between the post horses of the Tudors and the railways of Victoria.

In 1782 John Palmer, the son of a Somerset brewer, put before William Pitt the proposal that letters on the main postal roads should be carried by mail coach. Palmer as a West Country man was thoroughly familiar with the road from London to Bath and Bristol, the best and fastest of all the coach roads then existing, and was convinced that mail coaches on such roads could travel at least as quickly as stage coaches. The basic speed aimed at was eight miles per hour and this in fact was later to be achieved and in very many cases exceeded. Palmer's plan was not immediately adopted and meantime was referred to the postal surveyors and other postal officials who almost unanimously rejected it as impracticable and even ludicrous. Palmer had based his arguments for the adoption of mail coaches not only on the additional speed and security which it would mean for the mail, but on the grounds that in return for these advantages it would be reasonable to increase postal charges. One of his proposals for achieving greater speed for the mail was that the exemption from tolls, which horse mails had hitherto enjoyed, should be extended to the new coaches — an innovation which in Scotland at least was to give rise to a long and bitter controversy.

In 1784 Pitt, now First Lord of the Treasury as well as Prime Minister, again considered the plan and decided to adopt it, no doubt influenced by the prospect of collecting increased revenue for a heavily burdened Treasury.* The first

---

* So far as Scotland was concerned the new postal rates were as follows: For a single letter carried over one postal stage the charge was now 2d. Beyond one stage and up to 50 miles the charge was 3d and between 50 and 80 miles 4d. Between 80 and 150 miles the rate was 5d and beyond 150 miles 6d single. Letters

mail coach was run on the road between Bath and London, and following its complete success mail coaches soon made their appearance on the other main postal routes out of London. The Great North Road to Edinburgh was the last of the main roads to get the new coach service in the summer of 1786, the time between London and Edinburgh being then reduced from 85 to 60 hours each way. Two years later a direct mail coach service from London to Glasgow was started, soon to be among the fastest runs in the whole country.

It will be recalled that during the long controversy over the delay in the posts from Edinburgh to Aberdeen about 1792 it had emerged that even with an earlier despatch from Edinburgh the only real acceleration could come from the use of a mail coach which the growing weight of the mails was in any event making almost essential. Hitherto the bad state of parts of the road up the east coast had prevented this, but in the last quarter of the century Turnpike Trusts were, with the active encouragement of the Post Office, being set up on many of the main roads of South and East Scotland. In February 1792 Ronaldson the surveyor had recorded in his Journal that 'the general desire for the extension of the mail coach from Edinburgh to Aberdeen having become very prevalent in the country and the riding work having fallen much behind in consequence of the badness of the roads' he had examined the roads to see whether a coach was practicable. From this it appeared that a coach could not travel 'in winter under night with any certainty nor with any safety to the passengers' particularly between Dundee and Arbroath and between Montrose and Stonehaven.[6] In June 1793 the Aberdeen magistrates, referring to the delay in extending the mail coaches to Aberdeen owing to the state of the roads, claimed that 'several of them are newly made into good Turnpike roads. It is therefore now proposed that a small mail coach or diligence to contain three inside passengers should be established between Edinburgh and Aberdeen.'* But the state of the road to Aberdeen was not the only obstacle to starting a coach. Ronaldson was having difficulty in finding contractors to undertake the

---

between Edinburgh and London now cost 7d. (Howard Robinson, op. cit., ch. XI.)

* Robertson, the author of *Rural Recollections*, has recorded that in 1797 he found the road from Montrose to Aberdeen in a very bad state, but that by 1800 a vast improvement had taken place.

work. In view of the high speeds called for and the number of horses which thus had to be maintained and kept in constant readiness, few contractors were prepared to undertake the working of more than a short stretch of road. In fact at the date of the commencement of the mail coach from Edinburgh to Aberdeen no less than nine different sets of contractors were involved. New arrangements had to be made with post offices in Fife, Perthshire and Forfarshire to take account of the new time schedules which a mail coach would entail, and it was not until 1st August 1798 that the first mail coach ran from Edinburgh to Aberdeen. A week later Freeling had in his hands the first waybill of the Aberdeen coach. The first journey had been completed within an hour of the stated time.

The early success of the mail coach system and the rapid spread of Turnpike Trusts in the Lowland areas led to a steady increase in mail coach services in South and Central Scotland. The same year that saw the establishment of a coach to Aberdeen saw the start of a similar service from Edinburgh to Glasgow by Linlithgow, soon to be followed by a second service between the cities by way of Whitburn. In 1805 mail coaches started running from Edinburgh to Portpatrick by way of Dumfries and in 1807 from Edinburgh to Stirling.* The establishment of the Stirling coach at a cost of £150 per annum was justified on the ground that the postal revenue from places on this route amounted to £5000 per annum, and that the new coach would result in letters to Linlithgow, Bo'ness, Falkirk, Grangemouth and Stirling being sent off immediately after the arrival of the morning mail from the South instead of being held up till the afternoon. By 1813 the mail coach services in Scotland numbered 11, all in Central and Southern Scotland, save Edinburgh to Aberdeen and Aberdeen to Inverness.[7]

Palmer's plan for a mail coach service with its promise of higher postal revenue had been based on increased speed and security for the mails. In 1784, when the first mail coaches took the road, a standard speed of seven or eight miles an hour was aimed at, but stage coaches, which had for some time been carrying parcels and mail, were achieving this and more, and Palmer saw that his mail coach service must be at least competitive.

---

* The postal service between Glasgow and Portpatrick seems, almost throughout, to have been operated by horse post owing to the poor state of part of the road.

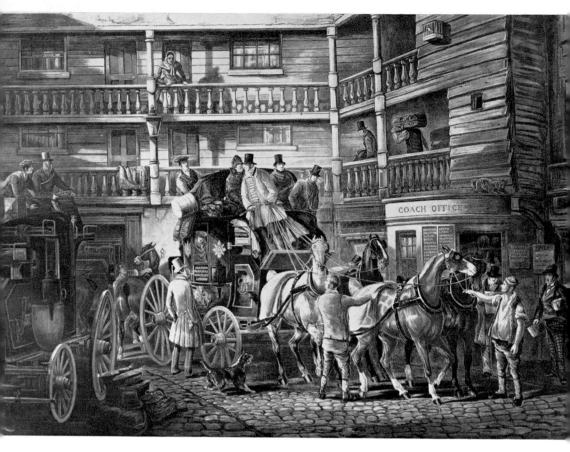

5. Glasgow mail coach leaves Bull and Mouth Inn, London, *p.* 81.

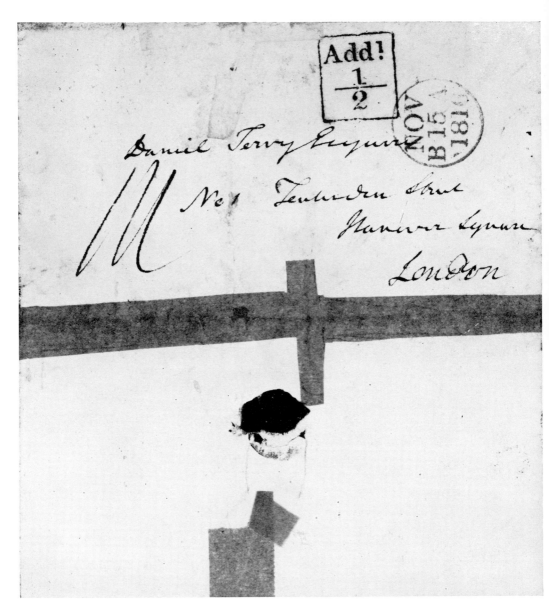

6. Mail coach surcharge on a letter by Sir Walter Scott, *p.* 90.

Stage coaches were primarily for passengers, and it was clear that while the new mail service might carry a few passengers the speed and safety of the mails must be paramount. The 'diligence' which operated the first mail coach service on the road between Bath and London does not appear to have been unusual except in the fact that both coachman and guard were armed, while no outside passengers were carried. In 1787, however, a far-sighted coachbuilder called Besant produced a 'patent' coach specially designed for the mail service. This proved so well fitted for the job that he, and later his partner Vidler, obtained and held for nearly forty years the monopoly of building, hiring out and maintaining mail coaches for the postal service. These coaches were hired to mail contractors who supplied horses and drivers and worked the coaches over those parts of the roads covered by their contracts. The usual rate of hire paid to the coach builders was 2½d a double mile out and back, and this included cleaning, greasing and maintaining the coach in constant running order and returning it to the coaching stages or inns for its next run. The great majority of the coaches northbound from London including those to Edinburgh and Carlisle started from the Bull and Mouth Inn in St Martins,* and here the coaches were delivered each evening ready for the road from Besant and Vidler's coachworks in Millbank. While 2½d a double mile was for long the usual rate of hire, evidence given before a Commission of Enquiry in 1830 shows that for some time previous to that date the rate for coaches on the Edinburgh to Aberdeen road was 3½d. These coaches on the Aberdeen road in common with so many others were supplied by Vidler, but in that same year (1830) John Croall of Edinburgh won a contract for the supply of two-wheeled 'curricles' for conveyance of mails from Edinburgh by Wooler to Morpeth and Newcastle. The contract provided that the vehicles must be capable of travelling 90 to 110 miles out and back each day at 10 miles per hour, the hiring charge to cover the maintenance of the vehicles in constant order, cleaned and greased, with lamps and oil.[8] These vehicles carried no passengers but only the driver and guard. It would appear that though Vidler was supplying standard 'patent' coaches for the road to Aberdeen and other Scottish roads, his monopoly

---

* In 1829 the Headquarters of the G.P.O. were moved to St Martin's-le-Grand.

did not extend to these two-wheeled vehicles which were, for reasons which will appear later, used on this inland road from Edinburgh by Wooler to Newcastle and on a few other Scottish roads.*

The mail coaches' initial speed of seven or eight miles per hour was later increased with the use of improved types of vehicle and the steady improvements of the main roads under the care of well-managed Turnpike Trusts. At least by 1830 speeds of 10 miles per hour were regularly maintained over some stretches of the main routes. Among the fastest runs by mail coaches were those between Carlisle and Glasgow where 93 miles were covered in 9 hours 33 minutes and between Edinburgh and Aberdeen where 134 miles were covered in 14 hours 22 minutes despite the crossing of the Forth at Queensferry. About 1836, when the mail coaches had reached the peak of their efficiency, the run from London to Glasgow (396 miles) was done in 42 hours, while on the London to Edinburgh road an average speed of 9 miles per hour including stops was maintained. One stage-coach was doing even better. A coach owned by Captain Barclay of Ury in Kincardineshire was, on the road between Edinburgh and Aberdeen, regularly attaining a speed of over 11 miles an hour with 15 passengers besides the driver and guard.[9] With this sole exception, however, it would seem that, in Scotland at least, the mail coaches in their heyday were the fastest vehicles on the roads. Joseph Mitchell, who was for many years Chief Inspector to the Parliamentary Commissioners engaged in the construction of roads and bridges in the Highlands in the first quarter of last century, wrote in his *Reminiscences* of the coaches of the Highlands in his day.

'In my early days coaching was very slow and imperfect. The coachmen's drive was limited to one stage of 10 or 12 miles; thereafter he tended his horses and prepared them for the return journey. His reward was 6d from each passenger.

---

* In a letter written to the Postmaster General in the autumn of 1832 Freeling recalled that the original proposal to run a mail coach on the route by Wooler to Newcastle had been opposed by those interested in the mail coach road by Berwick with which it would compete. After much negotiation it was arranged that on the Wooler road only a two-wheeled curricle would be run, incapable of carrying passengers. This would not only reduce the cost to the Post Office, but would obviate competition with innkeepers and others on the main road by Berwick.

The roads throughout the country became very much improved between 1830 and 1840 and coaches improved also and became numerous. A few years after 1840 coaching in Scotland was brought to its greatest perfection. A great impetus was given to it by an association of some country gentlemen, chiefly Mr Ramsay of Barnton, Mr Barclay of Ury, Lord Glenlyon and others. They started a coach between Edinburgh and Aberdeen. Their coaches were luxurious and handsome, the horses beautifully matched and of the first character, harness in good taste and of the best quality. The drivers and guards in their uniforms of red coats and yellow collars were steady and respectable men, great favourites on the road, obliging, full of conversation and local knowledge and several of these played with no mean talent on the bugle and cornet. Time was kept to a minute and so complete and perfect was the whole establishment that a highly paid veterinary surgeon was employed to tend the horses and see that they were perfectly looked to.'[10]

The high speeds demanded and achieved by mail and stage-coaches alike took a very heavy toll of coach horses. On the fast routes it was found that a change of horses was required every ten miles, and on such roads the contractor required to keep a horse for every mile of road worked by him in order to ensure an efficient service. On the main post road between London and Edinburgh 40 changes of horses were required, the usual day's work of the drivers being 30 to 40 miles out and back. With such high speeds to maintain over a distance the technique of changing horses was brought to a fine art. On high speed routes five minutes was all that was allowed for the change, while the deposit and taking up of mails was little more than a matter of seconds.* Even today, looking back on those coaching days, the achievement of maintaining a speed of close on 10 miles per hour over several hundred miles seems remarkable. To contemporaries such a speed must have seemed both stupendous and alarming. Lord Chancellor Campbell has recorded that when planning a coach journey from Edinburgh to London in 1798 his family sought to deter him from risking the damage to the brain which such high speeds were thought to cause.[11] It

---

* One postal historian has even recorded that at certain points on the Great North Road only one minute was required for the change of horses and mail.

was not only to the human frame, however, that damage was feared. In 1791 the Postmasters General had thought it prudent to issue a warning to the public to avoid so far as possible sending cash by post 'partly from the prejudice it does to the coin by the friction it occasions from the great expedition with which it is conveyed'.[12]

One of Palmer's main arguments in favour of the adoption of mail coaches was that the security of the mail would in this way be greatly improved. 'The mails', he wrote in 1783, criticizing the existing system, 'are generally entrusted to some idle boy without character mounted on a worn-out hack and who so far from being able to defend himself or escape from a robber is much more likely to be in league with him.'[13] Palmer's original plan was that the mail coaches should carry armed soldiers, but this was found to be impossible and in fact the arming of the coach guards proved an adequate precaution. Though the guards carried arms these were only used in case of real emergency, the penalty at one time for their improper use being – as railway travellers of a later age will readily guess – £5! Taking it all in all the position of a mail coach guard was no sinecure. Besides being ultimately responsible for the safety of the mails, he must enter in the time-bill entrusted to him the details of the journey, arrivals, departures and delay at any of the points where the coach stopped to change horses, deliver or take up mails. In the printed time-bill of the mail coach between Edinburgh and Aberdeen in 1798 appears the following note:

'The time of working each stage is to be reckoned from the Coach's arrival. Five minutes for changing 4 horses is as much as is necessary, and as the time, whether more or less, is to be fetched up in the course of the stage, it is the Guard's and Coachman's duty to be as expeditious as possible and to report the horse-keepers if they are not always ready when the Coach arrives and active in getting it off.'[14]

At the point on the journey where the guard was relieved from duty he must deliver to his relief the sealed clock by which the progress of the run was timed. He must, when required, give such help as he could in changing the horses, and at least in the early years of the 19th century he must keep a look-out for escaping French prisoners-of-war. His duties did not end even here. In the event of the coach breaking down it was his duty to take one of the horses and endeavour to take the mail to the nearest stage. The annals of the mail coach contain many instances of devotion to duty on the part of the men in charge. In the history of the post in Scotland there is perhaps none more striking than that which occurred on the road from Edinburgh to Dumfries in February 1831. Owing to heavy snowfalls the mail coach was unable to get beyond Moffat. The guard, driver and a post boy, all mounted, pushed on carrying the mails. At the Devil's Beef Tub the horses could get no further and were sent back to Moffat in the charge of the post boy. The guard and driver proceeded on foot carrying the mails, and five days later their bodies were found in the snow, the mail bags tied to a roadside guide-post. The Post Office paid £20 to the orphan daughters of the dead men, but came under severe criticism from the local press for keeping their employees so strictly to their duties that the men dared not give up their efforts to get the mail through.

If the state of the roads of Scotland at the end of the 18th century still left very much to be desired a vast improvement had in fact taken place since the middle of the century. Much of the credit for this must go to the Turnpike Trusts which were rapidly being set up following the complete and obvious failure of Statute labour. These trusts, which were now being set up in all parts of Scotland, were based on private Acts of Parliament obtained at considerable expense and by local initiative. These local Acts, which were very detailed, authorised the trustees to establish toll houses on, and to levy fixed charges for the use of, existing roads or in some cases to construct new roads. The revenue of the trusts was supplemented by local assessments and the trustees were also authorised to borrow money secured on the tolls. This power to borrow, essential as it no doubt was, was to prove a source of future trouble, for in very many cases the revenue of the trusts proved quite inadequate even to pay interest on the borrowed money, far less to repay it over a period, and before long many of the trusts were heavily in debt with arrears of interest accumulating.

The exemption from tolls which was granted to the mail coaches in 1785 does not appear, in Scotland at least, to have given rise to much early criticism. Those Turnpike Trusts which had already been set up were not yet so heavily in debt as they were to become, and in any event only on a very few roads in the Lowlands were mail coaches running. But with the steady extension of mail coaches a storm of protest arose. In February 1797 the chairman of the Glasgow Chamber of Commerce wrote to Henry Dundas with a Memorial prepared on behalf of the Turnpike Trustees. In particular he expressed the fear that if exemption were continued the effect on the Turnpike Trusts on the Carlisle to Glasgow Road would be such that this road would soon become impassable. He urged that toll exemption be discontinued and that to compensate mail coach contractors for having to pay tolls the fare for passengers on mail coaches should be slightly increased.[15] Dundas's reply was not encouraging. On 2 August 1798, the day after the opening of the mail coach service to Aberdeen, David Scott wrote to the Post Office complaining of the great loss he would suffer in Perthshire from the toll exemption. The complaint was referred to Ronaldson, the surveyor, who reported to Freeling a few weeks later that he had made enquiries of postmasters and innkeepers in Perthshire and Angus who had assured him that the mail coach had resulted in more private posting on the roads than ever before. The running of mail coaches, he considered, had made travel more popular, and as passenger accommodation on these coaches was strictly limited the demand for private chaises had increased, to the great benefit of the Turnpike Trusts.[16]

While Turnpike Trustees all over Scotland were protesting with growing vigour but continuing lack of success against the mail coach exemption, there was one case in which the toll-keepers met with better fortune. On the old road from North Queensferry through Fife to Perth a mail coach had, at the request of the city of Perth, been established in the last years of the 18th century. At Bridge of Earn, two miles south of Perth, the road crossed the River Earn by an old stone bridge recently improved at a cost of £1,000 by the magistrates of Perth, who claimed the right of 'pontage', an ancient customs levy on goods and vehicles crossing the river. In the autumn of 1800 the magistrates exercised their right and claimed payment of dues from the mail coaches. Kerr, the Secretary of the Post Office at Edinburgh, thought that the claim should be resisted, no pontage being paid at the bridge over the Tay at Perth and a similar claim having been successfully resisted at Montrose. The Solicitor to the Post Office pointed out, however, that the rights claimed by the city of Perth rested on a Charter of James VI, so distinguishing them from the toll duties imposed by Act of Parliament from which by the Act of 1785 mail coaches were exempt. The legal opinion seemed conclusive, and Freeling could do no more than record his view that Perth's claim was 'as shabby as any I recollect since I have known the office', since Perth itself had pressed for the running of the coach.[17]

Early in 1807 the postal arrangements in Strathearn were again causing trouble to Freeling and his colleagues. In March of that year Lady Perth and Miss Drummond had raised the question of a mail coach being substituted for the horse post on the road between Perth and Glasgow which, following the dispute between George Haldane of Gleneagles and Smythe of Methven in 1793, went by way of Crieff. Freeling wrote to the Postmaster General that this matter had already been raised two years before and that the Government would not agree to meet the cost of a coach. In any event strong opposition was to be expected from the Turnpike Trustees. Sir Patrick Murray and Colonel Graham as trustees on the stretch of road between Perth and Crieff had represented that this trust was burdened with a debt of £9,631 for which the trustees were personally liable. The annual expenditure exceeded the revenue by £68, and if a mail coach was put on the road it would supersede a stage-coach which paid tolls of £93.18/– per annum. On the road from Crieff to Stirling the debt due by the Turnpike Trustees was £6,894. The net revenue available for its reduction was only £179 per annum and the introduction of a mail coach would reduce this to £54. The Postal Surveyors, too, had reported to Freeling against a mail coach, so the ladies' proposal was turned down.[18]

As the years passed it became evident that the pressure for abolition of toll exemption for mail coaches was steadily increasing. The trustees of the Glasgow to Greenock road, where four mail coaches ran each day, had applied urgently for their reduction to two 'in order to prevent the road from utter destruction'. A Minute of 1809 refers to a Parliamentary Committee which was at that time considering the use of broad wheels by coaches for the preservation of turnpike roads,[19] and in the spring of that year Ronaldson had been asked by the Post Office to state the case for retaining the *status quo*. The surveyor had already formed the opinion in the application by David Scott in 1798 that mail coaches benefited Turnpike Trustees more than they damaged them and now he amplified his views. 'Mail coaches', he wrote, 'are a spur to travelling in general. . . . Without mail coaches not one in ten would find their way to the metropolis of Scotland who do so now, as posting and consequent expenditure is not for everyone's pocket. . . .' As to the contention of those who asserted that mail coach contractors made large profits he wrote, 'I believe there has been as many failures among mail coach contractors as in any other line of business in the same period.'[20]

But the case for abolition of toll exemption was being steadily built up. In 1809 a committee, appointed in the previous year by a meeting attended by representatives of many of the largest towns and counties in Scotland, reported that the ten mail coaches and six diligences then running affected 21 counties and meant an annual loss to them of £6865. The loss by the exemption in some cases amounted to one half the total revenue of the trust. The loaded weight of a coach could be as much as two tons. Such a vehicle travelling at 8 or 9 miles per hour did great damage to the roads and not a few stage-coach owners offered to carry mails for short distances and at low rates, solely to qualify for the exemption from tolls. The improvement of posts brought about by the introduction of mail coaches was for the advantage of the commercial interest in the country, who, it was argued, bore no part of the cost of road maintenance. Five years later, when matters had come to a crisis, it was reported that in Roxburghshire one-third of the revenue of the Turnpike Trusts was being lost and that no less than forty-five years' interest on the Trust's debt was in arrear. In Selkirkshire the position was almost as bad, while in Perthshire and Forfarshire the trusts were losing one-third and one-half respectively of their revenue with nineteen years' interest in arrears.[21]

But perhaps the most poignant appeal on behalf of the Turnpike Trustees came from the pen of an anonymous protagonist in 1808.

'By Mr Palmer's plan for mail coaches', he wrote, 'the commercial interest have attained despatch and security to their correspondence; the Government have more than doubled their old revenue; the contractors have made fortunes by the conveyance and the Trustees for the Roads have lost a large proportion of their tolls and are in many cases reduced to a state of bankruptcy. For this they have got no equivalent, unless it shall be said that in common with the merchants they have obtained despatch to their correspondence. But what advantage is this to a plain country gentlemen? He gets few letters and it is of very little moment to him whether they are hurried forward at the rate of 8 miles per hour by the mail coach or come at the more leisurely pace of the old saddled horse. The main objects with the Trustees are to afford good roads to all species of travellers and to keep their families free from loss by reducing from the revenue of these roads the money they have advanced and the engagements they have personally come under for making them; but they cannot keep faith with the public or do justice to their own families unless they obtain redress from the innovation introduced by the establishment of mail coaches.'[22]

The case for ending the exemption of mail coaches from payment of toll had by now reached formidable proportions. By 1812, a total of over 200 mail coaches were in use throughout Great Britain, and the Turnpike Trustees claimed that they were losing £50,000 each year. A Committee which had been set up by parliament in 1810 to consider the matter reported unanimously in favour of ending the exemption, an outcome which was perhaps hardly surprising since the interests in parliament of landed proprietors and Turnpike Trustees were at that time predominant. To add weight to the case against exemption, tolls had since 1798 been levied on mail coaches in Ireland, and it seemed illogical that the system in England and Scotland should be different. For a time the Post Office continued in the hope that the matter would be dropped, but this proved to be wishful thinking. In England the continued exemption of mail coaches from payment of toll duties was only achieved by a drastic reduction by the Post Office in the number of mail coaches in use, and between 1812 and 1815 the total number of mail coaches on the roads of Great Britain is believed to have fallen from 200 to 61.[23] So far as Scotland was concerned matters came to a head in 1813 when by an Act of Parliament of that year exemption from toll for vehicles with more than two wheels carrying mail was abolished. For two-wheeled vehicles toll exemption continued, provided they carried only mails and no passengers. To indemnify the Post Office for the tolls which would now be payable, every letter carried by mail coach over however short a distance in any part of Scotland was charged with an extra halfpenny of postage.

The Act of 1813 bore hardly on the Post Office in Scotland and led to results which had been no part of the intention of parliament. Turnpike Trustees in nearly every part of Scotland not unnaturally fixed the rate of toll at the very maximum allowed by the Acts which governed each trust. In many cases these Acts also permitted a toll charge for each outside passenger carried on a mail coach. These charges were all enforced, and there is evidence that in some cases Turnpike Trustees endeavoured in the face of violent Post Office opposition to discriminate against mail coaches by lowering toll charges on stage coaches. The extra halfpenny of postal charge allowed to the Post Office proved quite inadequate. Some years later, when the whole position was again under review, it was estimated that before 1813 mail coaches, but for exemption, would have paid £6865 per annum in tolls. After 1813 the total toll charges against mail coaches in Scotland, at the rates now in force, was approximately £11,760 per annum, of which less than £6000 per annum was recovered by the Post Office by means of the extra halfpenny.

To the outlook of both the Turnpike Trustees and the Post Office the altered circumstances had brought a radical change. On the road from Perth to Glasgow by Crieff the proposal for a mail coach in 1807 had been strenuously opposed by the Turnpike Trustees. Now, with toll charges in prospect, they were equally strong in supporting it. In April 1812, Sir Patrick Murray of Ochtertyre, who as a Turnpike Trustee had been so vehement in opposition to the earlier application for a coach, wrote to Lord Melville, then Secretary of the Admiralty, at his estate of Dunira near Comrie to say that as soon as the Act repealing toll exemption was passed the campaign for a coach between Perth and Stirling would be reopened and that the contest between the advocates of the routes by Crieff or by Auchterarder would be revived. The Auchterarder route, which Lord Kinnoul was supporting, was the shorter by 7 miles, but on this route 13 miles which had not yet been made turnpike were in winter almost impassable. For this reason Sir Patrick asked for Lord Melville's support for the adoption of the Crieff route. Lord Melville's reply was hardly encouraging, containing as it did more than a suggestion that in his view rural seclusion was preferable to postal facilities. 'If', he wrote on 4 May, 'the Admiralty office were at Dunira, I should have no difficulty in deciding against all Mail Coaches or Posts, or any other conveyance of letters.'*

The revival of the dispute over a coach between Perth and Stirling was no isolated case. On the part of the Post Office a change of thinking was equally apparent. Receptive as he was to plans for improvement of the postal services, Freeling had always a keen eye to post office revenue, and mail coach services were costly at any time. Now, with heavy tolls added, he and his colleagues at Post Office Headquarters had to look even harder at existing services, let alone new ones. Within months of the passing of the Act trouble arose on the road from Glasgow through Paisley to Greenock. Here the tolls now payable amounted to well over £900 per annum. The mail coaches had already been much injured by three 'newly erected steamboats'. Drastic economies were called for, but Ronaldson, the surveyor, rightly foresaw that his proposal to substitute horse posts would be strongly opposed by the Turnpike Trustees, themselves losing traffic to the boats; but the responsibility of the Post Office was to provide an equally good – or in this case a better – letter service as cheaply as possible, even if this meant less traffic at the toll bars or inconvenience to those who had hitherto travelled as passengers on the mail coaches. While the arguments in favour of Ronaldson's proposal for a horse post were considered by the Post Office to be conclusive, the people of Greenock viewed the matter in a very different light. Two years later Ronaldson wrote to Freeling confessing his complete inability to get the horse-post work on the Greenock road done in such a way as to satisfy the local people. Indeed the trouble over this whole matter had reduced the surveyor to such a state that he was considering retiral after forty years' hard service with the Post Office.[24] The trouble on the Glasgow to Greenock

---

* S.R.O. GD. 51/16/60. The impression that Lord Melville's mind was fixed on rural rather than postal matters is strengthened by the fact that among the papers is a letter addressed to him in the autumn of 1809 about the appointment of a postmaster at Comrie. Of Lord Melville's view on this matter there is no record, but in its place is a list of vermin killed on Dunira estate between January 1808 and May 1809. Though totally irrelevant, it may be of some interest to record that these included 15 martens and wildcats and 30 gleads(buzzards), and the total payment for 145 head of vermin amounted to £10.1.6d. (Ibid. 45. Nos. 1 & 2.)

road was to prove only one of many, and from now on the policy of the Post Office as regards mail coach services was one of contraction rather than expansion. Indeed it soon became apparent that so far as concerned the future of mail coach development in Scotland the results of the Act of 1813 and the subsequent policy of the Turnpike Trustees were likely to prove disastrous.

In 1824 the people of Inverness-shire submitted to the Post Office a Memorial asking for improved coach facilities, and Freeling summarized the position as he saw it in a Minute to the Postmaster General. The additional halfpenny of postal charge, he pointed out, did not produce more than half of what the Post Office paid in tolls in Scotland. The importance of mail coaches to the Turnpike Trustees was now such that these coaches were sometimes sought for this reason only, though in many cases the Post Office could convey the post more suitably and at less expense by carts or on horseback.[25] On some Scottish roads, too, such as that from Inverness to Fort Augustus, two-wheeled gigs or 'curricles' exempt from toll under the Act of 1813 had been introduced. Three years later, Freeling, smarting under a sense of injustice and anxious as always for the welfare of the Post Office, relieved his feelings in a further outburst to the Postmaster General.

'I have often had to notice the eagerness with which the Scotch pursue any point connected with their own interests and I do hope that the time is speedily approaching when the large sums which that Country is drawing from the Post Office for the payment of Turnpike Tolls from which individuals are enriching themselves will meet with the inquiry and remedy which perhaps ought long since to have been applied to it.

'The people of Scotland while anxious to reduce the amount of taxation as far as regards our Department never advert to the principal on which the Act of 1813 was founded, viz. "That an indemnity should be received for the loss which may arise to the Post Office from the payment of tolls". As I have before stated to Your Lordships the additional postage imposed by that Act does not repay one-third of the expense of the tolls and the Post Office consequently lose £10,000 a year.

'No one in Scotland has ever shewn any other feeling on

this subject, except a desire to liberate themselves and the persons connected with the Trusts from the burden and expense of keeping up the public roads in that country; hence has arisen the combination of mighty weight and interest to get those roads covered by mail coaches and the strongest threats if in any instance we have attempted to take them off or to alter the line.'[26]

The strained feelings between the Post Office and the Turnpike Trustees all over Scotland persisted, the latter losing no opportunity of extracting the last penny of toll-duty from the mail coaches. In the summer of 1828 attempts to charge tolls against two-wheeled mail gigs in the south of Scotland on the highly technical grounds that the drivers had on occasion taken up a passenger led to a further outburst from Freeling.

'I wish sincerely', he wrote to the Postmaster General, 'that the Trustees of all the roads in Scotland were more desirous of repairing and maintaining them than attempting to enforce what, under any circumstances, must be considered an unjust claim. I lament to add the fact that most of the roads in Scotland are kept up with Post Office money.'[27]

Again in the spring of 1831 a proposal to run a new stage coach between Glasgow and Perth, which would pay lower toll charges than the mail coach, was vigorously opposed by the Duke of Richmond, then Postmaster General. 'The best thing these Trustees can do', he wrote to Freeling, 'is to reduce the toll of the Mail to [that of] the proposed Coach. I can not consent to the Mail paying more than any other coach.'[28] Resentment against the Turnpike Trustees and the losses suffered since 1813 by the Post Office was by no means confined to Freeling and his immediate colleagues. In 1830, the Commissioners who had been appointed to enquire into post office revenue in Scotland recommended, to no purpose, that toll exemption should be restored to mail coaches or that failing this the extra charge on letters carried in Scotland by coach should no longer be limited to a halfpenny.

The controversial halfpenny charge on letters carried by mail coach in Scotland continued until the end of 1839 when it disappeared at the advent of uniform Penny Postage,* while

---

* On 5 Dec. 1839 an experimental uniform 4d inland postage rate was established as a step towards the introduction of uniform Penny Postage which in fact came into force on 10 Jan. 1840.

before many years had passed the Turnpike Trusts themselves were disappearing as their functions were increasingly taken over by the new Local Authorities. It is, perhaps, hardly within the proper function of the postal historian to attempt to adjudicate as to the rights and wrongs of the arguments of the Post Office on the one hand and the Turnpike Trustees on the other. It can hardly be doubted that in the early years of Turnpike Trusts very many of them suffered heavy losses in carrying out what was in most cases useful and disinterested work, and that with the advent of heavy mail-coach traffic they had a very real grievance against a privilege granted to the latter by Pitt at a time when postal revenue was sorely needed. But the Post Office, too, had its grievance in the losses which, after 1813, it had to bear. It can only be said that if in the closing years of the 18th century the work of the Post Office and the construction and maintenance of roads had alike been more clearly recognized as the public services which they were, an unhappy conflict of interests which should never have arisen might have been avoided.

When the Act of 1813 at length ended in favour of the Turnpike Trustees the acute controversy between them and the Post Office, mail coaches had already been operating in Scotland for rather over a quarter of a century. During nearly the whole of this period these services had been almost entirely confined to the Lowlands with the addition of the important route up the east coast to Aberdeen. With this latter exception the mails for the whole of Scotland north of the Forth were, till at least the year 1809, still carried on foot or on horseback. The reason for the absence of mail coach services in the central and western Highlands and in the country north of the Great Glen was not far to seek. The construction or maintenance of roads either by Statute labour or, still more, by Turnpike Trusts, depended on wheel traffic sufficient both to justify the labour and to help to meet the cost. Wheel traffic on any substantial scale depended on bridges, and with few exceptions bridges in this wide area were lacking. If this was the state of affairs during the first twenty years of the history of Scotland's mail coaches, important developments were in fact taking place which were soon to bring about radical changes. In the first year of the 19th century the Government, alarmed by widespread unemployment and economic distress in the Highlands with consequent threats of emigration on a growing scale, had determined on drastic steps. In the summer of 1801 Thomas Telford, an eminent civil engineer with wide knowledge of road and canal construction, was sent to Scotland to report on the improvement of communications in the Highlands. Following on his report work was started in 1803 on a great project which in the course of the next twenty years was to result in the construction, partly at local expense but mainly at Government cost, of over 900 miles of Highland roads, more than 1100 bridges, great and small and the making of the Caledonian Canal. There can be little doubt that the work which was thus done between 1803 and 1823 brought to the Highlands more lasting benefit than any project for Highland development before or since, and nowhere was its effect more marked than in the improvement of postal services. The absence of bridges at certain key points had for long been one of the principal weaknesses, involving the traveller in river crossings where, as Lord Cockburn was to recall forty years later, there were 'nothing but wretched pierless ferries, let to poor cottars, who rowed or hauled, or pushed a crazy boat across, or more commonly got their wives to do it'.[29] This great weakness was noted by Telford in his initial survey, and to this he and the Commissioners for Highland Roads and Bridges, for whom he worked, immediately turned their attention. The most urgent need was for bridges over the lower courses of the Tay and the Spey. On the lower Spey some progress had already been made by local proprietors in the building of a bridge at Fochabers, and with the help of the Commissioners this vital link on the road between Aberdeen and Inverness was completed in 1805. At Dunkeld the bridging of the Tay was soon in hand, and in the spring of 1809 the work on this, one of the finest examples in Scotland of Telford's genius, was complete. 'A considerable object', wrote the Commissioners in one of their annual reports, 'was thus attained. Dunkeld being, as it were, the portal of the Central Highlands and, more remotely, the access to all the Northern roads.' Over the next ten years major bridges were, in face of immense difficulties, constructed by Telford and his colleagues over the Dee, the Don, the Findhorn, the Conon, and the Beauly, and many another Highland river, with innumerable small bridges on the new roads which were thus being opened up.[30] For the spreading postal services this work was of immense value. In particular, with the building of the new bridges at Dunkeld and Fochabers, the direct roads from Perth and Aberdeen to Inverness were now, for the first time, available for through passage by wheel traffic, while with the bridging of the Conon and the Helmsdale, and the making of the great mound to carry the road across the mouth of the River Fleet, the way was now open for similar traffic to Wick and Thurso.

If any proof were needed of the value of the Commissioners' work in the Highlands, this was immediately supplied by the speed with which their new roads and bridges were put into use. By 1809 a mail cart using the new bridges over the Spey at Fochabers and the Findhorn at Forres was on the run from Aberdeen to Inverness, and by 1811 the local press reported this as a daily service.[31] This seems at first to have been only a two-horse vehicle, but later a four-horse coach was substituted, and James Shearer, the postal surveyor for the North, was soon deeply engaged in maintaining and improving this service. In an endeavour to meet the competing claims of towns and villages on the coastal road along the Moray Firth and those on the alternative route by Huntly, it was arranged that the coach would run alternately by Kintore, Inverurie, Huntly, and Keith, or by Turriff, Banff, Portsoy and Cullen, in each case crossing the Spey by the new bridge at Fochabers. Like so many compromises this one pleased neither party and led to bitter attacks both locally and in London against James Shearer, grappling as he was with the double problem of a growing load of mail and newspapers and local quarrels as to postal routes. Indeed the controversy over the Aberdeen/Inverness mail coach would appear to have been almost the worst example of the difficulty of pleasing postal critics in Scotland, of which Freeling so often complained. The attacks on the surveyor, led by an Inverness lawyer, were described by Lord Gray, the Postmaster General for Scotland, in a letter to Freeling as 'most illiberal and unhandsome' and even as 'a gross libel'. 'How so many respectable gentlemen should have lent their names to such a man', he wrote, 'I am at a loss to guess.'[32]

To the long journey up the north-east coast from Inverness to the Pentland Firth the new roads and bridges brought a similar transformation. For many years past the mail service from Inverness to Tain had been by horse post, runners taking

7. Peter Williamson, *p.* 107.

8. Letter by Peter Williamson's Penny Post to
Sir Walter Scott's father, *p.* 108.

the mails from there on across the dangerous ferries and un-
bridged rivers to Wick and Thurso. The completion of the
new roads and bridges in this the most northerly of the areas
to be improved by the Commissioners, was long delayed, but in
the summer of 1819, less than a year after work was complete,
the *Inverness Courier* was able to report that 'an elegant new
mail coach built on the "patent" principle' had started running
between Inverness and Thurso, leaving Inverness at 6 a.m.
and due at Thurso at 7.30 a.m. the following morning.[33] Coach
horses had been brought from Edinburgh and stables and inns
had been built by Lord Stafford. The Turnpike Trustees had
agreed to allow the coach to cross the new bridges free of toll
which, it was estimated, would have amounted to £760 per
annum.[34] The counties of Ross and Sutherland, together with
Lord Stafford, had each undertaken for two years to subscribe
£200 per annum towards the cost.[35] The Post Office, too, had
given their help by agreeing to allow the unusually high figure
of 6d a mile to the contractors for the working of the coach,
and the Government had remitted part of the mileage duty at
that time levied on all coaches. Despite the financial help thus
given to the Thurso mail coach its way was not to prove so
smooth or so easy as had been hoped. The local press had, it
seems, been somewhat over-enthusiastic, for in their annual
report for 1821 the Commissioners for Highland Roads and
Bridges wrote in rather more factual terms.

'It is not to be understood that this Northern mail coach (or
diligence as it is usually called) is exactly the same thing, in
form or speed, as those in the Southern parts of the Kingdom,
but it appears to be well calculated for its purpose. It carries
three inside passengers (one of them looking backwards)
three outside passengers, the driver, the guard, the mail and
other luggage. The coach itself is lighter by two or three
hundred-weights than the Southern mail coach and the speed
required is no more than six miles per hour; but it is drawn
by two horses in place of four, the horses generally, their
provender always, of an inferior kind. ... It would be unreasonable to expect that occasional snow storms and sudden
thaws added to the general influence of a humid climate and
(more than any of these causes) the inexperience and want
of accurate habits in the persons engaged in such an undertaking should not sometimes delay the arrival of the coach

beyond its stated time; but probably tacit allowance is made for such accidents as we do not find that the mail coach has ever returned to Inverness so late as to retard the conveyance of its letter bags southward.'[36]

The more cautious language of the Commissioners seems to have been fully justified, for in January 1821, less than two years after the start of the coach service, James Loch, agent on the Sutherland estates, was writing to Lord Melville asking for a meeting to discuss the question of the Thurso mail coach.

'I will', wrote Loch, 'add nothing to excuse the freedom and earnestness which I have taken in pressing this matter so important to the North of Scotland, and which the two Northern Counties have committed to my care and which I could only do by stating my deep interest in the improvement of my native country especially that part of it where I have received so much kindness and friendship and for which therefore I am bound to make every exertion.'[37]

Despite the help of the Turnpike Trustees, the Post Office and the Government, the service was, it seems, proving costly. The contractors, who appear to have been innkeepers on the coastal road, were unwilling to renew their contracts, and the counties which were already contributing heavily to the expense were faced with shouldering an increasing cost if the mail service, so valuable to the North-East, was to continue. On 17 June 1821 Loch wrote to Stewart Mackenzie of Seaforth informing him that the Government had agreed to remit for five years the whole mileage duty at that time levied on horse-drawn vehicles, on condition that the counties of Sutherland and Caithness doubled the amounts which they were contributing to the cost of the mail coach. Stewart Mackenzie replied on 27 June that in view of the mileage duty concession it was only fair that all four counties through which the Thurso mail coach passed should double their contribution.[38] The mail coach service survived, and seven years later Telford, looking back on the great changes which his work had brought to the North-East, was able to report to the Commissioners, 'Now in the year 1828 a mail coach passes daily from Tain to Bonar Bridge, the Fleet Mount, Dunrobin, Helmsdale and the Ord of Caithness to the extremity of the Island at Wick and Thurso without being interrupted by a single ferry.'[39]

On the new roads and bridges mail coaches were now running

from Aberdeen to Inverness and on to the Pentland Firth, but on one main route to the Highlands no mail coach had yet appeared. Telford's great bridge at Dunkeld had forged the missing link in the direct road connection between Perth and Inverness, and with improvements on the road northwards from Dalwhinnie, the whole 117 miles was open for wheel traffic. Though some improvements had taken place in the postal arrangements north of Dunkeld since 1799 when the Duchess of Gordon's Petition for a horse post to Blair Atholl had been so summarily turned down, the letters to and from Inverness still went by way of Aberdeen. An attempt to start a stage coach on the direct or 'Highland' road had been made in 1803, and though this was soon abandoned it was successfully restarted in 1806 when the 'Caledonian' coach did the journey three times a week in summer and twice a week in winter, taking 14 hours.* It is true that on 14 December 1809 the *Inverness Journal* reported 'We fear the Highland road is impassable. The Caledonian coach which should have arrived on Wednesday evening (12 December) is still on the road, but where we know not',[40] and nearly every winter brought delays and inter-ruptions; but still the coach ran for passenger traffic, and the postal delay caused by the diversion of mail by way of Aberdeen increasingly irked the people of Inverness and the North.

In 1809, the year which saw the completion of the Dunkeld bridge, an application was made to the Postmaster General for a direct mail service between Perth and Inverness, and the matter was remitted to Shearer, the surveyor, to report. The Secretary's own view both from the financial and the practical aspects was adverse. 'With respect to the revenue of the Post Office', he wrote, 'there would be a loss resulting from the diminished rate of postage on shortening the distance of the route', though he added, almost echoing sentiments expressed by the Duchess of Gordon in 1799, 'I may observe that perhaps as a question of public improvement and civilisation the loss of postage may not weigh against the utility of a post through the Highlands. . . .' The practical difficulties as reported by the surveyor were even more formidable. For each stage of 13 miles and for some stages of 10 miles Shearer reckoned that

---

* As this was before the completion of the Dunkeld bridge a ferry over the Tay must have interrupted the direct run.

six to eight horses would have to be kept, and there were few inns on the whole route where the innkeepers could afford to keep such large stables and to lay in the corn, hay and straw required. 'Nor', observed the surveyor, 'would people venture to go at the risk of their lives by such conveyance in the winter months' when, as he added, 'one thousand men would not keep this road clear of snow'.* When Shearer wrote his report the 'Caledonian' coach had already been running between Perth and Inverness for more than two years; but mail coaches built on the 'patent' principle were designed more for the safe transport of the mails than for the comfort of passengers, particularly on Highland roads, and even the 'Caledonian' was to find winter conditions difficult and often impossible. Not surprisingly Freeling opposed the project. 'It is properly stated in Mr Shearer's report', he wrote to the Postmaster General, 'and it is clearly shown that a Mail coach could not possibly travel this mountainous and comparatively unfrequented road during four of the winter months. In these months even the travelling on horse-back is difficult and dangerous and sometimes impossible, and therefore in that season none of the advantages of this road as a line of post communications could be felt.'[41]

During the next quarter of a century and more, petitions for a mail coach on the Highland road were to be regularly submitted to the Post Office and as regularly refused. Meantime, the 'Caledonian' coach was keeping up a regular service and on 10 February 1820 the *Inverness Courier* reported that from 1 March of that year the coach would run three times a week, covering the distance from Inverness to Perth in 17 hours. The innkeepers on the road had, it was reported, now become coaching contractors and horses were changed at every stage. By 1828 pressure on the Post Office for a mail coach service had increased still further. In that year a Petition was presented to the Treasury on behalf of the whole county of Inverness, when it was claimed that an area of country from which the Post Office drew a revenue of £12,000 per annum would benefit by the plan. Less than twenty years before, claimed the Memorialists, the only coach arriving at Inverness was a two-horse mail coach from Aberdeen. Now no fewer than seven mail and stage-coaches left Inverness regularly for various destinations, while

* See Appendix IX.

a four-horse stage-coach had been running for years on the Highland road, where every inn now kept post horses.⁴² In January of that same year, Joseph Mitchell, the resident engineer to the Commissioners for Highland Roads and Bridges, had reported to his chairman on plans, never proceeded with, to shorten the Highland road by alternative routes through Glen Feshie and Glen Geldie into the top of Glen Tilt or through Glen Tromie into Glen Bruar. The advantages claimed for these routes included the acceleration of the mail. 'For an advantage of such eminent importance', wrote Mitchell, 'it would be considered no more than a reasonable compensation should an additional 1d be levied on every letter. . . .'* But neither the growing traffic nor the prospect of a shorter route with even the possibility of a supplementary charge could move the Post Office, or the Treasury at their back, and it was not until 1836 that a daily mail coach at length ran on the Highland road, '. . . spick and span new, with new guards in new liveries and horses that find no difficulty even at the ugly Pass of Slochmuick in clearing 9 m.p.h.'⁴³ The length of the struggle to get it was to prove somewhat out of proportion to the period of its existence, for before thirty years more had passed the building of railways, first between Aberdeen and Inverness and soon after between Perth and Inverness, was to mark the end of mail coaches, not only on the Highland road but in the whole of the Highlands of Scotland.

REFERENCES

1. Hamilton, *The Industrial Revolution in Scotland*, 226.
2. Haldane, *New Ways through the Glens*, ch. 2.
3. Braid, *Postal History of Old Glasgow*.
4. Quoted in Oliver & Boyd *Almanac*, 1839.
5. Edinburgh was by this time becoming a well-known centre for coach-work. Henry Grey Graham has noted that by the end of the 18th century the city was exporting coaches to Russia and the Baltic countries. (Graham, *Social Life in Scotland in the 18th Century*, 60.)
6. N.L.S., Ronaldson, 8/23 Feb. 1792.
7. Post 40/168/1813.

* H.R. & B., 9th Report. Joseph Mitchell was a civil engineer and not a post office official and it may be that he had overlooked the fact that the produce of an extra 1d on each letter might well have been cancelled out by the lower postage on letters (still charged by distance) carried over the considerably shorter routes which he proposed.

8. Post 40/437/1830.
9. Joyce, op. cit., 426.
10. Quoted in Barron, *The Northern Highlands in the 19th Century*, vol. 11, xxxix et seq.
11. *Life of Lord Campbell*, vol. 1, 29.
12. Quoted by Hyde, op. cit., 56.
13. Quoted by Hyde, op. cit., 17.
14. Post 10/14.
15. S.R.O. G D. 51/5/563/1.
16. Post 40/50T/1798.
    Ibid./24v/1798.
17. Ibid./88B/1800.
18. Ibid./84D/1807.
    Ibid./48E/1807.
19. S.R.O. G D. 51/5/575/2.
20. Post 40/35N/1809.
21. Post 30/10. England 474K/1814.
22. Post 40/35N/1809.
23. Howard Robinson, op. cit., ch. XII. On 15 Feb. 1813 the House of Commons had before it a Petition for abolition of toll exemption for mail coaches presented by Turnpike Trustees in no less than 21 Scottish counties stretching as far north as Aberdeenshire.
24. Post 40/109/1815.
25. Ibid./459/1824.
26. Ibid./451/1827.
27. Ibid./649/1828.
28. Ibid./360/1831.
29. Cockburn, *Circuit Journeys*.
30. Haldane, *New Ways through the Glens, passim*. In one of their annual reports on the progress of Highland road and bridge building the Commissioners observed that on an average two bridges on every mile of road were required.
31. Barron, *Northern Highlands in the 19th Century*.
32. Post 15/133/1809.
33. Barron, op. cit.
34. H.R. & B., 9th Report, 1821.
35. Barron, op. cit.
36. H.R. & B., 9th Report, 1821, 33.
37. S.R.O. G D. 51/5/601/2.
38. S.R.O. G D. 46/17/57, fol. 334, 335, 336.
39. H.R. & B., 15th Report (Repair), 1829, App. B, 8/9.
40. Barron, op. cit., vol. 1.
41. Post 40/29M/1809.
42. H.R. & B., 14th Report (Repair), App. D, 43.
43. Barron, op. cit., vol. 11, xxxix–xli.

Ƒiᵫe

The Town and City Posts

Until the closing years of the 18th century the provision for postal services in the towns and cities of Scotland can only be described as rudimentary. It is true that as early as 1708 the postal staff of seven at the Edinburgh post office is reported to have included three letter-carriers. While this would appear to indicate some provision for a postal service within the city it must be borne in mind that Edinburgh was at that time, and for very many years to come, the centre of the entire postal system of Scotland, the whole of the letters of Scotland passing through the capital in order that the postal charge could be calculated and marked on each. It seems possible, therefore, that the carriers owed their existence at least partly to the work of the central Post Office for the whole country, and not entirely to a service for Edinburgh itself. The fact, too, that each of these carriers was for long in receipt of only 5/– a week and that their number on the establishment remained static till near the middle of the century certainly suggests that the postal service given to the citizens of Edinburgh during this period was very far from perfect. Apart from such service as Edinburgh had from its three carriers, London was till 1773 the only city in the British Isles with any organized service for the delivery of letters. Elsewhere any delivery of incoming letters in the towns seems to have been undertaken purely at the option of the local postmaster who made for the service such charge as he chose. Apart from this, those sending or receiving mail had to call at the post office. In 1773 a development took place in Edinburgh which was to be of much importance in the postal history of Scotland, but for any clear understanding of what then took place, or of the subsequent development of Scotland's town and city posts, it is necessary to review postal developments in England, and particularly in London, during the previous century.

In the closing years of the reign of King Charles 11 the postal service in England was steadily rising in importance. Up till this time postal development had been taking place despite rather than in consequence of official postal policy. Growing postal revenue was all too little used for development of postal facilities, a policy which resulted in criticism and discontent and inevitably to much use by the public of unofficial means of communication. London remained the great postal hub from which radiated the main postal routes. All letters continued to be routed through London, the great centre of wealth and population, but with the steady growth of towns to north, east and west a demand for direct cross posts between these centres built up to formidable and finally to irresistible dimensions. Many years were to pass before the regular system of Cross Posts, started by Ralph Allan in 1720, began to meet at all adequately the needs of the times, and meantime many a carrier, many a tramp and many a private messenger throughout the land acted as unofficial postmen.

In London itself the postal facilities were utterly inadequate. Only one General Post Office served the whole city of close on 500,000 people, and though after the Restoration the post office staff included over 30 letter-carriers, these appear to have been employed mainly in taking to the General Post Office letters handed in to receiving offices for destinations outside London. Arrangements for the delivery of letters coming to London from outside were primitive, most of these letters being called for at the General Post Office, while for postal communication between those living within London itself there appears to have been virtually no provision at all. Indeed it has been said that at this time it was easier to send a letter from London to Edinburgh than from Westminster to any other part of the city. The solution of the problem was to prove as surprising as the weakness from which it arose.

In April 1680 William Dockwra, a London merchant, announced that for one penny prepaid he was prepared to convey and deliver letters, and parcels up to 1 lb in weight, within an extensive area in London and, for an extra penny, to certain country districts on the outskirts. The system was to be operated by means of a small number of central sorting offices and hundreds of receiving offices scattered throughout London. Collections and deliveries were to be made ten or twelve times a day, and the penny charge was even to cover insurance of packages up to the value of £10. Letters could also be delivered through the new service to the General Post Office for conveyance outside London at normal postal rates. Dockwra's offer electrified London, but the success of his enterprise was its undoing. James, Duke of York, to whom postal revenue at this time belonged, could not fail to see in it a grave threat to income, present or potential, while for the Post Office it was a too-pointed criticism of the short-comings of the existing service. In November 1682 an action against Dockwra for infringement of the post office monopoly was successful, and his short-lived penny post came to an end. His enterprise had, however, served a most useful purpose. Before the end of the year a penny post for London, based largely on Dockwra's methods, had been established by the Post Office, the first step on the road which was to lead to a great reform of the postal service, not only for London, but later for the towns and cities throughout the land, and which was finally to bring the post to the remotest villages.[1]

The London Penny Post, which thus came into existence as a special department of the General Post Office in 1682, made slow progress. At the start of the 18th century the income from this source was nearly £5,000 per annum, but eighty years later the annual receipts had only doubled, a rate of increase far less than that of the Post Office in general over the period. Until well into the second half of the century the Penny Post was restricted to London alone and even here, by 1801, the charge had been raised to 2d a letter in the City and 3d in the suburbs; but with the rapid growth of the towns in the Midlands and the North the need for similar developments outside London was becoming apparent, and in 1765 penny, or local posts as they were frequently called, were legalized for any city or town in Great Britain or Ireland at the discretion of the Post Office. This power of extension was not immediately used, but in 1773 a penny post was started in Dublin, the first city outside London to have this service.

In view of the large part which the Penny Post, as legalized for general use in 1765, was to play in the development of the postal services both in Scotland and in England, it is of importance to define the nature and limitations of this post. The penny post of 1765 was little more than an extension of the service offered to London by Dockwra in 1680, and though its increasing use and popularity throughout the United Kingdom in the early part of the 19th century no doubt helped to pave the way leading to the uniform Penny Post of 1840, the two posts must not be confused. It is perhaps unfortunate for students of postal history that the same name has been given to two services so different in scope and object.

The penny post which came into existence in January 1840 was uniform throughout the United Kingdom, one penny carrying a letter up to a half-ounce in weight between any two post offices in the land, though free house-to-house delivery was only gradually conceded. The penny post of 1765, on the other hand, was intended for local correspondence, either within a Post town or city on Dockwra's model, or between such a centre and near-by villages which had no postal service. As time passed, the radius thus served by penny post from the centre extended, but it remained true that the service was only designed for, or extended to, places which had no postal service. Letters passing between two Post towns, even if in close proximity, continued for many years to pay the full postal rate for the distance. The penny paid under the penny post of 1765 was intended to cover delivery, again on Dockwra's model, though as will appear this rule was widely disregarded for a long time, and this penny post service was frequently used to bring in to the central post office letters intended for transmittal to a distance. Such letters paid the extra penny over and above the normal postal rate to the letter's destination. So, too, with incoming letters, the penny post system of 1765 was frequently used for their delivery, the recipient having to pay the extra penny as well as the normal postal charge on the letter, unless in areas where a free delivery had been conceded.

At almost exactly the same time as the start of Dublin's penny post in 1773, events of great importance in the postal history of Scotland were taking place in Edinburgh. About the year 1740 Peter Williamson, the ten-year-old son of an Aberdeenshire crofter, had been kidnapped in Aberdeen and shipped to America, apparently destined for a life of slavery in the plantations, but in fact launched on a career of astonishing adventure and enterprise. The ship in which Williamson sailed was wrecked, but he himself was saved and was subsequently sold for £16 into slavery in Philadelphia. Hugh Wilson, into whose ownership Williamson came, proved to be a humane and generous master who educated Williamson and left him on his death a sum of money which enabled Williamson to gain freedom and eventually to marry. Through his wife's family Williamson acquired a farm on the borders of Pennsylvania, but his misfortunes were not yet ended, for in 1754 he was captured by Indians. Escaping from them, Williamson served for a time with the British Army in America, till 1756 when he was wounded and again captured, this time by the French, finally reaching England where he was discharged from the Army.[2]

Williamson's memories of Aberdeen were bitter ones, and on his return to Scotland he devoted part of his time to claiming damages in respect of his kidnapping in 1740. In this he was ultimately successful, and in 1758 he moved to Edinburgh where he established inside the Parliament House a tavern which came to be known as 'Indian Peter's Coffee House'. The Parliament House in those days bore little resemblance to what it is today. Across what is now the Parliament Hall ran a wooden partition about 15 feet high, cutting off some 25 to 30 feet of the northern end. To the south of this partition was what would now be called the Outer House of the Court of Session.[3] In the days of Peter Williamson the roll of the fifteen judges of the Court of Session, under Lord President Robert Dundas, contained such well-known names as Auchinleck, Hailes, Kames and Monboddo, and each week one of the judges in turn, other than the Lord President, held in the southern end of the Parliament Hall, what we would now call Courts of First Instance; but in the smaller northern section on either side of the public space were the stalls of shopkeepers.[4] A description of the place about 1780 tells of two booksellers' stalls, a hat-maker's stall, a hardware merchant's store and Peter Williamson's coffee house. A few years later the booksellers' stalls had disappeared to be replaced by a jeweller's shop and a cutler's shop, where about 1792 Lord Cockburn bought his first pair of skates and was surprised to see figures in black gowns and white wigs walking about among the cutlery.[5]

Peter Williamson's coffee house flourished, but this was not the only outlet for a boundless energy unimpaired by earlier hardships. Having invented a primitive type of reaping machine in 1762, he turned to printing and in 1773 produced the first *City Directory* for Edinburgh. In his work at the coffee house Williamson had seen the need for frequent communication between lawyers and for postal service for those attending the court. So the second issue of the *Directory* in 1774 contained this announcement: 'The Publisher takes this opportunity to acquaint the public that he will always make it his study to dispatch all letters and parcels not exceeding 3 lbs in weight to any place within an English mile to the East, South and West of the Cross of Edinburgh and as far as South and North Leith every hour through the day for one penny each letter or bundle.'[6] Thus, rather less than a century after the start of Dockwra's short-lived penny post in London, a very similar service had come to Edinburgh.

Like his coffee house, Williamson's penny post flourished, perhaps because the two were naturally complementary and no doubt closely linked. Besides Williamson's main office 'at his printing house in Swan's Close a little above the guard North side' the service was run by means of numerous receiving houses, where letters for delivery were taken in, including the shops of nine grocers, a shoemaker, a tobacconist and a vintner on the shore of Leith. The letters and packages were carried by six postmen employed at 4/6 a week each and wearing hats bearing the words 'Penny Post'. Prepayment of postage was optional, the letters being stamped 'Penny Post Paid' in red, or 'Penny Post not paid' in black.[7]

Peter Williamson's enterprise and energy were rewarded with a degree of good fortune which had been denied to William Dockwra in London nearly a hundred years before, and for almost twenty years his service continued with apparent satisfaction to all concerned and a profit to himself which enabled him to live and bring up a family. Why the Scottish Post Office did not challenge this obvious encroachment on their monopoly over this long period is not clear. Perhaps they were well content that the troublesome business of the collection and delivery of local letters within the city should be in hands other than their own, and the experience of the Penny Post started in Dublin in 1773 had hardly been encouraging. Finally, however, in 1793 the Post Office took over the service, enlarging the delivery to include ordinary post office letters. In the previous autumn William Kerr, the Secretary of the Scottish Post Office, had written to Freeling

'. . . I have reason to believe that Williamson would be very well pleased with an annuity of £25 stg. or even £20 and as to any other claimant there can be none as the person who endeavoured for a short time to make a similar establishment to Williamson's finding it would not answer I understand now has a cart to carry parcels between Edinburgh and Leith.

Mr Edwards and I had some conversation with Williamson on Saturday. He informed us that his establishment stands him about £120 a year for runners etc. and that the surplus has largely contributed to rear up his family.

He did not mention the amount, but I suppose it may be towards £40 a year. He is sensible that the law can suppress his establishment and says he always had and always would give a cheerful obedience to it and that he left his case to the generosity of the Post Master General and would be grateful for whatever they were pleased to do for him.

The singularity of Williamson's character, the reflection of his sufferings and the expense of the establishment has rendered abortive any attempt to supplant or compete with him.

Wm. Kerr.

From the vicinity of Williamson's shop to this office etc. I suppose he could not be employed in the new establishment.'

Freeling forwarded Kerr's letter to the Postmaster General, observing as he did so, '. . . your Lordships will see that the produce of the letters under Williamson's management must have been near £200 a year, a sum far exceeding my expectations. I therefore presume your Lordships will find no difficulty in consenting to allow him a pension of £25 a year which it seems would not only content but make him extremely happy. His age and the situation of his house entirely preclude him from any situation in the new penny post establishment at Edinburgh of which your Lordships at one time had some idea. . . .'⁸

The profitability of Williamson's enterprise seems to have been a matter of some uncertainty. Kay, in his *Edinburgh Portraits*, records that in divorce proceedings against his wife in 1789 Williamson averred that his income was trifling, that the *Directory* paid him very poorly, and that his wife robbed him of three-quarters of the profit of the Penny Post. In corroboration of this he pleaded as a litigant on the Poor's Roll. His wife, on the other hand, claimed that his penny post was a very lucrative business.⁹ Whatever was the actual truth of the matter the Post Office in 1793 evidently accepted the more liberal estimate. The annuity of £25 was approved. No doubt Williamson, now in the sixtieth year of a hard and active life, was happy to get it, and with its receipt he passes from the picture to occupy a sizeable niche in the postal history of Scotland.

In the same year which had seen the beginning of Peter Williamson's delivery service in Edinburgh there had taken place in England an event which was eventually to have important consequences for the postal services in cities and towns throughout the whole of the United Kingdom. In the small Berkshire town of Hungerford in the Kennet valley lived in the year 1772 a family of the name of Smith. For some years past it had been the custom of Powdich, the Hungerford postmaster, to arrange for the delivery in the town of incoming letters on payment of a fee of a penny a letter. The payment of the fee had for long been acquiesced in by the Hungerford people, but Smith now contended that the Postal Act of 1711 had made it the duty of postmasters to deliver letters within the limits of Post towns without any payment beyond the normal postage charge. On the strength of this conviction Smith refused to pay the penny for delivery, whereupon Powdich refused to give up letters to Smith unless he called at the post office where he could get them free of delivery charge. This Smith refused to do and the dispute was referred to the courts. Meantime the question raised by Smith had also come up in other parts of England. Decisions in the lower courts had been against the Post Office, and, as a matter of principle of great importance was clearly involved, it was decided to treat the Hungerford case as a test case. In due course the case found its way to the King's Bench

Division where Lord Mansfield and his colleagues in 1774 supported Smith's contention and confirmed that free delivery of letters could be demanded within the limits of any post office as defined by the postmaster, though no attempt was made to lay down exactly how these limits were to be fixed.[10] In Scotland at least this decision was for long to remain a dead letter, but Lord Mansfield's decision was not forgotten, and in years to come it was to be recalled and invoked to the embarrassment and cost of the Post Office, but to the great and lasting benefit of the public.

The penny post system in Edinburgh which was taken over from Williamson by the Post Office in 1792 appears to have suffered the fate which has so often befallen private enterprise when first taken over by public authority. Williamson had offered deliveries within the city every hour of the day; but now this was severely cut down. In October 1795 Freeling wrote to the Postmaster General that the Penny Post in Edinburgh was not proving profitable despite the fact that, on Freeling's instructions, no rise in salary had been given to the post office officials. On enquiry he had learned that only two deliveries a day were being made, and he now recommended the employment of two additional letter-carriers at an annual cost of £25 each to give two extra deliveries.[11] Two years later the total number of letter-carriers in the city had grown to ten. Even with these it seems that only three deliveries daily were being given, but from now on the growth of the city and in particular the rapid building of the New Town forced on a somewhat grudging Post Office a steady extension in the service both of collection and delivery of penny post and ordinary post letters alike. In addition to house-to-house delivery many letters were still collected at the General Post Office.* Here, from a comparatively early date, the postal authorities had instituted boxes to be marked with the names and addresses of the recipients of

---

* The first site of Edinburgh's post office appears to have been on the first floor of a house near the Market Cross above an alley which was long known as 'Post Office Close'. Later it was moved to premises fitted like a shop on the South side of Parliament Square where letters were dealt with across a counter like ordinary goods. At this time the volume of mail for Edinburgh must have been small, for the whole delivery in the city is believed to have been done by one man. After the death of Lord Covington in 1782 the post office moved to his house behind Parliament Close and later to a house in North Bridge Street. The next move was to Waterloo Place and finally to the North Bridge. (*Traditions of Edinburgh*.)

letters. These boxes – at one time there were as many as eighty of them – were rented by shops, offices and private persons at small rents which were regarded as the perquisite of the 'window men', whose work it was to give out letters to callers at the post office or to place in the appropriate boxes letters addressed to those who rented them. In addition to such perquisites as they had from the renting of boxes at the post office, the window men appear to have received some remuneration in relation to the number of letters handled by them. When in 1793 a penny post service was arranged to Leith, an additional sum of 1/6d a week was allowed to the letter-carriers 'as an equivalent for their pence on letters and trouble'. It seems, too, that at the same time Robert Oliphant, the Deputy Postmaster General for Scotland, got £100 per annum for life 'for the loss of the Leith letters'.*

The object of the Postal Act of 1765 which legalized penny posts for any town or city in the British Isles was, as has been seen, to cheapen and facilitate correspondence between persons living in different parts of large towns or between dwellers in these towns and correspondents in near-by villages which had no post offices. Without such a service much of this correspondence would, in those days of growing postal rates, have been lost to the Post Office either from not being written or from being entrusted to unofficial carriers. In addition to encouraging local correspondence the penny post service came to be extensively used for letters sent through the general post service at full postal rates. Before the penny post was instituted and extended to the villages in the Edinburgh area a correspondent, for example, in the village of Currie five miles from Edinburgh, wishing to send a letter by the General Postal Service, would

---

* Post 40/143B/1793. It seems that for some time during the period 1789–95, Musselburgh, Dalkeith and Prestonpans had some form of postal service, and it has been suggested that this formed part of Peter Williamson's penny post, though no reference to it appears in his *Directory*. An advertisement issued by the Post Office in June 1793 refers to an extension of the post to these three villages at that time, while the report of a Select Committee on Finance refers to certain compensation having been paid in 1793 to Archibald Hume the Clerk of the English Road in Edinburgh 'who had all the Country Penny Letters near Edinburgh'. This suggests that at the time when Williamson was operating his penny post in Edinburgh the clerk was running a private country post serving the three villages.

This somewhat obscure matter is more fully discussed in a paper read by Mr (now Sir) Walter Mercer to the Postal History Society in Oct. 1948. (*Postal History Society Bulletin*, No. 47, 1949.)

have been put to much difficulty and expense in getting it to the Edinburgh General Post Office. Now by means of the new service he could do so at a cost of a penny pre-paid in addition to the normal postage rate on the letter. If his letter was addressed to a correspondent in Edinburgh he could, by leaving it at the penny post receiving house in Currie, have it conveyed to Edinburgh and delivered within the city for 1d only.* So the public got a real convenience while the Post Office got an increased revenue. Of this revenue it seems probable that the major part came from the increased number of letters collected for the General Postal Service by means of the penny post rather than from the 1d paid on letters for purely local delivery.

The limits of the penny post service had at an early stage been set at twenty miles. This limit was later reduced to ten miles, but in 1795 the limitation of area was abolished, and shortly after the Edinburgh post office took over Peter Williamson's enterprise a steady extension of the penny post service to include surrounding villages began. One of the earliest places to be brought within the limits of the Edinburgh Penny Post was the port of Leith, two foot carriers conveying letters between the city and the port four times a day. Far from looking on this as an advantage, however, the people of Leith resented the extra penny paid on their letters, or at least on so many of them as came from outside the penny post area. The trouble arose from the fact that some years before it had been conceded by the Post Office that, owing to the mercantile importance of the port, a special bag with letters from the South should be dropped at Leith by the mail coach from London. In the light of this concession Leith now took exception to being treated as

---

* The penny paid on letters sent through the penny post system was as has been seen intended to cover the delivery of the letter. While this was the official policy it is doubtful to what extent it was fully observed even in Edinburgh and Glasgow. Certainly in 1825 a delivery charge for penny post letters was still being made in Portobello and Tranent and only in that year was a free delivery given to them. At a later date when penny posts had been extended to many small towns and villages in Scotland complaints arose that a charge for delivery was being made. Freeling writing to the Postmaster General in 1825 about a complaint made by the people of Kilpatrick, pointed out that a delivery charge was out of line with the post office policy in England where no charge was made for delivering penny post letters, at least within the penny post area, and from then on, when complaints were received, the English practice was followed. The prepayment of the penny post charge was, in 1794, made optional.

an appendage of Edinburgh, through the penny post service. In
the spring of 1801 Freeling sent on to the Postmasters General
a Memorial by the Leith people setting out their grievances.
The Leith claim was, in effect, that they be regarded as a Post
town. Freeling advised against it. Edinburgh and Leith were
only a mile and a half apart, and to make Leith a Post town
would, he considered, establish a dangerous precedent, while
the probable cost of the post office revenue from the loss of the
penny post letters would be as much as £600 per annum. In
this, as in so many matters, Freeling's advice was accepted, and
Leith remained within the Edinburgh penny post area, an
arrangement whereby, however distasteful it may have been
to them in other respects, they continued to get four deliveries
of letters a day as against only a single delivery which they would
have received had the status of a Post town been given them.[12]

The first quarter of the 19th century saw a steady extension
of Edinburgh's penny post system. The village of Lasswade
had got this service as early as 1795, and in 1803 the Postmasters General, on Freeling's advice, agreed to a request by
Sir William Forbes of Pitsligo, the prominent Edinburgh
banker, and others that a penny post service be given to Colinton
at a cost estimated at £9 per annum for a runner and £4 to
someone to take charge of a receiving house in Colinton.[13] In
1804 the service was further extended to Corstorphine and in
1806 to Hermiston and Currie.[14] The rapid rise in postal rates
which took place during the Napoleonic war made the system
extremely popular throughout the country for local mail, which
by 1812 at ordinary rates would have been charged at 4d up
to 15 miles, 5d between 15 and 20 miles, and 6d between 20
and 30 miles. These high rates continued in force long after
Waterloo, and meantime the penny post service throughout the
country increased and extended by leaps and bounds. By 1830
Edinburgh's penny post served 21 surrounding villages, including Kirknewton near Midcalder, Tranent in East Lothian,
and Ford in Midlothian 13 miles from the General Post Office.
The extension to Kirknewton dated from 1826. The village had
applied for the establishment of a post office, but this was not
considered to be justified by the probable revenue. In the
circumstances the extension of the Edinburgh penny post area
to the village was proposed, and as Lord Meadowbank had
guaranteed to make up any difference between the penny post

9. New Post Office, Waterloo Place, Edinburgh 1829, *p.* 111.

10. 'St. Valentine's Day', *p.* 120.

revenue and the cost of the service this was somewhat reluctantly agreed to.[15] If the Edinburgh service had proved unprofitable to the Post Office in the early years its steady improvement and extension had entirely changed the picture. By 1825 the penny post revenue from the city and surrounding villages had grown to over £2,000,* and four years later the number of letters sent each day by penny post in the Edinburgh area was reported as being well over 2,300.[16]

In common with Edinburgh and certain other towns and burghs of Scotland, Glasgow from an early date claimed and exercised the right of maintaining a post of its own. During the first half of the 17th century Glasgow had grown steadily, if not yet spectacularly, in size and wealth. Her merchants were already carrying on an active trade in wine and salt, and consumer goods from France and the Low Countries, in wood from Norway, and in their own linen cloth and yarn sent south to the West of England and as far as London. Scottish emigrants to Ireland, too, and the people of Scotland's Western Isles bought wine and salt, imported to Glasgow, in exchange for hides, plaids, butter and oats.[17] It has been seen that as early as 1630 the burgh records note the appointment of a burgh post to carry letters to other towns and within Glasgow itself. Fifteen years later there appears a record of a payment of 6/8d to Donald Clark as post, together with the provision of clothes and shoes for him.[18] By the second half of the century Glasgow's growth in wealth was already outstripping that of any other large town in Scotland, her merchants and their ships adventuring across the North Atlantic, to the Caribbean and the plantations on the east coast of North America.[19] The Glasgow records of the second half of the 17th century contain periodical references to payments for postal services, but these would seem to have been rather of the nature of *ad hoc* payments for services rendered from time to time rather than regular salaries. In most cases the service appears to have been the conveyance of letters or messages outside Glasgow. Where the destination

---

* While no breakdown of these penny post revenue figures is available it is virtually certain that they included not only the penny paid letters for purely local delivery—the original object of the penny post system—but also the penny paid for conveying to the General Post Office letters intended for the General Post at full rate to more distant places. The normal postal dues on mail of the latter type would not, however, be included as penny post revenue.

is recorded this is most commonly Edinburgh, though there are early references to communication with Ayr and Port Glasgow.

By the end of the 17th century Glasgow's post office had grown to be of some importance, and when the Postal Act of 1711 established a general postal service for the whole United Kingdom, the Glasgow postmaster had a salary of £25 sterling per annum. This indeed was only half of what was being paid to the postmasters at Haddington and Cockburnspath on the great post road from London, but Glasgow's post office was already growing fast. In 1730 Daniel Montgomerie, then in charge of the office in Gibson's Wynd, received a salary of over £100, and twenty-five years later the postmaster's salary had grown to £200.[20] Up till the end of the 18th century the absence of any details as to the staff of the Glasgow office makes it difficult to form a clear picture of the standard of postal services within the city itself, but it is certain that at least by 1799 a regular delivery service within the city had come into existence. In that year, besides the postmaster, there were two clerks, a stamper and sorter of letters, and four letter-carriers. The carriers and the stamper got 10/6d a week each, and the clerks £30 and £25 per annum respectively. From his salary of £200 the postmaster appears to have given £10 a year to each clerk, besides paying over £30 for office rent, coal and candles.[21] As in the case of Edinburgh up till 1795, Glasgow at the end of the century had only two deliveries a day, and it is probable that, as in Edinburgh, a proportion of the Glasgow letters were called for at the post office. The pay of the Glasgow letter-carriers had been only 8/– a week up till 1793, when rather grudgingly it had been increased to 10/6d. The petition of the carriers for an increase at that date referred to rise in rents and food prices, the expense of shoes, the growth of the town area, and the risk of being given bad money by the recipients of letters.[22] In this latter connection the records of the post office make it clear that over a very long period letter-carriers, local postmasters, and even the officials of the General Post Office at Edinburgh, in collecting and remitting money, were held responsible for any bad coins and that no allowance was made to them on this account.

The success and rapid growth of the official penny post service which had been started in Edinburgh in 1793 made its early extension to Glasgow certain, and in 1800 the Glasgow penny post came into existence, at first on an experimental basis. It may be that twenty years experience of Peter Williamson's service had given to the people of Edinburgh a familiarity with the local collection and delivery system which Glasgow lacked. Whatever the reason, the growth of Glasgow's penny post service with three receiving houses was slow, and in the first six months Ronaldson, the surveyor for the West of Scotland, reported that the revenue from this source was less than £50 against an expenditure of £73.9.od. Ronaldson's view was that the people of Glasgow had not yet 'obtained that confidence which longer experience may bring to them . . .'; but Freeling was in doubt whether the continuation of the experiment in Glasgow would be justified. 'Glasgow', he wrote in disappointment, 'was the only place where I thought the penny post at all likely to succeed.'[23] Three years later, however, the critical stage had passed and revenue at last exceeded expenditure, though it was not till 1806 that Glasgow's penny post began to be extended to the suburbs. From then on the growth was steady, though for long it lagged far behind that of the Edinburgh service. In 1815, when the number of penny post letters carried each day in Glasgow was reported at 280, the gross revenue had reached £367 per annum,[24] and ten years later when the revenue from Edinburgh's penny post had reached £2200 that of Glasgow was still only £690.[25]

Reading the contemporary correspondence which passed between the Scottish postal officials and the General Post Office headquarters in London, it is hard to avoid the feeling that the relatively slow growth of Glasgow's penny post was partly the result of parsimony on the part of the London office. Francis Freeling was a great protagonist of the penny post system in large towns, but above all he looked for profits for the Post Office and disliked throwing his bread on the waters. Expenditure, except in anticipation of an assured future profit, was little to his liking. As a postal historian of last century has written, 'That the Post Office must sow before it can reap is a truism which those who hold the purse-strings have, at all times, found it hard to accept.'[26] So it seems to have been in Glasgow. The number of receiving houses on which so much depended tended to lag behind the needs and potentialities of the service. So too with letter carriers. It was perhaps hard for Englishmen to realize fully the extra burden which the tenements of Scottish towns placed on Scottish postmen compared with their opposite numbers in England, and many years later Anthony Trollope, with more than thirty years' experience as a post office surveyor behind him, recorded that accompanying a Glasgow postman on his delivery round was the hardest day's work he had done in his life.[27]

By the end of the first quarter of the 19th century the Glasgow penny post service was being rapidly extended to the suburbs and surrounding towns and villages. In 1830, 9 carriers were giving a postal service to 28 points on the outskirts, and the rapid extension of the service is shown by the fact that in 1833 18 letter-carriers were given 2/6d each for delivering in four days 21,000 penny letters in connection with the election of magistrates and councillors in the City.[28] By 1835 Glasgow's penny post reached out to 35 places including Cumbernauld, East Kilbride, Neilston, Dunglas, Milngavie, Lennoxtown, Strathblane, Killearn and Balfron. In the previous year the penny post revenue of Glasgow had reached £1400 per annum and Francis Freeling reporting to the Postmaster General on the city's improved postal service wrote: 'I hope I may be allowed the indulgence of some honest pride in seeing, as the parent of the country's Penny Post systems, that their use and extension have greatly facilitated the intercourse of the country, have accommodated thousands of persons in remote villages and districts and have produced immense sums of money each year into His Majesty's Exchequer.'[29] When in March 1835 Freeling reported to the Postmaster General on further improvements in the postal arrangements in the Glasgow area, he had at least some justification in writing of criticisms made by Robert Wallace, the great advocate of postal reform, '. . . we might fairly challenge the Member of Parliament locally connected with one of the places above mentioned [Greenock] who is so ardent in his representations affecting this office, to produce any instances of want of due attention and convenience on our part where the object comes within the limits of practicability.'[30]

While the penny post system, after a relatively slow start in the closing years of the 18th century, came in the first quarter of the 19th century to play a part of increasing importance, its primary purpose was for the collection and delivery of purely local mail. Letters which passed through the General Postal

Service at normal postal rates depended for their collection and delivery on carriers whose work it was to collect and bring to the General Post Office outgoing letters which had been handed in to the receiving houses, where these existed, and to deliver such incoming letters as were not called for at the post office of the city or town in question. It has been seen that by 1797 the staff of the Edinburgh post office included ten letter-carriers for the delivery of letters which had passed through the General Letter service, and at about the same date four carriers were employed in delivering similar letters in Glasgow. In this respect Edinburgh and Glasgow were exceptionally well served by contemporary standards, not only in the number of carriers employed but in the fact that the two cities, together it seems with Leith, were the only places in Scotland where a free delivery of letters was given. In the other Post towns of Scotland letters were still either collected by the recipients at the post office or were, at the option of the postmaster, delivered by carriers usually employed by him in return for what was known as a 'gratuity' which was generally at the rate of $\frac{1}{2}$d or sometimes 1d a letter. This was retained by the postmaster towards the wages of the carrier. This system of gratuities continued in nearly every Scottish town and even in some English towns long after Lord Mansfield's decision in the Hungerford case, and it was not until near the end of the first quarter of the 19th century that increasing protests from the Scottish towns forced the Post Office to recognize and give effect to a legal decision which up till then had been conveniently ignored.

It may readily be supposed that until that time came the delivery service in Scottish towns outside Edinburgh, Glasgow and Leith left much to be desired. The postal arrangements in Inverness about the year 1770 as described by contemporary witnesses are probably typical of those in many other towns in Scotland. In Inverness the duties of letter delivery were undertaken by one Angus Shaw or sometimes by his wife who were employed by Warrand the postmaster. The delivery charge was $\frac{1}{2}$d a letter, and though some of the Inverness merchants were in the habit of calling for their letters at the post office they often found that these had already been given for delivery to Shaw, who refused to part with them except in return for his $\frac{1}{2}$d. It seems that Shaw suffered from the appreciable handicap of not being able to read, and was in the habit of taking the letters

[119]

to a shop where the addresses were called over to those expecting letters who had congregated for this reason. Worse still, Shaw frequently took the letters to the Supervisor of Excise to have the addresses deciphered – a habit which perhaps explained what one aggrieved merchant regarded as an undue number of seizures by the excise officer. Illiteracy seems to have been no bar to employment as letter-carrier in the Inverness district at the time, for about the same date the carrier between Inverness and Tain stated that being unable to read he placed a mark on each letter before starting on his rounds to let him know where it was to be delivered. The arrangements for outgoing letters seem to have been equally primitive. A hole in the window of the post office acted as a letter-box, but at times when the post office was closed letters were left on the dresser of the postmaster's kitchen. Here the maidservants, who seem to have had educational advantages over Shaw and his colleagues, derived entertainment from reading the addresses or even on occasion from opening, reading and re-closing the letters.[31] No doubt Sir Walter Scott had in his mind's eye some such scene as that enacted at the Inverness post office when in *The Antiquary* he described the episode in the Fairport post office where Mrs Mailsetter and her gossips speculated on the contents of the incoming mail.* The arrangements for the delivery of letters addressed to the country districts round Inverness seem to have remained somewhat inadequate long after this period, for it is on record that up till 1829 the Inverness postmaster disposed of mail for these districts by calling over the addresses at the market cross each Friday, delivering the letters to the addressees or to those willing to accept and pay for the letters on their behalf.[32] Conditions in Hawick appear to have been at least equally primitive. The writer of the *New Statistical Account* for that town (1842) quotes a description of how 'previous to the establishment of the Post Office in Hawick about 70 or 80 years ago the letters which were brought from Jedburgh by a common hawker once a month were exposed on a stall in the street on a market day like so many cakes of gingerbread and the people used to look at them with as much curiosity as the

---

* It has been said that in the 18th century certain Catholic clergy who had been trained abroad, *e.g.* in Spain, habitually wrote to one another, while both were in Scotland, in the Spanish language to escape the prying eyes of the postmasters and postmistresses. (*The Innes Review*, vol. xiv, No. 2, p. 112.)

botanists of the present day would do at a few exotic plants from Van Diemen's Land.'[33]

If the illiteracy of 18th-century letter-carriers was a hindrance to improvement in the standards of postal service, it would seem that the carriers themselves had not a little with which to contend. Houses were of course unnumbered, streets largely unnamed, while in the Old Town of Edinburgh at least, the high tenements might house almost indefinite numbers of people – owners, tenants, servants, lodgers or passing visitors – a cross-section of humanity where the certain identification of the addressee of an occasional or unexpected letter would have taxed the patience and intelligence of the best. Writers of letters, in the hope of aiding their safe arrival, often resorted to forms of descriptive or geographical address sometimes helpful but perhaps more often not. 'For Captain Philip Anstruther off Newgrange' read the address on an early 18th-century letter 'att his lodging a little above the fountain-well south side of the street Edenborough'. Another of the same period was for 'Mr Archibald Dumbarr of Thunderstoune to be left at Captain Dumbarr's writing chamber at the Iron Revell third storie below the Cross North end of the Close at Edinburgh', while a third, directed to London, went to 'Mrs Mary Stowell at Whiteakers in St. Andrew Street next door save one to the Blew balcony near the sundyall near Longaiker'.[34]

When Lord Mansfield and his colleagues decided in 1774 that recipients of letters through the post were entitled to a free house to house delivery within the normal limits of Post towns, a principle of the utmost importance both for the Post Office and for the public had been laid down. It might reasonably have been expected that on the side of the public no time would be lost in seeking its enforcement; but in Scotland at least this did not happen, while even in England the custom of free delivery only gradually became universal. There can be little doubt that a sense of grievance over the continued delivery charge by the Post Office was growing in the mind of the public, but it was not till about 1823 that this reached formidable proportions. In September of that year Freeling wrote to the Postmaster General: 'Your Lordship is aware that on any representations which may have been made to this office from time to time by individuals that a gratuity has been paid of ½d or 1d over and above the postage for the delivery of letters in Post Towns orders have been immediately given for its discontinuance, the result being invariably an additional expense to the Revenue for providing a letter carrier at the place. I have always lamented the necessity of incurring that expense on the discontinuance of a practice having the sanction (as in all cases of the kind) of immemorial custom and usage, but as I said before, whenever it has been objected to it has been our duty to direct that it should not be persisted in. I lately received a remonstrance from a person at Greenock which I referred to the Secretary of the Scottish Post Office and in my correspondence with him upon the subject I learn for the first time that with the exception of Edinburgh, Glasgow and Leith there is not an allowance – *i.e.* by the Post Office – to any office in Scotland for a letter carrier. The custom, therefore, of an extra charge on the delivery of each letter is general thro' that part of the Kingdom and it is clear that this charge is readily paid or we should have had remonstrance against it.

'When I consider that there are upwards of 250 Post Towns in Scotland, that the salaries are for the most part very low, that the extra charge can in a few cases only be a source of profit to the Postmaster and is chiefly a mere remuneration to the person whom he employs to deliver the letters and finally that it would bring upon us a heavy increased expense of hundreds per annum if we were to provide letter carriers I confess I am overcome by the difficulties of the case.

'The Solicitor in his observations on Mr Godby's letter says truly that by a decision of a Court of Law many years since the Postmaster General is bound to deliver letters in Post Towns for the legal rate of postage only. I pray your Lordship, therefore, to consider whether it may be necessary to submit these facts to the Lords of the Treasury or to refer them to the Parliamentary Commissions when they commence their enquiry into this Department. I ought to add that there are probably some 50 or 60 places in England and Wales where the gratuity is still paid without objection and under the sanction of immemorial usage and that with a view to keep down the expenditure every Postmaster General during the long time I have been in the office has considered that enough has been done in ordering the custom to cease when it has been objected to by any individual.'[35]

Shearer and Reeves, the two Scottish surveyors, had prepared lists of the Post towns in their respective areas with annual postal revenues of over £600 where they considered that carriers would soon be needed.* In most cases one carrier was thought to be sufficient, but in the case of Dundee, Inverness, Perth, Greenock and Paisley two were recommended and four in the case of Aberdeen. These men would need salaries varying from £15 to £30 per annum, so the charge on the Post Office for a free delivery was likely to grow to formidable proportions, and Freeling's distress and perplexity were understandable. The only benefit to the Post Office from the improved service was likely to be a decrease in illegal carriage of letters.[36]

The application for a free delivery in Greenock was the beginning of a flood of similar applications from all parts of Scotland. The next few years saw free deliveries given in Stirling, Linlithgow, Dunfermline, Cupar, Blairgowrie, Perth, Dundee and Aberdeen in Central and Eastern Scotland; in Banff, Forres, Inverness, Wick and Kirkwall in the North; in Hawick, Selkirk, Melrose, Lanark and Girvan in the South, and in Inveraray, Bowmore and Tobermory in the West. In 1834 Freeling wrote to the Postmaster General, reporting perhaps somewhat prematurely, that there were now few Post towns in Great Britain where a charge was still made for delivery.[37] Arrangements for the delivery of letters in Aberdeen were the cause of much worry to Freeling and his colleagues. For many years letters in the city had been delivered by four carriers whose salaries were, as in the case of Inverness, met by a delivery charge of $\frac{1}{2}$d per letter which was estimated to bring in an average of 16/– to 18/– a week to each carrier, and it was not till 1829 that an application for a free delivery was made. In December of that year Freeling sent on the application to the Postmaster General recommending the appointment by the Post Office of three letter-carriers at an annual cost of £25 each. Some of the Aberdeen people, however, who had long been in the habit of collecting their mail at the post office, complained that the new arrangement deprived them of this privilege, and it was reluctantly decided that the privilege should be restored, Freeling cherishing the unfulfilled hope that this would enable the letter-carriers to be reduced from three to two.[38] Three years later similar complaints came from

* The total produce in 1823 of $\frac{1}{2}$d for each letter delivered in these 21 towns was reported to be approximately £460 per annum.

merchants in Dundee and Greenock where free delivery by letter carrier had been conceded. The postal authorities took the opinion of counsel who advised that the obligation of the Post Office was only to deliver letters to the addresses of the recipients and confirmed the existing policy and practice that letters would only be held at the post office for those who rented boxes for their retention.

The concession and growing extension of free delivery in Scottish towns and the success of the penny post system in Edinburgh and Glasgow brought new problems to the postal officials. The limits of both free delivery and penny post areas had been arbitrarily fixed by the local postmasters, and as time passed and population grew, these limits were becoming more and more out of date, while the growth or movement of population meant a constant demand for more receiving houses or the resiting of existing ones. In Edinburgh, especially, the rapid growth of the New Town to the north and north-west of Princes Street meant growing demands and constant complaints. Lord Mansfield's judgment in the House of Lords in 1772 and the arbitration award by the future Lord Eskgrove four years later had happily resulted in preserving the land immediately to the south of Princes Street as pleasure ground, so concentrating feuing and building activity on the land north of Princes Street and west of Hanover Street. St Andrew's Square had been largely feued before 1780 and in the last decade of the century building was progressing steadily along the north side of Princes Street and in George Street. At the west end of George Street the first building in Charlotte Square had been completed in 1792, but further building followed slowly and by 1800 only part of the north side of the square was complete, with open country behind sloping to the wooded banks of the Water of Leith.[39] In Queen Street the westward spread of building was only gradual, but in 1810 James Hope, whose work as agent for the Commissioners for Highland Roads and Bridges was to do so much to open up communications in the Highlands, had moved from the eastern section of Princes Street to a new office near the west end of Queen Street. To the north of Queen Street the building of Heriot Row, Abercromby Place and streets further to the northward on land largely belonging to the Trustees of Heriot's Hospital occupied the years from 1803 to 1823. This was fast becoming the fashionable part, especially for the legal profession, and in December 1810 Freeling had before him a Memorial signed by 15 Advocates and 13 Writers to the Signet and supported by local postal officials asking for the appointment of an additional letter-carrier for the area.[40] To the south of the city, too, similar postal problems were arising with the spread from 1806 onwards of new building on open land in what is now the Newington district on the route of the London mail coach.

The gradual improvements in the Edinburgh postal service at this period constantly lagged far behind the growth of population and the building of new houses 'occupied as soon as completed', and before many years had passed even the cautious and economical Freeling had to agree that the growth of the city would soon call for new arrangements both for receiving houses and for delivery services. The trouble arose largely from the fact that the new building was constantly extending into areas beyond the boundaries which had been long since laid down as the limits for free delivery both of ordinary mail and of local letters circulating within the penny post system. But if it was easy for the postal officials to see what was the source of the trouble, it was much less easy to explain or rearrange matters to the satisfaction of those in the new areas, and there was some force, if less pure logic, in the argument of those in the Henderson Row area who complained in the spring of 1830 that being within the limits of the city and liable to high rating assessments they were entitled to free postal delivery of letters, whether through the ordinary post or the penny post system.[41]

Looking back on this complex period of postal development in Edinburgh it must be confessed that there is much obscurity. With two parallel systems of postal service in the City – penny post and ordinary mail post – each with its own receiving houses, its carriers and its delivery areas, it is little wonder that no small degree of confusion and frustration existed in the mind of the post office officials, of the public and no less of the postal historian of today. Nor was the problem by any means confined to Edinburgh or indeed to Scotland. In varying degrees it applied to nearly all towns and cities in the kingdom, and it is probably true to say that at this time there were few places in the United Kingdom where the post office officials could say with certainty what would be the full postal charge for transmission and delivery of a letter addressed to another town.

As time passed and demands grew both for extended penny post facilities and improvement in the ordinary postal service of Edinburgh, it became increasingly clear that some degree of co-ordination of the two was called for and the same need was soon to make itself felt in Glasgow and other Scottish cities. From about 1824 onwards references appear to the extended use in Edinburgh of general receiving houses to deal with both penny post and ordinary mail, though ten years later Francis Freeling appears still to have been opposed to this as a general practice.* The Edinburgh letter-carriers, too, delivering letters within the free delivery areas, were increasingly used to deliver outside these areas in return for 1d a letter.

About this time the wages of the Edinburgh carriers had grown to £45 per annum, exclusive of anything they could earn from letters delivered beyond the free limits. By 1829 the number of carriers in the city had grown to 30. Despite the growth in man force and the relatively generous pay, the work of the city letter-carrier at this time can have been far from easy. The building of the New Town and the movement of population from the crowded areas around the High Street must in some respects have eased his task, but this movement itself must have brought problems to the postmen. Freeling, writing in 1834, refers to a *Directory* started 28 or 30 years before to help the Edinburgh carriers in their work, the profits from which were divided between the carriers and the post office official who compiled the publication. In the spring of that year John Gray, 'one of the proprietors of the North British Advertiser', had asked the Post Office to help in correcting the draft of a new Directory on which he was working, but the Post Office preferred their own *Directory* and refused to help in the preparation of a new one despite a threat of court proceedings.[42]

In comparison with the pay of the carriers, that of the officials at the receiving houses seems to have been miserable, for in the summer of 1825 when new receiving houses, partly to serve the extending Newington area, were recommended, the pay pro-

---

* 7 Feb. 1824. 'The public in this city have got an additional accommodation by all the penny post offices through the New Town and suburbs being rendered free receiving houses for country letters'. (*Book of the Old Edinburgh Club*, vol. 29, 149.)

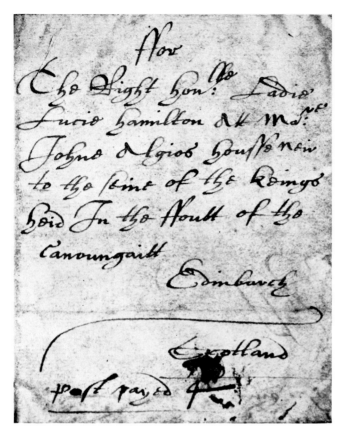

11. Early postal address (1662), *p.* 121.

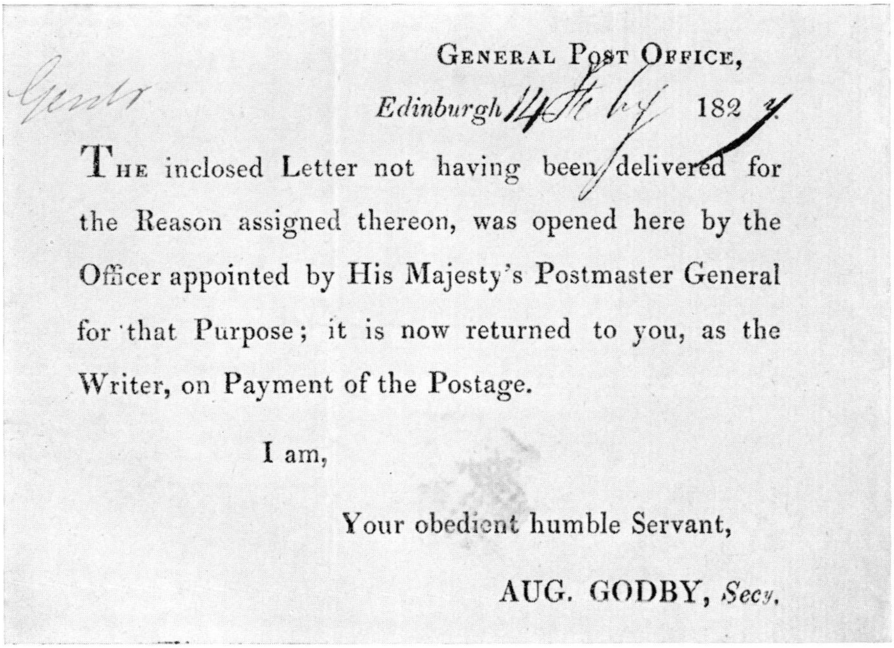

GENERAL POST OFFICE,

Edinburgh *14th by* 182

Gentr

THE inclosed Letter not having been delivered for the Reason assigned thereon, was opened here by the Officer appointed by His Majesty's Postmaster General for that Purpose; it is now returned to you, as the Writer, on Payment of the Postage.

I am,

Your obedient humble Servant,

AUG. GODBY, *Secy.*

12. Dead letters, *p.* 155.

posed was only £10 per annum for each.* It is small wonder
that, writing to the Postmaster General in 1834, Freeling
referred to the difficulty of getting receiving officers to accept
such a pittance for a day starting at 6 a.m. and not ending until
10 p.m. with no fewer than seven collections of letters bound
for the General Post Office. At least the Edinburgh receiving
officers were not expected to pay for the erection of posting
boxes at the receiving houses – a monstrous exaction which was
common in England.[43]

The story of the development of the postal services in Edinburgh and Glasgow has been told in some detail as illustrating
more fully than in any other town or city in Scotland the growth
of the ordinary mail and penny post systems both in the purely
urban areas and in the surrounding villages. Moreover, in the
case of Edinburgh especially, the rapid growth of the New
Town in the early decades of the 19th century brought with it
postal problems which at that period were peculiar to the city.
But if Edinburgh and Glasgow were the natural leaders, postal
development in other Scottish towns was soon to come. By the
middle thirties of last century, while free delivery of ordinary
mail in towns had become almost universal, over 80 towns and
urban areas in Scotland were enjoying the advantages of local
penny post. This, with a simultaneous and even more rapid
spread to villages had gone far to atune the thoughts, the habits
and the ambitions of the public to the Uniform Penny Post
which was soon to follow.

REFERENCES

1. Howard Robinson, op. cit., ch. VI.
2. Brodlie, 'On the Fringes of Fame', *Scots Magazine*, Nov. 1938.
   Mercer, 'Peter Williamson's Penny Post', *Postal Hist. Socy. Bulletin*, Mar.
   1949.
   Green, 'The Penny Post and Post Marks of Peter Williamson', *Philately in
   Scotland*, June 1933.
3. Chambers, *Minor Antiquities of Edinburgh*.
4. Boswell, *The Ominous Years*, 1774/6., App. B.
5. Cockburn, *Memorials of his Time*.
6. Brodlie, op cit.
7. Brodlie, op cit.

* By 1821 the number of penny post receiving houses in the city had reached 7
and these were steadily being added to.

8. Post 40/69B/1792.

9. Kay's *Portraits*.

10. *Smith* v. *Powdich*, King's Bench Division, 18 Nov. 1774.

11. Post 40/17H/1795.

12. Ibid./42E/1801.

13. Ibid./37N/1803.

14. N.L.S., Ronaldson, 21 May 1806.

15. Post 40/361/1826.

16. Ibid./470/1829.

17. Smout, 'The Glasgow Merchant Community in the 17th Century', *Scott Hist. Rev.*, XLVII, No. 143.

18. Quoted by Braid, *Postal History of Old Glasgow*.

19. Smout, op. cit.

20. Braid, op. cit.

21. Hyde, op cit., 97.

22. Post 40/117C/1793.

23. Ibid./43C/1800.

24. Braid, op. cit.

25. Post 40/65/1825.

26. Joyce, op. cit., 57.

27. Quoted by Hyde, op. cit., 66.

28. Post 40/867/1833.

29. Ibid./784/1834.

30. Ibid./191/1835.

31. *Miscellanea Invernessiana*, 1902, 56.

32. Penrose Hay, *Post Office Recollections*, 1885.

33. *N.S.A.*, III, 407.

34. Dunbar, *Social Life in Former Days*, 1st Series, 33/4.

35. Post 40/392/1823.

36. Ibid.

37. Ibid./509/1834.

38. Ibid./1088/1829.

39. Youngson, *The Making of Classical Edinburgh, passim*.

40. Post 40/49T/1810.

41. Ibid./734/1833.

42. Ibid./235/1834.

43. Ibid./511 1834.

Six

The Village and Country Posts of the Early 19th century

The development of postal services in Scotland during the latter years of the 18th century shows little sign that the process was being retarded by wars on the Continent and overseas. Indeed the records available make it clear that the rate of development increased after 1793 when Great Britain had become finally committed to the struggle with France. The next quarter of a century was to show that, in postal as in many other matters, the war on the Continent, far from retarding development, acted as a stimulus. The rapid progress which was to take place during the greater part of these twenty-five years was most noticeable in the rural and Highland areas of Scotland, and in nearly every case war was a potent factor if not a direct cause. The distress in the Highlands which followed the break-up of the clan system had led to a degree of disillusionment and consequent emigration directly threatening the supply of valuable recruits for both the Navy and the Army. It was largely to meet this threat that the great project of Highland road and bridge building was launched in 1803. In the same year a start was made on the building of the Caledonian Canal, not only to provide employment, but also to shorten for merchant and naval vessels alike the voyage between the east and west coasts and to avoid the threat from French privateers on the dangerous route

K   [129]

round the north of Scotland. In the agriculture of both Highland and Lowland Scotland the last years of the century saw a
great revolution in progress. Enclosing and reseeding of grass-
land, better drainage, improved ploughing and turnip cultiva-
tion as part of a wise rotation of crops led to better cattle to be
driven to the South where the consumption of beef by the navy
blockading the French ports was added to the demands of the
growing towns. In the hill country of the North and West the
rapid spread of sheep farming to which was due many of
the problems of the Highland economy had hastened a movement to the coast of displaced and landless clansmen who now
pinned their hopes on coastal fishing and the production of the
kelp which the war had made so valuable. On every side, and
more especially in the country districts, the impact of war was
apparent. So it is that, while the story of Scotland's postal
development up to 1800 tells largely of letter-carriage in and
between the towns, the interest during the next quarter-century
passes at least in part to the villages, the country districts and
the Islands.

The growth of Scotland's postal system during the 18th
century, measured solely by the number of post offices, had
been steady if not spectacular. The 34 Post towns recorded as
having been in existence in 1708 had grown by 1791 to 164,
but up to the end of the century little or no effort had been
made to recognize, far less to deal with, the postal needs of the
more remote country districts. As early as 1689 when John
Blair was Postmaster General for Scotland, the contract entered
into between him and the Privy Council which fixed postal
rates between the principal towns in Scotland had, as has been
seen, provided that any persons regularly employed in bringing
letters from towns, villages or country districts with no post
office to the nearest Post town should have 1/−(s) for each
letter.* Common carriers were also authorized to bring letters
to the nearest post, while the Act of 1711 gave authority for
arrangements to be made for the carriage of letters to the
nearest post office or postal stage more than six miles from the
General Post Office of London or the chief post office at
Edinburgh. About the end of the 17th century, at least some
local postmasters appear to have had as part of their remuneration a penny or twopence on each letter collected or delivered,

* See Appendix 1.

and in 1711 of the 34 postmasters then in office in Scotland only 12 are believed to have been paid by salary alone, the others getting as remuneration part of the postal charges on letters passing through their hands.[1] But such arrangements did little or nothing effectively to bring the post to rural areas, and all through the 18th century letters addressed to country addresses continued to be carried to the nearest Post towns only, their further carriage depending largely on chance, on the goodwill of the postmaster or on the initiative of those expecting letters.

The Post Office Act of 1765 had authorized the establishment, within a radius of 10 miles of any town, of a penny post based on the model of that started by Dockwra in London in 1680, and ten years later the result of the Hungerford litigation had made the Post Office responsible for free delivery of letters; but in each case the actual limits of the service had been left to the determination of the Post Office, and even within these limits free delivery was only slowly conceded. In 1794 the limitation of the area within which penny posts could operate was abolished, but the idea of rural posts in the true sense was still far off. So far as Scotland is concerned it was, at the end of the century, only in the case of Edinburgh and Glasgow that penny post services to surrounding country districts had come to be considered in any practical way. For the rest, in Scotland as in England, the postal needs of country dwellers continued to be met at best by the old provision whereby postmasters could if they so wished collect or deliver letters in return for a fee fixed virtually at their pleasure. It still remained open, however, for the country people to arrange at their own cost for regular messengers or private servants to carry letters to or from the nearest post office. Private letter carrying of this sort, which in the absence of an officially provided service was not looked on as a breach of the post office monopoly, was extensively used towards the end of the 18th century. It has been seen that about 1793 landowners in the parish of Kilmorack were having their letters carried to and from Inverness in this way. About the end of the century, residents in the Comrie district, who included Viscount Melville and Lord Advocate Dundas, got their mail to and from Crieff by this method*

---

* This private arrangement seems to have lasted till 1807 when with some hesitation Freeling approved the experimental establishment of a postal service from Crieff to Lochearnhead. (Post 40/78E/1807.)

and the first *Statistical Account* contains references to similar arrangements in other parts of Scotland.

In 1801 the Government took what at first sight appeared to be a real step towards rural posts. An Act of that year authorised postmasters to make special arrangements for the collection and conveyance of letters for towns and villages which were not Post towns, while it also empowered the Post Office to accept guarantees in respect of local posts of this sort which would not otherwise pay the expense of operating them. This Act remained, however, largely a dead letter, and so far as true rural posts in the United Kingdom are concerned their history starts in the year 1808 when the Post Office decided to use their powers to extend to villages in rural areas the system of penny posts hitherto confined to the neighbourhood of the large towns. From now on an increasing part of the official correspondence which passed between the Scottish postal officials in Edinburgh and the Post Office headquarters in London concerned the rural post in Scotland. By no means all of this concerned the growth of the penny post system. A steady extension of the ordinary postal services was also by now taking place, and by the end of the third decade of the century, though the postal map of Scotland still showed many blank spaces, the network of postal routes served by coach, by gig, on horseback or on foot had spread out to include many a village and many a remote district where the note of the coach horn, the beat of a post horse's hoof or the knock of a letter-carrier had been unknown sounds.

Postal development in Scotland in the second half of the 18th century had centred mainly on the principal postal routes running from Edinburgh through Aberdeen to Inverness and the far north, and from Glasgow north to Dumbarton, Inveraray and Fort William. In addition to these, certain cross-country postal routes had in the last years of the century started to make their appearance, notably from Stirling through the Breadalbane country to Argyll, and from Dingwall to the west coast at Strome Ferry on Loch Carron and at Ullapool on Loch Broom. For the rest, postal development in the purely rural districts of Scotland was still extremely limited, dependent on the initiative of local interests rather than on official policy or widespread demand.

A study of postal development in the early years of the 19th century shows in general the same broad pattern. The emphasis is still on improvement in the east coast route to Aberdeen and the north where mail coaches had made their first appearance in 1798, with better and more frequent posts to the west coast from Edinburgh, Glasgow and Inverness. At the beginning of the century postal policy both in England and in Scotland was coming more and more to be dictated by Freeling in London, and in Scottish matters a steadily growing volume of correspondence passed between him and the post office staff in Edinburgh. All matters of policy, and indeed many of detail, were, it is true, subject to the final decision of the two Postmasters General, but among the countless Minutes which passed between them and Freeling, the vast majority bear only the briefest endorsement 'approved'; on only a few have the Postmasters General indicated hesitation in accepting the Secretary's advice, while seldom if ever was an adverse view expressed.

In these early years of the 19th century postal policy and postal development in Scotland were dictated in the main by three considerations – the rapid increase in the weight of mail, the improvement in the standard of certain roads, and the developments, particularly in North and North-west Scotland, which were first put in hand in 1803. The volume of mail which had been carried by the foot posts during much of the 18th century had been relatively small, but as the French wars dragged on and developed in intensity, newspapers, newsletters and official publications came to form an ever-growing, though largely unprofitable, part of the postman's load. Scotland's roads, which had over much of the century been almost a byword, had come, through the efforts of Turnpike Trustees and military roadmakers, by the end of the century to be to some extent improved, while after 1803 work on the Caledonian Canal and on new roads in the North and North-west was drawing not only labour and capital, but men's interest and attention, to areas which had long been neglected.

The problem of accelerating the mail from Edinburgh to Aberdeen, which had given rise to such bitter controversy in the last decade of the 18th century, had at last been solved by the introduction of mail coaches between the cities in 1798. Little more than ten years later the bridging of the Spey and the Findhorn had made possible the extension of the coach service to Inverness. Beyond Inverness the postal service, at least north of Tain, appears to have been a foot post till 1809. In that year Freeling had before him a Memorial by local landowners asking for a horse post from Tain to Thurso to serve 'that inexhaustible source of national wealth the Fisheries', from which, claimed the memorialists, came 40,000/50,000 barrels of herring each year worth £60,000 in bills or promissory notes.[2] The fate of the petition does not appear from the correspondence, but certainly long before 1819, when the first mail coach reached the north coast over Telford's new bridges, the mail was reaching Thurso by horse post.

On the cross-country route from Stirling to Argyll a foot post had been established in the first years of the century, and this was soon extended through Tyndrum to connect at Dalmally with the post north-bound from Dumbarton and Inveraray. It is clear that postal traffic from Stirling to Argyll had grown rapidly, for by 1808 the annual revenue to the Post Office on this route had reached £2000.[3] The payment allowed by the Post Office to the contractor who worked these mails was based on the cost of foot posts, but the increase in the weight of mail and particularly of newspapers, had been such that he had been forced to use horses. In the summer of 1808 Freeling had before him a report by Ronaldson, the surveyor, recommending that a horse post should be allowed at the cost of 3d per mile. Not only, wrote the surveyor, was this the main route from Edinburgh to Oban, Fort William and the Western Highlands, but it would serve the growing needs of 'the Caledonian Canal now going forward'.[4] The high hopes of the new canal were in the end to be disappointed, but in 1808, with construction work already in full swing, prospects indeed seemed bright. Each summer the total labour force rose to 1200 or 1400 men and, though each winter saw a big falling off, Fort William as the centre for work on the west end of the canal was busy and thriving as never before.[5] In the spring of 1809, Cameron of Lochiel asked the Post Office to institute a six-day post between Fort William and the South in place of the service three days a week then in operation. Work on the new roads, the canal and that enticing but elusive will o' the wisp 'The Fisheries' were urged and accepted as reasons for the extended service, but before many months had passed it had become clear that the experiment had failed, and the post reverted for a time to three days a week.[6] Despite the continuing activity on the canal, decreasing trade at Fort William and the absence of many local landowners on Army service were blamed for the falling off in traffic.[7] Meantime, however, the hopes of the West Coast Fisheries and increased droving traffic led to an extension of communications between Fort William and the districts of Moidart and South Morar, and one of the earliest roadmaking projects approved and put in hand by the Commissioners after 1803 was the construction of a road to 'Keppoch in Arisaig' to serve a district 'from which it is apprehended much emigration might take place if the inhabitants were not to find sufficient employment'. Here in the summer of 1802 Freeling had already approved an application by Clanranald for the establishment of a post office to serve the needs of drovers from Skye and the Outer Isles and fishermen at the fishing station at Arnisdale on Loch Hourn.[8]

Freeling, as always, was slow to recommend extensions of service and expenditure by the Post Office till the need and the profit were beyond all doubt. The failure of the six-day post to Fort William may well have increased his doubts, for it seems that it was not till 1826 that the Secretary finally recommended the substitution of a horse for a foot post between Tyndrum and Dalmally at an annual cost of £40;* but by then the post road from Glasgow by Dumbarton and Inveraray to Oban, Appin and Fort William had claimed the growing attention of the postal authorites. On this route the mail from Glasgow by Inveraray and Dalmally to the crossing of Loch Etive at Bonawe had for long been conveyed entirely by foot posts; but the growing loads, swollen by prints of Acts of Parliament and Army Reports, were increasingly taxing the strength of the runners. It was now proposed to give the runners small additional allowances to enable them to keep ponies, so increasing their average speed from three to four miles an hour. If the foot posts on the route to Inveraray were heavy-laden, to no-one can the new plan have been more welcome than to the post runner between Inveraray and Dalmally. This unfortunate

---

* Post 40/145/1826. While April 1826 is undoubtedly the date of the letter reporting the institution of a horse post between Tyndrum and Dalmally, it should be noted that in a report by Charles Reeves dated 4 Oct. 1823 the surveyor refers to the substitution of horse for foot posts on the postal routes from both Edinburgh and Glasgow to Argyllshire which met at Dalmally.

man was due to leave Inveraray with his heavy load at 4.30 p.m. on the arrival of the mail from Glasgow, reaching Dalmally at 9.50 p.m. There he had just over an hour's rest before starting on the return journey to Inveraray, where he was due at 4 a.m. in time to catch the mail for Glasgow. This double journey of 32 miles covered largely by night he did three times a week.[9] At the same time the post from Bonawe to Fort William and Inverness was improved. On this part of the journey, also, two runners each walked 32 miles at a stretch three times a week, and a night's rest at Ardchattan seems by now to have been a thing of the past; but even these achievements were rivalled, if not surpassed, by those of the foot post between Tarbert and Clachan in Kintyre who on six days a week regularly covered the double journey of 24 miles between the hours of 10 p.m. and 4 a.m. Not till 1833 was his pay at last raised by £10 per annum to allow him to get a pony.*

To the surveyors it had long been only too evident that the current rates of pay were much too low. Ronaldson, reporting on the posts of Argyll in 1805, referred to some runners who were getting as little as 4/– to 5/– for a week's work involving three long tramps. This compared badly with the pay of 'twentypence or two shillings a day' which could now be earned 'from working at the Canal or other labour'.[10] If those at Post Office headquarters showed little real appreciation of the work of the Argyllshire foot posts this ignorance was not confined to the West. At the end of 1809 Shearer wrote with indignation of a suggestion, apparently accepted by those at headquarters, that children of 12 or 14 years old were carrying the mails through Sutherland and Caithness. The length and difficulty of the walks, the weight of mail and the dangers of the ferries made the suggestion ridiculous. 'It is not bairn's play', wrote the angry surveyor, though he agreed that at times the postal officials were hard put to it to get anyone to do the work.[11]

On the post road from Inveraray to Campbeltown, ponies were introduced in 1823. Reeves, the surveyor, considered this innovation necessary to prevent many letters going by boat and with a view to 'rescuing our runners from the disgraceful practice of literally begging their way up and down

---

* Post 40/90/1833. Less than 20 years later the daily work of a letter-carrier was very different. Anthony Trollope has recorded that about 1851: 'Our law was that a man should not be required to walk more than 16 miles a day'.

the country'. In the same year even Freeling reported to the Postmaster General that in postal matters the Western Highlands and Islands had been 'miserably neglected'.[12] But the troubles on the road northward from Glasgow were not yet at an end. In the spring of 1824 it was reported that a contractor who conveyed the mail between Inveraray and Arrochar had failed 'after destroying all his horses'. Reeves had been over the route, and in view of the difficulties of Glen Croe and Rest and be Thankful 'probably the most difficult and laborious stage in the Kingdom' had arranged that this part should be done on foot.[13] The service on the road between Bonawe and Appin, where mail traffic was increasing as a result of the establishment of a branch of the Bank of Scotland at Fort William, was soon to be further improved by an increased payment to the runner on condition that he, too, kept a pony. In making his recommendations the surveyor noted that the runner in addition to having to cross two ferries had to make his way through Glen Salach:

> 'the wildest Pass in the whole Highlands. . . . I scarcely met any Highland gentleman who had ever been through it. . . . The present individual, his Father and Mother have performed this journey with the mails for above 25 years with zeal and astonishing regularity.'*

Despite the successive improvements which had taken place on the postal route from Glasgow to Fort William, this post had with the exception of the premature experiment in 1809 for long continued to be only on a three-day-a-week basis, but in the autumn of 1826 Reeves had submitted an application by the people of Inveraray that they should have a daily post to Glasgow and this was granted. From Inveraray north the three-day post appears to have continued for another seven years, but in the summer of 1833 Reeves, who had been making a detailed study of the Argyllshire posts, recommended that a daily post be granted. For many years past the route had been from Inveraray to Dalmally and so down the Pass of Brander to Bonawe, but the surveyor's sketch plan shows that it was now proposed to revert to the old route in use at the beginning of the century, ferrying Loch Awe near Cladich and reaching Bonawe through

---

* Post 40/237/1824. See Appendix x. Despite the recommendation of a horse-post on this route, a report by Charles Reeves, the surveyor, in the following year (1825) describes Glen Salach as having 'no road yet practicable for a horse'.

Glen Nant, Dalmally to be served by post runners from Cladich. The total cost of the improved service to Fort William, including ferry charges at Loch Awe, Bonawe, Creagan and Ballachulish, would be over £350 per annum; but substantially increased revenue was expected, and as illegal and competing traffic up the coast by boat had, it seems, been prevalent the new plans were approved.[14]

While the postal services from Edinburgh and Glasgow to the seaboard of Argyll and south Inverness-shire were thus being steadily improved, the services in other parts of rural Scotland were receiving some, if less marked, attention. These latter improvements were isolated and widely scattered, showing no distinct pattern save in so far as they illustrated the continuing dependance of postal development on local initiative and enterprise. As time passed increasing use came to be made of the provision in the post office legislation which allowed local interests to guarantee the Post Office against loss on services which might not of themselves prove profitable – a provision which underlined still further the importance in postal development of the rôle of the landowners. Despite their authority to accept guarantees either from single persons or groups of individuals, the Post Office showed not unnatural reluctance to do so, preferring where possible to make the continuance of doubtful services dependent on their proved profitability. In the closing years of the 18th century postal services had, with some hesitation, been granted to Campbeltown in Kintyre and Drymen in Stirlingshire, the continuance of the service in each case to be dependent on results rather than on the guarantees offered by the Dukes of Argyll and Montrose respectively. In the autumn of 1804 McLean of Ardgour had asked for a post office at 'the North Ferry of Ballachulish' where the runners from Fort William, Appin and Strontian met and exchanged bags. Neither the surveyor nor the Edinburgh office appear to have pressed the application, but a receiving house was suggested and to this Freeling agreed, though whether on the north or the south side of the Ferry is not clear. Early in 1805 came an application by the Duke of Gordon for a post office at Muir of Rhynie at the head of Strathbogie, ten miles south of Huntly. Here the duke claimed to have lately established a village and 'various manufactures'. Both the surveyor and Freeling himself supported the application, which was agreed to on an experimental basis, without, it seems, any guarantee.[15] How the experiment turned out does not appear. There is in the later correspondence no evidence of its failure and it must be presumed that it justified itself, though unless the 'manufactures' established by the duke were on a larger scale than seems probable, Rhynie was a small place to get a post office at a time when larger places achieved them with difficulty. The details of the contemporary postal system in this district of Aberdeenshire are far from clear. At this time the main postal route from Aberdeen to Inverness went by Old Meldrum to Turriff and so down the Deveron to Banff and along the coast by Fochabers and Elgin. Within a few years, however, an alternative route from Aberdeen to Inverness was to be by way of Huntly. No postal route appears to have extended up the valley of the Don beyond Alford, though in 1793 a post extending up Deeside as far as Aboyne had been agreed with offices at Banchory, Kincardine-O'Neil and sub-offices at Tarland and Strathdon, guaranteed by local proprietors who had claimed that hitherto their only postal connection with Aberdeen was by 'country carriers or accidental private'. This post appears to have been on the basis of three days a week until 1804 when, on the application of the Earl of Aboyne and other landowners, a daily post was agreed to, the offices at Tarland and Strathdon being made full post offices.*

In central Perthshire the Earl of Breadalbane was a frequent and persistent advocate of postal improvement. In the early years of the century he had successfully pressed for a postal connection from Callander by Lochearnhead to Killin and finally on to Tyndrum and Dalmally, and before long he was again to be in the queue of urgent applicants. In December 1809 Freeling had before him what seemed a reasonable complaint that letters between Aberfeldy and Killin went round by Perth and Dunblane, a distance of about 100 miles as compared with

---

* In the contemporary records up to 1836 frequent references appear to 'daily posts' and to 'six-day a week posts' and it is by no means clear in many cases whether 'daily posts' can be literally so interpreted. Certainly by 1835 Sunday posts appear to have been quite common. In that year when supporting the continuance of a Sunday post at Balfron in Stirlingshire in face of the representation of the local minister, Freeling wrote: 'If he disapproves of it he need not avail himself of it, and I think it would be hard to deprive respectable gentlemen residing in the district of their Post on Sunday which is common all over the country merely to satisfy the religious scruples of anyone.' (Post 40/251/1835.)

the actual 24 miles between the two places, and were charged accordingly. Now a foot post by Kenmore up one side of Loch Tay and down the other was asked for, and Freeling's Minute of recommendation to the Postmaster General came back marked 'approved'.[16]

Aberfeldy's main postal connection with the South about this time was by Dunkeld, and by the end of the first quarter of the 19th century four posts a week were in operation, with a less frequent connection on to Rannoch. In the spring of 1825 Colonel Stewart of Garth wrote to Freeling in vigorous terms complaining that four posts a week were quite insufficient. Eleven new distilleries had, it was claimed, lately been established in the district and while these were designed to check illicit distilling, the absence of a daily post resulted, said Stewart, in the smuggling of letters. Colonel Stewart pointed out, with more force than relevance, that large sums were at that time being spent by the Government on Highland roads and bridges, but added that he and other proprietors were ready to make up any loss suffered by the Post Office on the extended service. Freeling opposed the application on the ground that the postal revenue did not warrant it, and four months later a still more vigorous letter from Stewart directly threatening to smuggle letters appears to have met with a similar reception.[17] Early in 1827 a further application for an improved post for Aberfeldy, this time from Sir Neil Menzies, was on Freeling's table. This too was refused on the ground that the matter had been fully gone into in 1825, though the attitude of the Post Office seems to have been influenced by the fear that any concession to Aberfeldy would quickly bring applications from Lord Breadalbane for further improvement of the Kenmore and Killin posts. In sending on the papers to Freeling, Augustus Godby, who had succeeded William Kerr as Secretary of the Scottish Office, ignoring the eleven new distilleries referred to by Colonel Stewart, described Aberfeldy as 'a small Highland village only with little or no trade beyond a few retail shops . . .'[18] If Stewart of Garth had overstated his case as to the needs of Aberfeldy in 1825, it is difficult to avoid the feeling that Godby's information in 1827 was somewhat incomplete. In 1833 a horse post six days a week between Dunkeld, Aberfeldy and Kenmore was agreed by Freeling, who seems unlikely to have granted such good facilities to a place which only seven years before had been a small village with little trade; but perhaps Freeling's apprehension in 1827 of Lord Breadalbane's intervention in the argument had proved well founded.[19]

Whatever part Lord Breadalbane may have played in the controversy over the Aberfeldy and Kenmore posts it is clear that his interest in postal communications was as intense as ever. In June 1835 Freeling wrote to the Postmaster General as to proposals Lord Breadalbane had put forward for extensive alterations in the postal arrangements for the Breadalbane country; but unfortunately Breadalbane's plans were accompanied by the suggestion that the appointment of postal officials in the area was his prerogative. To this suggestion Freeling took great exception, but for the rest he advised acceptance of Lord Breadalbane's offer to provide at very moderate cost to the Post Office a mail cart to replace the three elderly men who had hitherto carried the mail between Kenmore, Killin and Tyndrum.[20]

The important policy decision of the Postmaster General in 1808 which now made possible the wide extension of penny posts, hitherto intended and used for towns and their surrounding districts, had shown the intention of the Post Office to make postal services available to rural areas hitherto neglected. In Scotland at least, the power to extend penny posts was not extensively used for some years to come, but meantime the more liberal policy of the Post Office was showing itself in the extension of ordinary mail services in many parts of the country. The first quarter of the century was marked by steady postal progress. Writing to the Postmaster General in the summer of 1813 immediately after the abolition of toll exemption for mail coaches, Freeling had listed eleven mail coach services in Scotland, including those from Carlisle to Edinburgh and Portpatrick, from Edinburgh to Glasgow, Stirling and Aberdeen, from Glasgow to Greenock, Ayr and Carlisle, and from Aberdeen to Inverness. Ten years later when the question of free delivery in towns was under consideration, Freeling referred to the fact that more than 250 Post towns existed in Scotland, while in giving evidence about the work of the Post Office in 1824 James Shearer, the surveyor, stated that in his district of North and East Scotland he had at that time 800 miles of horse post and over 250 miles of foot post under his control. While few, if any, of these were penny posts a great extension of the penny post system in all parts of rural Scotland was in fact about to take place.

One of the earliest places outside the immediate neighbourhood of Edinburgh or Glasgow to get such a service was the small community of Easdale, ten miles south of Oban. Here an application in 1824 led to the establishment of a post runner to take mail to and from Oban on a penny post basis, the local people guaranteeing the Post Office against loss – a guarantee which in fact proved unnecessary.[21] Polmont in West Lothian got a similar service in the same year, while Kilpatrick near Glasgow, and Leslie and Markinch in Fife followed close on their heels. As in so much of the detail of postal service, especially in the country districts, the influence of the surveyors was of first importance. In the establishment of penny posts James Shearer in the North and East seems to have been less active than his colleague Charles Reeves in the South and West, perhaps because Shearer appears to have taken exception to the fact that where penny post facilities were granted a delivery charge was regularly made for newspapers which were exempt from postal charges if sent by ordinary mail.* Writing in the summer of 1829 Freeling refers to only three penny posts in Shearer's area compared with thirty-four in Reeves', a total which by 1831 had in the latter case grown to 76.

With the third decade of the century applications for penny posts came from all parts of Scotland. In the great majority of cases these were granted, though sometimes with local guarantees. As the years passed the policy of Freeling and his colleagues in London and Edinburgh, though still inhibited by extreme caution and a passion for economy, was in this respect at least becoming rather more liberal and more flexible. Penny posts, for so long regarded with doubt and conceded with caution even in the neighbourhood of towns and cities, were coming at last to be recognized by the Post Office not only as public services to rural areas long overdue, but in fact as useful sources of revenue, and it has been estimated that before the end of the third decade of the century 81 towns and 199 villages in Scotland had a penny post service. For the year 1828/9 the total

---

* Exemption from delivery charges was never conceded to items of mail such as franked material or newspapers which had not borne full postal dues.

revenue from the country penny posts was quoted by Freeling as £3167, a figure which presumably excluded the cities and large towns of Scotland.

Within the course of a very few years penny posts in Aberdeenshire were bringing the mail to Monymusk on the Don, with a guarantee by Grant of Monymusk, to Pitsligo, Strichen and Rosehearty in Buchan and to Macduff and Aberchirder in Banffshire. The service to Aberchirder was one of the relatively few penny posts subsequently discontinued as being uneconomic, though the village continued to have some postal connection with Huntly and Banff. In Aberdeen itself and the immediate neighbourhood the first reference to a penny post appears to be in the autumn of 1831 when a net profit of £171.11.1d was reported on the first year's working. About the same time Alva and Clackmannan, St Ninians and Bannockburn got penny post services from Stirling, the 'mineral springs at Strathpeffer' from Dingwall, Kinloch Rannoch from Pitlochry, and Scone, Methven and Bankfoot from Perth, but in 1834 an application for a penny post between Fort William and Arisaig was turned down on the grounds that the distance (40 miles) was too great. In the South of Scotland Bonchester Bridge got a similar service from Hawick in 1835, while in the previous year the penny post had started to carry letters between Whitburn and the works of the Shotts Iron Company in West Lothian. Even the small group of houses at Kilchrenan on Loch Awe had a penny post, its success as reported in 1835 being no doubt due to the fact that it lay immediately on the new line of the post between Inveraray and Bonawe through Glen Nant and could thus be served with the minimum of expense to the Post Office.[22] Certain districts in both Skye and Mull got penny posts in the thirties, together with Kinlochmoidart in Moidart and Corran in Ardgour, while one of the most surprising was in the Knoydart district of Inverness-shire. Here in the spring of 1834 the factor for Aeneas Macdonell of Glengarry had written to the Post Office intimating that Glengarry had taken up permanent residence at Inverie on Loch Nevis, and asking that a penny post be established between here and Invergarry, with a runner four times a week who would serve a large area including part of the district of Glenelg. Reeves, not surprisingly reported that there was no prospect of such a service proving economic, but Glengarry had guaranteed the Post Office against loss, and Freeling recommended that it be tried for one year.* As in certain other cases no record of the subsequent withdrawal of the service appears in the post office papers, so it may well be that Glengarry and his people in this remote part of Scotland continued to enjoy it.†

When the penny post service was originally instituted first for the cities and their surroundings and later for villages and country districts, the intention had been that the penny charge would cover delivery of the letter. This remained, throughout, the official policy, but in fact there appear to have been many cases both in the smaller towns and villages and even occasionally on the outskirts of cities where a delivery charge was made. Portobello and Tranent in the Edinburgh area and Kilpatrick near Glasgow all complained of it in 1825. In each of these cases the charge was stopped, while eight years later when Galston in Ayrshire made a similar and successful protest Freeling, evidently conscious that other cases of delivery charges still existed, wrote to the Postmaster General that demands for free delivery could not be resisted.[23] Far to the north-west, a further postal link across Scotland to the Atlantic sea-board had been forged. In the autumn of 1828 Shearer, the surveyor for the North of Scotland, had recommended the establishment of a foot post from Bonar Bridge to Assynt and Lochinver, a runner to make the journey once a week. Freeling approved the plan on an experimental basis, the runner to be paid £20 per annum, with £5 per annum to each of the sub-post-masters at Lochinver and at the school-house at Assynt.[24]

While the establishment of penny posts and the steady increase in the number of receiving houses to serve villages and country districts hitherto without regular postal services was indicative of the growth of a rather more liberal policy at the Post Office, Freeling and his colleagues still lay open to the

---

* Guarantees of penny posts seem to have been accepted more readily than guarantees of ordinary posts, probably because the latter were more difficult and costly to establish and could not so easily be withdrawn.

† Post 40/132/1834. In claiming that a penny post service to Inverie would serve part of the Glenelg district, Macdonell's factor was probably somewhat optimistic. As late as 1842 the writer of the 'Account of Glenelg Parish' in the *New Statistical Account* referred to the only postal connection for the parish as being through Lochalsh. 'Thither we send in the meantime at our own expense by the ferry of Loch Duich.' Shortly after this date a penny post service three times a week was established betewen Glenelg and Lochalsh.

criticism that postal charges remained too high. The ordinary
postal charge for even the shortest distances was still in general
4d, and critics of the Post Office could point with every justification to the fact that postal rates had not fallen from the peak to
which they had risen in the last years of the Napoleonic wars.
While this was true of the United Kingdom as a whole, the
last years of Freeling's life saw a concession of some significance
in which certain of the small towns and villages of South and
Central Scotland shared. As far back as 1818 it had been
decided to reduce to 2d the charge for letters passing between
Plymouth and the near-by post towns of Stonehouse and
Plymouth Dock (later renamed Devonport). As the minimum
rate for single letters passing between Post towns up to a limit
of fifteen miles was at that time 4d this was a substantial concession but one which Freeling after consultation with the post
office solicitor believed the Post Office had power to make. The
Plymouth concession appears to have remained unique throughout the country till 1833, when a similar concession was granted
for correspondence between Edinburgh and Leith, Freeling's
Minute on the matter to the Postmaster General referring
specifically to the Plymouth arrangement of 1818 as a precedent.
The legality of the reduction seems not to have been questioned
in 1833, and within the next two years Twopenny Posts came
into force between other adjoining Scottish Post towns including Greenock and Port Glasgow, Paisley and Renfrew, Kin-
cardine-on-Forth and Alloa, Leven and Kennoway, Melrose
and Galashiels, and Earlston and St Boswells. The opinion
which Freeling had obtained from the post office solicitor at the
time of the original concession to Plymouth in 1818 is missing
from the records, so there is no means of knowing how he was
persuaded of the legality of a concession which at that time and
for many years to come had no legislative basis; but persuaded
Freeling clearly was, and in approving the new arrangements
for Melrose and the other Border towns in 1835 he even went
out of his way to distinguish these new concessions from the
existing penny posts. The latter, he pointed out, had been
designed to serve places or districts where postal services were
inadequate or lacking, whereas the new plan applied to carriage
of letters by ordinary mail services already in existence.[25] It may
well be that, in sanctioning a concession which seems in fact to
have been clearly beyond his powers or those of the Postmaster

General, Freeling was influenced less by the fact that the legal charge of 4d was a heavy one for the transport of letters between places within a few miles of one another than by the knowledge that, in some of these cases at least, postal revenue was being lost to illegal carriers. Whatever the reasoning and whatever the motives it seems clear that in 1818 the Post Office, albeit illegally, conceded the only reduction in ordinary postal charges to take place for over twenty years from the end of the Napoleonic wars, and that in the last years of that period the concession was widely applied to country posts in South and Central Scotland.*

REFERENCES

1. Corrie, *The Dumfries Post Office*, 19.
2. Post 40/47P/1809.
3. Ibid./12K/1808.
4. Ibid./12K/1808.
5. Haldane, *New Ways through the Glens*, ch. 6.
6. Post 40/28N/1809.
7. Ibid./59T/1810.
8. Ibid./81.1/1802.
9. Ibid./249/1823.
10. Ibid./53Y/1805.
11. Post 15/133.
12. Post 40/449/1823.
13. Ibid./237/1824. See Appendix XI.
14. Ibid./416/1833.
15. Ibid./11V/1805.
16. Ibid./74P/1809.
17. Ibid./285 and 502/1 1825.
18. Ibid./41/1827.
19. Ibid./596/1833.
20. Ibid./438/1835.
21. Post 40/549/1824. The establishment of a penny post for Easdale was no doubt at least partially due to the important slate quarries at that time in active operation.

* Early in 1837 Colonel Maberly, who had succeeded Freeling as Secretary to the Post Office in the previous year, reached the conclusion that the concessions made by Freeling to Plymouth in 1818 and many years later to other towns both in England and in Scotland were in fact illegal. For a short time the postal charges of 2d for letters between those towns which had received the benefit of the concession of 1818 were further reduced to 1d in order to make them at least ostensibly legal on the basis of the Penny Post legislation. The position was only clarified when in 1838 a general postal rate of 2d for letters carried up to 8 miles was introduced, though it is not clear whether even this change in rate had any statutory basis. This was one of the many anomalies and perplexities which were finally resolved by the introduction of Uniform Penny Post in 1840.

22. Ibid./10/1835.
23. Ibid./213/1833.
24. Ibid./773/1828.
25. Ibid./314/1835.

Seven

The Work of the Country Postmaster

That the quality of a service can be no higher than that of the men and women who operate it, is a truism perhaps too obvious to warrant statement. Yet it is probably true to say that nowhere and at no time have the qualities of the servants been of such paramount importance as in the early history of the Post Office. When it is recalled that collection of postal charges at the receiving instead of the despatching end was for long the rule rather than the exception, and that till well on in the 18th century there was little possibility of keeping an effective check on postal dues for very many letters passing between adjacent or near-by offices, it becomes apparent that any shortcoming in the reliability of postmasters or the standard of their work, would strike directly at the quality of the service and the revenue of the Post Office.

The earliest post offices in Great Britain – and these were on the main roads of England – were almost invariably inns. This was a sensible and almost an essential arrangement since the innkeepers, who were also the postmasters, were in the best position to provide horses for those 'riding post' with the royal despatches or occasional urgent private messages which before the post became a public service made up the whole of the postal traffic. Whether the three postmasters on the road between

Edinburgh and Berwick in the early 17th century were also innkeepers is not known. Certainly they kept horses both for the use of State messengers and for hiring to others, and Arnot of Cockburnspath had a supplementary income from, but also the obligation to keep in repair, the harbour at Cove. But though the English inn was far more a centre of social life and of passing traffic than its counterpart in Scotland ever became, it is a reasonable assumption that in Scotland, too, some at least of the early post offices may have been of the nature of inns. Archibald Campbell at Inveraray certainly kept the local inn in 1734 and there were probably others who, like him, added farming to their postal activities. But save on the Berwick road the hiring of horses never seems to have been common among Scottish postmasters at least till the coming of the coaching age. Writing to William Kerr, the Secretary of the Scottish Office in 1797, Francis Ronaldson, the postal surveyor, pointed to the difference between Scottish postmasters and those in the South who were 'common hyrers or letters of horses'. 'In proof of this', he added, 'there is not now a single Postmaster on the road from Edinburgh to Aberdeen, I may say from Edinburgh to Jony Grotts, who keeps or lets horses for hyre.'[1]

If the keeping of an inn by the postmaster was looked on by the authorities as desirable in the 16th and 17th centuries and was at least accepted as natural during much of the 18th century, a great change took place as speed in the conveyance of mail became of growing importance, and particularly after the introduction of mail coaches in 1784. From now on, regular time-keeping, and consequently the quality of the horses, came to be of the first importance, and it became necessary for the Post Office to appoint postmasters other than innkeepers to keep an independent check on the contractors who were now increasingly working the coaches, and to regulate the arrival and departure of the mails.

'Persons who keep horses for other uses and particularly innkeepers', wrote a postal surveyor in 1792, 'may assuredly more conveniently and at less expense work the mails than those who keep horses for that business only; but on the other hand it may be observed that innkeepers so far from paying Government service the compliment of employing in it their best horses too often send their worst with the mails; and as to their riders they are in general the dregs of the stable yard and by no means to compare to those employed by the Postmasters in private stations.'[2]

But it was not only of the horses and their riders that the Post Office complained. Postmasters who were innkeepers or farmers frequently delegated their postal duties to others. Waiters and chambermaids often attended to receiving and sending on the mails. Letters were sorted in bars and public rooms, and the lack of privacy complained of in the post office of Inverness in 1770 could very surely have been matched in many parts of contemporary Scotland. 'The head ostler', wrote a postal surveyor regarding an English office in the mid 18th century, 'was often the Postmaster's Prime Minister in matters relating to the mails', and in the last years of the century, Helen Anderson, the postmistress at Dunfermline, was refused an increase on her meagre salary partly on the grounds that she sometimes employed her servant maid and a young boy in the duties of the post office.[3] Freeling's view in the closing years of the 18th century was that innkeepers should not be appointed as postmasters. In a long letter to the Postmaster General in January 1793 after arguing at length the pros and cons he came to the conclusion that innkeepers should be ineligible, but as this might not always be possible no pains should be spared to see that where they were appointed they were fully qualified.[4] For the postmasters, too, as time passed, the attraction or even the possibility of running a subsidiary business so demanding as innkeeping or farming steadily diminished. The volume of postal traffic was increasing. Long hours and greater responsibility were ill recompensed by small salaries, reduced as they were by the expense of providing at the postmaster's own cost coal, candles, paper and sealing wax, while increasing use of the Post Office as an instrument of taxation meant constant and peremptory calls for periodic remittances to Edinburgh. So the progressive divorce of postal duties from other activities seems to have come about in most cases as a matter of policy on the part of the authorities and of necessity if not actual preference on that of the postmasters. Today in many a sub post office in rural areas the combination of post office and small shop works smoothly and perhaps to the benefit of both; but innkeeping or allied activities have long since ceased to go in double harness with postal work. The new policy had already been long established when in December 1832 Freeling was in correspondence with the Postmaster General regarding the suggestion that the post office in Kirkcudbright should be situated in a retail spirit shop. On that occasion the proposal was reluctantly agreed to on the understanding that the post office business must be kept quite separate and that should the shop prove to be of low character the appointment would be terminated.*

From a very early date it had been the custom to require an applicant for the position of postmaster to provide a satisfactory surety or guarantor who would guarantee the due performance of the postmaster's duties and particularly the periodic remittance to Edinburgh of the postage collected. It will be recalled that in 1603 an Edinburgh burgess acted as guarantor for Arnot the postmaster at Cockburnspath, and from this time on it would seem that no appointment of a postmaster was ever made till a bond of surety or guarantee had been signed.†
With the spread of rural posts in the early 19th century these guarantees became more than ever necessary, and no small part of the official correspondence at this time deals with this topic. The guarantee, which might be by more than one person, was required to be for the full amount of postage collected by the postmaster in question – presumably calculated on the basis of a yearly average – and for £50 to £100 in addition to cover expenses in the event of failure of a postmaster making it necessary to call on the guarantee. Heavy penalties were imposed on postmasters who failed to intimate the death or bankruptcy of their guarantors, and until 1817 the expenses of executing the bond had to be met by the postmaster. In that year the Post Office decided to pay the expenses in cases where the salary of the postmaster was under £20 per annum, a

---

* Post 40/931/1832. In 1966 the post office authorities instituted an enquiry with a view to ascertaining which post office in the United Kingdom could claim to be the oldest post office building still in use as such. The result of the enquiry was to establish the claim put forward by Sanquhar in Dumfriesshire. The earliest known evidence of the existence of a post office in Sanquhar is an entry in the *Edinburgh Almanack* of 1763 and it is understood that the office there has been in the same building at least since 1800.

† When James Cowie, postmaster in Dundee, died in 1778, Alexander Hill, baker in Dundee, and James Bisset of Bridgend, Perth, his guarantors, who had completed title to Cowie's estate as Executors-dative *qua* creditors, paid £251.11.2d sterling being the balance due to Robert Oliphant, Deputy Postmaster General, by Cowie, and partially recouped themselves by the sale of Cowie's household furniture. (S.R.O., Com. Brechin Tests, 26 Aug. 1778.)

concession which seems to have been not only fair but sensible and useful. 'There must', Freeling had written a few years earlier, 'be the greatest difficulty in getting proper persons where the expense of the Bond is more than the salary of the first quarter.' These guarantees required from postmasters were throughout strictly enforced and scrupulously adhered to. In 1825 Freeling had before him an application from a correspondent at Abergeldie on Deeside that the use of the old name 'Tullich' be abolished in favour of 'Ballater', the former place being now only a small group of cottages and the post office having been moved to Ballater, two miles off. Freeling opposed the application largely on the grounds that the existing guarantee which was in respect of the postmaster at Tullich would be invalidated by the change of name.[5]

The system of requiring sureties for the performance of contracts of all kinds was very common in Scotland in the early 19th century. It is by no means unknown today, but bankers' references and other sources of information, then virtually unknown, have in many cases taken its place. When the Commissioners for Highland Roads and Bridges were adjusting the complex contracts, often involving large sums, which were necessary in connection with road and bridge construction work in the Highlands between 1803 and 1823, one of the main worries of James Hope, the Commissioners' Edinburgh agent, was to get adequate guarantees.[6] In that instance it may be that the guarantor, perhaps a local merchant, received some advantage such as the contract for supplying meal for road workers, but in the case of a guarantee for a local postmaster it is difficult to see how this could have been other than very largely disinterested. The cynical may suggest that the return made to the guarantor may have been in the form of some valuable concession at the post office, such as preferential treatment in the receipt of news, the reading of *Gazettes* or perhaps even the opportunity for pleasurable gossip about other people's letters; and indeed in some instances the cynics may be right. Whatever be the truth, however, the giving of a guarantee to a postmaster was by no means a mere formality, and in the Journal of Francis Ronaldson the postal surveyor covering the years 1786 to 1814 appear constant references to the default or bankruptcy of local postmasters.

As in the time of James Anderson in the early years of the

18th century, the collection of revenue from local postmasters was always a major preoccupation of the Postmaster General, and the monthly journals of the surveyors over a long period contain many references to attempts 'to force up the remittances to Edinburgh'. Only ten to twelve days' grace was allowed to postmasters in arrears and after that legal action followed, postmasters and sureties alike being liable in the last resort to horning, caption, poinding and sale of goods and every weapon in the formidable armoury of Scots law. The only concessions granted were in cases where the arrears due to the General Post Office by the local postmaster were offset by balances due to him from the General Post Office in respect of salary, outlays for the postal service or other items. In such cases delay was to be allowed, though in the late 18th and early 19th centuries there were frequent and bitter complaints by postmasters that their rights as creditors of the Post Office were unfairly subordinated to their obligations as debtors. In the great majority of cases the law took its course without favour or forbearance. With such uncompromising action on the part of the authorities it was inevitable that on occasions guarantors should suffer. In February 1823 Freeling was in correspondence over the case of Donald Ross, the postmaster of Tain, who had resigned. Ross had been constantly in arrears with his remittances. His sureties had had to pay up on two occasions and had now withdrawn. But Sir James Riddell of Ardnamurchan was made of sterner stuff. Some time prior to 1825 he had become surety for the postmaster at Strontian, who proved a constant defaulter. Here, too, the guarantee had been called on twice. Sir James, who was clearly acting in the interests of the local people, was prepared to renew it once again, but recommended that a new postmaster should be found at a higher salary than the £8 per annum which was all that had been allowed hitherto. Freeling minuted to the Postmaster General that if a new appointment were made the Scottish officials should report on the adequacy of the salary. So Sir James' intervention seems likely, at some cost to himself, to have been to the ultimate benefit of the local postal service.[7]

If some guarantors bore their losses with equanimity there were others who took a different view. In the spring of 1803 complaints reached Freeling that all was not well at the Perth post office. Perth at that time was the most important office north of Edinburgh, with an annual revenue of some £4000, and James Shearer, the surveyor, was sent to report. The nomination of the postmaster at Perth was, it seems, at that time virtually in the gift of the Duke of Atholl and the duke had nominated one Duff, a youth under twenty years of age, with no experience and little sense of responsibility. The complaints of the people of Perth were, therefore, fully justified; but the grounds for criticism went far beyond mere inefficiency on the part of the youthful postmaster. His predecessor had gone bankrupt and the guarantors had been called on to make up considerable shortages to the Post Office. To recoup themselves for their loss, the guarantors had, it transpired, induced the Duke of Atholl to nominate Duff who by a private arrangement had agreed to hand over to the guarantors part of his salary and any other profits he made from the office. Freeling in reporting the matter to the Postmasters General observed that it was for them to decide whether the right of nomination should again be offered to the Duke of Atholl. The Postmasters General in their minute in reply appear to have evaded this delicate issue, but left no doubt that the duke must be informed that in this instance his right of nomination had been unwisely used.[8] Despite the insistence on adequate guarantees, the vigilance of the Edinburgh office and the activity of the post office solicitor, the accumulation of arrears due by postmasters between 1810 and 1820 reported by a Committee of Inquiry in 1830 as irrecoverable was £1000, but the same committee found that from 1820 to 1830 no loss had fallen on the Post Office from this source.[9]

To a 20th-century reader accustomed to the busy atmosphere of even a rural post office it will readily occur to ask what was the work of a country postmaster in the 18th or early 19th centuries. He had no stamps or postal orders to sell, no telegrams to send or letters to register, and in many cases little or no direct responsibility for delivery of incoming letters. As has been seen it was only after 1774 that the Post Office became in law if not in practice responsible for delivery of these, and even then only in an unspecified and limited area in or around Post towns. In the real country districts, even when after 1808 the penny post system came increasingly to be extended to them, it is doubtful whether this meant for many years to come more than at the most delivery to a local receiving house, leaving the recipients of letters to call there for them. About the end of the period covered by this book growing attention came to be given to the question of free delivery, and at a slightly later date one of the great advocates of such a development of the postal service in this country was Anthony Trollope, who for many years combined the activities of a highly successful novelist with those of an able and energetic postal surveyor. But a free nation-wide house to house delivery was long delayed and was only achieved on the Diamond Jubilee of Queen Victoria in 1897.*

So in the early part of the 19th century delivery of letters outside Post towns was at most only a small part of a postmaster's work. Those expecting them must call to collect them; those hoping for them must call on chance. But in widely scattered rural communities expectant or only hopeful recipients, perhaps in poor circumstances, could ill afford the time to call at an office often many miles from their homes, while others might well hesitate to pay heavy postage dues in order to collect letters for friends or neighbours. Writing, in 1793, the account of Campbeltown in the *Statistical Account of Scotland*, The Rev. Dr John Smith pertinently complained of a system whereby many letters were returned as 'dead' to the General Post Office because, in the absence of second sight, the addressees were unaware of their arrival at the local office.[10] At least until 1829 the practice was for these letters to be retained in the local office for three weeks if the addressees could not be found, or for one month if the letter were marked 'to be called for' after which the letter was returned as 'dead' to the General Post Office. The postage due on such 'dead' letters was deducted from the total for which the local postmaster had to account to the General Post Office, a practice which, as will be seen, gave rise to considerable abuse. The prevalent absence of second sight noted by Dr Smith in 1793 no doubt went far to explain how it came about that in the closing weeks of 1806 three clerks at the Edinburgh office were occupied for thirty-five days in

* Describing his work as a postal surveyor about the year 1851, Trollope wrote: 'The object was to create a postal net-work which should catch all recipients of letters. In France it was, and I suppose still is, the practice to deliver every letter. Wherever a man may live to whom a letter is addressed, it is the duty of some letter-carrier to take that letter to his home, sooner or later. But this, of course must be done slowly. With us a delivery much delayed was thought to be worse than none at all.' (Anthony Trollope, *Autobiography*.)

examining 142,924 dead letters. The postage on these, lost to the Post Office, amounted to £3256, and 433 of the letters containing currency, bills or documents had to be returned to the senders.[11]

While the country postmaster had in these early days little direct responsibility for the delivery of letters, he was responsible for seeing that postage was collected from the recipients of incoming letters where, as in most cases, this had not been prepaid. It has been seen that in certain cases local landowners sent servants or private messengers to collect their mail. In such cases it is probable that the local postmaster kept an account of postage dues which was settled at irregular and often long intervals, and it is known that up to 1802 when a sub office was established at Lochmaddy in North Uist, the postmaster at Dunvegan in Skye had been forced to keep postal accounts with thirty people in the Long Island.[12] The problems of the Dunvegan postmaster were certainly not peculiar to him. In 1771 Captain Torquil Macneal of Lossit in Kintyre paid the Campbeltown postmaster a postage account covering the past twelve months. Twelve years later the accounts of the Duke of Argyll's Kintyre estate show a payment for postage on letters covering the period from October 1781 to October 1783 and there is no reason to doubt that these instances were typical of what was happening all over Scotland.[13]

As to outgoing letters, the position seems to have been still more complicated. For the dues on letters prepaid on despatch – and a few were prepaid – the postmaster was of course responsible. In the vast majority of cases the dues fell to be collected at the delivery end, but even in respect of these the despatching office had, at least by the 19th century, no little responsibility. Originally the 'taxing' of these letters – that is the marking of the postage due on them – was done by clerks at Edinburgh through which centre all Scottish mail was routed. At one time when letters were comparatively few in number the same clerks both sorted and taxed the mail, carefully examining each letter to see whether it consisted of two sheets or more or had the least enclosure which would make it liable to double postage; but later, as correspondence increased, special taxing clerks were employed. Still later taxing of unpaid letters came to be done by the postmaster of the first Post town to handle such letters. Certainly early in the 19th century taxing had become part of the duty of postmasters except possibly in the case of some of the smallest offices. Taxing of letters was always a difficult and responsible job and never more so than in the early years of the 19th century when postal rates were periodically increased. At the beginning of the century Francis Ronaldson, the surveyor for the West of Scotland, was making long and frequent journeys of inspection, at least part of which were taken up in instructing local postmasters in new rates and correcting records of mileage between Post towns, which even then were in many places faulty.

Though the country postmaster had for long little or no responsibility for delivery of letters, he was, if his office were on a through route, responsible for seeing that the mail for forward dispatch was promptly sent on its way. When the mail coach was introduced the working of the coaches became the responsibility of contractors who hired the coaches from the coach-builders; but before this time came, and when the mail was still being carried on foot or on horse-back, the arrangement for and payment of these services was often done by the postmaster. In such cases he was allowed a fixed sum to cover the cost, and could retain this sum, together with his salary, from amounts due by him to the General Post Office when remitting. This system of allowing postmasters to arrange for the transport of mails to the next stage was unsatisfactory, for there was always the temptation to them to make a profit on the deal by employing cheap or inferior labour, and those employed not being in the direct employment of the Post Office their shortcomings were the more difficult to check or cure.

If the amount of work falling to postmasters in some of the smaller country offices in the early 19th century was often relatively small, their hours of duty were long. Many a time they might have to wait far into the night for horse or foot posts delayed by bad weather or heavy mails. Postal time-tables, altered or adjusted to take account of new timings on main routes, might mean late arrivals at many smaller connected offices, and when in 1809 James Stewart, the postmaster of Auchterarder, sought an increase – the first for fourteen years – on his old salary of £10 per annum, Shearer the surveyor explained that new postal arrangements with near-by Dunning kept Stewart up till 10 or 11 p.m. each night to make up the last of the five postal bags for which he was daily responsible.

Stewart and his father between them had held the office of postmaster at Auchterarder for over thirty years during which period the net revenue of the post office there was estimated to have increased to £160 per annum. The revenue of the office, the central position of Auchterarder and the difficulty of maintaining the connecting services converging on it entitled the postmaster in Shearer's view to an increase in salary to £18 per annum.[14]

When in the autumn of 1815 Freeling, writing of the expenses involved in the bonds of guarantee required of postmasters, remarked on the difficulty of getting suitable people, his observation was applicable alike to postmasters and to those who became their guarantors. Throughout the records of Scottish postal history from the early years of the 17th century until the second quarter of the 19th century there are few references which occur with greater frequency than those relating to the financial straits of postmasters or petitions for increased pay. Looking back over these two centuries and more, there seems little doubt that from first to last the Post Office, or the Treasury always at their back, were niggardly paymasters and that many of the troubles which so often afflicted the service were caused by the salaries of postal officials failing to match the responsibilities which they carried and the temptations to which they were laid open. The earliest postmasters' salaries of which there is a record in Scotland were those of the men stationed on the Berwick road in the early years of the 17th century – £25 sterling to the postmaster at Cockburnspath, £20 and £12.10/– to those at the foot of the Canongate and at Haddington respectively. Such payments at that period would almost seem generous, but the work and conditions of service of these three men on this the earliest and for long the most important postal route in Scotland were in many ways exceptional. In any event it has been seen that despite their salaries and such perquisites as they had, none of the early holders of these postmasterships prospered. In the early years of the 18th century the majority of the thirty-four postmasters then in office are reported to have been remunerated by means of a percentage of the postal dues of letters passing through their hands, while in the cases where the actual cash remuneration is known the figures for that period apply only to the larger towns. At the time of the Union of the Parliaments the postmasters of

Glasgow and Aberdeen received £25 and £28 per annum respectively, those at Dundee, Montrose and Inverness £15 each and at Dumfries and Ayr £12 each, while the postmaster at Edinburgh, who was virtually the manager of postal services for the whole of Scotland, got £200.[15] The spread of rural posts during much of the 18th century was slow, and it was not till the end of that century that salary figures for rural or small town offices became available. Meantime those paid at Edinburgh and Glasgow had risen to £312 and £255 respectively, at Aberdeen to £120, at Dundee and Falkirk to £50 and at Greenock to £47. The salaries seem to have borne in many instances no close relation to the post office revenue of the towns in question. Most, judging by contemporary comment, were inadequate; few if any were generous.*

By the early years of last century the postal network was spreading out to include many small and some quite remote places, though with few exceptions these were still on or closely connected with the main postal routes. In some cases the payments to postmasters appear to have included certain small but unspecified remuneration in respect of purely local or '*by*' letters though as time passed there were increasingly frequent complaints from postmasters that extra work for them and extra revenue for the Post Office was not rewarded by adequate increases in salary. Some of the smallest salaries went to persons who merely kept receiving houses where letters could be deposited for delivery or collection either within the ordinary postal system or, after 1808, as part of the penny post service. Of the records of payments to postmasters of truly country offices some of the earliest relate to the extension of the Dumbarton road through Inveraray to Appin and Fort William. By 1793 the Inveraray postmaster was getting a salary of £30 soon to be increased to £32. North of Inveraray the Oban postmaster had only £6 until 1793 when he got an increase to £15, while at Bonawe and Appin the payments were in the same year raised from £6 and £5 respectively to £8 each. Even at Fort William at the same date the postmaster only got £15.[16] When in 1800 an extension of the postal route from Callander into the

---

* The cash accounts of David Ross for the years 1773/7 show that during this period his salary as Secretary and Accountant of the General Post Office in Edinburgh was only £23.15/- sterling per quarter. (S.R.O. RH. 9/18. Papers of David Ross.)

Breadalbane country was agreed to on the urgent request of the Earl of Breadalbane the salaries for the postmasters at Lochearnhead and Killin were each fixed at £5 with £4 for the man at Luib. In the extreme north the Thurso postmaster in 1792 had £47 per annum, but this was to cover the expenses of runners to and from Dunbeath thirty miles away, while far to the south-west the New Galloway postmaster's salary at about this date was raised from £6 to £8, In the Islands the pay was no more generous. At Achnacraig in Mull, where the ferry boat with the mails from Oban came in, the salary in 1793 had just been raised from £5 to £8; and some twelve years later Freeling rejected an application put forward by the British Fishery Society that the postmaster at Tobermory who was responsible for the mails for Coll and Tiree should have his salary increased from £5. As to the Outer Islands, when in 1802 the Post Office at length agreed to meet the cost of an office at Lochmaddy their contribution was only £6 per annum as salary for the postmaster, the cost of the boat to Dunvegan in Skye continuing to be met by the local people.

Small as these cash payments were – and it is clear that many of them were recognized even by the senior post office officials themselves as being inadequate – they were often still further reduced by outlays which had to be met by the postmaster. It has been seen that until 1817 all postmasters had to meet the cost of obtaining guarantors. In addition many had to pay the most ordinary and necessary office expenses. At Aberdeen and Arbroath about 1793 and at Dunfermline in 1796 the postmasters had to meet the cost of rent, fuel, sealing wax, candles, stationery and string, while at Paisley about the same time it was claimed that similar outlays reduced the total salary of £33 by fully one-half.[17] In common, too, with the letter carriers in the towns, postmasters all over the country had to make good any losses from bad money, for in remitting to the General Post Office in Edinburgh no allowance for this was ever made. The risk of losses from this source must have been considerable, for while postage dues on many incoming letters were no doubt paid by the recipient calling at the post office or by messengers collecting mail on behalf of local landowners, it seems certain that as time passed an increasing part of the responsibility of collecting postage must have been delegated to letter-carriers

13. 'The Village Post Office', *p.* 166.

On REMITTANCES, &c.

To the Postmaster of

YOU are to pay by Inſtalments on the 10th of every Month, the net Revenue ariſing within your Delivery.

The Inſtalment for your Office is eſtimated at £   per Month, which muſt be paid to the Receiver-General, or remitted to me on the Day appointed in a good Bill, or Bills, payable at 21 Days at leaſt from ſuch Day, to the Order of John Mortlock, Eſq. Receiver-General of the Poſt-Office Revenue.

No one can be allowed to withhold Payment of the Sum required, beyond the Day appointed, the Object being, that the Poſtmaſter ſhould pay the Money into the Office, or remit it on that Day in good Bills, to be accepted by the Party on whom drawn when preſented for that Purpoſe.

You are also on the Receipt of your *Quarterly Account Current* with this Office, to remit ſuch Part of the Balance as may remain undiſcharged; that is, the Sum which may remain due after deducting ſuch Bills as may have been remitted before Quarter-Day, but which for the Reaſons hereafter ſtated, are not placed to the Credit of the Account; and alſo the Sum you may have paid ſubſequent to Quarter-Day, as the firſt monthly Inſtalment being towards diſcharging that Account; the ſecond and third Inſtalments being on Account of the current Quarter.

Although it will require ſome Time after Quarter-Day to make out all the Accounts with the ſeveral Poſt-Maſters in this Kingdom, yet as the Receiver-General muſt neceſſarily cloſe his Accounts with the Exchequer on each Quarter-Day, being the 5th January, 5th April, 5th July, and 10th of October, no Credit can be given for ſuch Bills as are not due *before Quarter-Day*, nor any Money paid thereafter, but will of courſe be allowed in the Account for the Quarter in which the *Money* is actually paid.

In making your Remittances to this Office, it is neceſſary you ſhould take every Precaution recommended to the Public ſo often by Advertiſement from hence, not to ſend whole Notes when payable to Bearer; and you ſhould be careful in entering at the Foot of your Letter Bill, any Money Letter you may addreſs to me.

I am

Your aſſured Friend,

GENERAL POST-OFFICE,
APRIL 3, 1800.

Francis Freeling,
SECRETARY.

The following Form of a Bill of Exchange is recommended to ſuch Poſtmaſters as may obtain Bills for the Purpoſe of making their Remittances on Account of the Revenue:

£100   *April* 10*th*, 1800.
    " Twenty-one Days after Date, pay to John
" Mortlock, Eſq. or Order, Receiver-General of the Poſt-
" Office Revenue £. s. d. for Value received of C. B.
" being His Majeſty's Money."

                C. D.

" To Meſſrs.

    " London."

When Bills want Indorſement, the following is a proper Form:

    " Pay John Mortlock, Eſq.
" or Order, Receiver-General of
" the Poſt-Office Revenue."

who would often be of low intelligence and little education.* As for pension rights, the postmasters had none. As late as April 1836 James Shearer the postal surveyor had supported the application for a pension which a post runner in Orkney had had the temerity to make. In refusing the application Freeling pointed out with some vigour that pensions were never granted even to postmasters, far less to runners on a weekly wage.[18]

Yet for all the evidence against the Post Office as hard task-masters and niggardly payers the records seem to show that far from being disliked the office of postmaster was much sought after. Indeed the only instance which has been found among contemporary records of a post office official in Scotland threatening to relinquish his office failing a substantial rise in pay was at Invergarry in Inverness-shire as late as 1835. Here the local schoolmaster who had been appointed receiver for the penny post service to Inverie on Loch Nevis asked that his salary be more than doubled. This service, it will be recalled, had been started at the request of Macdonnell of Glengarry and since it was quite uneconomic it is probable that the schoolmaster's pay for the work was very low indeed. His request was reluctantly agreed to, Reeves the surveyor reporting that the schoolmaster was the only person in Invergarry capable of the work – a fact of which the schoolmaster himself was no doubt well aware.[19]

The reason for the popularity of an apparently ill-paid and harrassing job lay almost certainly in the fact that the cash payment was not the whole, and sometimes only a relatively small part, of the total benefits. In the early days of the Post Office it is clear that some postmasters possessed and prized the monopoly of horse hiring. How valuable this was may be doubted, particularly in Scotland where travel on horseback or by private coach or chaise was never as easy, as comfortable or as common as in England, but it may be that at least in the first half of the 18th century there were cases even in Scotland of

---

* A letter written by a senior post office official in London to Robert Oliphant the Scottish Postmaster General in 1790, makes reference to losses in respect of bad money falling on letter carriers. While this may have been in theory the position both in the towns and the country districts, it would seem that postmasters must have had difficulty in making good claims against men earning only a few shillings a week and in practice the risk fell on the postmaster. (Post 15/124/1790.)

14. Notice as to remittances, 1800, *p. 205.*

postmasters to whom the possibility if not the monopoly of horse hiring was a consideration. It is clear, too, that some of the postmasters on the main through roads acted as contractors in the transport of mails to the adjoining stages. Where transport of mails was undertaken in this way by postmasters it was almost certainly confined to foot or possibly horse transport. Contracting for working mail coaches after 1785 was a more serious undertaking, involving considerable capital resources for the provision of horses, stabling and fodder, and it seems unlikely that postmasters even on the principal mail coach routes would be in the position to provide these. Allowances to postmasters to cover horse or foot transport services provided by them were relatively common, and though the sum allowed, generally at the rate of 3d a mile, was not generous, it seems that some postmasters found ways and means of making a small profit on the business. Some, too, both in towns and certain country districts, could supplement their salaries by charging for delivery of letters where free delivery had not been conceded by the Post Office. In the early period of postal development in Scotland this factor was probably a very appreciable one, though it seems doubtful whether at a later stage the delivery charges did much more than pay the expense of the letter carriers employed by the postmasters. A further possible source of income arose from the long-standing system of 'franking', of which more will appear at a later stage, in which in varying degrees some local postmasters appear to have participated.

Finally, in considering the financial benefits, real or potential, which attached to the office of postmaster, it would be unrealistic to ignore the question of '*by*' letters – that is those letters which did not pass through Edinburgh or any other office where postal dues were calculated and marked, but which passed between smaller and often near-by offices. It was largely the difficulty of assessing such revenue and its frequent loss to the Post Office which led after 1715 to the appointment of postal surveyors.* Till that time came, there seems little doubt that much postal revenue found its way into the pockets of postmasters, particularly in rural areas; and even after the advent of surveyors brought much closer supervision there is some reason to think that, if only from faulty accounting rather than from bad faith,

* See Chapter x.

some postal revenue continued for a time to be lost to the Post Office.

Besides the monetary benefits, direct or indirect on which he could count, there was a less tangible but no less powerful consideration which would weigh with the local postmaster as an attraction of his office. Throughout the early period of Scottish postal history and indeed until well into the 19th century news and gossip, always precious in the rural areas, must have had a high scarcity value. The Post Office, whether a busy office on a main postal route or only a humble receiving office in a remote district, was clearly a natural centre for both, while the postmaster as the recipient and potential retailer would hold a position carrying with it prestige and perhaps at times no little local influence. When, in the early years of the 19th century, news grew more plentiful and its transmission more easy the Post Office remained the natural centre of communication, and with the widespread and intense interest in military and political events the position of the postmaster would be still further enhanced in importance.

Writing to William Kerr at the Edinburgh General Post Office in 1800 in answer to enquiries as to perquisites of Highland postmasters, James Shearer the surveyor reported that he knew of none save that possibly at one time something might have been made from payments to them as contractors for 'riding work' or from the use of money retained in the postmaster's hands till remittances to the General Post Office were due.[20] It has been seen that profit on the former was probably only marginal, while the vigilance of the accounting department at Edinburgh and the activity of the post office solicitor would seem to have precluded much benefit from the latter. Shearer seems, however, to have overlooked or at least made no mention of what was at one time the commonest and most valuable perquisite of all, though it is probable that this was enjoyed more frequently by Lowland than by Highland postmasters. This perquisite, which arose from the remarkable arrangements long in force for the circulation of news in these islands, was so complex and in some respects so illogical that at this distance of time it is not easy to comprehend, still less to explain clearly, its exact nature. Indeed official Minutes and notes endorsed on the margins of many of the contemporary documents relating to this matter make it clear that senior postal officials, and not least the

Postmasters General themselves, found it hard to understand.

Newspapers, newsletters or 'gazettes' as they were for long called, made their first appearance during the latter days of the Commonwealth, and from the early years of the 18th century these publications had been subject to a tax – originally at the rate of $\frac{1}{2}$d per sheet but subsequently and progressively raised to as much as 4d a sheet at the end of the Napoleonic Wars. These 'gazettes', to use the generic term most commonly applied to them, were, in their origin at least, semi-official in character, and in the collection of the news and other information contained in them those responsible for their compilation had received very great assistance from certain post office officials. In particular they received valuable help from the Clerks of the Roads who were the members of the staff at the headquarters of the General Post Office in London responsible for the organization and operation of the postal arrangements on the six main postal routes into which England was long divided. While the oldest of these gazettes, dating from about 1665, was known as *The London Gazette*, others came to be called *The Post Boy*, *The Postman*, *The Flying Post*, titles which served to commemorate their close connection with the Post Office to which they came to owe so much.

Almost from the start it had been the practice to allow such publications to go free through the post though nearly a century was to pass before this practice came to have any statutory basis. This valuable concession was granted, or at least acquiesced in, by the Government, since it greatly facilitated the circulation of official intelligence and, after 1711, increased the yield from the government tax of $\frac{1}{2}$d on each sheet which was introduced in that year. In acknowledgment of their original services as news-collectors and in recognition of the highly important part played by the Post Office in its transmission, the Clerks of the Roads at the General Post Office headquarters together with certain other Government officials had from at least the latter years of the 17th century been allowed to participate in the profits of this news business by having the monopoly of 'franking' gazettes or similar publications through the post.[21] Since any gazettes sent through the post at full postal rates would have paid postal charges of at least 4d and possibly as much as 6d a copy in addition to the publishers' price for the paper itself, the ability of the clerks to 'frank' them constituted a perquisite of very great value. The clerks were thus in a commanding position to undercut gazettes supplied through almost any other channel, and in effect they were, over nearly the whole country outside London, for long almost the sole newsagents. The exact method adopted by the clerks to turn to account their advantageous position with regard to the gazettes supplied through them is not altogether clear. Full advantage of their perquisite could clearly most readily be obtained through the local postmasters on each postal road, and it is certain that for this reason the clerks passed on to very many of the postmasters copies of the gazettes on advantageous terms, leaving the local men to make what they could from the copies so supplied. The usual charge made by the Clerks of the Roads against local postmasters for franking the papers supplied to them appears to have been 2d a copy in addition to the publishers' price for the paper. In the contemporary documents there is curiously little evidence as to how these payments reached the clerks; but reach them they certainly did, and by 1764, when extended rights of franking granted to and grossly exploited by members of parliament began seriously to cut into the clerks' profits, the annual proceeds of their franking privilege is believed to have grown to not less than £8,000.[22] This was, at that time, an immense sum for distribution among six clerks, though their salaries purely as Clerks of the Roads were for long little more than nominal. The profit from this newspaper perquisite appears, however, to have been looked on to a large extent as the property of the post office service as a whole. Since this profit arose so largely from the exemption of newspapers from postal dues, it was not unnatural that the money so earned should be regarded as virtually post office revenue, and in fact much of it had for long been used to pay certain post office pensions or to supplement inadequate salaries. By the end of the 18th century the profits of the clerks had been so far reduced by the extension of franking rights that these were no longer sufficient to cover their own salaries – now increased to £300 per annum each – and to meet the other calls hitherto made on them. Among the contemporary documents is a letter of 17 March 1792 from the Postmaster General to the Treasury renewing an annual application for a payment of over £600 to enable the clerks to supplement certain other post office salaries as in the past.[23]

[165]

All through the second half of the 18th century and at least during the first decade of the 19th century interest in naval, military and political events continued to be intense. At the date when mail coaches first appeared in 1785 nearly 10,000 papers left London each day.[24] Ten years later this number had been doubled, while papers in growing numbers were being printed in and circulated from Edinburgh and Glasgow. A list prepared by one of the Clerks of the Roads in England in 1809 shows that by this time, in addition to certain commercial and shipping lists, over 40 newspapers were regularly being sent from London to the provinces, including 10 morning and 7 evening papers each day.[25] At this period readers of newspapers were far more numerous than individual purchasers. Indeed regular ordering of copies by households or individuals does not appear to have become common till about 1835.[26] Previous to this papers passed largely from hand to hand. They could be and often were subscribed for by groups of persons who were willing to wait for days or even weeks for a chance to see a paper. Indeed it is on record that about 1750 the town council of Montrose were glad to receive gazettes as much as months old. To be able to read up-to-date news in the local post office would therefore be a privilege dearly prized and readily paid for, and it can easily be understood that, especially in the days when local post offices were still in many cases inns or at least places of common public resort, the receipt of a paper would be amongst the most valued perquisites of a postmaster. Readers of *The Diary of a Country Parson* will recall that in 1761 Parson Woodforde in Somerset paid as much as 7½d a time to read a newspaper at the local inn, and contemporary records describe the eagerness with which all over the country the arrival of the mail with news was awaited. From contemporary evidence available as to the salaries paid to postmasters it is clear that the supply to them by the Clerks of the Roads of gazettes on advantageous terms was so fully recognized and so widespread that it was regularly taken into account by the Post Office in fixing salaries. So the Post Office got some return for carrying newspapers free of charge, by using at least part of the profits of the Clerks of the Roads and of the local postmasters to help with the salary bill.

The exact nature and extent of the early trade in newspapers in Scotland is somewhat obscure, but it is certain that in the second half of the 17th century newsletters or gazettes of some sort were being published in Edinburgh and that in their circulation and probably also in their compilation the Post Office was, almost from the start, playing here as in England a considerable part. It is on record that in 1661 Robert Mein, who at the Restoration had been reappointed to his former post as Keeper of the Letter Office at Edinburgh, was authorized to publish a weekly paper to prevent the circulation of false news,[27] and it has been seen that in 1667 the postal contract between the magistrates of Aberdeen and John Wells included an obligation on the latter to supply them regularly with weekly and daily papers and newsletters from the South.[28] Such a clause in a contract of the mid-17th century has a surprisingly modern ring, but the further reference to newsletters and gazettes in the Aberdeen negotiations of 1674 would seem to put it beyond doubt that at this time such publications were in fact being produced and regularly circulated. James Anderson, the Deputy Postmaster General at Edinburgh in 1715, appears to have enjoyed much the same privileges as the Clerks of the Roads in England. It is at least clear that he engaged in newspaper circulation on a considerable scale, even if on his own evidence he made little profit by it, though it would appear from such records as are available that he supplied papers direct to customers and not through local postmasters. The list of papers supplied to Mrs Shields in Glasgow by Anderson in 1717 shows that by then many publications were in circulation, and Anderson's own letters refer also to King's Speeches, Lords' Addresses and 'Articles of Impeachment' as being regularly received by him.[29] Many of these publications clearly came from the South, but without doubt some would be printed in Edinburgh, and in November 1715 Robert Thomson, the postmaster at Glasgow, published the first newspaper in that city, the *Glasgow Courant*.[30]

It seems that shortly after this date questions had arisen in connection with the privileged position of the Clerks of the Roads with regard to the circulation of newspapers, for the post office records contain the following order dated 23 June 1737 and under the heading 'Newspapers, Scotland': 'Resolved that the priviledge of sending Newspapers into the Country by the Officers of the General Post Office was originally priviledged to the Clerks of the Roads: And it is hereby ordered that no other Officers do presume to intrench upon them, or send any papers by Contract, or Agreement for proffitt unless by a special allowance of the Postmaster Genl. in order to prevent for the future the Inconveniencys which have attended the Contrary practice.'[31] At the end of the century Helen Anderson, the Dunfermline postmistress whose plea for an increase in salary was refused in 1796, stated that one newspaper, originally allowed to her but subsequently taken away, brought her in two to three pounds a year,[32] and it can hardly be doubted that about this time many other postmasters in Scotland enjoyed similar perquisites. As to the Clerks of the Scottish Roads it seems clear that they enjoyed privileges similar to those of their English colleagues, for in 1794 following on certain changes affecting newspaper distribution in Scotland, they applied successfully for compensation to make good their losses. Their income from franking had, it seems, amounted to nearly £350 a year largely divided between four clerks and hitherto treated as part of their salaries.[33] In England the sole remuneration of the postmaster at Dorchester was at one time the receipt of four newspapers a week. These were only a few of very many instances of early newspaper distribution throughout the country, and in the postal records of the late 18th and early 19th centuries complaints of the growing weight of newspapers and official publications carried on foot and at last perforce on horseback bear witness to the wide circulation of official and semi-official publications even in the remotest areas reached by the post.

Till well past the middle of the 18th century the Clerks of the Roads, using local postmasters throughout the country as their distributing agents, remained in unchallenged control of the newspaper trade, but after 1764 substantial franking privileges were extended to members of parliament through whom they became widely, though often corruptly, available. Finally an Act of 1825 empowered any member of the public to send newspapers through the post free of postage. Meantime the growing demand for news, stimulated by the American and later by the French wars, had led to the publication of more and more papers. Newsvendors and newsagents had entered the trade on a growing scale, and with their monopoly of franking diminished and finally abolished, the post office clerks found themselves in open and often hostile competition with these new interests. The newsvendors accused the clerks of abusing their position by bringing pressure to bear on local postmasters to favour papers sent through their own agency by giving preference in the delivery of such papers. It was also claimed that papers sent post free through the clerks regularly contained other items which were not entitled to exemption from postal dues. It is probable that this practice did in fact prevail, and indeed the early gazettes sent through the post by the agency of the post office clerks are even believed in some cases to have included a blank section for a letter which would thus go post-free with the paper. That the practice persisted is shown by the fact that on 30 March 1798 *The Times* published the following notice: 'No person has a right to abuse the privilege of free carriage which the newspapers enjoy for the encouragement of the Stamp Duties by smuggling under cover any private correspondence.'[34]

In the growing struggle between the clerks and the newsagents which was now developing Freeling, resentful as always of any criticism of post office practice or ancient privilege, fiercely defended the clerks' rights. Far from being open to challenge by the newsvendors, he contended, the clerks had a real grievance against these newcomers encroaching on rights enjoyed by postal officials almost since the first establishment of the Post Office. By the early years of the 19th century, too, local postmasters had ceased to regard themselves as obliged to act solely as agents for the clerks and in fact not a few now acted as agents for London newsagents who offered them better terms. By now only about one-tenth or at most one-seventh of the papers sent each week from London to the country went through the clerks, but even so, and with their franking privilege gone, the profit to the clerks and so to the Post Office remained substantial. In Freeling's eyes the case for the clerks was an unanswerable one. The clerks who enjoyed this ancient privilege were in all cases old post office servants, to whom it appears to have been given as a reward for long service, often at low salaries. To abolish this privilege would, contended the Secretary, greatly add to the cost of administering the postal service. The right of sharing in the newspaper trade, too, was for these officials no mere sinecure. The papers had to be purchased from the publishers through one source only – another post office official who had his own profit from the traffic. In 1811 in the course of one of the many enquiries into the whole involved matter it was claimed that the clerks required a combined capital of £15,000 to enable them to finance their dealings. It may be, too, that in his defence of the clerks' position Freeling was not unmindful of the fact that no small part of his own remuneration at the Post Office reached him in the form of compensation for the abolition of franking privileges in respect of newspapers sent overseas which he had once enjoyed. So, in one way or another, the Post Office and its officials had valuable vested interests in the newspaper trade.

But the newsagents and newsvendors were not to be denied, and though for some years Freeling with the support of successive Postmasters General was able to maintain his position, the days of the post office privilege were running out. Postal administration and the whole complex of involved and obscure custom and practice evolved and built up over generations past was coming under increasing scrutiny and mounting criticism, while the authority of Freeling himself was being questioned and at last undermined. Finally in the early weeks of 1834 Lord Althorp, the Chancellor of the Exchequer, informed the Postmaster General of the Treasury decision that the privilege of the clerks in sending newspapers through the post was to be discontinued in return for increased salaries, and a Minute of 12 February brought to an end one of the oldest and certainly one of the most complex chapters of postal history. There can be little doubt that latterly, and indeed for many years past, the favoured position of the Post Office in newspaper sale and circulation had been both an anomaly and an anachronism. If this must be conceded it can, however, be fairly claimed for the Post Office that for many years during its early history the part played by it ensured for much of the country outside London a circulation of news which without it would have been impossible.[35]

REFERENCES

1. Post 14/335/1797.
2. Quoted by Hyde, op. cit., 295/6.
3. Post 14/337/1796.
4. Post 42/52A/1793.
5. Post 40/697/1825.
6. Haldane, *New Ways through the Glens*, ch. 4.

7. Post 40/375/1825.
8. Ibid./67M/1803.
9. *20th Report of Commissioners of Enquiry* (P.O. Revenue, Scotland), 1830, vol. XIII, 15.
10. *O.S.A.*, X, 559.
11. Post 40/25z/1806.
12. Ibid./80.1/1802.
13. Information from papers in Lossit House, Machrihanish.
14. Post 15/134/1809.
15. Joyce, op. cit., 117.
16. Post 40/117c/1793.
17. Hyde, op. cit., 100/1.
18. Post 40/171/1836.
19. Ibid./549/1835.
20. Post 14/337/1800.
21. F. George Kay, *The Royal Mail*, 85 et seq.
22. Joyce, op. cit., 192.
23. Post 24, Clerks of the Roads, 1791/1834.
24. Howard Robinson, op. cit., ch. XII.
25. Post 24, Clerks of the Roads, 1791/1834.
26. *History of 'The Times', 1785–1841*, ch. III.
27. R.P.C., 3rd Series, vol. I, 115.
28. *Aberdeen Council Letters*, vol. IV, 297.
29. N.L.S., Anderson MS, 141.
30. Braid, *Postal History of Old Glasgow*.
31. G.P.O. Orders 1737–1771, p. 3.
32. Post 40/8.1/1796. See Appendix IV.
33. Ibid./160A and 194A/1794.
34. *History of 'The Times', 1785–1841*, ch. III.
35. Post 24. Clerks of the Roads; Newspaper privilege; Correspondence 1791–1834.

Eight

The Island Posts

In July 1796 certain of the inhabitants of the Shetland Islands prepared for submission to the Postmaster General a Memorial dealing with the history, and the inadequacy, of the postal arrangements to their islands. A copy of this was sent in February 1797 to Henry Dundas, Secretary of State for War, the member of the Government who dealt with Scottish business, asking his support for their request for an improved service. As far back as the middle of the 18th century efforts had been made to establish a postal service between Leith and Lerwick. It seems probable that originally these arrangements were private ones made with traders between the two ports, but early in 1763 they came to have some degree of official recognition and support. The postal rate at that time was fixed at 6d a letter, and the Post Office paid £60 per annum to a firm of Leith merchants towards the cost of a sloop which made the passage five times a year. This contribution proved to be totally inadequate, and not unnaturally the carriage of mails came to be entirely secondary to the shipping of goods.[1]

In this unsatisfactory state the Shetland mail remained till 1789 when contractors in Aberdeen offered to take the mail to Lerwick twelve times a year for the same price as had been arranged by the Leith shippers, an offer which was accepted.

It is hardly surprising that the Aberdeen effort failed and the people of Shetland had to fall back on the old arrangement with Leith. This suited neither party. The islanders got only a spasmodic and infrequent mail service, while in the summer of 1793 Strong & Company, the Leith owners of the packet *Elizabeth* which had been on the Shetland run, wrote to Robert Oliphant, the Deputy Postmaster General, complaining that the post office contribution was no less than three years in arrear. No interest was being charged on the outstanding balance, and the shippers were in addition involved in heavy war risks insurance on the passage to Shetland. They now asked for immediate settlement of their overdue account and an assurance of quarterly payments in future.[2] Despite the apparently unsatisfactory terms on which they were operating, Strong & Company continued to stress the advantages of the service from Leith, perhaps because almost simultaneously an Aberdeen firm, Brebner & Company, had again offered to make the passage to Shetland once a month, except in January and December, for an annual payment of £120. Whether the Leith firm got their arrears is not clear, but the postal officials in Edinburgh advised the acceptance of Brebner's offer.

In the Memorial prepared by the Shetlanders in July 1796 it was claimed that the Islands' export trade, mainly in fish and wool, amounted to £30,000 per annum, while the Islands were of considerable importance for the trade with Norway, Archangel and the Baltic. Two thousand Shetland men were serving with the Navy and there was much enemy activity in the neighbourhood, news of which, in the absence of a frequent postal service to the mainland, had to be sent by open boat to Fair Island and thence to the post office at Kirkwall in Orkney.[3] Despite all this, Post Office Headquarters in London or more probably the Treasury, refused to raise the post office contribution above the old figure of £60 per annum, and in order to avoid a return to the Leith service the people of Shetland were forced in a seven year contract with the Aberdeen firm to make up the balance of £60 per annum.[4]

Brebners found their contract unprofitable. The Customs officials raised difficulty over the carriage of goods and mail in the same ship, and Freeling's suggestion to the Treasury that in the circumstances some extra payment by the Post Office would be reasonable seems to have fallen on deaf ears. The

people of Shetland, burdened with their annual contribution of
£60, enlisted the help of the Admiralty, who supported them
in pointing out that in these wartime days the importance of
the Shetland service should not be measured only in terms of
money. Lord Chesterfield too, one of the Postmasters General,
was sympathetic to the islanders, but could only refer the
matter to the Treasury 'without whom', he wrote, 'we cannot
stir a step'.⁵ But constant friction can wear down even a stone,
and by 1802 the government contribution to the Shetland
service is at last referred to as £120 per annum. At that date
the Lerwick mails were going ten times a year from Aberdeen.
Shetland wanted a more frequent service, urging that the packet
boat would be most useful in reporting privateers. On this
occasion the rejoinder of the Post Office was short and in the
circumstances pertinent. The less the packet boat saw of
privateers the better they would be pleased.⁶

No improvement on the Shetland postal service seems to
have taken place for the next 10 years, and in 1812 the Islanders
returned to the charge asking that the post office contribution
be increased from £120 to £300 per annum for a service
twice a month, though whether from Aberdeen or Leith is not
clear. Both Freeling and the surveyor considered this to be
quite out of the question, the net annual revenue from Shetland
letters being now only £75. Freeling's suggestion was that the
present contract with the Aberdeen shippers should be cancelled
and that Shetland letters should now go as ship letters by every
ship sailing to or from Leith at a charge of 4d a single letter,
2d a letter being paid to the commanders of ships, and the
Customs officials at Leith and Lerwick being instructed to
prevent any vessel starting to unload cargo till it had been
certified that all letters had been handed over.⁷

While the people of Shetland were thus, in the face of many
discouragements, struggling to achieve an improved letter
service, Orkney's postal arrangements, too, had been far from
satisfactory. No arrangement for regular conveyance of letters
from Leith or Aberdeen to the Islands appears to have been in
existence, the only postal route being by open boat across the
Pentland Firth. For long the post to Orkney had been only
a weekly post, but in 1804 Shearer wrote that he had tried
the experiment of a post twice a week. The Baltic trade and the
periodical concentration of the North Sea whaling fleets in the

Island justified, in the surveyor's view, the increased service which would also help to bring early information of enemy cruisers. Shearer's action had been approved and he had even earned the praise of the Postmasters General, an event which, as will later appear, was for him by no means an everyday occurrence.[8]

In 1828 the merchants of Leith wrote to the Post Office urging that letters from Orkney should be carried by vessels trading with Kirkwall. Sir David Wedderburn, then Deputy Postmaster General at Edinburgh, considered that this would not only speed the Orkney mail but would bring in to the official post many letters at present sent illegally by sea. Wedderburn's plan raised the question of postal charges. The mileage by sea from Leith was only 240 miles, and at current rates this would mean a charge of only 1/– a single letter, compared with 1/2d by the route to Wick and across the Pentland Firth at present in use. Reluctant though he always was to reduce charges, Freeling advised that the new plan be tried in the expectation that it would increase correspondence, the shipmasters to get, as on the Shetland route, 2d for the carriage and delivery of each letter.[9] The old route across the Pentland Firth was however to remain in use, and it is known that in April 1830 in accounting to the Edinburgh post office for the balance due for the preceding quarter Archibald McGamoch, the Kirkwall postmaster, still showed a payment of £10 made by him to a contractor for taking mails across the Pentland Firth.[10]

About the time when the first rudiments of a postal service to Shetland were taking shape a postal link was being forged between the west coast of Ross-shire and the Island of Lewis. As early as 1741 when Alexander Hamilton, the Deputy Postmaster General in Edinburgh, was believed to control a total of over one hundred post towns in Scotland, postal bags both to Kirkwall in Orkney and to Stornoway are mentioned. Authentic records of a regular post to Lewis do not, however, start until 1756. In the spring of that year George Mackenzie, 'Steward and Receiver of Lewis', presented a Memorial to the Earl of Leicester and Sir Everard Fawkener, the Postmasters General, asking post office support for a regular postal packet from Stornoway to Poolewe and a foot post on to Inverness. The lack of any regular communication with the mainland was, Mackenzie claimed, a great disadvantage. The absence of a post office on the Island caused difficulty in the provisioning and paying of the Government troops which since 1745 had been stationed on the Island, despite the fact that the population of 6000 or 7000 were all Protestants and well affected towards the Government. Shipping too was handicapped. Commanders of vessels putting in to Stornoway for repair or for provisioning could not raise funds save by sale of part of their cargo, and it often happened that vessels were stormbound for weeks on end while their owners, in ignorance of their safety, had to arrange extended insurance. For these and other reasons the islanders asked that the Post Office provide for Stornoway a small decked vessel with a master and six men to sail to Poolewe once a week in winter, a six-oared boat to cross in summer and calm weather and two foot carriers from Poolewe to Inverness.[11] The outcome of this approach was a letter from the Secretary of the Post Office giving orders to treat with Mr Mackenzie 'upon the best and most reasonable terms you can for the carrying this Service into Execution so that the same may as effectually answer the Ends proposed as possible'.[12] Agreement, it seems, was quickly reached, for in November 1758 certain inhabitants of North and South Uist, Harris, and Barra complained that 'our Neighbours of Stornoway have had Interests to obtain a Packet on the Publick funds and yet we may affirm with Truth they have not half our Correspondence'.[13] This latter claim, needless to say, was contested by the Lewismen, who appear to have had the better of the argument.[14] When, in 1776, George Gillanders, the Earl of Seaforth's chamberlain, was appointed postmaster at Stornoway he was to receive £70 each year towards the upkeep of the packet, payment of runners to carry the mail to Inverness once each week, and his own salary.[15]

Some thirteen years later the problem of the postal arrangements for Lewis again arose. In March 1789 Mackenzie of Seaforth, the owner of the Island, was in communication with the post office authorities. The annual contribution of £70 per annum previously arranged had become inadequate and the loss in maintaining the service fell on Mackenzie. The vessel on the Poolewe crossing had become worn out, and after negotiation with the Edinburgh office it had been proposed that £30 be allowed for her repair, the annual contribution to the service to be raised from £70 to £85. Before these arrangements could

I GEORGE MAIN Deputy Post-Master-General of that part of GREAT BRITAIN called Scotland, do hereby impower and Nominat *John Adam* to Receive and uplift the Port of all Letters and Pacquets, due to Her Majesty to and from the Town of *Elgin* and to do whatsoever else is incumbent to him, as Post Master Depute, as fully and freely in all Respects as I might do my self, if personally present: But it is hereby specially provided, that the said *John Adam* shall make just Compt and Payment to me Monthly, for the Port of all said Letters and Pacquets due to Her Majesty, and that immediatly whenever the Accompt is sent, he always being allowed *the fourth of all Inland Letters to & from Edinburgh & Elgin as his Salary* out of the first End thereof. In Witness hereof I have Subscribed thir presents, and caus'd affix the Seal of this Office, at *Edinburgh* the *Seventeenth* day of *December* one thousand seven hundred and *Eleven* years. Before these Witnesses *George & John Main's my sons*

George Main witnes

John Main witnes

George Main

15. Nomination of the Elgin postmaster, 1711, *p.* 208.

16. Francis Ronaldson, *p.* 228.

be put in hand, however, the vessel sank, and though she had been raised she was now said to be beyond repair. Mackenzie proposed that the Post Office secure a good second-hand boat of 40 to 80 tons which would cost about £40; that the vessel be handed over to a contractor who would fit her out receiving an annual sum of £100 for a weekly service, and that Mackenzie himself would guarantee the service for fourteen years. These proposals were, however, turned down by the Post Office who refused to increase their annual contribution. Matters appeared to have reached a deadlock and it is not apparent how the Stornoway postal service was in the meantime kept up. Mackenzie threatened to withdraw all support from the Poolewe packet, and a meeting of merchants and others at Stornoway in August 1792 could only suggest that he be asked to relent and that all shipowners taking passengers between Stornoway and the mainland should charge for their passage and account to the master of the postal packet. Kerr, the secretary of the Edinburgh office, in a letter written to Mackenzie a few weeks after the meeting in Stornoway, indicated that he saw no alternative to abolishing the packet altogether. Certainly the figures were not very encouraging. In the previous year the wages of the master and crew of the packet boat amounted to £33, with £16.18/– for seven barrels of beef and eight bolls of meal for provisions. The two runners on the mainland got £3, with 4/– for wallets and six bolls of meal costing £4.16/–,[16] while running repairs to the boat and other incidentals were put at £12.5/–. This, with a salary of £5 to a substitute postmaster at Stornoway, brought the total outgoings to £75.3/–. To meet these the yearly allowance from the Post Office was still £70, while the income from freight charges for the years averaged £18. The balance to the contractor who undertook the service was thus less than £13, a modest return even at contemporary values, while the return which the Post Office got in revenue in respect of their £70 seems problematical.[17]

The next record of developments in the postal service between Lewis and the mainland appears in the narrative of a Petition to the Post Office submitted in 1821. The annual contribution of £70, to which the Post Office had agreed over half a century earlier, had proved only sufficient to provide one post every fifteen days. In course of time trade between the Island and the mainland improved and a weekly post was arranged. The post office contribution, however, remained at £70, the people of Stornoway making up the balance of cost. Now, in 1821, trade had again fallen off and Stornoway was seeking an increased contribution by the Post Office towards the maintenance of the service which was costing a total of £250 per annum. Freeling, as always, looked closely at the figures. These showed that following a steady rise till 1817 the nett revenue to the Post Office from the Lewis service had fallen sharply, and the Lewis application was refused.[18] At the end of 1824 a further effort was made to get increased help from the Post Office to the cost of the Lewis service. The weekly post was still being kept up, the maintenance of the mail packet costing Mr Stewart Mackenzie, the proprietor of the Island, £120 a year. The two runners who carried the bags from Pool House at the head of Loch Ewe along the north shore of Loch Maree to Achnasheen were now costing £8 a year and 10 bolls of meal. Worse still, the packet boat *Glenelg* had recently been lost, at a cost to Mr Stewart Mackenzie of £400 besides a sum of £59 paid by him for a temporary replacement. Again the Post Office seem to have proved unsympathetic. Mr Stewart Mackenzie's claim for compensation for the loss of the boat was turned down on the ground that there was no contract between him and the Post Office, and that the main purpose of the boat was to serve his own interests as owner of the Island.[19] In writing to the Postmaster General, however, in 1825 about the loss of the *Glenelg* Freeling refers to the contract for a new 'permanent packet' involving the Post Office in much additional expense, so it may be that in the event more generous feelings had prevailed. Certainly the proprietor of Lewis could not be criticized for lack of energy in the interests of the Island. In 1816 efforts by the Commissioners for Highland Roads and Bridges to arrange the construction of a road from Achnasheen through Glen Docherty to the east end of Loch Maree had failed owing to the high cost. More than ten years later no further progress had been made. 'I have', wrote Mr Stewart Mackenzie in April 1827, 'within the last three days with difficulty and at the risk of my health and life scrambled up from Lewis to attend the Circuit Court at Inverness, but arrived too late to do my duties as Juror owing to the want of a road from Poolewe at Achnasheen.'[20] In the following year he wrote to Joseph Mitchell, the Commissioners' engineer, again urging the construction of this road which would enable the Lewis post to run twice a week to the benefit of the coastguards and the excise officers. Six years later success had been achieved, and in February 1834 Freeling was able to report that a post to Lewis twice a week had been arranged, besides a payment of £250 for the packet boat and an extra runner on the road between Poolewe and Achnasheen.*

While postal communications were gradually and in the face of great difficulty being established between Lewis and the mainland, similar problems confronted the inhabitants of North and South Uist, Benbecula and Barra. From very early times contact between this part of the Long Island and the mainland had been maintained largely through Dunvegan on the north-west coast of Skye, and when during the second half of the 18th century postal problems for these Outer Islands were for the first time being actively debated, it was inevitably through Skye that their solution had to be sought. When in the course of certain litigation which took place in 1770 evidence was given regarding the working of the Inverness post office, a postal route to Loch Carron and Skye was mentioned as one of those for which the Inverness postmaster was responsible.[21] There appear to be no records of the exact date when this line of communication was opened up nor of the frequency of such postal service as then existed, but it may well be that about the time when a regular post to Lewis was started in 1756 the first letter-carriers were to be seen on the roadless country which lay between Inverness and the Kyle of Lochalsh.

If the exact date of the opening of regular postal communication to Skye must be to some extent a matter of conjecture, there is direct evidence that about the time when a post to Stornoway was being established the people in the southern portion of the Long Island were cherishing similar ambitions. In the autumn of 1758 a Memorial, already mentioned, by 'heritors, ministers, farmers and merchants' of the Uists, Harris and Barra was presented to Lord George Beauclerk, Commander-in-Chief of the Government forces in Scotland, asking for his assistance in obtaining support for a packet which they had established to

---

* Post 40/97/1834. Despite the relatively satisfactory state of the Lewis postal arrangements at this date, the *N.S.A.* (1842) records that at that time the mail packet to Poolewe sailed only once a week, weather permitting, with a Government contribution of only £150 per annum.

operate weekly to Dunvegan. The memorialists based their claim for support partly on a not unnatural sense of the isolation of 'these Islands wherein we live unguarded and defenceless, exposed to the rapine of our open and avowed enemies, obnoxious to the annoyance and devastation of their privateers the fatal effects of which these places have felt in all the wars with France for many years back. . . .'[22] Whatever the merits of the islanders' claims, they produced an angry retort in the form of 'Observes', anonymous but almost certainly emanating from those in Lewis. The Uist Memorial is described as a gross misrepresentation of the facts. In particular the only so-called 'merchant' in Uist was said to be one Donald McLean who owned a small sloop for bringing meal from Caithness and exporting kelp. The anonymous writer dismissed the Memorial as inspired by jealousy of the packet service to the mainland enjoyed by the people of Stornoway.[23] Appeals to an Army commander, preoccupied in 1758 with problems of settlement and roadmaking on the Scottish mainland, were in any event virtually wasted effort. The Memorial of 1758 remained unanswered save perhaps in a negative sense, and for the next thirty years and more communication between the southern portion of the Long Island and the mainland by way of Skye was to be maintained by the unaided efforts of the islanders.

But the postal needs of this part of the Long Island were at last to be met, if only partially, through the efforts of their neighbours in Skye. In the last days of December 1789 a most informative Memorial was prepared at the instance of Alexander Lord Macdonald urging the claims of the people of North Uist for improved communications through Skye to Inverness. If the Memorial of 1758 had relied for its appeal on a sense of isolation, that of Lord Macdonald was based on more solid economic grounds, though the memorialist's description of North Uist as 'the most fertile of all the Western Isles' may suggest to a reader of today some degree of over-statement. In the latter part of the 18th century and for many years to come North and South Uist and Benbecula shipped through Lochmaddy to Dunvegan considerable numbers of black cattle to be driven south, together with beasts from Skye, for sale at the trysts of Southern Scotland and eventually in the markets of England. North and South Uist and Benbecula were also at this time producing large quantities of kelp from the seaweed grown along their shores or driven in by the Atlantic storms, a valuable product shipped to the south to supply a demand which grew rapidly all through the French wars. This trade meant frequent correspondence with Liverpool, Newcastle, Hull and other towns in England, and the Memorial of 1789 laid stress on the traffic in bills and promissory notes sent to the Islands in payment for kelp and cattle, bills which were later to be returned to the mainland to pay for timber, iron and general supplies needed by the islanders. Lochmaddy, too, was a common resort for fishing boats and for larger craft engaged particularly in the Baltic trade. As in the case of the Stornoway petition, Lord Macdonald's application was for help from the Post Office in establishing a packet boat, in this instance between Lochmaddy and Dunvegan, which he undertook to maintain and operate at his own expense. Since an effective postal service to this part of the Long Island depended on adequate communication between Skye and Inverness, a postal runner three times a week to go by way of the Kyleakin Ferry was also needed. Reference to the activities of the existing runner made it apparent that a regular post between Skye and Inverness was already in existence though the service seems to have been neither satisfactory nor frequent.[24]

Lord Macdonald's Memorial of 1789 failed in its purpose, but it had the incidental effect of greatly alarming the people of Stornoway who appear to have seen in it a danger that the direct postal link between Lewis and the mainland might be abandoned in favour of one by way of Dunvegan. Almost simultaneously with Lord Macdonald's Memorial came another addressed to the Postmaster General, this time from F.H. Mackenzie, the proprietor of Lewis. Mackenzie argued that if the Lewis post were to be routed by way of Dunvegan this would entail the postal packet from Skye sailing along a dangerous coast and past 'some most iminently dangerous rocks' on the way to Stornoway. Any alternative plan to land the Stornoway letters for example at Rodell or Tarbert in Harris would involve a two- or three-day journey north by a foot post over rough and boggy country intersected by lochs or arms of the sea where no ferries could be maintained. Such a plan, he considered – as well he might – to be impracticable and not to be compared with the straight sea crossing between Stornoway and Poolewe, a port which to some extent served also the coastal

country at least as far north as Ullapool. Stornoway, he claimed
with some justice, was the undoubted centre of trade in the
whole of the Long Island, a town of about fifty 'sash and slated
houses' having nearly £20,000 'vested in shipping and trade',
with twenty-five decked vessels of her own besides being the
centre for other shipping and fishing boats. Mackenzie's
Memorial contained much of common sense and incontrover-
tible reasoning, but rather less of friendly feeling towards his
neighbours. 'Your Memorialist', he wrote, 'is no stranger to
the many ill-judged attempts daily made by his neighbours both
North and South [against] the prosperity of Stornoway, insti-
gated, he supposes [by] a desire to make her pay for their private
accommodation where they cannot afford it themselves.'[25]

Though Lord Macdonald's Memorial on behalf of North
Uist fell, like many another, on stony ground, at least it was
preserved in the post office archives where it remained till
rescued from oblivion in the first years of last century. Meantime in 1798 his lordship had again taken up the postal cudgels on behalf of Skye and the Outer Isles, this time with the
support of MacLeod of MacLeod, Macdonald of Clanranald
and others. By this time the local proprietors in Uist, despair-
ing of support from the Post Office, had established a packet
boat between Lochmaddy and Dunvegan and a post runner in
North Uist at an annual cost of £72.17/–; but the postal arrangements between Inverness and Skye remained inadequate.
Post offices had been set up at Sconser between Broadford
and Sligachan, and at Dunvegan, but it is hardly surprising to
learn that the sums allowed by the Post Office for their running were so small that much of the cost of maintaining the
offices fell on local subscription. The sums allowed for the foot
runners to and from Inverness, too, were miserable. For the
round trip from Skye to Inverness and back, a distance of 226
miles including six ferry crossings, the runner received only
5/–. Not surprisingly he acted as general carrier on his journey,
a function which, if it eked out his pay, delayed his mails. To
shorten his journey too, the runner appears often to have
adopted the expedient of sailing between Skye and Loch
Carron, a short-cut which added to the risk of his journey and
no doubt also to the irritation of the inhabitants of those districts
in Skye and on the mainland thus deprived of his services. To
remedy these defects in the service the Post Office was asked to

increase their annual grant by £40 per annum to put the posts in Skye on an efficient footing, to make a reasonable allowance for a runner from Skye to convey letters to Loch Carron where he would hand over to a runner from Inverness, and to appoint a postmaster in North Uist responsible for the local distribution of letters. The arguments in the Memorial were reinforced by an estimate that 3,000 tons of kelp and 7,000 black cattle went south each year from Skye and the Outer Isles. To this the Island fishermen added several hundred tons of fish each year, while fishing villages established by the British Fisheries Society at Stein in north-west Skye and by Lord Macdonald at Lochmaddy and Portree were dependent on adequate communications.[26]

These Memorials had for long lain unnoticed, or at least unanswered, at the headquarters of the Post Office in London, but with the end of the 18th century the attention of the Government was coming to be focussed increasingly on the needs and problems of the Highlands and Islands. In the autumn of 1799 James Shearer, one of the post offices surveyors, had sent a complaint from Skye that only one post a week linked them with Inverness though the gross postal revenue of the Dunvegan, Sconser and Loch Carron offices had grown to over £300 per annum, with payments to postmasters and runners of only £56.10/–. An increased service was clearly not only justified but long overdue. Shearer in sending on the Skye complaint had written: 'I confess my knowledge of that island is very limited as neither I nor anyone now in this office have ever been there.' But Freeling's eye to postal profit was a keen one, and this rather than detailed knowledge dictated his policy. The Skye revenue figures spoke for themselves, and a second runner between Inverness and Dunvegan was granted.[27]

The establishment at local expense of a packet boat between Lochmaddy and Dunvegan had removed the fear of major commitments which had weighed with the Post Office in refusing earlier appeals for help. In the summer of 1802 William Kerr, the Secretary of the Scottish Office, wrote to Freeling recommending the expenditure of £6 per annum involved in starting a post office at Carinish in North Uist.* This, he added,

---

* The office at Carinish was closed in about 1830 and transferred to Lochmaddy where the Carinish postmark continued to be used for some time following the transfer.

would greatly ease the burden of work on the postmaster at Dunvegan who up till now had been forced to keep postage accounts with at least thirty people in the Uists and Benbecula. Kerr's recommendation with the supporting papers were submitted to and approved by the Postmaster General. Nothing was said of financial support of the packet which appears to have remained a burden on the local people; but at least and at last, after close on fifty years of deferred hope and constant effort, the people of North Uist had got a post office.[28]

Though the last year of the 18th century had seen the granting by the Post Office of a second runner between Inverness and Dunvegan, the state of the Skye post was still far from satisfactory. Much of the cost of keeping up offices in Skye itself still fell on the local landowners and in 1808 the office at Sconser had been closed owing to the default of the postmaster. In the following year, however, Lord Macdonald and other Skye landowners had undertaken to guarantee to the Post Office payment of postage dues on all letters delivered there. The annual postal revenue from the Island had now grown to £500 and with this in mind the Postmasters General, on Freeling's advice, agreed to the re-establishment of the Sconser office with a receiving house at Kyleakin for the deposit and collection of letters.*

Meantime, on the mainland, important developments were taking place. The building of a road from Dingwall by Achnasheen to Loch Carron had been one of the first of the many projects placed before the Commissioners for Highland Roads and Bridges and approved by Thomas Telford their engineer. Soon contracts had been let and work put in hand. By 1813 the Commissioners were able to report that the unfinished road was already in use for conveyance of mail; but six more years were to pass before it was complete. Two successive road contractors on the stretch from Dingwall to Achnasheen had failed, while on the western section to Strome Ferry, competing claims for routes north or south of Loch Carron had brought further delay. Not till 1819, ten years after the start of the work, was the road completed following the north side of the Loch and so

---

* Post 40/510/1809. Collection of the Skye revenue seems to have been not without its difficulties, for in 1814 the Postmaster General had to resort to a summons against Macleod of Macleod for payment of arrears in respect of the Dunvegan office. (Dunvegan Muniments, Box 35.)

by means of the ferry at Strome, on to the Kyle of Lochalsh.[29]
With the completion of the new road to Skye came new life and
unaccustomed activity. 'When our ferrymen were loitering on
the South side', wrote Lord Cockburn of the Strome Ferry
crossing about 1820, 'it was curious to hear them agitated to
activity by the mail horn on the other. I had forgot in these
solitudes that there was a post.'[30] Five years later the Skye post
graduated from runners to riders. In the summer of 1825
Reeves, the surveyor, writing from Broadford, sent to Freeling
plans for a horse post three days a week between Dingwall and
Skye. The rate of pay to the contractors was to be £3 per annum
for each mile of road as far as Strome, with a higher rate for the
steep section on to Kyle of Lochalsh, and the post was to travel
at six and a half miles an hour. By now the postal revenue on
the Skye route had risen to nearly £1,000 per annum, and as
Lewis and the southern part of the Long Island would also
benefit from the improved service it was clearly and fully
justified. The postal needs of the people of Skye, so long neglected, were now being closely watched, and in 1833 Reeves
put forward further plans for improvement. Despite the completion of the new road from Dingwall to Kyle of Lochalsh
there was, as yet, no public conveyance or public carrier and
only the horse post passed three times a week, 'passing only 3
or 4 houses in 56 miles'. Reeves now proposed that the horse
post should be replaced by a gig to carry passengers and parcels.
A two-wheeled gig would be exempt from toll on any part of
the road which might be Turnpike and the contractor might
be able to give a service on four days a week. Freeling, however,
turned the suggestion down, since the security rules of the
Post Office did not allow passengers to be carried with the
mail.*

On the Island itself the years were bringing further improvement, not only on the main postal route from Kyleakin to
Portree and Dunvegan, but on local and connecting services as
well. Gone were the days when the post office surveyor must own
that neither he nor anyone in the Edinburgh office had ever
been to Skye. Charles Reeves, who had taken over much of the
surveying work in the West of Scotland, now paid regular

---

* Post 40/641/1833. It seems that this rule applied to gigs with a single driver.
A limited number of passengers were regularly carried on mail coaches which had
both a driver and a guard.

visits, and even Freeling and the Postmaster General in London were, at least on paper, becoming familiar with the Island and its postal problems. In 1823 the Post Office agreed to contribute £5 a year towards the cost of a runner three days a week between the parishes of Kilmuir and Snizort in the far north-west and Portree, the balance to be made up locally. When in 1829 this dual control was causing the trouble which might have been expected, a penny post service from Portree was agreed, extending 20 miles into the district of Trotternish.[31] At the south end of the Island the postal arrangements had long been primitive. No official post service existed south of Broadford, and for many years past the only means of conveying letters to and from the district of Sleat had been by private letter-carrier maintained at the expense of the local people, who carried mail between Armadale and Broadford at a charge of 2d per letter. Four years after the establishment of the penny post at Trotternish a similar service was established between Armadale and Broadford, with a receiving house for letters at Isle Ornsay on the Sound of Sleat.[32]

In the transformation which had taken place in the Skye posts during the past two decades the making of the new roads both on the mainland and on the Island had played a vital part – a part which did not go unnoticed or unacknowledged. 'The communication of our letters and newspapers by the Mail', wrote a resident in Portree in 1828, 'is very different now to what it was about 20 years ago. Previous to the completion of the roads we had first only one and afterwards two Mails a week, and these were only carried on runners' backs. There was only one runner from Inverness to Janetown and there being no piers or landing places or indeed regular ferry-boats the detention at the ferries must have been occasionally very considerable. We are now very differently situated. We have a regular communication three times a week with Dingwall with a change of horses at different stations to the ferry of Kyle-Laken. And as an instance of the facility of communication I receive a London Sunday newspaper regularly here (Portree) every Thursday, which must appear to a stranger almost incredible and which, of course, is solely attributable to the Roads made under the authority of the Parliamentary Commissioners.'[33]

The steady improvement in the post to Skye had not been without its effect on the postal service from Dunvegan by boat to Carinish or Lochmaddy in North Uist; but much of the cost still fell on the local people who bore the expense, not only of the packet twice a week across the Minch, but of the conveyance of letters south from Carinish. In 1814 James Shearer, the surveyor, who had been investigating an application by the local people for an increase in the contribution of only £6 per annum which the Post Office paid for the cost of running the Carinish office, recommended that this be raised to £20. The outcome does not appear from the papers. Shearer's advice was by no means always accepted at the Post Office Headquarters in London, but the Carinish revenue had grown to £100 per annum. This in Freeling's mind would at least be a powerful argument and it may well be that some increase was granted. For the next twenty years and more no further development in the post to the Outer Isles seems to have taken place. As late as 1842 the writer of the account of the parish of North Uist in the *New Statistical Account* recorded that the 60-ton packet which crossed twice a week from Carinish to Dunvegan was supported by an assessment which bore heavily on all the local inhabitants. A small sum only was allowed by the Post Office, so it is doubtful to what extent Shearer's recommendation in 1814 had been acted on. None the less the service seemed to be giving satisfaction, for the writer of the *Account* refers to letters and papers being received from Edinburgh in the short time of four days.[34] Within the Long Island itself the letter service to the south of Carinish across the fords and the ferries to Benbecula, South Uist and Barra continued to be arranged and paid for by local enterprise, but in 1834 Mr Stevenson the lighthouse engineer offered on behalf of his Board to share the expense of a regular postal service to Barra, where a lighthouse at Barra Head had lately been built, supplementing the boat which sailed to Tobermory once a month on behalf of the Board. The Post Office agreed to the plan, a runner going at post office expense twice a week from Carinish to the Sound of Barra, the Board paying the cost on to Barra Head.[35]

The difficulty which has been found in fixing the exact date of the establishment of postal services to Lewis and Skye recurs in the case of Mull and the adjacent Islands of Coll and Tiree. Throughout the 18th century when postal services on the mainland of Scotland were slowly extending from Edinburgh, and later from Glasgow, the greater part of Mull, the whole of

Tiree and part of Coll formed part of the great Argyll estates. So when in the last quarter of the century postal services first reached the three islands, their growth was closely linked with the work of estate development carried out by John, the fifth duke, which in continuance of the great work of his predecessors had already made Inveraray the central point of the Western Highlands. Until well past the middle of the century Mull and the Islands had suffered from extreme isolation. In 1768/9 James Turnbull, the Land Surveyor, took five weeks on the return journey between Edinburgh and Tiree, and for at least the next fifteen years slowness of communication was to add greatly to the difficulties of estate management.[36]

In 1786 the 'British Society for extending the Fisheries and Improving the Sea Coasts of the Kingdom', commonly known as the British Fisheries Society, had been founded with the fifth duke as its Governor, and three years later the society established a fishing station and village at Tobermory on the north-east coast of Mull. Like so many of the society's activities the development of the settlement at Tobermory was to fall far short of expectations, but in the early years prospects seemed bright. In October 1789 James Ferrier, w.s., the Duke's Receiver General and agent in Edinburgh, sent to James Maxwell, the Argyll Estate chamberlain in Mull, directions from the Duke on a number of matters relating to the management of the Mull estates. These included plans for a post office at Tobermory. 'As soon as any of the Customs House Officers are settled at Tobermory,' wrote Ferrier, 'you may draw up and get signed by them and the settlers and gentlemen in the neighbourhood a Memorial stating the necessity and propriety of having a Post Office at that place and send it to me and I will correspond with Lord Frederick Campbell [Lord Clerk Register and brother to the fifth Duke] about it.'[37] Shortly before the start of the Tobermory Settlement a post office had been established at Aros on the Sound of Mull with a post once a week from Oban. It seems that there had been doubt whether a post office in Mull would prove profitable, but in the Petition which Maxwell subsequently prepared for the Postmaster General asking for a post office at Tobermory and a post three days a week, it was claimed that the postal revenue since 1786 had shown a steady increase with an average net return of over £53 per annum, and prospects of further increases from the new settlement.

The Petition appears to have been successful, for in 1806 an application for an increase in the salary of the postmaster at Tobermory refers to 'the Post Office lately established at Tobermory' with a gross revenue for the past year of £71.9.9d. Though an increase in salary was refused to the postmaster it is clear that Mull's postal services were in fact growing. In support of the application the secretary of the British Fisheries Society had written that besides mails for his own district there were also mails to be made up for Coll and Tiree, and accounts to be kept for the offices in these Islands. At the western end of the Ross of Mull, too, a receiving house had been set up at Bunessan, with a runner paid by the local people to carry letters between it and the post offices at Aros and Achnacraig at the south-east corner of the Island. In the accounts of the Argyll estates in Mull for 1804/5 James Maxwell, the chamberlain, has recorded the payment of £4 'to assist the expense of a runner betwixt the Post Office of Achnacraig and Bunessan paid at Mr Ferrier's desire' and similar entries appear in the accounts for the next three years. The entry for 1806/7 refers to carriage of letters 'betwixt the Post Offices of Achnacraig and Bunessan', though it seems doubtful whether at this date the office at Bunessan was more than a receiving house.

While the postal service to Mull was thus gradually being put on a regular footing, the Duke of Argyll was also turning his attention to the needs of Coll and Tiree. The Islands, with a total population which a quarter of a century later was estimated at 5000/7000, exported whisky, grain and flax, but no regular communication had so far existed between them and Mull or the mainland. 'Consider', wrote the Duke in October 1801 to Malcolm McLaurine, chamberlain of Tiree, 'of establishing a regular Packet between Clyde and Tiree. I will willingly be at some expense supporting it and perhaps something may be got from the Post Office.'* A few months later McLaurine was able to report that a small packet to carry letters and passengers once a week had been established between 'Croig or Pollach' on the north coast of Mull and Tiree, and the Post Office was approached for support.[38] In a Petition signed by James Ferrier on behalf of the landowners and people

---

* This would appear to be undoubtedly a reference to a proposed service between Tiree and the Firth of Clyde, an ambitious project support for which from the Post Office was highly improbable.

of Tiree the petitioners asked that the Post Office should pay the salary of the postmaster at Scarinish, a request which was granted. The amount of the contribution made by the Post Office does not appear, but in view of the scale of salaries then considered appropriate for postmasters in the Islands it is hardly surprising that it proved inadequate. In October 1803 the duke wrote to the Tiree chamberlain: 'It was your fault that Government allowed so little for the Post Office. You insisted that it would be sufficient and it will now be difficult to get an addition; but it may be tried.' How far the blame lay with McLaurine rather than with the parsimony of Freeling may be doubted, but it seems that the outcome was in the event reasonably satisfactory for a few months later the chamberlain was able to report, 'The allowance for a runner along with the Postmaster's salary is a good object to our Post Office.'[39]

Though no direct references to it appears in the contemporary correspondence over the Mull Posts, an additional burden appears about this time to have been placed on the Postmasters either at Tobermory or at Aros. Despite the extension of the postal service across Corran Ferry to Strontian in the early years of the 19th century, the postal needs of the Morvern coast on the Sound of Mull were served three times a week by ferry from the Island. In the autumn of 1824 Freeling had before him an application for a more frequent service, when it transpired that since the introduction of steamboats on the west coast the passenger traffic between Mull and Morvern, on which the ferry largely depended, had become negligible.[40]

For some years to come no great change seems to have taken place in the post of Mull and to the adjacent islands, though in 1814 the two runners who carried the mail between Mull and the mainland had applied for increased pay, partly in view of the cost of the ferries from Oban to Kerrera and from there to Achnacraig. Shortly before 1830, penny posts which were about this time being started in Skye were successfully introduced in Mull, first between Aros and Bunessan with a local guarantee subsequently dispensed with, and rather later in the district west of Tobermory where the post runner was to take the mails three times a week delivering 'at the houses of the gentry'. About the same time a direct mail boat once a week between Tobermory, Coll and Tiree, proposed by McLean of Coll and Colonel Campbell of Knock, factor for the Duke of

Argyll, got post office approval and an annual grant of £15, and in 1833 this service was put on an official Penny Post basis, with a post office contribution of £10 per annum.

Postal communications for the islands of Jura and Islay appear to have lagged some way behind their development in Mull, Skye and the Outer Isles. The exact date on which a postal service to Islay first came into being does not appear from the contemporary records available, though in 1760 one of the duties of the ill-paid postmaster at Inveraray was the dispatch once a week of a bag to Islay and one authority refers to a post office having been established 'in the Sound of Ila' as early as 1767.[41] Francis Ronaldson in his Journal for 1799 recorded a journey in the West of Scotland between 15 and 25 August in which the following passage occurs: 'Proceeded from Rothesay by Tarbert to Bowmore in the Island of Islay regulating the packet boat and Post to that Island by establishing the office at Port Askaig and Instructing a new Deputy Postmaster....' In December 1804 Freeling was in correspondence with the Postmaster General as to a successor for the postmaster at Port Askaig who had recently been dismissed. At that time Mr Trotter, the Deputy Postmaster General in Edinburgh, referred to Port Askaig as having been for five or six years past the main post office for the Island, mails being landed there as the most convenient point and from there taken on to Bowmore in the south or across the Sound to Jura. This appears to have been the main, and probably the only, postal route till July 1812 when Francis Ronaldson in the course of a two weeks' journey in Argyllshire was able to report the establishment of a new postal route from Lochgilphead by Crinan to Keills on the Sound of Jura and so across the Sound to Jura and on to Islay.[42] At that time the only postal link between Lochgilphead, Edinburgh and Glasgow was by Inveraray, but three years later Freeling agreed to a request by Lord Breadalbane, Campbell of Melfort, Campbell of Jura and other local landowners for authority to convey mail through Lochgilphead to Oban, thus forging a second link with Central and Eastern Scotland. The Post Office agreed to bear the expense of receiving houses at Kintraw on Loch Craignish and at Clachan in North Kintyre, the local landowners meeting the cost of the runners until such time as the Post Office took over the service.[43]

In the Islands themselves the expense of the two runners who conveyed the mail between Lagg in Jura and Bowmore in Islay was for some years met partly by the Post Office and partly by the local people. As in the case of the service to Snizort and Trotternish in Skye this arrangement proved unsatisfactory. In the autumn of 1825 Charles Reeves had been in the Islands and with the surveyor's report before him Freeling wrote to the Postmaster General that the local people 'occasionally assume the control and make the posts subservient to individual rather than public accommodation'. The postal revenue of Islay alone had, by this time, grown to £260 per annum and the Secretary advised that in future the Post Office should pay the whole cost of the Islay runners.[44] A few years earlier a post office had been started on an experimental basis at Bowmore. This, with the older office at Port Askaig, had proved successful and in the last weeks of 1821 Freeling agreed, on the recommendation of the surveyor, that they be made permanent for the benefit of the people 'in this remote corner of the King's Dominions' who carried on a considerable trade in cattle, grain and malt.[45] By 1833, though Islay was getting three posts a week 'by way of the Ferries' – by Keills to Jura and so across to Port Askaig – a steamboat running once a week from Glasgow carried many letters which paid no postage. In view of this it was decided to make a virtue of necessity and send one post each week by boat as well as the three by runner. In the same year a free delivery of letters was given in Bowmore and this, with the four posts a week, may have gone far to make this corner of the king's dominions seem less remote.[46]

So from Shetland to Islay the Island posts had in the course of some seventy-five years grown from the most rudimentary beginnings till by the end of the third decade of the 19th century, though still far from perfect, they had achieved the status of a regular and reliable public service. Development had been beset with difficulties, human and geographical. Progress had in the early years been slow. For the Western Isles at least a quickened rate of advance had come after 1803 as more thought and more money came to be given to Highland development, while better roads on the mainland and in the Islands alike, brought a changing picture with the passing years. By the end of the first quarter of the century, too, the steamboat was emerging, first as a competitor and then as an essential ally of the old foot and horse posts, while the Penny Post, first designed

for the cities and their surroundings, was playing a growing part
in bringing the post to the furthest rural areas.

REFERENCES

1. S.R.O. GD. 51/5/562: Caledonian Mercury, 28 February 1763.
2. Post 40/74c/1793.
3. S.R.O. GD. 51/5/562.
4. Ibid.
5. Post 40/67m/1796.
6. Hyde, op. cit., 71.
7. Post 40/269/1812.
8. Ibid./77t/1804.
9. Ibid./164/1828.
10. 'St. Martin's Letter bag', *St Martin's-le-Grand Magazine*, 456.
11. S.R.O. GD. 46/13/99(5).
12. Ibid., (6).
13. Ibid., (7).
14. Ibid., (8).
15. Ibid., (9).
16. A boll of meal contains 140 lbs.
17. S.R.O. GD. 46/13/99 (4, 20-38) *passim*.
18. Post 40/193/1821.
19. Ibid./410/1825.
20. Quoted by Haldane, *New Ways through the Glens*, 140.
21. Noble, *Miscellanea Invernessiana*, 1902, 56.
22. S.R.O. GD 46/13/99 (7).
23. Ibid., (8).
24. Post 40/80.1/1802. See Appendix III.
25. G.P.O., Palmer's Papers. Miscellaneous Papers, 1775/92 (Part III), No. 15.
26. Post 40/80.1/1802. See Appendix V.
27. Ibid./54y/1799.
28. Ibid./80.1/1802.
29. Haldane, *New Ways through the Glens*, ch. 7.
30. Cockburn, *Circuit Journeys*.
31. Post 40/506/1829.
32. Ibid./640/1833.
33. H.R. & B. Appendix to 9th Report.
34. *N.S.A.*, XIV, 178.
35. Post 40/853/1834.
36. *Argyll Estate Instructions, 1771/1805*. Cregeen, Scott. Hist. Soc., Introduction.
37. Ibid., 159.
38. Ibid., 57 and 62.
39. Ibid., 77 and 82.
40. Post 40/557/1824.
41. Walker, *Economical History of the Hebrides*, 11, 338.
42. N.L.S., Ronaldson, 15/31 July 1812.
43. Post 40/29/1815.

44. Post 40/578/1825.
45. Ibid./413/1821.
46. Ibid./631 and 633/1833.

Nine

The Postal Budget – Credits and Debits

★

The earliest posts both in England and in Scotland were, as has been seen, almost entirely for the use and convenience of the crown or the state. Till the early years of the 17th century the system of posts set up in England for the transmission of official despatches was maintained almost solely at the expense of the crown. Such limited and closely scrutinized public use of this posting system as was tolerated brought no direct contribution to the cost, but only small and uncertain hiring profits to those who kept horses for crown use on the few established postal routes. At the time of the Union in 1603 the annual cost to the crown of the maintenance of the posts was steadily mounting. Increasing use was by now being made by the public of hiring facilities, but postmasters appointed by the crown were complaining of abuse of these facilities resulting in damage to horses and unpaid hiring charges, and often, too, of delay in payment of their own salaries. By 1609 it was estimated that a net annual loss of some £ 3400 was being incurred in the upkeep of a service often unsatisfactory to the crown and of little real use to the public.[1] A proclamation in the first year of the reign of James I of England had sought to limit the use of the posting service to those who could show that they were genuinely engaged on public business, while giving postmasters the exclusive right of letting horses for use by travellers. Six years later a further order prohibited anyone not authorized by the crown from taking any part in the collection, carriage or delivery of letters. While this monopoly of letter-carrying had all the appearance of an attempt on the part of the crown to reserve to itself the profits from a true postal service, its real object was in fact to put into the hands of the state a means of detecting and defeating conspiracies against itself. A postal service open to the public was still regarded as highly dangerous, while as a source of profit it seems hardlys a yet to have been considered.

Though the introduction in the early years of the 17th century of the crown monopoly of letter carriage was at the time intended and looked on as a police rather than a fiscal measure, it came in the years ahead, to have an important, if unintentional, result. Horse hiring on the roads of England, whether for travel or for transmission of news, had thus come in theory and at least largely in practice to rest in one hand — the hand of the state — a development which now for the first time made possible a real organization of the posting service. The word 'post', hitherto implying little more than travel from place to place, was at length coming to bear something of the meaning which we now attach to it, and when in 1635 Thomas Witherings, as Master of the Posts in England, got royal approval of his plan to organize the posts and to levy fixed charges for carriage of messages, a great step towards a true postal service in these Islands had been taken.

During the early years of the Commonwealth the idea of postal revenue went little further than the mere relief of the state from loss on the system, but the vision of actual profit was growing clearer as the years passed. In 1644 when Edmund Prideaux became Master of the Posts, a condition of his appointment was that he was to relieve the state of the whole financial burden of the posts retaining any surplus; but soon he was being asked for an annual rent of £5000 for his office, and with its payment the revenue of the Post Office had for the first time come into being. By 1653 the office of Master of the Posts was being put up for auction and the rent paid by the successful bidder had risen to £10,000.[2] At the Restoration this had grown to £21,500, thereafter growing by successive and rapid stages, and by the end of the 17th century the net income of the Post Office from all sources had risen to about £150,000.[3]

In Scotland, prior to the Union of 1603, certain of the larger towns like Edinburgh, Glasgow, Aberdeen and Dumfries had private messengers, but apart from this there were virtually no arrangements either for the carriage of messages or for the service of travellers, and even for royal despatches there were no regular facilities such as those which had grown up in England under Henry VIII and Elizabeth. After the Union a separate Scottish postal service with separate revenue and under the control of a Postmaster General for Scotland came into existence and remained in being for over a century, though part of the Great North Road which ran between Berwick and Edinburgh was long maintained from London as an extension of the postal route to the North. Shortly after the Restoration the Scottish parliament fixed postal charges within Scotland, but the extent of the revenue earned by the Scottish post office during the greater part of the 17th century can be little more than a matter of conjecture. That it was not great seems certain, for in the latter years of the century successive Postmasters General received a salary as well as any surplus they could make after meeting the cost of maintaining the service, and as has been seen at least one found even this a bad bargain. In 1689 the office of Postmaster General for Scotland was, for the first time, put up to auction and by the beginning of the 18th century the rent fixed by this method had risen to £1194 sterling.[4] The last provision of the Scots parliament with relation to the Post Office in Scotland was the Act of 1695 which gave to the Postmaster General for Scotland a monopoly of letter-carrying, and fixed postal rates. The charge for hiring post horses was then fixed at 3/– (s) a mile, but this was retained by the postmasters at each post and was not truly part of postal revenue.[5]

The establishment of letter-carrying as a royal monopoly in the early years of the 17th century had opened the way for the organization of the post as a public service and the collection of revenue on the basis of fixed postal charges. The institution in 1711 of a combined post office for England and Scotland marked a further step in the same direction, while with the organization of Cross posts, in England at least, some progress was being made towards adapting the postal service to the growing needs of the times.

[197]

The Act of 1711 and the adoption by the Post Office of corrected measurements of distances based on Ogilby's Survey and the standard mile of 1760 yards, had meant both in England and in Scotland greatly increased postal charges, while with regular and statutory weekly contributions to the Treasury, the Post Office for the first time had come to be looked on as an instrument of taxation. Ralph Allen's work between 1720 and 1764 in devising a widespread system of Cross posts between the main postal routes of England, went far to remove the long-standing grievance that the routing of all letters through London led to needless delay and expense. The new Cross posts legalized much cross-country postal traffic hitherto carried by unofficial methods, and diverted to the Post Office no small amount of revenue which had up till now found its way into the pockets of common carriers or private messengers; but the higher postal rates increased the temptation to use unofficial methods, for which ample opportunity still existed, and the first post office surveyors appointed in 1715 faced a formidable task in their efforts to check this.

The growing postal revenue which fell to the crown or the state during the second half of the 17th century from the monopoly of letter-carrying had been used for a wide variety of purposes, and only partially for the improvement of the service to the public. This short-sighted policy was to continue for many years to come. With the notable exception of Allen's work, the first three-quarters of the 18th century saw equally little attempt to keep pace with the increasing postal needs of the country, and it was not until 1784 that the adoption of Palmer's plan for using coaches for transit of mail brought a further great development in the postal service. Palmer's mail coach plans were based on a real conviction that by this method the speed, the security and the general efficiency of the postal service could be vastly improved. His belief in the new project was to be most fully justified, but it is doubtful whether in the face of the extreme conservatism of post office officials, he could have won such speedy approval for it had he not been able to reinforce his arguments with the prospect of increased postal revenue. The revenue of the Post Office, originally a crown prerogative, had been partially given up by the crown in 1711, and in 1764 had been surrendered to the public in its entirety in exchange for a Civil List grant. Pitt, who had become Chancellor of the Exchequer in 1782, faced with a national debt higher than ever before, was seeking for revenue from every source. A proposed tax on coal had to be dropped in the face of great popular outcry, and the prospect of a rise in postal rates which would enable the Post Office to increase the weekly contribution to the Treasury was a compelling argument in favour of Palmer's plan. Pitt approved the plan. Postal charges both in England and Scotland rose steadily. A letter between London and Edinburgh now cost 7d. In Scotland the charge for single letters up to 50 miles rose to 3d, between 50 and 80 miles to 4d, between 80 and 150 miles to 5d and over 150 miles to 6d, while the weekly contributions made by the Post Office of the United Kingdom to the Treasury was now raised from £700 to £2300.[6]

The rise in postal rates and fixed contributions to the Treasury which had been provided for by the Act of 1711 had the avowed purpose of helping Great Britain to continue to finance the costly war on the Continent. The increase in both charges and contributions which now helped to solve Pitt's problems at the Exchequer was followed by a series of further rises, each reflecting the military, political and fiscal problems of the times. In the years immediately following the outbreak of war with France the rapid expansion of the armed forces had thrown a massive burden on the finances of the country. A ship of the line cost £10,000 to build, and by 1795 the fleet had one hundred of these besides thousands of smaller craft, while nearly half a million fighting men had to be fed and equipped all over the world. To finance this huge outlay meant borrowing on an unprecedented scale, and within a few years Pitt doubled the national debt. To help to meet the needs of the Treasury, the revenue of the Post Office was again called on, and the year 1797 saw a further rise in postal rates for all stages, increasing the cost of a letter from London to Edinburgh to 8d; but even this was little more than the beginning of a progressive rise which was to continue almost up to the end of the Napoleonic wars. Pitt's resignation in 1801 brought no halt to the rise in postal rates, or in the general cost of living throughout the country. In a year which saw grave shortages of food, wheat prices higher than ever before and near-starvation among the poorer classes, letter rates for all the larger distances were again raised. A letter from London to Edinburgh now cost 11d, and mileage marking was now used on letters to assist in the exact calculation of the postage charge.

Four years later, with the ailing Pitt back in office and the fortunes of the war in Europe hanging in the balance, postal rates rose still further. Finally in 1812 Nicholas Vansittart, then Chancellor of an almost exhausted and bankrupt Exchequer, called on the Post Office for an annual contribution of £200,000. In the hope of increasing its revenue, postal rates were once again raised. With the letter charge between London and Edinburgh now 1/1½d and as much as 1/5½d for the longest postal routes in the country, postal rates rose to the highest points ever reached in the history of the British Post Office.[7]

In pursuing the policy of raising postal charges and using postal revenue for Treasury purposes, Pitt, Addington, Vansittart and their successors had found a ready ally at the Post Office. Francis Freeling, able administrator and loyal public servant as he proved himself, appears to have been almost throughout obsessed with the idea of increasing postal revenue. To this was due, at least in part, the reluctance with which, during his long service as Secretary to the Post Office, increases in salaries and expenditure of all kinds were conceded and, no less, the avidity with which the monopoly of the Post Office was defended. Despite the almost penal levels to which postal rates rose in the late 18th and early 19th centuries, and the consequent and continuous losses caused by illegal carriage, franking and abuses of all kinds, postal revenue rose steadily, though in the years immediately preceding the introduction of uniform Penny Post in 1840, net revenue was showing an actual decline, all the more marked in view of the rise in population. To attempt to quote a large number of detailed figures over a long period would be wearisome and possibly misleading, for while some authorities quote net figures, others quote gross returns; but the trend is reasonably clear. In England between 1650 and 1680, when the post office revenue consisted solely of rental paid by those who worked or 'farmed' the post, this rose from £5000 to £43,000. At the time of the Revolution of 1688 the total receipts of the Post Office had grown to approximately £90,000 and in the early years of the 18th century the total revenue in England had risen to well over £150,000. The middle years of the century showed a gradual but steady increase till 1784, when the introduction of mail coaches and higher postal charges brought a sharp rise, the net income rising to almost £480,000 in 1796. Thereafter the rise continued steeply to over

£1,000,000 in 1806, and over £1,500,000 in 1815.[8]

Of Scotland's contribution to the United Kingdom total it is hardly possible to write with anything approaching certainty, at least before the second half of the 18th century. Here too the figures available seem sometimes to be gross totals and sometimes net, while some sources refer to postal receipts at Edinburgh, leaving the reader in doubt as to whether these referred to Edinburgh alone or more probably to the revenue from Scotland as a whole collected through Edinburgh. Scottish revenue for 1754 is reliably reported as £8927,[9] while the total collected at Edinburgh towards the end of the century is quoted in the *New Statistical Account* as having risen to £40,000. About this period official figures showing the net revenue become for the first time available and these show steady growth to £35,879 in 1784/5, just before the introduction of mail coaches, £55,334 in 1792/3 and £92,871 in the last year of the century.[10]

A few figures for the towns outside Edinburgh and Glasgow in the 18th century are given in the first *Statistical Account*. Here again no indication as to the basis of calculation appears, but such as they are the figures give some indication of the trend of postal earnings and the spread of postal services. In Argyllshire, the Campbeltown office, no doubt benefiting partly from the postal needs of the Argyll estates, but even more from the town's important trade connections with the American colonies, and constant visits of the west coast herring fleet, showed a revenue of £250 per annum.[11] In Central Scotland Dunfermline returned a total of over £400.[12] The Dunkeld office had a revenue of £138 in 1786 and £279 in 1798,[13] while in the north-east Banff, despite the loss by illegal carriage complained of by Freeling, in 1792 had a revenue of £800.[14] In the extreme north, Thurso in 1796 brought in a net sum of £221.[15] In 1793 Kerr, the Secretary of the Scottish Post Office, sent on to Freeling applications by a number of postmasters for increases in salary based in each case on the gross revenue of the office. Oban's revenue was stated at £200, that of Fort William and Inveraray at £107 and £450 respectively. From the smaller offices came figures of £63 from Appin and £39 from Bonawe, £120 from Auchnacraig in Mull and £47 from New Galloway.[16]

With the publication of the *New Statistical Account* (1842) a host of figures became available for various dates mostly in the first quarter of the 19th century. Of the larger centres Aberdeen claimed revenue of over £9500,[17] Perth £4000[18] and Dumfries £2500.[19] Of the smaller towns Hawick showed a revenue of £1000,[20] Wick £1200[21] and Crieff £740.[22] The Islands too were now adding a quota not to be despised. By 1824 the revenue from Skye had risen to £1000 though this probably included letters from the Long Island and certain inland places on the long route from Skye to Dingwall. Islay about the same time returned a figure of £260 and Stornoway £330.[23]

The increasing calls of the Treasury on postal revenue during the 18th and early 19th centuries necessarily resulted in growing pressure on postmasters throughout Scotland and on those in Edinburgh responsible for the remittance to London of postal revenue collected by the local offices. The Act of 1711 had called for a weekly contribution of £700 from the Post Office. When James Anderson held the office of Deputy Postmaster General in Scotland in 1715 many of the troubles experienced by him came from difficulty in meeting the urgent calls for money from the South. 'His Majesty having been graciously pleased to appoint us his Post Master General', wrote Lord Cornwallis and James Craggs to each postmaster in March 1714, 'you are to remit to us the profits of the letters of your stage in good bills or money and to transmit such accounts as you shall judge may be for the service of His Majesty and the advantage of this Office.'[24] But it was one thing to ask for money and accounts from local postmasters and quite another to get them, and Anderson's Letters are eloquent of the difficulties. No record of the amount or regularity of the contributions made by the Edinburgh post office to the General Post Office in London during the greater part of the 18th century has come to light, but there is little reason to doubt that the troubles which afflicted James Anderson in his short tenure of office from 1715 were fully shared by his successors. The first available figures showing the amount of the remittances to London from Edinburgh are for the period between 1780 and the end of the 18th century. In 1780/81 a total of £20,000 was remitted to the Receiver General in London in respect of postal revenue from Scotland. Five years later this had grown to £29,000 and in the year 1795/6 the total was close on £49,000, while for the whole period 1780/1800 a total of £788,000 was remitted from Scotland to London.[25] A settlement of accounts was called for each quarter, but where possible weekly remittances were made, to correspond with the weekly contributions due by the Post Office to the Treasury. From 1790 the hand of Francis Freeling, that watchful guardian of postal revenue, becomes increasingly apparent. Many local postmasters were in arrear with their payments, and in the summer of that year quarterly returns of these arrears were called for, with reports on the adequacy of the guarantors. The tone of the Minutes passing between London and Edinburgh grows more peremptory, and from this even senior officers are not exempt. In the spring of 1792 Freeling protested to Robert Oliphant, then Postmaster General for Scotland, of the retention by him of £1000 from quarterly remittances to London of £8000, presumably to meet contingencies. This, writes Freeling, must be paid forthwith otherwise the post office Solicitor will be instructed to proceed against the Edinburgh officers.[26] A further rise in postal rates in 1801 had reflected the growing strain on the Treasury. This in turn showed itself in increasing pressure for remittances to the South, and the records of 1803/5 contain frequent references to the use by the Edinburgh office of bills of the Bank of Scotland, the Royal Bank, and Sir William Forbes & Company drawn on Messrs. Coutts at forty days, for the remittance of money.[27] By now the revenue from the ordinary postal service was being supplemented by revenue from the growing volume of 'by'-letter traffic. This traffic, between adjacent or near-by offices, had for long proved almost impossible to control, and for a time much of this revenue was lost to the Post Office. The appointment of surveyors in England and at last in Scotland* had gone some way to check this loss of revenue, and by the beginning of the 19th century the income from this source was becoming substantial. For the third quarter of 1802 it reached over £9000, though Ronaldson reported that a falling off in the rate of increase from the corresponding quarter in the previous year had been due to less shipping correspondence following the Peace of Amiens.[28] Soon, too, the Penny Post, first in Edinburgh then in Glasgow and finally in nearly every district in Scotland, was to add its increasing quota to the growing total.

For local offices, both in the towns and especially in the country districts, the growing pressure of the London and Edinburgh offices brought troubles and problems, while the

* See Chapter Ten.

frequent changes of postal rates during the Napoleonic wars added to their difficulties and those of the surveyors. In the summer and autumn of 1795 two long journeys by Ronaldson took him through Perthshire, Inverness-shire, Moray and Aberdeenshire, explaining the new rates and supervising their application. The work involved must have proved extensive, for at the end of 1797 Ronaldson and his colleague Edwards asked for some recognition of their trouble in preparing new rate tables,[29] and in the spring of 1801 Ronaldson was again on the road, this time at Carlisle, looking into a further change in rates and checking distances throughout Scotland. Accurate calculation of mileage was of prime importance to the Post Office, since letters were still charged strictly according to the distance they were carried. This distance might be quite unnecessarily large, for only gradually and unwillingly did the Post Office relax the rule that all letters must be routed through Edinburgh or other central points. The absurdity of letters between Aberfeldy and Killin going round by Perth was too obvious to be ignored and in that case a direct post had been granted in 1809,[30] but till at least the beginning of the second quarter of the 19th century proposed alterations on postal routes which promised greater convenience and better service at the expense of the post office revenue were looked on with a critical eye. As late as 1827 Freeling wrote to the Postmaster General regarding Memorials by the Incorporated Trades of Dundee and Dumfries who had urged that where for the convenience of the Post Office letters were sent circuitously the charge should only be on the direct distance from point to point: 'The principle of charging letters according to the distance they are actually conveyed is recognised by the Act of Parliament and has not in any instance been departed from.'[31]

From postage dues collected by him on incoming letters the postmaster could deduct his own salary and sums paid by him to foot or horse carriers on behalf of the Post Office, besides an allowance for such letters as had been redirected or those dead letters which were not collected. With all this it was small wonder that the arrears accumulated during the ten years to 1820 had grown to over £1000.[32] If there was thus no lack of practical difficulties and accounting problems to be faced by postmasters often ill-fitted by education or perhaps by intellect to deal with them, there was one major problem to which curiously little reference appears. The extensive post office records which from 1792 onwards throw light on so many aspects of postal organization and practice in Scotland, tell almost nothing of the means by which local postmasters remitted to Edinburgh the revenue collected by them. Francis Ronaldson's Journal constantly refers to his work all over his wide district in 'forcing up remittances to Edinburgh', but neither here nor in any other of the many sources is there any substantial reference to the exact method by which these remittances were made. It will be recalled that in the latter part of the 17th century the transmission of funds between Edinburgh and London was a major problem and that when, in the spring of 1715, James Anderson took up his appointment, one of the first communications received by him from the Postmaster General in London was an instruction to remit post office revenue periodically in good bills or money. While Anderson's subsequent papers are full of references to the difficulties which he encountered in keeping his postmasters up to date, nothing appears as to how in fact remittances from them reached Edinburgh. At the end of the 18th century one of the main preoccupations of the Scottish postal surveyors was still to ensure that postal revenue reached Post Office Headquarters, but enquiry into the method of transmission by the local offices seems not to have been an important part of their duty.

In the spring of 1800 Freeling sent to local postmasters a circular containing instructions as to the monthly remittance of revenue. This was to be sent in the form of good bills payable within twenty-one days to the credit of John Mortlock, at that time the Receiver General of the post office revenue, and in addition to the monthly remittances, quarterly returns were called for when any balances in hand were to be accounted for. In Freeling's circular, as in that of 1715, while the emphasis was on the use of bills the alternative possibility of remitting in money appears in the closing paragraph of the instructions. 'In making your remittance to this office it is necessary you should take every precaution recommended to the public so often by advertisements from hence, not to send whole notes when payable to bearer.'[33] The reference to payment to the Receiver General suggests that these instructions were addressed at least primarily to postmasters in England, for Scottish postal revenue went to the Edinburgh office; but there seems little reason to doubt that

Freeling's instructions at least as to the form of remittances were equally applicable to those made within Scotland.

Money in the form of cash was scarce in Scotland in the 18th century. Though the Bank of Scotland had been founded in 1695 and the Royal Bank some thirty years later, it was not till the middle of the century that banking facilities became widely available in the rural districts; but while money was short, credit was long, and promissory notes or bills of exchange were in active circulation. It was by means of promissory notes or cash credits, obtainable with surprising ease from the banks, that the drovers of the 18th and early 19th centuries largely financed their hazardous and speculative trade. Promissory notes appear to have been much used in the fishing and kelp industries, and the construction of Highland roads and bridges by the Parliamentary Commissioners in the early 19th century was largely financed in this way. With the establishment of branch banks in the country towns in the latter part of the 18th century, the obtaining of drafts for remitting money through the post became possible, while soon small banking companies which sprang up all over the country started to compete with one another and with the more stable institutions to put into circulation notes of questionable value.[34]

This over-rapid growth of banks and credit facilities in Scotland, checked though it was by widespread failures about 1772, must have provided for postmasters in or near country towns the ready means of making the frequent remittances for which Edinburgh was constantly pressing; but for many in more remote areas no such facilities were available. It needs small imagination to picture the predicament of an 18th-century postmaster in the Islands or indeed in much of the northern or western Highlands threatened from Edinburgh with dismissal or even legal action for failure to remit money, much of it perhaps owed to him by distant and dilatory landowners, its eventual collection dependent on the whim or the solvency of his debtors or perhaps not least on the intelligence or honesty of illiterate letter-carriers. The money when it reached him would be in small denominations, pennies, sixpences, shillings and only occasional notes, with the ever present risk of bad coins for which no allowance was ever made by his masters at headpuarters. For such a postmaster widely removed from banking facilities, a bill of exchange or a bank draft would be far to seek, while notes, if unobtainable locally, could only be got at some risk by messenger from the nearest town. With all this it is small wonder that postmasters fell into arrears, and that throughout the country many guarantors were finding to their cost that their place and function in the financial organization of the Post Office was no formality. Even in the more highly organized districts of England, remittance of postal revenue was not without its problems. In 1806 Freeling was in correspondence with the postmasters of Bristol and Birmingham on the subject. Banking facilities were readily available to them, but post office regulations required bills payable at twenty-one days' notice. By current banking practice thirty-five to forty days' notice was the normal period allowed for payment of a bill, certain expenses for commission and stamps being charged if a shorter maturity were required. Faced with this expense, the Post Office agreed, if necessary, to accept bills payable at longer dates.[35] In many districts, however, remittance in cash was evidently common. Only a month after his correspondence with Bristol and Birmingham Freeling was writing to the Postmaster General about extra help required at headquarters following on new regulations for more frequent remittance made in the critical year of 1805. In six days between 11 and 17 March 1806 there reached the London post office 425 remittance letters containing 620 bills and 473 bank-notes. Of the bills and notes 627 had, as recommended, been cut in half, enormously increasing the correspondence involved.[36] If these conditions prevailed in London it can fairly be assumed that Edinburgh too had like problems, increased in this case by further accounting with London. As for the smaller towns and villages from which came a growing part of the Scottish postal revenue, difficulty in remittance to Edinburgh may well have contributed in no small degree to the delays in settlement of postage accounts complained of by James Anderson in the early 18th century and by Francis Ronaldson at a later date. As late as 1830 the Commissioners who were enquiring into the revenue of the Scottish Post Office referred to remittances from country offices being made to Edinburgh in the form of cash, bank-notes or bills payable in as little as ten days, though how the latter were arranged in rural districts is not explained.[37] Such problems and difficulties can only increase the degrees of wonder that despite it all the office of postmaster was keenly sought after and eagerly retained.

While the revenue of the Post Office in Scotland was steadily rising from growing postal rates, spreading postal routes and increasing traffic, the expenses of the service were mounting. Much of the rise in cost was the natural consequence of the extension of the service, but part arose from less welcome causes, and in particular from the inflationary conditions brought about by the French wars. Before the Union of the Parliaments, the main objective of post office administration had been to avoid loss rather than to make profit. This limited objective would appear to have been largely achieved and it was only after the Union, and particularly after the merging of the Scottish into the British Post Office in 1711 that the need for, or even the possibility of, constructing a true postal budget arose. The total annual cost of the whole post office establishment in Scotland at that time was believed to have been approximately £1000.[38] With the exception of the postmasters at Cockburnspath and Haddington, Scottish postmasters even at the largest centres received little more than £25. Some appear to have got no fixed salary, being remunerated on the basis of a proportion of the postage collected by them. Of the total cost of the establishment in 1711, the largest single item was the cost of the Edinburgh office. Here the postmaster received £200, the accountant and clerk each £50 and an assistant £25.[39] By the middle of the century the Edinburgh staff had risen to 11 including the three letter-carriers, and to over 30 in 1793 when Robert Oliphant of Rossie was Postmaster General for Scotland with a salary of £321 a year, and William Kerr was getting £100 as Secretary to the Post Office.[40] In Glasgow, by the end of the century, the staff had grown to 9 including four letter-carriers, soon to be still further increased in number with the introduction of the Penny Post to the city. Here the total salary bill was rather under £400 of which the postmaster got £200.*

If the pay of Scotland's postmasters, inadequate from the first, bore little relation to the growing burdens placed on them by the developing service, the foot posts of the country fared no better. The earliest foot posts were little more than messengers

---

* Hyde, op. cit. The rise in establishment expenses during the last two decades of the 18th century may be judged from the fact that in 1780 the Edinburgh salary bill amounted to just over £1800 and in 1800 to nearly £3200. In 1780 the salaries for the country offices, excluding payments for 'by'-letters, was just under £5500 and in 1800 nearly £10,000. (Post 9/87.)

employed mainly by the large towns as and when required, their remuneration of the nature of payments for specific journeys rather than fixed wages or salaries. As correspondence became more frequent a small payment for each letter came to be given, a basis of payment long to be continued for delivery of letters in and around towns or in the country districts, served at his option by the local postmaster. By 1715 when James Anderson was Postmaster General the volume of correspondence had grown to a point where regular foot services were needed on 'the western road of Scotland' and it will be recalled that £40 per annum was paid to runners for a service three days a week between Edinburgh and Glasgow, £32 10/– for a similar post between Glasgow and Ayr, and £43.6.8d for a post twice a week between Ayr and Portpatrick.[41] Herbert Joyce in his *History of the Post Office* states that at about the time of the Post Office Act of 1711, runners between Edinburgh and Aberdeen were paid £60 per annum, between Aberdeen and Inverness £30 and between Inverness and Thurso £18. The payment on the Aberdeen route in particular seems high compared to the wages of foot posts at a later date, but it may well be that out of the £60 the cost of two ferries in either direction would have to be met.[42] In a Memorial about the poor state of the post between Edinburgh and Aberdeen, undated but probably written about the middle of the 18th century, the memorialist referred to the pay of the foot posts for the return journey being as little as 6/8d, eked out by the unofficial carriage of parcels 'without which it seems understood they could not live'.

By the end of the 18th century the rate of payment for foot posts in most parts of Scotland was approaching somewhat nearer to a common standard, though wide variations were still apparent. At this time and for many years to come, surveyors and other postal officials were constantly calling attention to the underpayment of both letter-carriers and postmasters, but postal officials in the South were slow to respond, partly with a view to keeping up the net revenue of the Post Office and partly no doubt from lack of knowledge of the country and of the local conditions. Postal services in the country districts were at this time only slowly developing, and in many of the remote areas the deliveries were still so infrequent that some letter-carriers were paid so much for each journey, though others on a weekly basis, In either case the pay was miserable, though no doubt in those hard times the carriers, like the postmasters, were thankful for even a pittance. In 1798 on the newly established post to Skye the carrier got 5/– for a return trip between Inverness and Dunvegan, though in the following year this seems to have been increased to 7/6d.[43] When in 1829 Alan Macdonald, the foot carrier between Fort William and Glenfinnan, pleaded unsuccessfully for a pension on his retiral after over thirty years' service at the age of 78, his Petition showed that from 1798 to 1821 he had been getting less than 3/6d for a week's work during which he regularly covered eighty miles. Only after twenty-three years' service was this raised to 4/6d.[44] In the same district in 1802 when a postal service to Arisaig was under consideration Ronaldson estimated that the cost of a foot post going twice a week to and from Fort William would be 7/– a week.[45] At the beginning of the century 1/– a journey was paid to a foot post from Lochearnhead to Killin and 2/– from Callander to Lochearnhead,[46] and at about the same time 9/– a week was paid to the foot post who went four days a week between Castle Douglas and New Galloway.[47] In 1805 many of the Argyllshire runners were getting 4/6d to 5/– for a week's work entailing three tramps of twelve to fourteen miles, and in the same year the post boy who was accused of robbing the mail on the road between Dingwall and Tain got 5/– a week, though the distance covered by him was not stated.[48]

In the first years of the 19th century work was scarce in Scotland, particularly in the Highlands, but soon work on the Caledonian Canal was in steady progress, and between 1803 and 1812 the average day's wage of a labourer in the Great Glen rose from 1/6d to nearly 2/6d.[49] Labour, too, was coming to be in demand for the many roads under construction by the Parliamentary Commissioners throughout the Highlands. With competition for labour the general wage level rose, but with it the cost of living, the price of meal rising in these nine years from 20/– to 36/– for a boll of 140 lb. By the end of the first quarter of the century letter-carriers' pay had risen to about double what it was before 1800, though wide and puzzling variations were still apparent. The 9/– week paid in 1823 to the post runner for a twice-weekly tramp between Inveraray and Dalmally, though much less than what could be earned on the heavy road and canal work, was not far short of what was coming to be considered a fair wage for the carrier's job. Many carriers, too, made

extra money, tacitly approved or at least not actively disapproved at headquarters, by carrying parcels and letters collected en route, while some, like the carriers between Poolewe
and Achnasheen, got an allowance of meal. About 1830 Argyllshire carriers in Jura and Islay, in the Kintyre peninsula and in
Mull were earning wages not far short of 10/– a week. In
Central Scotland a carrier's pay in the Stirling area was about
the same, and in that year Charles Reeves, the post office surveyor, giving evidence before a Post Office Commission of Enquiry, stated that carrier's wages varied from 7/– to 14/– a
week.[50]

In Edinburgh, which for many years enjoyed the only free
delivery service in any Scottish town, three carriers were employed at a weekly wage of 5/– each. Williamson in the last
quarter of the 18th century paid 4/6 a week to the carriers employed by him, but his service was a purely private enterprise
and the cost found no place in the post office budget. When in
the last years of the century the Post Office took over Williamson's undertaking as part of an official service, the wage for each
of the ten carriers then employed was soon raised to 12/– a
week.[51] In Glasgow in 1799 the carrier's wage was 10/6d.[52]
For many years Edinburgh, Glasgow and Leith remained the
only Scottish towns to have a free delivery service either for
letters passing through the ordinary mail service or for those
circulating under the Penny Post service. In the other Scottish
towns letters not collected at the Post Office were commonly delivered by the postmaster who made a charge of ½d or 1d a letter
for delivery. This charge paid the cost of the carrier with little or
no surplus, the delivery of these letters thus involving neither a
credit nor a debit entry in the accounts of the Post Office. Early
in the 19th century, however, the legal liability of the Post Office
for the free delivery of letters, at least in towns, came increasingly
to the notice of the public, and in one Scottish town after another
objection was taken to the delivery charge. By 1823 the agitation
for free delivery had grown clamant and widespread, and
Shearer and Reeves were called on to supply lists of the towns in
their district where carriers would soon be needed. The pressure
for free delivery, first started in Greenock, soon spread to
Aberdeen, Perth, Paisley and Dumfries and from them to the
smaller towns. In 1834 Freeling, approving a free delivery in
Dunfermline, noted with satisfaction that there could not now

be many places in Scotland with post offices where charges were still made for delivery,[53] and by 1836 the cost of delivery in towns and villages had become a large and regular item on the debit side of the Post Office budget.

While the cost to the Post Office of conveying mail by foot post was gradually rising a still more serious item was swelling the debit side of the Postal Budget. The mails on the road between Edinburgh and Berwick had from very early days been carried on horseback, but with this exception mails in Scotland were carried by foot post till 1715 when James Anderson introduced the horse post between Edinburgh and Stirling. Soon after, a horse post was established between Edinburgh and Glasgow, but till far on in the 18th century horse posts appear to have been confined to the main postal routes from Edinburgh to Glasgow, Aberdeen and Inverness, the latter being later extended to Thurso. The standard payment for horse posts for long remained 3d a mile and, with these posts employed only on the main routes, the total cost was probably not a major item. But as the 18th century drew to a close, the general rise in prices began to tell its tale, while soon the effects of the Napoleonic wars were making themselves widely apparent. By this time the transport of mails by horse was coming to be largely in the hands of contractors receiving a fixed mileage charge. Early in 1793 Ronaldson, struggling with delays in the mails up the east coast of Fife, had to report failure in getting runners to do the work at the current rates ' ... from the nature of the service (being night duty)', he noted in his Journal, 'increased weight of bags by Newspapers and high price of labour in every part of this country any acceleration appearing impracticable to be obtained by runners, recommended horse-post'. In the autumn of 1791 the surveyor had been forced to pay 4d a mile to the contractor on the road from North Queensferry to Perth, as no one could be found to do the work on better terms.[54] In the spring of 1792 a similar increase had to be given on the roads from Glasgow to Greenock and Dumbarton,[55] and in the following year even Freeling, never lavish with increases of pay, wrote to the Postmaster General that 3d a mile was no longer enough for riding work.[56] The rise in prices was by now making its effect felt all over Scotland, and in November 1796 the mail contractors on the road from Aberdeen to Inverness joined in the general protest against the 3d rate.

'The destruction of horses', they wrote in a Memorial to the Post Office, 'the very increased price of provender the high accounts paid for mail carts, the saddlers, blacksmiths and the additional wages now paid to riders far exceed upon a fair calculation what the Post Office has hitherto allowed for this very necessary branch of the public service.'*

In the last year of the century the surveyor for the North of Scotland wrote:

'It is impossible to obtain any other contractors to ride the mails at 3d out or 1½d per mile each way. On this account we have been so much distressed with mail riders that we have sometimes to submit to the mails being conveyed by mules or such species of horses as were a disgrace to any public service'.57

Transport difficulties seem to have been particularly acute in the north of Scotland where in the first years of the 19th century poor crops added to the problems. Drought in the summer of 1801 had caused a failure of the hay crop and a poor corn harvest. The price of corn in the north had risen to 24/– a boll compared with 16/– round about Edinburgh, and hay was now 1/8d a stone as compared with 8d in a normal season. Good horses were needed to carry the great weight of mail in these wartime days, and the increased demand for cavalry horses for the Army had doubled their price. The calls of the Services, too, were making young riders difficult to find, and in both 1802 and 1803 Shearer the surveyor had been forced to raise the mileage rate to the contractors to 5d and even 6d a mile,58 In the west, Ronaldson was having his problems in maintaining an efficient service to Argyllshire and the Islands in the face of the rising cost of fodder, the ever increasing weight of mail and a general wage rate which by 1807 had risen to 2/6d and even 3/– a day.

The years to come brought, for the Post Office at least, no end to the spiral of inflation, and till long after the end of the French wars wages of postal carriers on foot or on horseback were constantly, if grudgingly, increased and as constantly failing to keep pace with the general rise in costs. New rates for the pony post from Inveraray by Dalmally to Bonawe had been fixed in 1823, but two years later the continuing rise in the price of corn

---

* Post. 40/27M/1796. With the great increase in the weight and bulk of newspapers and official publications at the end of the 18th century the horse post contractors were often forced to use mail carts.

had already put them out of date. Charles Reeves, who had succeeded Ronaldson as Surveyor for the West of Scotland, suggested a moderate increase which Freeling approved. 'Even a Highland pony, the latter conceded, 'must be fed with corn to perform so much work.'[59] In the Kintyre Peninsula, always a difficult and costly postal route, the same pattern was apparent. On the long road from Inveraray to Campbeltown the riders' pay for each of the four stages had already been raised to £40 per annum to enable ponies to be used and the mail to be quickened. In 1826 Reeves was forced to give a further increase to provide better food for the beasts and to raise the speed from 4 to 5 miles per hour.[60] A few years later the cost of taking the mail from Bonawe to Oban had to be nearly doubled to pay for a horse to carry the mail bags which had now grown to 40 and sometimes 50 lb. in weight,[61] while on the road from Arrochar to Inveraray Reeves had been compelled to increase from £84 to £100 per annum the payment to the contractor who had complained of the weight of mail, the price of fodder and the hard road through Glencroe and over the Rest and be Thankful.[62]

The increase in the cost of transporting the mails was not confined to those carried by foot posts or on horseback. Up till 1784 when Palmer introduced his mail coaches the annual allowances to stage coaches carrying mails had in England varied from £4 to £8 a mile depending on the weight of the mail, the coach owners paying the tolls from which the coaches were at that time not exempt. After 1784 the terms on which the mail coach owners conveyed the mails were exemption from tolls and 1d a mile in addition. The toll exemption was a valuable consideration and the new terms were estimated to be the equivalent of an annual payment of £3 a mile. Before many years had passed, however, the mail coach contractors were rueing their bargain, and when in 1797 a duty of 1d a mile was imposed by Act of Parliament on all public carriages including mail coaches matters came to a climax. Now the mail coach contractors found themselves in effect carrying the mails in return for no consideration except the toll exemption. Since mail coaches, unlike stage coaches, were severely limited in the number of passengers they could carry, the margin of profit had almost disappeared. Proposals to alter the construction of mail coaches to accommodate more passengers were rejected by the Post Office and to make matters still worse a bad harvest in the last year of the century caused a big rise in the cost of fodder for horses. The Government refused to concede to mail coaches exemption from the new duty on vehicles, and faced with a threatened breakdown of the whole mail coach system the Post Office was forced to concede to the coach owners first a temporary increase of $\frac{1}{2}$d a mile and finally in 1804 a more permanent increase which brought the cost to an average rate of $2\frac{1}{8}$d a single mile or $4\frac{1}{4}$d a double mile.[63]

So far as Scotland is concerned, it may readily be imagined that the almost total withdrawal in 1813 of the toll exemption hitherto enjoyed by mail coaches led to something not far short of a crisis in mail coach administration. It is true that the number of mail coach routes in Scotland was only a fraction of those operated in England, but none the less the additional cost falling on the Post Office after 1813 was substantial and it is hardly surprising that in Freeling's eyes it constituted an almost intolerable burden. From now on the problem of keeping mail coach payments to a minimum was never far from the minds of Post Office officials both in Edinburgh and London, while for the Scottish surveyors it was a constant worry. In some instances the toll charges appear to have been paid by the contractors, so reinforcing their constant demands for increased mileage charges, but in the majority of cases the payment appears to have fallen directly on the Post Office. The direct result was a reduction of existing mail coach services in Scotland, refusal of nearly all applications for new services and the introduction when possible of two-wheeled gigs exempt from toll. In a few cases the Post Office was able to negotiate favourable terms with Turnpike Trustees, as on the roads between Glasgow and Perth, and Edinburgh and Stirling, but these were exceptional and in most instances the trustees, heavily in debt as most of them were, exacted every penny which could be charged. On the difficult road from Inverness to Thurso, despite the fact that their mail coaches were granted freedom from toll on the new bridges, while the unusually high rate of 6d per mile was allowed to the contractors by the Post Office, the difficulties of maintaining the service were such that, almost from the first, the Treasury was forced to remit the licence duty levied on horse-drawn vehicles together with half and finally the whole of the mileage duty on mail coaches.[64] The big expense of keeping and feeding horses necessarily led to the existence of many small contractors, and this in its turn involved the Post Office in heavy costs for preparing many separate contracts. In an effort to reduce this outlay Freeling in 1828 proposed to resort to printed forms; but even here the scope for economy was limited since the 'testing clause', or details of attestation added after the signing and witnessing of a deed, unknown in English documents, had to be written 'and', as he somewhat sourly observed to the Postmaster General, 'so important is that clause considered in the Law of Scotland that the most trifling error or the slightest deviation in form vitiates the whole Deed. . . .'[65]

The rapid growth of the postal system in Scotland in the late 18th and early 19th centuries brought yet another item of rising cost to the Post Office. Up till then the passage of foot, horse or wheel traffic on main and side roads alike had been interrupted by rivers or arms of the sea which could only be crossed by ferry. After 1803 the work of the Commissioners for Highland Roads and Bridges resulted in the bridging of many of the largest rivers, but in the west of Scotland particularly, there remained lochs and many arms of the sea where ferries alone sustained the traffic. Hitherto the cost of such crossings had been relatively small. In the first half of the 18th century when the post between Edinburgh and Aberdeen was still carried on foot the payment allowed to the carriers for the double journey included an allowance of only 1/6d for the crossings in either direction of the ferries at Queensferry and Dundee, and no doubt crossings of river or loch on such roads in the north and west as had postal services were proportionately small. When the increased cost of a daily post between Aberdeen and Inverness was being calculated in 1792, only £10 per annum was allowed for the crossings of the ferries on the Spey and the Findhorn, and in the autumn of 1802 when a daily post between Dornoch and Wick was under consideration only £5 per annum appears to have been allowed for ferry crossings at Helmsdale and the little ferry over Loch Fleet.[66] But with the more frequent and more dependable services demanded by improving posts, ferries came to play a more vital part – a fact which would not be lost on those who worked them. On the road from Edinburgh to Aberdeen the ferries had from the first been a source of weakness and worry, and as the posts were speeded up so the ferries, here as in other parts of Scotland, came to have still more importance as links in the chain of communication. In December 1793 Ronaldson had been dealing with complaints of delay to the mails at South Queensferry and in the spring of 1796 he had to be present when the boats from the south side of the ferry were let by contract for the season to ensure that the boatmen who offered for them were under obligation to convey the mails. Meantime the boatmen on the north side had combined to demand more pay.[67] The crossing at Queensferry was to be a source of worry to the Post Office for many years to come. In 1826 Freeling considered but rejected a proposal that a survey of the ferries over the Firth of Forth should be undertaken with a view to the possible adoption of a crossing to Kinghorn.[68] A letter at this time from Godby at the Edinburgh office refers to the use of open boats for the Queensferry crossing in view of the cost of steamboats. Some four years later the Kirkcaldy Chamber of Commerce asked that their mail from the South be directed by way of Leith and Newhaven and so across the Forth by steamboat to Pettycur in Fife. This plan, too, was turned down on the grounds that the piers were inadequate, while the route suggested would place the Kirkcaldy mails in the charge of skippers over whom the Post Office would have no control.[69]

On the difficult post road from Inveraray to Fort William ferries were among the many recurrent problems. In 1800 delays at the ferries over Loch Awe, Loch Etive and Loch Creran had led to proposals to use the diversion by Dalmally to cut out the ferry over Loch Awe, while Loch Creran was to be crossed at Creagan in place of the wider and more exposed Shian.[70] Till 1823 the crossings of Loch Etive at Bonawe and Loch Creran cost only 3d a time,[71] but ten years later the Bonawe crossing cost £15 a year for a daily crossing, Creagan Ferry £13 and Ballachulish £18.5/–.[72] Meantime the charge for crossing Loch Linnhe at Corran three times a week had been increased in 1826 from £2.12/– to £7.16/– per annum, and in 1833 when the post service from Corran to Strontian was increased to six days a week the ferry charges at Corran Ferry were increased to £9.2/– per annum.[73] Acceleration of the posts, too, meant in some cases higher charges for crossings out of working hours. On the route to Skye up to 1824 the men on either side of the ferry at Kyleakin had had £3 a year for crossing three times a week.[74] Now quicker posts meant frequent crossings at night, and Freeling approved increases. At Strome, too, where the crossing was often made at night, the charge for a service six days a week was increased in 1826 from £4. 10/– per annum to 6d for each crossing.[75] In the Long Island in 1834 the cost of taking mails from Lochmaddy to the Sound of Barra twice a week included £5 per annum for the crossing of the dangerous North and South fords between North Uist, Benbecula and South Uist.[76] By now 6d a time had come to be recognized as the usual charge for night crossings, though in that year Freeling, with his eyes as always on economy, wrote to the Postmaster General:

> 'It has always been impressed on the District Officers that they are always to obtain the best bargains they can for permanent services, such as private tolls, passage of gates, bridges and ferries, and not to accede to the same rates as are levied on casual passengers where a composition on better terms can be effected.'[77]

So in the two centuries which had elapsed since the establishment of letter carrying as a public service, the annual budget of the Post Office had changed out of all recognition. Till well into the first quarter of the 17th century the entries had been solely on the debit side, the crown bearing an annual loss of several thousands of pounds for the maintenance of a service designed and used virtually for it alone. The postal organization undertaken by Thomas Witherings in 1635, growing public use of the post and increasing insistence on the state monopoly of letter carrying introduced for the first time credit as well as debit entries. Postal revenue made its appearance at first in England and then in Scotland in the form of rent paid by those who 'farmed' the operation of the service and later as direct operational profit earned by the Post Office itself. After 1720 the Cross posts of Ralph Allen increasingly directed into the coffers of the Post Office much revenue hitherto earned by unofficial carriers, while in urban areas and later in rural districts Penny and local posts brought further items into the credit side of the account. With the increase in postal facilities and postal usage came increase in postal charges partly justified by the growth of operating costs, but largely aimed at raising revenue for a needy Exchequer.

On the debit side of the account, many items which in the early days of the service had been absent or of small significance made there first appearance or grew with the passing years. Salaries of postmasters grew both in number and in size, for even the strictest economy of Treasury and postal officials could not ignore the needs of an expanding service and the impact of the general rise in costs. So, too, with the pay of letter carriers, many of whom now required horses to carry an ever increasing load of mail and to meet a constant demand for greater speed in its transport. In cities and towns, too, and soon in villages throughout the land, the cost of delivering letters, for long passed on largely to the recipients, came grudgingly, but at last with growing resignation, to be accepted as a charge payable by the Post Office. With the introduction of mail coaches, contractors who for a time had been content with 3d a mile were soon demanding 4d and more, while after 1813, the ending of the toll exemption in Scotland, so bitterly resented by the Post Office, added to the difficulties and the cost.

Yet, despite the growing costs, Post Office charges rising to their peak in 1812 kept receipts well in excess of expenditure. In 1784 with the introduction of the mail coach the weekly contribution of the Post Office to the Treasury fixed in 1711 at £700 a week had risen to £2300, and by 1812 the Treasury were receiving an annual payment of £200,000 from a Post Office which had long been regarded by the state and accepted by the public as an instrument of taxation as well as a public service.

REFERENCES

1. *The Post Office. An Historical Summary*, GPO, 1911.
2. Howard Robinson, op. cit., 40/1.
3. Howard Robinson, op. cit., 81.
4. Joyce, op. cit., 117.
5. Howard Robinson, op. cit,. ch. VIII.
6. Howard Robinson, op. cit., ch. XI.
7. Howard Robinson, op. cit., ch. XII. Joyce, op. cit., 356.
8. Joyce, op. cit., 341. Howard Robinson, op cit., *passim*.
9. Lang, *Historical Summary of the Post Office in Scotland.*
10. Post 9/7.
11. *O.S.A.*, X, 559.
12. Ibid., XVI, 478.
13. Ibid., XX, 431.
14. Ibid., XX, 358.
15. Ibid., XX, 513.
16. Post 40/117c/1793.
17. *N.S.A.*, XII, 96.
18. Ibid. X(1), 97.
19. *N.S.A.*, IV, 22.

20. *N.S.A.*, III, 407.
21. Ibid., xv, 157.
22. Ibid., x, 516.
23. Ibid., xvi, 136.
24. N.L.S., Anderson's ms, 3.
25. Post 9/7.
26. Post 15/124/1792.
27. Post 15/130, *passim.*
28. Post 40/32L/1802.
29. Post 14/337/1797.
30. Post 14/74P/1809.
31. Post 40/451/1827.
32. *20th Report of Commissioners of Enquiry.* (P.O. Revenue, Scotland), 1830, vol. XIII.
33. Post 40/29A/1806.
34. Haldane, *The Drove Roads of Scotland*, 46/51; *New Ways through the Glens*, 50/51.
35. Post 40/29A/1806.
36. Post 40/50A/1806.
37. *20th Report. Commissioners of Enquiry into Collection of Revenue*, Part III (Scotland), 9.
38. Joyce, op. cit., 118.
39. Hyde, op. cit., 95.
40. Post 40/202C/1793.
41. N.L.S., Anderson ms, 138. See Chapter Two, p. 44.
42. Joyce, op. cit., 118.
43. Post 40/54Y/1799.
44. Ibid./130/1829.
45. Ibid./80.1/1802.
46. Ibid /66B/1800.
47. Ibid./46P/1803.
48. Hyde, op. cit., 19.
49. Haldane, *New Ways through the Glens*, 107.
50. *20th Report of Commissioners of Enquiry* (P.O. Revenue, Scotland). 1830, vol. XIII, 320.
51. Post 40/202C/1793.
52. Hyde, op, cit., 97.
53. Post 40/509/1834.
54. N.L.S., Ronaldson, 25 Sept. 1791.
55. Ibid., 11/22 May 1792.
56. Post 42/232C/1793.
57. Quoted by Hyde, op. cit., 13 et seq.
58. Post 40/49H/1802. Ibid./58P/1803. See Appendix VIII.
59. Ibid./465/1825.
60. Ibid /372/1826.
61. Ibid./802/1832.
62. Post 40/746/1828.
63. Joyce, op. cit., 337 et seq.
64. S.R.O. GD. 51/5/601/1–3; GD. 46/17/57, fol. 334–6.
65. Post 40/411/1828.
66. Post 42/94A/1802.
67. N.L.S., Ronaldson, 8/18 March and 7 May 1796.
68. Post 40/187/1826.

69. Post 40/955/1830.
70. Ibid./66B/1800.
71. Ibid./249/1823.
72. Ibid./416/1833.
73. Ibid./423/1826.
74. Ibid./129/1824.
75. Ibid./81/1826.
76. Ibid./853/1834.
77. Ibid./501/1834.

Ten

Abuses and Evasions of the Post

From the very earliest period in the development of postal services in these Islands up to the beginning of the Victorian era, one of the chief preoccupations of those responsible for postal organization has been the prevention or at least the limitation of practices which have from time to time threatened the security, the efficiency and above all the economy of the post. In the long battle waged between those who sought to defend these aspects of postal services and their opponents the weapons available to each and the degree of success achieved have varied from time to time, but the continuing struggle has throughout played an important part in postal history.

The earliest posts, both in England and in Scotland, were, as has been seen, intended solely for royal or Government service, and for at least 100 years virtually the only abuse feared was the transmission of news or messages likely to imperil the peace or security of the state. The expense of maintaining the system of horse posts established in England under the Tudors was met entirely by the crown, and so far as cost was concerned the occasional use of this system for private messages was not of much consequence; indeed it was probably of some small advantage in so far as it brought some horse-hiring business to the postmasters on whom the Royal Postal Service depended.

[222]

Though the conception of posts as a public service dates from the first half of the 17th century the idea that in them lay a potential source of revenue came slowly, and while posts and posting continued to be closely guarded as a royal monopoly the reasons for this continued to be political rather than economic. In the early years of the Commonwealth, however, the posts of England came for the first time to be let or 'farmed out' to men who paid an annual rent and made what they could from the enterprise. The rents so paid steadily increased in amount, and with the emergence of this, the first real revenue of the Post Office, came at last the idea of the Post Office as a real source of profit. The monopoly of the posts thus came to be even more closely guarded, by the tenant as directly affecting his pocket and by the crown both for security reasons as in the past, and now in addition for the protection of rights which had come to be of monetary value.

In Scotland the development of the idea of postal services followed a very similar course. Up till at least the middle of the 17th century the post continued to be regarded and maintained mainly as a service for King and Parliament. Here, as in England, the monopoly claimed and enforced was largely for reasons of security or for the benefit of postmasters appointed by the crown for the transmission of Royal Mail. In the last quarter of the 17th century the Register of the Privy Council contains many references to measures aimed at preventing the carrying of 'false news' or 'seditious and treasonable Pamphlets' by 'common poosts' and others particularly in the southern and south-western counties. Proclamations of 1684 and 1685, clearly with unofficial news-carrying in mind, sought to prevent pedlars and packmen from travelling in the counties of Ayr, Roxburgh, Berwick, Selkirk and Peebles without passes. In the summer of 1689 the town council of Dumfries ordered that in view of the risk of suspicious correspondence by 'disaffected persons' the post bag with letters for despatch should be brought to the council's clerk so that any suspected letters could be opened before the bag was sealed, and the bag with letters from Edinburgh was also to be brought to the council.[1] Towards the end of the century, however, arrangements in Scotland for letting out the contract for the running of posts came into being and, as in England, the monopoly of letter-carrying came to assume a commercial as well as a political importance. In the dispute between John Grahame and Alexander Farquhar over the postal service on the Aberdeen road in 1686 it is clear that what was then at issue between the Deputy Postmaster General and the Aberdeen postmaster was less the security of the post than the revenue derived from it.[2]

At the close of the 17th century the postal service in England was still organized on the basis of six main postal routes radiating from London, through which centre all mail was routed. By now, however, a steadily growing demand had arisen for Cross posts between the main routes. For this little, or no provision had hitherto been made by the postal authorities, and so an increasing amount of correspondence began to be carried by common carriers, stage waggons and even stage coaches, for by the last quarter of the 17th century increasing numbers of coaches were, despite the poor roads, coming into use. The Postmaster General and his staff in London had little means of keeping any check on such traffic or on any postal dues which could be levied on it and which were regularly and even, it seems, with official cognisance retained by local postmasters or carriers. As time passed this loss of revenue became too obvious to be ignored, and matters were made worse by the Act of 1711 which increased for the whole country the rates of postage and thus the temptation to use and exploit the growing opportunities for smuggling letters. By 1715 matters had reached such a pitch that, after initial opposition, the Treasury at length agreed, on the urgent recommendation of Lord Cornwallis and James Craggs the Postmasters General of the time, to the appointment of three postal Surveyors. Their duty was to check the returns made by the local postmasters with particular reference to cross-country or 'by' letters, to restrict the unofficial carrying of mail and to prevent abuse of the franking system, which had arisen out of a privilege granted to Members of Parliament in 1654 whereby within certain limits their correspondence could pass free through the post.[3]

When the first appointment of surveyors was made in 1715 it was intended that they should be merely temporary. In fact they had come to stay, and for the next two centuries and more the surveyors of the Post Office were to be among the most valuable members of the whole Post Office organization in the British Isles. Ralph Allen in his great work of developing the Cross posts of England between 1720 and 1764 made full use of these surveyors, and in 1787, three years after the establishment by

17. Page from the Journal of Francis Ronaldson, 1792, *p. 229.*

Journal Account
How and where Employed

			Days out
		Brot forward	16

Feby 24 & March 16 in

From Aberdeen to Ellon Peterhead and Fraserburgh examining & correcting abuses in the offices their Runners &c and from thence to Banff Portsoy Cullen Tochabers Elgin Tochabers Ports Nairn Ft George and Inverness upon the same employment & in charging some of the Postmasters for Gross neglect and abuses of their offices by sending letters free, &c &c ——— 22

March 17 & 3 in

From Inverness to Beauly the Deputy there having fallen behind in the Revenue and also for contracting for the Riding work betwixt Inverness & Dingwall which had been thrown up by former contractor and Returning from thence by Inverness to Elgin and Banff From Tochabers to Keith & Huntly correcting abuses in the offices there and return by Tochabers to Banff Turriff old Meldrum & Aberdeen upon the great road regularly the Riding work there &c &c and return by Stonehaven & Laurancekirk to Montrose examining the Roads there with in case the Riding &c by Bervie &c should be stopt as was nearly the case, Contracting anew for it by Bervie in consequence of the fear of Office taking this line of road which is rather better, tho a little longer than ye other & returning to Edinr ——— 58

5 To a Journey to Haddington with the Solicitor taking a precognition in regard to an Assault or Interruption of the Mail Coach ——— 1

Days out in Lady day Quarter 1792 | 57

57 days at £1. 1/ ⅌ day is £59. 17/—
Settled ⅌ receipt 5th. April 92

618 mo

ROBBERY OF THE MAIL.

GENERAL POST OFFICE,
EDINBURGH, 1st *August* 1802.

WHEREAS the POST-BOY carrying the MAIL from *Falkirk* to *Edinburgh* was, about Three o'Clock this Morning, attacked by Two Men on Foot near a Place called *The West of Sight Hill*, Three Miles West of *Linlithgow*, where they took from him the MAIL, containing the BAGS of LETTERS for *Edinburgh* from the following Places, viz.

Air,	*Hamilton,*	*Port-Glasgow,*
Auchterarder,	*Inverary,*	*Renfrew,*
Beith,	*Irvine,*	*Rothsay,*
Cumnock,	*Kilmarnock,*	*Stewartoun,*
Douglas,	*Kilsyth,*	*Stirling,*
Drymen,	*Kirkintilloch,*	*Stranraer,*
Dumbarton,	*Lanark,*	*Airdrie,*
Dumblane,	*Largs,*	*Kincardine,*
Falkirk,	*Mauchline,*	*Arrochar,*
Girvan,	*Maybole,*	*Cairndow,*
Glasgow,	*Neilstoun,*	*Luss,*
Greenock,	*Paisley,*	*Alloa.*

ONE of them is described to be a Stout Man, about Five Feet Six Inches High; had on a Blue Great Coat, Half Boots, and Gray Stockings; and the other Man not so Tall, had on a Gray Short Coat, with a White Night Cap or Handkerchief tied below his Hat; and both wore their Hair short cut.

A Reward of TWENTY POUNDS is hereby offered to any Person or Persons who shall give such Information as will lead to a Discovery of the Perpetrators of this ROBBERY; and a further Reward of FIFTY POUNDS is hereby offered to any Person who shall apprehend the said MAIL ROBBERS, and commit them to the nearest Jail, to be paid upon Conviction of the Offenders.

By Order of the Postmaster General,

WILLIAM KERR, *Secretary.*

Palmer of the Mail Coach Service, their number was increased to six, one for each of the areas based on the main postal routes into which England was at that time for postal purposes divided. Francis Freeling, who was later to play such a great part in postal development, started his work for the Post Office as one of Palmer's surveyors, and throughout the forty years during which Freeling was Secretary of the Post Office he, too, made the fullest use of these essential and hard-worked men.

The work of the early surveyors was confined to England, and many years were to pass before similar appointments were made in Scotland. There is no reason to believe that illegal carriage of mail or fraudulent practices by postmasters or carriers was less common north of the Border than south of it. Smuggling of letters on the Aberdeen road did not end with Alexander Farquhar. The progressive rise in postal rates from 1711 onwards greatly increased the temptation to send letters by unofficial means, and till well into the 19th century letter-carriers on post roads all over Scotland were supplementing their poor pay by carrying letters which paid no dues to the Post Office. James Anderson, in his short time as Deputy Postmaster General for Scotland, had no lack of trouble in protecting the monopoly and collecting the revenue of the Post Office, and the 'apprehender of private letter carriers' included in Archibald Douglas's staff in 1738 no doubt found his time well occupied. But in Scotland the middle decade of the 18th century saw only a slow growth of the postal network. Cross posts between the main post roads with the opportunities they offered for suppressing dues were still almost unknown, and since the postal revenue collected by the Edinburgh office amounted to only a fraction of that collected in London it is hardly surprising that the Treasury grudged the expenditure on surveyors in Scotland of the £1 a day which was being paid to those south of the Border. The first appointment of a surveyor on Scottish post roads took place in 1760 when a Mr Kerr was appointed to the post, but little is known of the work which he accomplished. On Kerr's death in 1782 his son William succeeded to the surveyorship, while Francis Ronaldson, whose name has already frequently appeared in these pages, at that time started a long and useful career in post office service as Assistant Surveyor. In 1789 William Kerr became Secretary to the Scottish Post Office and to succeed him as Surveyor the Postmaster General appointed a

18. Robbery of the mail, 1802, *p. 231.*

Mr Edwards of the English Post Office. Edwards' appointment over the head of Ronaldson caused much ill-feeling, and with a view to remedying this position Ronaldson was appointed Joint Surveyor. So it came about that from 1789 Scotland had two postal surveyors, an arrangement which, though apparently unintentional at the time, was soon to show itself to be most fully justified.[4]

The rapid development of postal services both in England and in Scotland in the last quarter of the 18th century had enormously increased the extent and complication of the work falling on postal surveyors, and the task which faced Ronaldson and his colleague was no light one. At each office which he visited the surveyor must examine the books and accounts of the postmaster, noting all balances due by or to him. He must enquire into the adequacy of the guarantees given by postmasters on their appointment and the solvency of the guarantors. The correct marking on letters of the postal charge must be watched and any evidence of illegal carriage of letters must be noted. The rates paid to foot posts, to horse posts and in the later years to mail coach contractors must be reported and the use of franking or other concessions to the public must be looked to.[5] To add to all this the surveyors in England and Scotland alike had to deal with the frequent grievances of ill-paid postmasters or of those whose salaries were in arrears, of riding or mail coach contractors who found their modest rates insufficient, and of members of the public who complained of delays in the mail or missing letters or who wanted postage times or even postal routes altered for their convenience. 'The Surveyors', read an official circular of 1847, 'are the eyes and ears of the Post Office.' In their dealings with the public their duty as defined in sweeping terms at the same date was 'not only to remove the grounds of just complaint but to anticipate the reasonable wants of the public'.[6] Indeed there was virtually no aspect of the work of the postal service both in rural districts and in the towns which was regarded as being outside the scope and responsibility of the surveyors, and the officials at Headquarters were not slow to lay at their door the blame for frauds, abuses or complaints. Writing to a fellow surveyor in somewhat cynical vein in 1867, Anthony Trollope, looking back on over thirty years as a postal surveyor, wrote: 'You have married no wife, keep no hunter, go to no parties, read no books, but have become a machine for grinding and polishing Post Office apparatus. This is not good enough for any man, though there are worse ways of spending life.'[7] Reporting to the Postmaster General in 1806 Freeling wrote of the surveyors:

'The Surveyors must be versed in all the business of the Post Office, must be of respectable description, high character and unexceptionable integrity and of good education. They have to confer with persons of consideration in all parts of the Kingdom. They must maintain the most decided control over all Post Masters and Agents. The salary and allowances are not equal to the constant duty, trusts and responsibility and expense.'[8]

When the first surveyors were appointed in England their pay of £1 a day was intended to cover travelling expenses, but subsequently in order to encourage them to spend as much time as possible on tours of inspection they were given small salaries and relatively generous subsistence allowances while on the road. In the autumn of 1793, Freeling, reporting on the staff employed at the Edinburgh office, mentions two surveyors, almost certainly Edwards and Ronaldson, at annual salaries of £150 each and a subsistence allowance when travelling of 10/– a day. By the early years of last century when Francis Ronaldson and James Shearer were the two Scottish surveyors they received in addition to the fixed salary a daily subsistence allowance which had been increased in 1787 to £1.1/– and later to £1.6/–. In addition they were allowed at first 6d and then 8d a mile to cover actual travel expenses. These increases are reflected in steep rises in the total payments reported in respect of surveyor's journeys in Scotland. For the year 1780/1 these appear to have amounted only to £24.15/– while for 1799/1800 they had grown to £410.8/–.[9] These expenses were always closely scrutinized and constantly called in question, but even Freeling, careful custodian as he always was of post office finance, recognized that the position of the Scottish surveyors was a special one. They had to contend with peculiar travelling difficulties, while as regards travelling expenses the scarcity of coaches meant that private chaises or horses had often to be hired. Moreover, as Government servants, they were expected to keep up a certain standard while they were on the road and no doubt the charges at inns were adjusted accordingly. 'It must be remembered' Freeling wrote to the Postmaster General many years later, 'that the whole of Scotland is divided between two Surveyors only, the offices are more scattered than in England and that consequently the Scottish Surveyors must have much more ground to go over which will in some measure explain the high sums incurred for mileage.'[10]

Francis Ronaldson, the man who in 1789 started work as one of Scotland's early postal surveyors, seems to have possessed many of the qualities which Freeling recognized as being necessary for the post. The man who in later years found a place among Kay's *Portraits* of Edinburgh characters was clearly regarded as a personality among his contemporaries. Ronaldson was a man of unusually short stature, a fact, however, which did not interfere with his membership of the Royal Edinburgh Volunteers recruited in the city during the Napoleonic wars. Kay's *Portraits* depicts him strikingly posed beside a fellow-volunteer called Osborne, a man as much above the average stature as Ronaldson was below it. On one occasion Ronaldson had the misfortune to be in the rear rank on parade immediately behind his massive colleague by whom he was completely obscured. The sergeant in charge, seeing what appeared to be a gap in the rear rank behind Osborne, ordered Ronaldson's neighbours in forceful terms to fill it. Their apparent refusal to do so threatened a crisis of military discipline till a small voice came from the invisible Ronaldson, 'I can't cover, I do all I can.' Kay further records that finding his musket too heavy for him Ronaldson had one specially made for him, a degree of unusual enterprise which was not only approved but which on one occasion earned the official commendation of an Inspecting Officer.[11] His lack of inches seems to have been no handicap to Ronaldson in dealing in forthright fashion with the wide cross-section of postal officials and members of the public with whom he came in contact, while the sense of humour with which he was credited would not come amiss.

One of the duties of the postal surveyors was to keep a full record of all their journeys, to serve the double purpose of commenting on the postal arrangements of the various offices visited, and of justifying the claims for subsistence and travel allowances which they made. It is fortunate that Ronaldson's journal from 1786 to 1814 has survived, for from this source it is possible to get a fair picture of the development of postal affairs in Scotland during that period, and particularly of the shortcomings and abuses on the part of both postal servants and of the public which it was the surveyor's duty to remedy or remove. In Ronaldson's case at least, the policy of the Post Office in offering generous travel allowances seems to have been fully justified by the number and length of his journeys. In the early years of his service while still an Assistant Surveyor, these journeys, generally with William Kerr whose work he was soon to take over, were mostly short in distance and duration; but as time passed he ranged further afield. His area seems at one time to have covered practically the whole of the Scottish mainland. Even Kirkwall fell within his territory, and over the years there can have been few offices which remained unvisited either by him or by his colleague James Shearer. A long journey from mid May to early July 1791 is typical. Ronaldson's route took him by Perth and Dunkeld to Inverness, perhaps considering the possibility of the direct post through the Grampians for which the Post Office was being constantly pressed. Then by Cromarty and the Black Isle he journeyed north to Wick and finally to Kirkwall. From Inverness on the southward journey he turned down the Great Glen to Fort William and so by Appin and Bonawe to Inveraray and Dumbarton and back to Edinburgh after fifty-six days on the road. Two years later another long summer journey took him by Callander and Tyndrum to Fort William, Oban and Mull and south to Campbeltown and Bute; then crossing to the Ayrshire coast he visited Largs, Greenock and Glasgow. Sometimes he went south-west to Ayr and Portpatrick and along the Solway coast to Dumfries and Carlisle; again to Ellon, Portsoy and Banff and the fishing villages on the Moray Firth, everywhere 'correcting abuses', enquiring into 'irregular and confused conduct' and dealing with 'gross neglect'.[12] On occasion Ronaldson's work took him even across the Border. In January 1790 delays in the mail coach from London took him as far south as Newcastle to reprimand the Scottish mail contractors whose responsibility extended to this point, and in the following month both Ronaldson and Kerr visited London and subsequently Bristol, Bath, Oxford and York making notes on postal improvements introduced in England with a view to their adoption in Scotland. Honest ignorance, stupidity or pure indolence among postmasters were often his main enemies, but not infrequently there was deliberate fraud or calculated dishonesty.

The frequent changes of postal rates in the late 18th and early 19th centuries brought tribulation to the postmasters and to the

[229]

surveyors who tried to keep them right. The French wars, besides calling for increased revenue from the Post Office and so for constantly changing postal rates, brought other worries. As the wars dragged on more and more men were drawn into the Services, and in not a few rural districts postal services which had been established or expanded early in the century now became uneconomic, for the growing load of gazettes, newspapers and official documents which travelled free did nothing to replace the private mail of the men and especially the landowners fighting on the Continent or overseas. By an Act of 1795, too, sailors, soldiers and non-commissioned officers in both services had been given the privilege, whether at home or abroad, of sending and receiving letters for a postal rate of only 1d prepaid, the letters sent off by serving men being certified by their officers before despatch. So the revenue of the Post Office, especially in rural districts, already diminished by the calls of the Navy and Army, was still further eroded; and worse still the concession laid itself open to easy abuse, a fact which did not escape the notice of a certain section of the community.

'I have had occasion formerly to observe to you', wrote one of the Scottish surveyors in 1797, 'that a very great evasion of the Post Revenue has taken place – particularly in the North of Scotland – from the privilege granted to soldiers, under cover of which not only a very general opportunity is taken by the common people there to have their letters carried by soldiers to be freed by their officers, but even in certain instances which I observed and detected persons in higher rank have availed themselves of this circumstance.'[13]

Postal employees, too, were alive to the possibilities offered by the war-time concession, and in 1801 Ronaldson was engaged in the prosecution of a clerk aged 14 at the Port Glasgow office who had found it profitable to forge on paid letters attestations to make them appear to be service letters.[14]

Reckonings of mileage used in calculating postage dues on letters were still inaccurate. The English surveyors since 1794 had been supplied with measuring wheels known as 'perambulators' to check distances;[15] but there is no record of their use in Scotland, and well into the 19th century calculation of distance in many rural districts was still rough and ready. In the course of a Memorial prepared for the Postmaster General by F. H. Mackenzie of Lewis in 1789 regarding proposed changes in the postal route between Stornoway and the mainland, Mackenzie referred to the distance from Poolewe to Dingwall as 'called 30, but is about 55 miles' and that between Loch Carron and Inverness as 'called 40, is about 70 miles';[16] and these are only two instances among many. Imperfect knowledge of Scotland's geography was not confined to local postmasters. For Senior Officers even in Edinburgh, and still more at the Post Office headquarters in London, much of Northern and Western Scotland was a remote and little known country, though the purchase, recorded in 1792, of a number of copies of John Ainslie's *New Map of Scotland* for the use of postal officials must have helped.*

Complaints of delays in the post, of missing letters and of thefts by postal officials were everyday events and all found their way to the surveyors for enquiry, remedy or more drastic action. Sometimes, indeed, characters were cleared if time was wasted, as when prolonged search for a missing letter containing money ended with its discovery, unposted, in the pocket of the writer, or when a sinister hole in the mail bag on the Portpatrick crossing proved to be the work of rats; but more often than not investigation of a complaint proved that the Bill was a true one. The working of a country post office in the early 19th century and the complex system of accounting then in force gave countless opportunities for honest mistakes and dishonest practices, and the surveyors on whom so much depended had need for sharp eyes, ready wits and strong constitutions to detect and correct all that went amiss in the wide and growing areas under their charge.

One of the most frequent causes of trouble was the low rate of pay allowed by the Post Office. Such perquisites as the postmasters had, such as that from dealing in newspapers, seldom made up their whole remuneration to a fair wage, and it was an honest man indeed who could resist the temptation to make what he could 'on the side', often by means that would hardly bear close scrutiny. The palpable inadequacy of the pay of so many country postmasters was regularly commented on by the

---

* Post 15/124/1792. In 1799 Ainslie stood cautioner for Alison Ainslie, presumably a relative, when she was appointed postmistress in his native Jedburgh. (S.R.O., Register of Deeds, Durie, vol. 282. fol. 385.) It seems probable that prior to this date Adair's maps were in use by the Post Office. The library of John Inglis, Secretary to the G.P.O. in Edinburgh who died in April 1751, included a set of Adair's *Maps of Scotland*. (S.R.O., Com. Edinburgh Tests., 18 Sept. 1751.)

surveyors. Senior officers at Headquarters, too, were fully alive to it; but salaries constantly lagged far behind the growing work and responsibility as the service spread and developed.

One of the main duties of the surveyors on their first appointment in 1715 had been to stop the loss of postal revenue from 'by' letters passing between adjacent or near-by offices. Local postmasters acting in concert could all too easily suppress and keep for themselves postage dues on letters circulating locally. Indeed it was at least partly for this very reason that until the early years of the 18th century the revenue from such letters had in very many cases come, perforce, to be accepted as allowable, if not strictly legitimate, perquisites of postmasters. Such practices were hard to detect and still harder to stop, and well into the 19th century large numbers of letters continued to pass through the post which paid no dues to Edinburgh or London. But if the Post Office complained of loss of revenue suppressed from 'by' letters, the postmasters on their side felt themselves aggrieved at what they often considered to be undue pressure for the remittance to Headquarters of receipts from this source. The Post Office in some cases made concessions where sums due to them by local postmasters were offset by payments due to these local officials. But this was not always so, and it is certain that cases occurred not infrequently where real hardships were suffered. Reporting in 1793 on the growing burden falling on the shoulders of a country postmaster, a surveyor in the North of England wrote:

'To add to his distress – for he is not rich – he has been so closely pressed from the Bye-letter Office for his balance due there as to have been compelled to borrow money to discharge them at the very time he could not obtain any account from the General Office nor warrants for payment of as large sums due to him.'[17]

In making the periodical returns of postage collected at local offices, for which the Edinburgh office constantly pressed, the local postmaster could deduct his salary, and any outlays he had made to foot or horse posts carrying mail to the next office. He could also deduct from the sums due by him postage on 'dead' letters or on letters misaddressed or misdirected, on none of which had postage been collected. Here, too, was an opportunity for much abuse, and it was not unknown for postmasters themselves to forge numbers of such letters, the postage on which they then deducted in making their returns to London or Edinburgh. In the spring and summer of 1824 the postmasters at Golspie, Dornoch and Inverness came under suspicion for unusually large deductions under this heading and the papers were sent to the Procurator-Fiscal for investigation. The outcome is not apparent from the correspondence but, as so often, the Surveyor was blamed for lack of vigilance.*

If the low pay of the postmasters and constant opportunities for dishonesty made them prone to temptations which often proved irresistible, still worse trouble came to the Post Office from the men who carried the mail on foot, on horseback or even latterly by coach. As time passed and the postal service grew, more and more of the actual transport of mail from point to point came to be done by outside contractors at a fixed rate per mile; but in the early days transit of mail was often arranged by local postmasters who were allowed by the Post Office a low mileage rate making what they could from the business. The carriers so employed, whether by postmasters or by contractors, were sometimes dishonest, often indolent and usually of limited education and intelligence. Like the postmasters themselves they were grossly underpaid, but unlike the postmasters they were in many cases not under the direct control of the Post Office and had little to lose if their misdeeds were detected. On investigating in 1805 a theft of mail between Tain and Dingwall, the solicitor acting for the Post Office found that the total wages of the post boy accused of the theft were 5/– a week. 'Of course,' he reported, 'it may fairly be presumed that no respectable man will be got to perform this duty. Dismission [*sic*] to such a man for committing a fault is no punishment; and the safety of the conveyance of the mail which the public had a right to require seems to render some regulation in this respect necessary.'[18]

Increases in pay came only slowly, and meantime the mail too often remained at the mercy of every form of fraud, neglect or abuse. With a view to speeding the post the Post Office had from an early date used way-bills on which was recorded the date

---

* Post 40/250, 298 and 374/1824. Abuses of this nature were evidently of long standing. As early as 1731 Ralph Allen, writing to one of the postal surveyors about the 'manufacture' of 'dead' letters—in this case by the Carlisle office—referred to it as 'a Blamable Contrivance by some people in that office to expect money from me for bits of paper never sent by the post, but made by themselves. . . .' (Post 16/17.)

and hour of despatch and, at a later stage, the number of paid and unpaid letters in the bag. To conceal or explain delay on the route the hour of despatch was often altered, while theft of letters was hidden by tearing or obliterating the way-bill. Sometimes, in an attempt to trace a theft in the post, a surveyor would put marked letters into the bag and watch its progress, or again, as on the road far up the north-east coast, he would see the bag sealed and despatched at one post office going on by sea to await its arrival at the next. All too much of the surveyors' time had to be spent in investigating thefts and tracing the culprit, a part of their work for which they can have had little enthusiasm when, as so often, the culprit proved to be an ignorant boy of 14 years old or little more, underpaid and ill-clad, covering in all weathers distances far beyond his strength. At the General Post Office in Edinburgh, too, the solicitor to the Post Office was never done investigating and prosecuting. Thefts of letters containing money were so common that the Post Office sought to dissuade the public from sending money by ordinary post. If notes were sent through the post it was advised that they be sent in two halves, the second only to be despatched after the first had been acknowledged by the recipient.* In 1792 Freeling was in correspondence with the Deputy Postmaster General for Scotland regarding the advertising in the Scottish papers of the post office recommendation on this matter. The people of Scotland, it was then reported, were unwilling to adopt the procedure advised by the Post Office. This was hardly surprising, for a proposal by Lord Walsingham the Postmaster General that postage dues on the letter containing the second half of the note should, on satisfactory proof, be remitted, had been found to be contrary to law. The recommendation of the Post Office, therefore, would involve the sender of a bank-note in double postage dues.[19] The worries of postal officials about money sent through the post was still further increased by legal complications. In the summer of 1801 the Post Office got, at a cost of 5 guineas each, the opinions of the Lord Advocate and the Solicitor General on various points in connection with illegal carriage. Like many another legal opinion that of the law officers merely added to the complexities. The Post Office, they pointed out, was not liable for money sent by post, and accordingly this could be sent by carrier and a letter

* From this arose the practice of printing the number on *both* ends of the note.

with it. Carriers could already convey goods and letters directly relating to those goods, and it was doubtful whether the Post Office had any right of search. Little wonder that the harassed Freeling minuted on the papers, 'This is in my mind a most alarming opinion.'[20]

The common custom for the recipient to pay the postage meant that, in the days before house-to-house delivery was instituted, large numbers of unclaimed letters were conveyed and later returned to the GPO at the sole expense of the Post Office. Besides this it opened wide the way to still further abuse by the public. Sometimes the mere arrival of a letter, or perhaps its method of address, conveyed all the information required by the addressee who would hand it back unopened and unpaid to the Post Office. Some postmasters in Ireland were, it seems, even in the habit of allowing correspondents to get a sight of the contents of a letter before refusing to take delivery, and though the practice was not thought to be prevalent in Scotland the Post Office considered the risk warranted a special warning to Scottish postmasters.*

While the surveyors thus laboured to detect, correct or prevent the mistakes or misdeeds of post office servants, the post office officials in Edinburgh or London and their law officers spent no small part of their time protecting the post office monopoly and the post office revenue against constant attrition by the public. Illegal carriage of mail was as old as the postal service, and as postal rates increased so did the inducement to evade them. Writing to the postmaster about a prosecution for illegal carriage at Port Glasgow in 1801, Freeling expressed the opinion that this was more widespread in Scotland than in England; and contemporary records suggest that he may well have been right. Commenting in 1792 on a Memorial by the people of Peterhead asking for better post communications with Aberdeen, Freeling recalled that a few years earlier it had been found necessary to alter the postal route between the towns because nine-tenths of the letters were being carried illegally, a percentage which even Alexander Farquhar would have acknowledged as comparing creditably with his own achievements in 1686.[21] In 1794 a petition for a daily post between Dundee and Brechin by way of Forfar led to the disclosure that great

---

* For further detail see Howard Robinson's *The British Post Office*, 282/5.

numbers of letters were being carried on this route by the local carrier. Some years later it emerged that the Shotts Iron Company had for long been in the habit of sending their letters enclosed in parcels between Whitburn and Edinburgh, while in the north-east of Scotland it transpired that merchants in Banff and Forres were using the local carriers for the transport of parcels containing many letters for delivery in near-by villages.[22] In 1802 when the loss of revenue from illegal carriage was estimated at £6,000 per annum the Solicitor for the Scottish Post Office had in hand no fewer than 1200 prosecutions for abuses and evasions of all sorts. William Kerr, the Secretary of the Post Office at Edinburgh, had assured Freeling that in nearly every case a conviction was obtained, but that since many of the defaulters were poor people the penalty of £5 for each offence imposed by the Act of 1802 could often not be recovered. The Secretary in Edinburgh was confident that 'numberless letters which otherwise would be sent by carriers are now sent by post', but Freeling was alarmed at the prospect that legal costs might grow to as much as £1000 a year, and it was decided, despite the strongest protests of Beveridge, the post office Solicitor, that only in cases where there seemed a good chance of recovering the penalty would action be taken.[23]

In the autumn of 1801 the case of Robert Lawson, the enterprising owner of a 'caravan' operating between Perth and Dundee, had illustrated the scale of illegal carriage which threatened the post office revenue. Investigations through a Perth lawyer had established that Lawson's caravan took two, three or even four dozen letters between the cities each day, inflicting a loss of over £100 per annum on the Post Office, but providing a convenient means of correspondence which was believed to be commonly used by 'many respectable businessmen' both in Perth and Dundee. The outcome of Lawson's case illustrates the remarkable contrast between the treatment by the Post Office of illegal carriage of letters by the public and any dishonesty on the part of those engaged in the postal service. In Lawson's case much correspondence passed between Edinburgh and London as to what steps should be taken, and it was only after it had been established that his family were well provided for that a fine of £5 for each of ten of his many offences was imposed. Lawson was to be imprisoned till the fines had been paid while he was also ordered to execute a Bond of Caution for £100 as security against any future postal offences, but since he was believed to have saved £100 per annum during each of the last three years from his activities, neither of these provisions seems likely to have caused him much inconvenience. Beveridge, the post office Solicitor, expressed his views on the whole matter in a letter to Freeling '. . . the exaction of penalties', he wrote, 'is not with a view to enriching Government or Individuals or unnecessarily distressing the offenders, but merely a measure of precaution to prevent the continuance of a fraud of which we have so great reason to complain'. Freeling on his part wrote to the Postmaster General that the fines imposed on Lawson were as lenient as they could possibly be in the circumstances. He added that he was considering drafting a Bill for Parliament to impose penalties for illegal carriage of letters on the sender as well as on the carrier.[24] A further ground for complaint by the Post Office at this time was as to the lack of publicity given by the Press to postal prosecutions.

'At the present day', wrote a postal historian in 1893, 'a single prosecution undertaken by the Post Office would be the subject of comment in every newspaper in the Kingdom. Eighty or ninety years ago, numerous as the Post Office prosecutions were, there was not a newspaper in the Kingdom that gratuitously published particulars or even announced the fact. Often did the post-masters lament this reticence, believing as they did that to make known their repressive measures and the amount of penalties inflicted, must have a deterrent effect upon the illicit traffic; and at length for want of any better means of securing publicity they gave directions that wherever a prosecution took place, handbills giving full particulars were to be struck off and affixed to the doors of the local inns.'[25]

The considerate and almost tender treatment of Lawson was typical of the attitude of the Post Office towards the public at this time, and many other cases of illegal carriage and countless flagrant abuses of franking regulations were virtually ignored or leniently dealt with. In marked contrast dishonest postmasters or post boys got no mercy. In 1796 the postmaster at Kirkwall had been executed for a theft of only £9 from letters passing through his hands. Other postmasters found guilty of dishonesty or even only of negligence suffered instant dismissal and sometimes imprisonment, and in 1827 the postmaster at Achnacraig in Mull only suspected of dishonesty which could not be proved against him lost his job.[26] A postal historian of last century quotes the case of a post office servant who had been detected carrying forty unposted letters. 'This man, whose wages did not exceed a few shillings a week, was sued upon each letter and adjudged to pay 40 separate penalties of 10/— apiece.'[27] As for defaulting post boys their treatment was both summary and severe. Their youth made little difference to their sentences and in the late 18th and early 19th centuries there were countless cases of boys of 14 and 15 being sent to sea or transported for seven years.

A further anomaly in the postal service at this time arose directly from the strict application by the Post Office of the long-standing regulation that any letter containing more than one sheet or the smallest enclosure must be charged double or, it might be, treble postage. This led to much unproductive labour and endless delays in London, Edinburgh or other postal centres where officials employed for the purpose examined with the aid of a lighted candle letters suspected of containing additional sheets or other contents. When in the third decade of last century sweeping reforms of our postal services were being urged by Robert Wallace and Rowland Hill, they did not omit to point out that failure to charge letters by weight rather than by number of sheets led to injustice, to waste of labour, and to delays in the post absurd to a degree almost beyond belief.

If the methods used by dishonest letter-carriers, postmasters and other post office officials were occasionally subtle and often difficult to detect, there was always in addition the possibility of the more direct line of attack. Palmer's introduction of the mail coach in 1784 had almost put out of business the colourful highwayman who had preyed on the stage coaches of the mid 18th century. The arming of mail coach guards had come to be looked on as almost superfluous, their weapons of more danger to themselves, to their passengers or to innocent wayfarers than to possible attackers. In the history of Scottish postal transport there appear no figures cast in the mould of Dick Turpin; but on the early post road between Edinburgh and Berwick the post boys were not immune from attack. In 1688 the postmasters at Cockburnspath and Berwick were instructed not to allow post-boys to ride at night to avoid interception, and in the same year orders were given for horsemen to be stationed on the Berwick road to guard the mail, 2 at Berwick, 4 at Coldingham, and 2 each at 'Coperpatch', 'Brokesburne', Haddington and Tranent, a reward of £50 sterling to be given to anyone giving information about robbery of the mail.[28] Despite these precautions there were at least three occasions in the last decade of the 17th century when the mail was robbed. Neither in England nor in Scotland does the arming of horse posts appear to have been seriously considered until near the end of the 18th century. Since 1794 Freeling had been advising this, and in March 1796 he wrote at great length to the Postmasters General on the subject. Fire-arms, he advised, should not be supplied to the present post boys, some of whom, as he pertinently pointed out, were barely 14 years old. In future only men of good character between 18 and 45 years old should be employed, each to be armed with a Birmingham cutlass, a brace of pistols and a strong cap, with a thick coat every second year. The proposed arrangements were not to apply to Scotland nor to foot posts, as the latter carried only letters and not packages.*

While the arrangements which were finally made for the regular arming of horse posts appear initially to have been confined to England, it is evident that in Scotland, too, the security of the mails was giving rise to some anxiety. In the closing weeks of 1802 a year after he had won his long battle with the Treasury, Freeling was in correspondence with the Postmasters General about the guarding of the mail conveyed by horse post between Edinburgh and Glasgow. Hitherto this mail had been unguarded and though there is no record of any attack having been made on it, William Kerr the Secretary of the Scottish Post Office and Ronaldson the surveyor had been considering new arrangements for both conveyance and security. Four riders were required to maintain this daily post and Ronaldson now advised that four guards were also needed. An officer in the Mid-Lothian Cavalry with thirty years' service in H.M. Dragoons had offered to undertake the mail contract at a total cost of £450 per annum, including four armed guards at 14/– a week each. Ronaldson advised that the offer be accepted on the basis that 'able and active Dragoon Riders' would be employed as guards and that if this were agreed to 'the arms etc. that may be deemed

---

* Post 42/107.1/1796. Despite Freelings recommendation, arming of horse posts in England did not take place until 1801, following a long argument with the Treasury over the cost of prosecuting mail robbers. (Post 10/8–9).

necessary be ordered down for the service'. The Postmasters General expressed some hesitation on the ground of the cost involved, but finally agreed to the proposal.[29] For some years no further record appears as to trouble over security of the mails, but in 1820 Freeling approved the arming of horse posts on the 87-mile ride between Glasgow and Stranraer, fifty of which were covered at night. Seven years later the horse posts between Edinburgh and Blackshiels, Whittinghame and Morpeth, and Paisley and Glasgow were armed, the last being in the neighbourhood of 'towns infested with loose and improper characters'.[30]

If the right of search which the Post Office could enforce over inland transport was in doubt, their control over letters carried by coastal shipping or coming from overseas was even smaller. Here they must rely on Customs officials at the ports to see that letters arriving by boat were collected and put into the post. Shipmasters were entitled to 1d for each letter so handed over, and a payment of 1 guinea per 1000 letters was by long-standing practice allowed by the Post Office to the Customs officials for letters collected by them; but despite this a steady sea-borne traffic was carried on between Scotland and England and between Glasgow and Belfast in smuggled letters which paid no dues to the Post Office. At one time the Post Office had the services of one Turner, an officer described as 'Informer General to various Boards of Revenue' whose unenviable duties seem to have borne more than a little resemblance to those of the 'apprehender of private letter carriers' of Archibald Hamilton's day; but his work seems to have been a source of some embarrassment to the Post Office. Writing in the summer of 1828, Freeling refers to forty cases of smuggling of letters unearthed by Turner, some frivolous, some unsupported by proof and others of doubtful validity. Keen as he always was to defend the monopoly of the Post Office, Freeling was torn between anxiety to avoid expense on useless proceedings and unwillingness to discourage the informer.[31] The fact, too, that the Act of 1802 had provided for the division between the crown and the informer, of fines imposed on defaulters created a monetary interest in tale-bearing, which could on occasion throw doubt on the reliability of the evidence. It seems, too, that as the years passed Freeling's attitude towards illegal carriage of letters may have become tempered by a degree of reason and common justice which at an earlier date did not always characterize his actions in postal matters. In January

CAUTION to POST-BOYS.

BY the Act of 5th of *Geo*. III. If any Poſt-Boy, or Rider, having taken any of His Majeſty's Mails, or Bags of Letters, under his Care, to convey to the next Poſt Town or Stage, ſhall ſuffer any other Perſon (except a Guard) to ride on the Horſe or Carriage, or ſhall Loiter on the Road, and wilfully miſpend his Time, ſo as to retard the Arrival of the ſaid Mails, or Bags of Leters, at the next Poſt Town or Stage.—Every ſuch Offender ſhall, on Conviction before One Juſtice, be committed to the Houſe of Correction, and confined to hard Labour for one Month. All Poſt-Boys and Riders are therefore deſired to take Notice of this, and are hereby cautioned not to fail in the regular Performance of their Duty, otherwiſe they will moſt aſſuredly be puniſhed as the Law directs. And it is hoped and requeſted, for the Benefit of public Correſpondence, that all Perſons, who may obſerve any Poſt-Boy or Rider, offending as aforeſaid, will give immediate Notice to — *Johnson Wilkinson* Surveyor of the General Poſt-Office, &c.

19. Caution to post boys, 1765, *p.* 233.

GENERAL·POST·OFFICE,

SEPTEMBER 22d, 1792.

TO prevent the Loss of entire Notes or Drafts payable to Bearer in Letters put into any Post Office or Receiving House, the Postmaster General repeat the Recommendation so often inserted in the London Gazettes, and circulated by Hand-Bills throughout the Kingdom; namely To cut all such Notes or Drafts in half in the following Form, to send them at two different Times and to wait for the Return of the Post till the Receipt of one Half is acknowledged before the other is sent.

And when any Cash, in Gold or Silver, or when any Rings, or Lockets, &c. are sent per Post from London, particular Care should be taken to deliver the same to the Clerk at the Window, or to the Clerk of the Money Book, at the General Post Office; and when any such Letter is to be sent from a Country Post Office it should be delivered into the Hands of the Postmaster.

By Command of the Postmaster General,

ANTHONY TODD, Secr.

N° 108 / N° 108

February 9th, 1782.

I Promise to pay Demand the Sum of / to John Doe, - - - - - or Bearer, on

𝕿𝖊𝖓 Pounds.

London, the 9th Day of February, 1782.

£ 𝕿𝖊𝖓

Entd. Thomas Styles.

For the Governor and Company of the Bank of England.

Richard Roe.

N.B. The Note is to be cut exactly where it is marked with a black Line, first writing the Date and Year at one End of the Note, and the Number at the other End, by which Means each Part will contain a sufficient Specification of the Whole.

This Specimen will be put up at every Post-Office in the Kingdom.

20. Postage of banknotes, *p.* 234.

1833 Sir William Lees, then Secretary of the Scottish Office, had complained of the frequent illegal carriage of letters to Shetland and had proposed that the Customs officers be empowered to search all vessels. Freeling in referring the matter to the Postmaster General reminded him of the unsatisfactory postal service to Shetland and expressed his opinion that the suppression and punishment of illegal carriage should be pressed for only where postal facilities were such as to leave no excuse for the smuggling of letters, a view with which the Postmaster General agreed.[32]

With the end of the first quarter of the 19th century came steadily increasing use of steamboats on the coastal as well as on the overseas routes. Even as early as 1813 Ronaldson had reported that steamboats were cutting deep into the traffic of both the stage and the mail coaches on the run between Glasgow and Gourock, and ten years later Charles Reeves, who had in 1822 become surveyor of the Western district of Scotland, warned the post office officials that on the route from Inveraray down the Kintyre Peninsula to Campbeltown the post runner must be replaced by a horse post to speed the service and so check the smuggling of letters by boat.[33] As the years passed the position grew worse. Steamboats from Glasgow were taking so many smuggled letters to Islay and Campbeltown that it seemed best to try to make the smugglers honest men by paying the owners of the boats fixed sums for letter-carrying, the latter undertaking to give passage to no unpaid letters. Between Skye and Mallaig, too, the boats were stealing postal revenue, but Reeves' highly original suggestion of having locked boxes on board to collect en route letters for postage at the end of the voyage was turned down on legal grounds.[34]

Among the principal duties with which the postal surveyors had been charged at the time of their first appointments in 1715 was the prevention of abuse of the franking system. The coming years were to prove that the other tasks which these men were to be called on to undertake would amply fill their days and tax their strength without the addition of one which for well over a century to come was to defy the efforts of post office officials, legislators and politicians. Franking, or free carriage of letters through the post had started in 1654 when free carriage had been conceded for letters addressed to or despatched by Members of Parliament. In 1660 the privilege came under

R   [241]

critical review, the House of Lords entirely opposing it, while even the House of Commons seem to have viewed it with little enthusiasm. None the less, the privilege continued in existence, covering correspondence of some of the principal Officers of State as well as that of Members of Parliament. By the last quarter of the 17th century the loss to the Post Office resulting from franking had reached such a pitch that in reckoning the post office revenue as a basis for fixing their salaries, the Post-masters General were regularly allowed to bring into the calculation a substantial sum representing lost dues on franked letters – £4000 in 1670, £6000 in 1674 and £7200 in 1677.[35]

Some attempt to restrict franking was made in William III's reign. At this time Members of Parliament enjoyed the right of free postage during sessions of Parliament and for forty days before and after each session, while similar rights were allowed to five Government officials including the Secretary for Scotland; but franking continued to grow, and by 1714 it was estimated that it represented an annual loss to the Post Office of £25,000. Members of Parliament seem to have been always careless and often unscrupulous in the exercise of rights which, according to contemporary evidence, they frequently sought to retain even after they had ceased to sit in Parliament.

In the very early stages of postal development in Great Britain the use of the post by the public both in England and Scotland for transmission of treasonable messages, or official apprehension that it might be so used, led to the opening or suppression of mail on a scale which caused much complaint, and which at times reached the dimensions of a public scandal. This in its turn led to the practice by the public of addressing many letters to persons other than those for whom they were ultimately intended, the messages being passed on to the real recipient. Throughout the 18th and much of the 19th centuries, long after opening of letters for security reasons had ceased to be common, the public continued, for reasons of economy, a practice initiated to defeat the activities of the censor. Letters continued on a large scale to be addressed to those who in their official capacity were entitled to receive franked mail, the latter accommodating the writers and defying the regulations by forwarding the letter or its contents to a further address. Of the prevalence of such glaring and palpable abuses the Post Office was well aware, but of strong action to curb them there was little or none, while the occasional expostulation was mild in the extreme. In 1714 the annual value of franked material in England was reckoned by Ralph Allen to be £50,000, and by the time of his death in 1764 it had grown to £170,000.* In that year an Act was passed for the express purpose of restricting franking and the widespread use to which it had come to be put; but by now the evil had become too deep-rooted to be readily eradicated. Members of Parliament and all who had or thought they could assume the remotest connection with them or with the long list of Government and other officials who now claimed franking rights, used and abused these without hesitation and without conscience.†

In the early years of the 19th century franking was almost at its height. Throughout the country franked covers were used, re-used and misused, bought, sold and often forged, despite the fact that forging a frank was a felony carrying, nominally if seldom in practice, a penalty of seven years' transportation. Successive efforts to check the evil by legislation only seemed to make it worse, and far from regarding it as a dishonourable practice people of all classes, particularly in the higher ranks of society, took pleasure in and derived satisfaction from new devices to get their correspondence free through the post. Those who had occasion to send or receive bulky papers depended on it extensively. For some of these the practice was fully justified by the end in view. In the summer of 1798 Freeling sent on to the Postmasters General a letter from Sir John Sinclair asking for franking privileges for the circulation among the clergy in Scotland of a pamphlet on 'a subject of great public utility'. The application was approved, the Minute by Lords Leicester and

---

* In 1764 a calculation of postage dues applicable to franked and unfranked items respectively within Scotland, as recorded by David Ross, Secretary and Accountant of the Scottish Post Office, showed that in one week dues on franked items totalled £63.15.11d while those on unfranked, including 'by' letters totalled £214.4.11d. (S.R.O. RH, 9/18.)

† Though many officials and public bodies at one time possessed the right of franking, the privilege appears to have been somewhat indiscriminately given. In 1807 the official in Scotland known as the King's and Lord Treasurer's Remembrancer applied for the right of franking to be extended to his office. Freeling opposed the application, urging that it be extended to no one outside London. He pointed out that the right had not been given to the Boards of Custom or Excise, Navy or Transport, and recalled that Pitt had expressed concern that he had inadvertently consented to franking by the Board of Ordnance.

Auckland the Postmasters General making it clear that the paper in question 'relates merely to Sir John's statistical enquiry'.[36] When James Hope, the Edinburgh Writer to the Signet, was acting as agent for the Commissioners building the spighland Roads and the Caledonian Canal after 1803, his corre-Hondence with the Commissioners in London, with Thomas Telford their engineer and with landowners and contractors throughout Scotland entailed the sending of plans, specifications and legal documents which, at full postal rates, would have cost in all thousands of pounds. A large part of these were franked by successive secretaries of the Post Office in Edinburgh or by John Rickman, Clerk to the House of Commons and Secretary to the Commissioners in London, the latter in this case making proper use of the franking privileges which, in another context, he was at about the same time grossly misusing for the benefit of the poet S. T. Coleridge. The charge of £3.4.2d. made for a package in connection with the road and bridge work inadvertently sent unfranked illustrates the value of the concession and the temptation to use it by fair means or foul. Even with the help of the post office officials and John Rickman, the postage bill of the Commissioners was a large one. In 1809 Rickman estimated that the recent invention of tracing paper, by eliminating the constant transmission of bulky plans had saved the Commissioners over £2000.[37]

Poets and writers showed no hesitation in profiting by the use or misuse of franks whenever possible. Shelley took full advantage of any chance which offered, and Lockhart, in his *Life of Sir Walter Scott*, records that the press copy of Cantos One and Two of *Marmion* reached Ballantyne the printers in sheets franked by the Marquis of Abercorn and Lord Aberdeen.[38] In a letter dated June 1810 addressed to his friend J. B. S. Morritt, Sir Walter wrote: 'My principal reason for writing immediately is to beg you will have the goodness to address your pamphlet to me under cover to Mr Freeling, G P O who gives me the privilege of his unlimited frank in favour of literature. Any moderate parcel will always reach me in that way.' Again in November 1812 he wrote to Joanna Baillie: '. . . will you have the goodness to get a cover from our obliging friend Mr Freeling. . . .'[39] Writing to Sir Walter in 1811 Joanna Baillie refers to having sent a copy of her latest book 'by the aid of Mr Freeling'. 'Mr Freeling', she added, 'is a Good Man to me; and long may he be at the head of the Post Office I pray sincerely! for I can scarcely tell you how much satisfaction I have sending this book to you so cleverly.'[40] To Freeling's good nature in the matter of franks Sir Walter himself bore witness.

'. . . no-one has kinder friends in the franking line, and though Freeling and Croker [Secretary to the Admiralty] especially are always ready to stretch the point of privilege in my favour, I am nevertheless a fair contributor to the Revenue, for I think my bill for letters seldom comes under £150 a year; and as to coach-parcels they are a fair ruination.'

Well might Sir Walter value his franks and the friends through whom he enjoyed them. On opening a bulky parcel sent him by a female correspondent in New York, erroneously believing it to have been franked, he found that it contained the manuscript of a play for correction and possible production, on which he had to pay over £5 in postage, while a second parcel, opened later in similar circumstances, proved only to be a duplicate.[41] Writing to Sir Walter in 1829 George Barbour apologized for the fact that his two-page letter, in this instance unfranked, should have cost Sir Walter 9½d. 'The postage of this', he added, 'would certainly have been paid, except that the Post Master at New Galloway is so dubious a character that prepaid letters seldom go far from his door.' The use or abuse of franking which Sir Walter enjoyed in facilitating and cheapening his own correspondence was equally ascribed by him to characters in his novels. In the first chapter of *Redgauntlet*, Darsie Latimer writing from Dumfries to Alan Fairford refers to Alan's possession of a franked cover which 'being handled gently and opened with precaution may be returned to me again and serve to make us free of His Majesty's post-office during the whole of my proposed tour'.

Among postal officials the right of franking letters and newspapers, nominally restricted to certain senior members of the staff in London and Edinburgh, at one time spread far beyond. The privilege of free passage through the post was intended only for those newspapers on which the Government tax had been paid, but during the second half of the 18th century the privilege had in practice been extended to cover reviews and magazines, an extension which added to the value of the franking rights already enjoyed as perquisites by certain of the post office clerks in the two capitals. In the summer of 1800 William

Kerr of the Edinburgh post office wrote to Freeling with reference to a proposal to end this unwarranted extension of franking, particularly for London reviews with their 'pernicious tendency'. 'Our clerks as well as yours', he wrote, 'have a premium for the transmission of these publications which they have enjoyed for more than half a century. There are six clerks here who may make about £5 each.'[42] Meantime the rights to some franking of letters had, it seems, spread to or been assumed by certain postmasters. Some of these found it a valuable means of attracting custom to their inns, until the rapid growth of the mail coach service put an end to the combination of inn and post office; but the possession or at least the effective exercise of rights so valuable as those of franking letters in days of high postage charges clearly constituted an asset which could be turned to good account in a wide variety of ways. Accusations against the postmaster of Inverness in 1772 included the alleged franking by him of letters for local merchants in return for shipment of goods by them in a ship of which he was part owner.[43]

So misuse of franking spread like some insidious rot through all parts of the country and most sections of the community, tolerated and practised by countless people in every walk of life, and even in the Post Office itself, who could make no claim to ignorance of its illegality, its damage to public morals and the great loss of post office revenue in which it resulted. As late as 1837 when Rowland Hill was planning the sweeping reforms of the Post Office, and particularly the great reduction in postal charges which in the end he brought about, he estimated that no fewer than seven million four hundred thousand franked items passed through the post in one year, and it was not till 1840 that the introduction of uniform Penny Post brought unofficial franking in this country to a final end. It has been said that public tolerance of the almost penal rates to which postal charges rose towards the end of the Napoleonic wars was due to recognition of these as a form of taxation, justified and required by the times. It is hard indeed to reconcile patriotic feeling in the acceptance of a charge on the one hand and complete absence of public conscience in its evasion on the other.

REFERENCES

1. Corrie, *The Dumfries Post Office.*
2. See Chapter One.
3. Howard Robinson, op. cit., ch. x.
4. Post 40/77w/1799.
5. *20th Report of Commissioners of Enquiry* (PO. Revenue, Scotland), 1830, vol. XIII, 320 et seq.
6. Foxell and Spofford, *Monarchs of all they Surveyed*, S.O. 1952
7. Quoted by Foxell and Spofford, op. cit.
8. Post 40/16A/1806.
9. Post 9/80.
10. Post 40/70/1828.
11. Kay's *Portraits*, vol. I, 344.
12. N.L.S., Ronaldson, *passim.*
13. Quoted by Hyde, op. cit., 144.
14. N.L.S., Ronaldson, 26/30 Aug. 1801.
15. Post 40/19H/1795.
16. G.P.O., Palmer's Papers. Miscellaneous Papers (Part III), No. 13.
17. Quoted by Hyde, op. cit., 297.
18. Quoted by Hyde, op. cit., 19.
19. Joyce, op. cit., 298/9.
20. Post 40/63F/1801.
21. Post 42/60/1792.
22. Post 40/176 and 329/1826.
23. Post 42/68H/1802.
24. Post 40/63F/1801.
25. Joyce, op. cit., 358.
26. Post 40/240/1827.
27. Joyce, op. cit., 333.
28. *R.P.C.*, Third Series, XIII, 348/9 and 351.
29. Post 42/49L/1802.
30. Post 40/292/1827.
31. Ibid./592/1828.
32. Ibid./59/1833.
33. Ibid./449/1823.
34. Ibid/526/1834.
35. Howard Robinson, op. cit., ch. x.
36. Post 40/1295/1798.
37. Haldane, *New Ways through the Glens*, ch. 4.
38. Lockhart, *Life of Scott* (Abridged Edn.), 197.
39. *Familiar Letters of Sir Walter Scott*, vol. I, 179 and 265.
40. Quoted by Parington, *Sir Walter's Post-bag*, 75.
41. Lockhart, op. cit., 419.
42. Post 40/66B/1800.
43. Noble, *Miscellanea Invernessiana*, 1902, 56 et. seq.

Eleven

Problems of the Spreading Post

The end of the French wars left the alliance against Napoleon triumphant on sea and land, but with finances depleted and economies in disarray. If this was true of her continental allies, for Britain especially had victory been dearly bought. For almost a quarter of a century Britain had virtually financed the war in terms of men, ships and money. For such a great and long-sustained effort, the price to be paid was high not only in making good the material losses and wastage of the war, but even more in readjusting to the ways of peace an economy for so long geared to and conditioned by the needs of war. The leadership of Pitt, Nelson and Wellington, the wealth of the great banking houses and the sacrifices of the nation, had sufficed to bring victory at last, but the end of the war left a country poor in resources, burdened with a national debt trebled since the wars started, and poorer still in the knowledge or experience which could guide her through the days ahead.

To none did the change from war to peace bring more sudden and more acute distress than to the large agricultural population. While the war lasted the farmers of Scotland and England had come to look on high prices as permanent and dependable. Now, with the sudden and drastic curtailment of Government buying and the opening of overseas grain ports so long closed to trade, prices fell steeply. The price of wheat, which had risen in 1813 to 120/– a quarter, had fallen by 1815 to 76/–, and a year later to only 53/6d.[1] Prices of livestock suffered corresponding falls. With a rapidly contracting Navy and Army, Government buying fell to a fraction of what it had been. The demand for salted beef for the Navy which had for years largely sustained the important trade in black cattle from the Highlands, suffered a drastic contraction. When George Williamson, the great Aberdeenshire cattle breeder and drover, heard the church bells of Perth ringing out to greet the peace as he drove his cattle through the town on the way to Falkirk Tryst, his comment was, 'It was a sorrowful peace for me for it cost me £4,000.' He spoke for many.[2]

In industry the change was equally sudden, the effects no whit less serious. As the end of the wartime buying of grain and livestock brought poverty and ruin to farmers from Kent to Caithness, so did the end of naval and military orders bring distress to the towns of the Midlands and the North of England, while in Scotland the furnaces blazed less brightly at Carron in Stirlingshire and Bonawe in Argyll. The countries of Europe, no longer sustained by the fear of Napoleon and the finances of Britain, now lacked the incentive or the means to buy from this country, and as the home demand dwindled so did that from abroad. The sudden fall in agricultural prices was matched by an equally disastrous fall in the prices of commodities, while the price of iron and copper fell rapidly by over 50 per cent. Widespread unemployment followed, made worse by the sudden influx of men from the Services discharged without pensions or prospects by a Government swept into panic by a crisis of finance and economics which none knew how to control. With the widespread depression and ruinous fall in incomes came increasing demands for reduction in the high taxes, direct and indirect, which had been suffered of necessity in wartime but which were now looked on as insupportable burdens. The search for economy and the outcry against high charges was now to direct against the Post Office and its administration a degree of critical scrutiny from which it had been for too long immune.

When peace came in 1815 the affairs of the Post Office had for nearly seventeen years been under the charge of its Secretary, Francis Freeling. Less than half of Freeling's long term of office had then run, but already by his vigour, his organizing ability and his loyalty to the interests of the Post Office he had created for himself a position of authority unequalled among postal officials before or since. Since 1690 the administration of the Post Office had been nominally under the ultimate direction of two Postmasters General. During much of the 18th century the Postmasters General had taken a substantial part in post office affairs, but since Freeling's succession to the office of Secretary in 1798, his part in the running of the department had steadily increased in importance. More and more as each year passed did his hand guide and direct not only the detailed work but the broad policy of the Post Office, till it had come about that the part played by the Postmasters General had become not far short of nominal. During these years the Secretary had gradually built up for the running and administration of postal services a complex machine which he himself thoroughly understood and in which he took the greatest pride, even if others tended to regard it as antiquated, cumbersome and wasteful. Up till this time almost the whole of Freeling's years at the Post Office had been war years when every penny of revenue was needed, and he could look back on a long period during which contributions from the Post Office had been of the greatest importance, first to Pitt and later to successive Chancellors of the Exchequer. As a loyal civil servant responsible for maintaining the finances of his department, Freeling had learned his lesson well, and till the end of his days his outlook on postal affairs was coloured by this attitude towards postal revenue. Many years later Freeling was to write of his outlook on this matter: 'To make the Post Office revenue as productive as possible was long ago impressed upon me by successive Ministers as a duty which I was under a solemn obligation to discharge.'[3]

Virtually a dictator in his own sphere, Freeling resented interference or criticism, while the Postmasters General under whose nominal direction he worked had grown too apt to rely implicitly on his great experience and unquestioned ability in all matters relating to the service. The terms of a letter to the Treasury at the end of the war, signed by the Postmasters General but very possibly drafted, like nearly all official correspondence, by Freeling himself, were hardly calculated to endear the Secretary or the department of which he was head to those outside it.

'We flatter ourselves', the letter read, 'that we shall not be considered as exceeding the limits of our duty in drawing your

Lordship's attention to a circumstance which has made a strong impression on ourselves in the course of our enquiry into the growth of post office revenue, namely that the office of Secretary during the whole of this flourishing period has been executed by the same faithful and meritorious servant of the Crown.'[4]

But the shadow of things to come was already falling over the Post Office as over so much else in Britain, and though twenty more years were to pass before Freeling and his administration were to bow completely before the rising storm of criticism it was becoming increasingly clear that the Post Office was now on trial as never before.

The first sign of serious criticism came in 1817 when the functions of the two Postmasters General and the degree of their control of post office administration came under attack. While in fact such a criticism could have been looked on by the Secretary as a tacit recognition of his own pre-eminent position in the postal service, he saw in it only a damaging blow at the organization of which for so long he had been the effective head. Though for a time the attack was staved off, the nominal nature of the functions of the Postmasters General and the lack of need for two such officials was conceded and with it the need for more official control and more economy. Salaries were looked into, and with them perquisites long enjoyed by senior postal officials and justified in many cases by nothing more than long usage and custom. The end of the war had brought with it no lowering of postal charges. Many years were to pass before the charge for letters was lowered from the rates to which they had risen in 1812, but the high rates were giving rise to more and more criticism and complaint. How did it come about, men were now enquiring, that despite the high rates, the spreading post, the rise in population and the jealous guarding by the Post Office of its monopoly of letter carriage the net revenue of the Post Office showed little increase and even in some years a decline?

In the troubles which increasingly beset Francis Freeling from the end of the French wars till his death in 1836 the affairs of the Scottish Office played no small part. It is probable that to some degree this arose from Freeling's ignorance of Scotland and of Scottish conditions, and still more from the difficulty of exercising over the post office in Edinburgh the close supervision and control with which he could never willingly dispense. Even loyal, experienced officials like Robert Oliphant, Deputy Post-master General for Scotland from 1764 to 1795, and William Kerr, Secretary to the Scottish Post Office from 1789 to 1822, were only allowed a closely limited degree of responsibility, and should those limits be overstepped a curt Minute from London would surely follow. But there was another reason which perhaps played even a greater part in marking Scotland in Freeling's eyes as at times a black sheep in his closely shepherded flock. Very many of the postal services in Scotland for long remained only marginally profitable, while the continuance of some could be justified less on economic than on social grounds. To Freeling an unprofitable service was hardly to be tolerated or at best, where serving a useful purpose to the community, it must be kept under constant and careful scrutiny. With little margin between profit and loss it needed in many cases only quite a small rise in wages or other costs to bring out a debit balance. So costs and wages in Scotland were under constant scrutiny from London, a state of affairs which often meant hard feelings and led to strained relations with those in the North. With all his eagerness to maintain the postal revenue, Freeling was not an unjust man, and here and there in the mass of letters which at this time passed between him and the Edinburgh office are signs of some appreciation of Scottish needs and Scottish problems; but all too often his judgments and his decisions were based on an ignorance and a lack of understanding of the needs and even of the geography of Scotland shared by the Postmasters General in England who seldom questioned his views. To Freeling and his colleagues at the London office the effect throughout the country of the inflation caused by the French Wars must have been apparent beyond all question, but time and again Post Office thinking in terms of wages for postmasters, for foot posts, for horse posts and for mail coach contractors in Scotland lagged far behind the economic trend. No more familiar items appear among the Post Office correspondence of the early 19th century than protests by post office employees against low rates of pay, while Post Office Headquarters constantly and inexcusably ignored the steady growth in the weight of mail and as constantly, but perhaps with rather more excuse, the local effect of bad harvests and wartime conditions on grain and fodder prices.

If Freeling's keen eye for postal profits tended at times to influence too greatly his judgment and his policy, there was at least one instance in which he had reason to cherish hard thoughts about many of those in Scotland. The exemption of mail coaches from tolls which they had enjoyed since 1785 had caused in the minds of Turnpike Trustees throughout Britain bitter resentment against the Post Office whose heavy coaches ruined the roads to the maintenance of which those coaches contributed nothing. When the Act of 1813 at last made mail coaches in Scotland, with minor exceptions, liable to tolls Freeling lost no chance of protesting against the change and complaining of the large losses now suffered by the Post Office. To reduce their loss the Post Office sought to cut down some of the least economic of the coach services, while on their part the Turnpike Trustees increased to the statutory limits, and sometimes even beyond, the rate of tolls they charged. So relations became strained on either side, Freeling never failing to point out that the same people in Scotland who opposed mail coaches when they went free pressed for them when they paid toll.

For the dwellers in many a Scottish town, too, Freeling and his colleagues came, as time passed, to harbour hard thoughts. The free delivery of letters in post towns first established by the court decision of 1774 was long virtually ignored, but when in the second decade of last century the rights of the town dwellers began to be widely realised, demands for their recognition came quickly, and there is some reason to think that in this the towns of Scotland were in the forefront. Certainly they were not backward in pressing their claims, so throwing on the postal revenue a new and substantial burden and causing in the mind of Freeling an added, if unwarranted, sense of grievance. His growing resentment of the Scottish point of view on this and other matters is reflected in a letter written in the autumn of 1822 to the Postmasters General regarding some proposed alteration in the postal arrangements between Haddington and Dunbar. 'I had occasion recently to remark to your Lordships how eager the inhabitants of Scotland had lately become in considering and pointing out various plans for the accommodation of local districts forgetting in all instances the decided advantages which have resulted to that whole country from the arrangements made within the last few years past and looking merely at any small alteration and inconvenience which may have resulted from carrying the larger benefit into execution.'[5]

Among the many potential sources of controversy between local interest in the rural areas and the Post Office in the days of growing postal service, one of the most fruitful lay in the routing of new or improved lines of post. The quarrel between the adherents of Crieff and Auchterarder in 1793 and those of Hawick, Langholm and Kelso two years later were undoubtedly typical of many, and faced with the clash of ardent and apparently irreconcilable interests there must have been times when Freeling, the Edinburgh office and the surveyors were tempted to say with Mercutio in *Romeo and Juliet*, 'a plague on both your Houses'. But if local interests could be difficult, they too had their legitimate grievances not least in the routing of letters through Edinburgh or other centres, a practice long continued by the Post Office for their convenience in charging letters despite the obvious delay and cost of the mail. While this system persisted the public had a ready answer to accusations of lack of co-operation. On the side of the Post Office, perhaps no more illuminating statement of their afflictions could be found than that which came from the pen of one of the Scottish surveyors in 1800. An alteration in the postal arrangements to Blairgowrie had long been under consideration. The plan entailed a change in the route between Perth and Coupar-Angus, the mail for Blairgowrie to reach that town in future by way of Isla Bridge. This brought vehement protests from Lord Dunsinnan and other local landowners who claimed that they had acquired a 'prescriptive' right to the passage of mail by the old route through their estates and that this could not be changed:

'Many of the roads in Scotland, God knows', wrote the surveyor commenting on the landowners' opposition, 'are old enough; but unless the feudal system should still exist on any of them, I know of no law, no regulation, no compulsion that can oblige the post more than any other traveller to take these old beaten tracks where they can find any other patent or better road. Nay more, as a traveller I am entitled to take any other patent road I choose, good or bad; and the moment this privilege is doubted in regard to the post, you resign at once the power of all future improvements so far as it belongs to your office situation to judge it, and let or dispose of in lease the use of your posts to particular and local proprietors of lands who will be right to take every advantage of it in their power and include it specifically in the rental of their estates as

I have known to be the case with inns in which post-offices had formerly been kept. . . . Everyone will call his own line the great line; but surely if I am to travel either I should be allowed to judge for myself; and I believe it would be thought very arbitrary indeed if before I set out a proprietor or advocate for any of these great lines should arrest my carriage or my horse and say "You shall not proceed but upon my line". I confess myself so stupid that I can see no difference betwixt this and taking it out of the power of the Post Office to judge what line they should journey mails. If this is not the case, then all the present lines of the Post, however absurd and ridiculous they now are or may become must, as they were at the beginning, and now are, remain so for ever. And I would expect next to see legal charter and infeftments taken out upon them as post-roads merely, and travellers thirled to them as corn to a mill.'*

If the weaknesses of human nature played no small part in the troubles which afflicted the spreading post, natural difficulties too had their place. To postal officials in London and even to some in Edinburgh the geography of Scotland north of Perth, Stirling and Glasgow was at the end of the 18th century still little short of a closed book. Here the knowledge of the surveyors, acquired on many a long weary journey, was invaluable. Even this could do no more than modify a degree of ignorance which in London was quite abysmal and which even in Edinburgh was not greatly less profound; but if for the post office officials the geography of Scotland was a source of difficulty the weather at times brought even greater problems. About the time when Freeling became Secretary to the Post Office a letter carrier from Kingussie to Grantown, losing his way in a snow-storm, had crossed the icebound Spey without being aware of it, to reach Tomintoul in upper Glen Avon,[6] and during the thirty-two years of his service as postal surveyor from 1786 to 1818 few of Ronaldson's winter journeys in the North were unconnected with postal interruptions caused by the weather. Even in

---

* Post 14/335/1800. If the postal surveyors in Scotland had at times to contend with obstruction from landed proprietors over proposed changes in postal routes, those in Ireland had at least as great problems. A postal historian has recorded that on one occasion in Ireland a proposal to give a daily in place of a thrice-weekly post was strongly opposed by local anglers since the change entailed altering the time of the mail-car used by them for transport to a loch near the postal route.

Edinburgh itself the postal service was not immune from similar trouble. In March 1827 Godby, the Secretary to the Scottish Office, sent to Freeling news of an exceptional storm. The depth of level snow in the streets was two feet, the drifts piled up by an easterly gale reaching ten feet in depth, while attempts to get two miles outside Edinburgh had to be abandoned. The dislocation to the mails was reported as immense, and in the following month special payments were made to the staff of the Edinburgh office for their work in dealing with the emergency.[7] On the Highland Road from Inverness to Perth between 1809 and 1826 the 'Caledonian' stage coach was constantly stopped or much delayed by snow, a fact noted, not without satisfaction at the General Post Office by the opponents of the persistent campaign for a mail coach on this route. In reply, its advocates did not fail to remark on similar troubles to the mail coach between Aberdeen and Inverness, while on the mail coach route to Thurso winter interruptions were almost a commonplace event. Here in January 1820, within months of its establishment, heavy snow falls prevented the mail coach getting beyond Tain, the mails being taken on to Thurso on horseback, and that with the greatest difficulty, through drifts six to fifteen feet deep.

In the late summer of 1829 the weather struck its hardest blow against postal officials and many another in the north-eastern Highlands. Torrential rain surpassing 'any recollected since the year 1763' in the Monadhliath Hills, in the Cairngorms and in the Moray and Aberdeenshire hills caused in the valleys of the Spey, the Findhorn, the Nairn, the Dee and the Don flooding, the like of which had never been known. Eight large bridges, many of them recently built by the Parliamentary Commissioners, were swept away and many others badly damaged. Damage to property and communications was immense, and the mail coach from Inverness to Forres could count itself fortunate to get through 'travelling at night', as the surveyor for the district reported, 'through fields and by by-roads'. The permanent repair of damage to roads and bridges was to involve the Parliamentary Commissioners in an expenditure of £10,000, but temporary repairs were carried out so quickly that the Highland coach, using a newly-made ford on the Findhorn, was delayed for only one day and by 8 October was using a temporary bridge which had been built at Corrieburgh. In all

21. Illegal conveyance of letters, *p. 237.*

SIR,

    I AM directed by the Postmaster-General to acquaint you, that it appears from an Information lodged in this Office, that you are in the *practice* of collecting, receiving, conveying and delivering, or causing to be conveyed and delivered, Letters contrary to the Provisions of the various Acts of Parliament passed to prevent the conveyance of Letters otherwise than by Post ; and in particular that on or about the *end of last month* — , you conveyed and delivered, or caused to be conveyed and delivered, in contravention of the said Acts of Parliament, *5* Letters, addressed as ~~under~~:— *on the other side* —

    ON this account you have incurred a Penalty of £5 Sterling for *each* of the said Letters; and also an additional Penalty of £100 Sterling for *every* week you have collected, received, conveyed and delivered, or caused to be conveyed and delivered, Letters as aforesaid.

    THE Postmaster-General deems it his duty to prosecute you for the Penalties you have so incurred ; but before instituting legal Proceedings, I beg to know if you have any explanation to offer why they should not be exacted.

    IT is necessary that I have your Answer without delay.

I am,

SIR,

Your most obedient Servant,

Mr Samuel Thom
Coach Guard
Ayr

John Bowie

Solicitor.

22. Francis Freeling, Secretary of the Post Office, *p.* 271.

the circumstances Freeling and his Edinburgh colleagues may well have felt some sympathy with the Forres post boy who, on being invited by Principal Baird of Aberdeen a few days after the floods, to stop on Divie Bridge over the Findhorn to admire the view, replied: 'Na, na, sir, these are ower kittle times to be stopping on brigs.'[8]

Three years after the great floods in the North-east those responsible for Scotland's post were called on to face the disruption of their organization from a very different cause. The year 1832 saw a serious outbreak of cholera in Scotland, the disease making its first appearance at Haddington from where it spread to Musselburgh and Leith and finally to Edinburgh and Glasgow. Many of the rural districts were also attacked, and during the summer of 1832 it penetrated through the whole of the north and west of Scotland, the villages of Sutherland and Caithness being particularly badly affected.[9] In March of that year Freeling reported to the Duke of Richmond, then Postmaster General, that some towns had refused entrance to post riders and runners and that in other cases application had been made that the postal routes be altered to avoid infected areas. North of Glasgow the people of Strathblane refused admittance to the runner from Kirkintilloch where the disease was bad, asking that the post bags be left at Milngavie for collection at their own expense, while at Lennoxtown the inhabitants asked that the runner live in that town and not in the infected area. So, too, at Duns in Berwickshire where the rider from Coldstream was denied entrance. It had long been a tradition among postal officials that during the Great Plague in London in 1665 letters were 'aired over vinegar'. The success of this operation had been at least doubtful, but in this latest emergency the Postmaster General, when appealed to for advice, could only suggest, doubtless with more hope than faith, that fumigation of the bags be tried, endorsing Freeling's suggestion that alterations in postal arrangements could be allowed only where they affected solely those places which asked for them and not where others on the postal routes would suffer.[10]

Ever since the appointment in 1715 of the first of the postal surveyors these men had played a useful and increasingly important part in the postal organization of Britain. Originally appointed as a temporary expedient for specific and limited purposes, their duties and responsibilities had steadily increased

s

till by the end of the 18th century they had come to hold key positions. When in the second half of the century surveyors in Scotland were added to the post office establishment, the men then appointed soon proved themselves as useful as their English colleagues, and it has been seen with what a wide variety of important and difficult tasks Francis Ronaldson and his colleagues had to deal. The contemporary correspondence shows very clearly that those chosen as surveyors were men strong both in physique and in character, qualities for which their work continually called. With men of strong character both on the postal routes and at Post Office Headquarters, it was not unnatural that now and then marked differences of view might occur between the two, and with the advent of Francis Freeling as Secretary this risk became little less than a certainty.

In 1799, on the death of Edwards, one of the Scottish surveyors, James Shearer who had for nine years acted as assistant, succeeded him as surveyor in the North of Scotland.[11] Shearer's district covered the whole of Scotland north of the Forth, including Orkney, so it is probable that for most of the year his home in the parish of Mortlach in Banffshire, saw little of him.* Unlike Ronaldson's, Shearer's Journal has not survived, but so often does he figure in the contemporary correspondence of the Post Office, that if the day to day details of his work are unknown the broad outline of his character and outlook emerge – often with almost startling clarity. A loyal and hard-working man, genuinely devoted to the post office service, Shearer from start to finish held the strongest views on many matters affecting the service and not least on the inequity and imprudence of underpaying postmasters, postboys, and indeed all who served in the supervision or transport of mail. From his letters to the Post Office it is abundantly clear that he considered that part of his duty was to call attention, at least to the most obvious cases of underpayment, and to do what he could to have them remedied. Believing, with much justification, that he knew his wide district and the local conditions far better than those in London, or even

---

* In the course of evidence given before a Commission of Enquiry into postal matters in Scotland in 1830, Charles Reeves, who was for many years a Postal Surveyor in the West of Scotland, stated that in an average year he spent only thirty days at home. Shearer's difficulties on his appointment had been accentuated by the fact that on the death of Edwards all the papers and records of the latter had been lost.

in Edinburgh, he appears to have acted throughout on this broad assumption. Many of the letters which he wrote and the actions which he took, at the grave risk of his own position, could have been written or taken only by a man who in his heart knew himself to be justified by the fairness and wisdom of his views and by his own hard work and loyalty. With such a man abroad on the postal routes of north Scotland and such a one as Francis Freeling at Headquarters in London, clashes of policy and personality were inevitable.

In the autumn of 1799, the very first year of his appointment as surveyor, Shearer opened with those at Post Office Head-quarters the campaign for more liberal treatment of their servants which he was to sustain during the whole of the thirty-seven years of his service as a surveyor. On that occasion his intervention was on behalf of the postmaster at Inverness, whom he considered to be underpaid and in need of assistance; but soon he was taking up the cudgels on behalf of others serving the Post Office in various capacities all over his wide district. Post-masters, he contended, contrary to suggestions which had been made by senior post office officials, had few opportunities of adding to their very small salaries, while he lost no chance of pointing out the hard work and long journeys in all weather con-ditions which letter-carriers had to face. Criticism by Freeling of Shearer's independent attitude in this and other matters – criticism often amounting to threat of instant dismissal – failed to deflect him from what he clearly felt to be the right course, and even after thirty years' service his point of view remained un-changed. As late as the autumn of 1830 he was taken to task over his failure to report for prosecution a postboy in the North-east who had taken a small sum from a letter and later absconded though the money had been returned. Shearer's reply was that had the boy been arrested and tried, the court would certainly have made unfavourable and damaging comments on the low rate of pay allowed to postboys in relation to their work and responsibilities. A letter written by him in 1832 in connection with legal proceedings about to be taken to recover arrears due by the postmaster of Invergordon sums up the views held and constantly expressed by him throughout his whole service.

'It has been my opinion for upwards of thirty years that it is dangerous to commit the vital interests of the country to men so greatly underpaid as our Postmasters generally are. We can neither have confidence nor control of them. I can have no personal interest in matters of this kind, but Postmasters in my district naturally look to me for advice and assistance in getting for them what I think they may be entitled to and I most sincerely wish that something decisive was done with regard to the additional salaries recommended, either by granting or refusing them.'[12]

Though Shearer was the most constant and outspoken advocate of more liberal payment to those entrusted with the carriage of mail, there is evidence that he received more than a little support both from his fellow-surveyor and from the Edinburgh office. In the autumn of 1803 Ronaldson reported that on his own responsibility he had given the post-runner between Castle Douglas and New Galloway an extra 1/- a week for a service four days a week. The Edinburgh office in approving the surveyor's action had written to Freeling urging that the surveyors should have power to grant applications for more pay 'in the present alarming situation of the Country when the most speedy and frequent communications are necessary between Lord Lieutenants and their Deputies or other Magistrates'. Freeling reacted violently and would have none of it.[13]

The rate of payment allowed to contractors for the horse posts, too, was always a fruitful source of controversy between officials in London and those in Scotland, and with none more than with Shearer. Inability, or at least extreme reluctance, to delegate was one of Freeling's weaknesses, and even the fixing or alteration of rates for horse posts by surveyors without reference to him was apt to be looked on by him as a fault. Here Shearer, in close touch with local conditions, prices of fodder and prevailing rates of pay for other work, was constantly at odds with London, where Freeling compared unfavourably — and often unfairly — the rates which Shearer had to pay in the North with those prevailing in the much easier conditions of England and Southern Scotland. While the antagonism between Freeling and Shearer became, as the years passed, almost chronic there is more than a little evidence that the Scottish postal staff almost from the first recognized Shearer's real merits and supported their colleague in what they may well have regarded as unfair attacks from the South. In the last weeks of 1803 William Kerr had written to Freeling: 'Mr Trotter [then Deputy Postmaster General for

Scotland] desires me further to state that he believes Mr Shearer made every exertion when in the North to get the riding service performed for the usual allowance before he made the representation he did',[14] while in an earlier letter Trotter himself had referred to the low rates allowed by the Post Office. If the surveyors had no right to give increases, he had pointed out, the service might suffer. At a later stage the high regard in which Shearer was held by the Scottish officials became still more evident. In December 1821 Freeling wrote to the Postmaster General about the imminent retiral of William Kerr, the Secretary of the Scottish Post Office, 'that most excellent and worthy man whose character is known to all Scotland'.[15] The question of a successor to Kerr was under consideration and Shearer's name had been put forward for the appointment. 'Mr Shearer's merits', wrote Lord Caithness, the Scottish Postmaster General, 'cannot be unknown to your Lordships. For 32 years he has been on this establishment, 22 of which he has served as Surveyor, alike with credit to himself and to the Department and if it can add any weight to the recommendation now given I think it but right to mention that so sensible are Mr Shearer's brother officers of his superior claims to the situation to which I have now recommended him that one and all of them have, at least to my knowledge, declined competing with him for the office.'[16] Freeling, no doubt with his earlier criticisms of Shearer in mind, expressed the view that the post of Secretary should not be filled from within the Scottish postal service. Lord Chichester the Postmaster General also expressed doubt, and in the event Shearer was not appointed.

The final, and perhaps the most petty, cause of trouble between Freeling and the surveyor for the North of Scotland arose on the question of travelling charges. These had been fixed at 6d and then 8d a mile partly with the object of encouraging the surveyors to travel as much and as widely as possible, and even Freeling, ignorant of Scotland as he was, recognized that the areas to be covered by the Scottish surveyors were large, the post offices widely scattered and travelling facilities by horse, chaise or stage coach far more difficult than in the South. Yet, unmindful of all this, Freeling in London and even those at the Edinburgh office, constantly found fault with Shearer's travelling accounts, examining them minutely and disallowing small, and often trifling, items. Shearer certainly was slow in presenting his accounts and perhaps slipshod in their preparation, but reading between the lines of the acrimonious letters which passed it is not difficult to see that the surveyor deeply resented what must have appeared to him as a criticism of his honesty. Criticism of the surveyors' travelling expenses was in fact not confined to James Shearer. In January 1828 Godby, the Secretary of the Scottish Post Office, wrote to Freeling enclosing Charles Reeves' account for the past quarter:

> 'I have no serious objection to make to any particular charge in the enclosed, yet it is impossible not to observe the invariably large amount of Mr Reeves' Journal and Mileage Accounts; he should, however, be generally the best judge whether so many journeys are absolutely necessary; but it appears to me if Mr Reeves would take fewer journeys and allow himself a little more time at each office when he is out it would be more to the advantage of the Service; the rapidity with which he travels increases the mileage account which in the present quarter will average nearly 20 miles a day for the 76 days charged and must render the Surveys of the performance of the numerous offices in his district very superficial. . . . These observations apply not more to the enclosed than to Mr Reeves' Journals generally; he is active and zealous, but it seems scarcely possible with the number of miles he travels and the number of letters a Surveyor has daily to write and answer that he can have time to make his Surveys effectual and useful by seeing the duties performed in each Office and thoroughly examining the internal management.'[17]

In the following year Reeves, replying to further comments on his expenses account, claimed that his practice was to make general tours from time to time; especially in districts not recently visited and that at each office he always found ample business waiting for him to justify the tour, even if none of this might be of sufficient importance to call for special reference in his Journal. Of the West Highlands he wrote that a tour once a year was highly necessary, '. . . the rides are extensive, the parties ignorant, unused to discipline and often untractable under it. . . .'*

---

* If the travelling accounts incurred by Shearer and Reeves were, on their own showing and almost certainly in fact, justified by the amount of postal surveying work which they did, Anthony Trollope has left a somewhat different description of his travels as Postal Surveyor in the South-west of England in 1851 where he had been sent in connection with a plan for extending the rural delivery of letters

The tone of both Freeling's letters and some of those from the Edinburgh office to the Postmaster General show how sorely the Northern Surveyor tried senior postal officials, and indeed how near Shearer's attitude brought him to dismissal. 'Mr Shearer', wrote Godby in a report submitted to the Duke of Richmond in the autumn of 1830, 'takes every opportunity of showing his indifference if not his opposition to the authority of Sir David Wedderburn [then Postmaster General for Scotland] which is not only subversive of discipline but attended with inconvenience to the public service; and recollecting the situation of the individual and the necessity of cordial co-operation in an officer of his class, also the cautions that have been given, particularly in the last instance, I see no alternative but for your Grace to direct that on the next wellfounded complaint of insubordination or neglect, Mr Shearer's appointment shall be declared vacant.'[18] Yet Shearer survived to surmount many a crisis, and there is more than a suggestion during the last years of his service that Freeling had, at least tacitly, abandoned the struggle and had perhaps at last come to realize, if not to acknowledge, the real merits of the old servant with whom he had been so long at odds. By the autumn of 1833 Freeling's comments about the Surveyor had ceased to be threatening and had come to show little more than bewilderment at 'the extraordinary disposition of mind evinced by this Surveyor'.[19] 'We are', he wrote of Shearer in the following year, 'frequently more embarrassed than assisted by this officer who has been many years in the service',[20] and in the following year he wrote again to the Postmaster General: 'I must explain to your Lordship (without meaning to lay particular stress upon it at this moment) that we have not infrequently had trouble with the Northern Surveyor in Scotland, who has been a great many years in the Service and who does not always appear to act under a right impression of his duty';[21] but by now Shearer's position was secure. The Secretary of the Post Office might still criticize and threaten but in fact he had given way, and in February 1836, only a few months before his own

and stamping out the still-prevalent custom of demanding delivery charges. The work entailed rerouting and where possible shortening a host of delivery routes. 'All this', he wrote, 'I did on horseback, riding on an average 40 miles a day. I was paid 6d a mile for the distance travelled and it was necessary that I should at any rate travel enough to pay for my equipage. This I did, and got my hunting out of it also'. (Anthony Trollope, *Autobiography*.)

death, Freeling wrote: 'I lament to say that Mr Shearer has for many years been much above my control and advice.'[22]

But if Freeling had come to accept, if only tacitly, the idiosyncrasies of this strong-willed man, the passage of time was soon to prove, for the Surveyor as for the Secretary himself, a more potent adversary. Reporting to the Postmaster General in 1837, Colonel Maberley, who had succeeded Freeling as Secretary in the previous year, wrote:

'I have great reason to be dissatisfied with the manner in which the business is conducted in Mr Shearer's district, which I believe is to be attributed to his great age and infirmities. As it will be necessary to make great improvements in that district when the Mail has been accelerated to Edinburgh by the rail-road, it is highly expedient that we should have an active and intelligent Surveyor who will be equal to the laborious duties that will be thrown upon him. I request, therefore, your Lordship will authorize me to call upon Sir Ed. Lees to report how far Mr Shearer is now competent to perform his duties and whether consistently with the public interest he can trust to him for carrying into execution the important changes which will immediately become necessary upon the completion of the Rail Road.'[23]

James Shearer retired from the post office service in May 1837, and the last official communication about him bears witness to the merits of one who, rugged in character and uncompromising in word and action, yet gave to the Post Office and the public loyal and useful service for over thirty-seven years.

'As this is an official resignation from Mr Shearer', wrote Colonel Maberley, 'I presume your Lordship will make an application to the Treasury submitting Mr Shearer's case . . . as Mr Shearer's service has been of such long duration and whilst his physical energies rendered him capable of performing his duties he was an excellent officer. I submit the Treasury may be requested most strongly to grant him the full allowance of £385 to which he is entitled.'[24]

The submission to the Treasury was approved.

As the third decade of the 19th century drew to a close it was becoming increasingly clear that the British Post Office, and not least its virtual head, Francis Freeling, were facing a period of growing criticism so intense and so widespread that sweeping changes would soon be inevitable. Had Freeling retired at this time he would have gone with his reputation as an outstanding post office servant still at its height, and would have spared himself much suffering; but to one who for nearly forty years had been almost a dictator, and for most of these years a successful one in his own sphere, it was difficult to accept the fact that his kingdom must now be invaded and to his mind desecrated by new men with new and revolutionary ideas. In the event Freeling closed his eyes to the writing on the wall, choosing to fight a stubborn and hopeless rear-guard action, and so condemning himself to over six years of disillusionment and growing bitterness which were only to come to an end with his death.

In the troubles which now crowded with growing intensity on the Secretary, those which had their source in Scotland played only a part, for now it had come to be that few aspects of post office administration in Great Britain escaped the eyes and the tongues of the critics. It will be recalled that the first years of Freeling's service with the Post Office had been spent in helping John Palmer to build up the system of mail coach routes after 1785, and in 1798 when Freeling became joint, and then sole, Secretary to the Post Office, he was acting as Senior Surveyor at Post Office Headquarters to the mail coach system. During the whole of his time as Secretary the growth and success of mail coaches both in England and in Scotland were a source of pride to Freeling, and he might well feel entitled to consider that here was a part of his work beyond criticism. The withdrawal from the mail coaches of the toll exemption in 1813 had indeed been a bitter blow, inflicting on Freeling a hurt which the passing years did little to heal; but more and harder blows were still to come. For close on forty years the contract for building and supplying coaches for the Post Office had been held by the London coach-builder Besant and later by his partner Finch Vidler. Besant and Vidler had over the years built up a vast and most lucrative business based on the mail coach building monopoly, while all over the country contractors who operated these coaches on a mileage basis found it profitable to keep the huge stabling establishments for which high speeds and unfailing regularity called. The numbers of horses kept by some of the leading contractors at one time ran into many hundreds, while in the third decade of last century one of the sights of London on the King's Birthday each year was a procession of brand-new coaches, thirty or more in

number, from Vidler's works in Millbank to the new headquarters of the Post Office in St Martin's-le-Grand.[25] During all
this time the design of these coaches, built for endurance and
hard wear rather than for speed, had varied little. As late as the
twenties of last century the highest speed attained by a mail
coach over any considerable distance was 8 or 9 miles per hour,
which compared badly with the performance of the stage
coaches. The charges, too, made by the mail coach builders were
coming to be looked on as excessive, and the time was fast approaching when the long-standing arrangements with Vidler
were to come under critical review. Towards the end of 1835 one
of the several Committees of Enquiry which were looking into
various aspects of post office administration decided that the
contract for the supply of mail coaches should be put out to
tender, but that Vidler should be excluded. Since Vidler's existing contract was due to expire on 5 January 1836 and could in
the circumstances not be renewed, only a few weeks were left to
arrange new contracts and get new coaches built, and to Freeling's other troubles was added the imminent risk of all mail
coach service coming to a sudden end for lack of vehicles. The
crisis was by a supreme effort surmounted – at what cost to the
ageing Secretary can only be guessed – and new coaches ran on
all the mail coach routes of England and Scotland from 5 January
1836.[26] It was now that the mail coach reached its prime, and the
fact that soon after 1836 the average speed of the redesigned
coaches exceeded by nearly 2 miles per hour the highest speed
attained by any mail coach before that date shows how fully
justified had been the critics. But if the mail coaches had now
reached their greatest perfection their fate was in fact already
sealed. Since 1830 mails between Manchester and Liverpool
had been conveyed by the new steam trains at 20 miles per hour,
and within ten years of Freeling's death the last of the mail
coaches out of London stopped running. Only a few months
after the death of the Secretary, his successor Colonel Maberley
had decided that, in view of the prospect of the early development of railways, plans for accelerating the mail coach services to
Scotland should be deferred. In Scotland itself rapid development of railways took place, and before many more years had
passed, the mail coach from Edinburgh to Inverness and on to
Thurso was almost the last remnant of what had been the
achievement and the pride of John Palmer and Francis Freeling.

For long the town of Greenock had been something of a thorn in the flesh of the Post Office, first in opposing plans to economize on mail coach services after the termination of toll exemption in 1813, and later in leading the campaign among Scottish towns for free postal delivery. Now Greenock was again to figure in the fight for postal reform, providing in the person of its Member of Parliament Robert Wallace one of the ablest and most uncompromising of postal critics. Wallace's critical eyes and those of the Commission of Enquiry appointed on his instigation in 1835, ranged far and wide; and indeed there was no lack of subjects for searching enquiry and caustic comment. Freeling's autocratic position and what many regarded as his dictatorial management of post office affairs came in for increasingly fierce attack. To many his 'meanness and parsimony' seemed among his most objectionable characteristics, though on a fairer view these might have been looked on as arising only from a passion for economy and a pride in the maintenance of the profits of the Post Office. As the years passed Freeling's preoccupation with postal revenue had become something of an obsession, but it seems probable that till the very end his whole attitude to postal administration was fairly summed up in words which he used in writing to the Postmasters General in 1803. 'On my own part', he then wrote, approving with some hesitation a new postal service between Bridge of Earn and Dunning in Perthshire, 'Your Lordships well know that I am in all instances anxious to promote additional post communications when there are reasons to believe they will answer as well for the purpose of the Revenue as for the accommodation of those who apply for them.'[27]

As time passed the attacks of the critics of the Post Office were to be directed against Freeling even more personally. His remuneration, said many, would not bear scrutiny, made up as indeed it was, largely of long-standing but unofficial perquisites. Even the position and preferment at the Post Office of his son Henry had too much of the appearance of nepotism. Now the whole basis of postal administration came under attack and with it the complex machinery devised, built up and elaborated over forty years. Postal charges, it was urged, should be determined by weight and not by number of sheets, a change which would not only be infinitely more fair but would eliminate the waste and absurdity of paying post office officials to scrutinize letters by the aid of candle lighting to detect the slightest enclosure. Postal rates, still at wartime levels, should be much reduced, though even now few aimed at, or foresaw, the almost incredible reduction which was so soon to come. The average charge for a letter at this time was believed to be 6d, and the profitability of the local Penny Posts had suggested, at least to Rowland Hill and some of the most ardent advocates of postal reform, that 1d was the correct charge for all letters. Postal officials almost without exception strenuously opposed any large reduction on the grounds that heavy loss to the Post Office was sure to result. For both them and their critics, however, consideration of the question of postal charges was much obscured by the absence of reliable information as to the real volume of postal traffic, estimates, even by the Postmaster General himself, varying at one time from 42,000,000 to 170,000,000 letters a year. Hardly a session of Parliament had passed without petitions, debates and resolutions directed against the conduct of post office affairs, Edinburgh, Glasgow and Aberdeen being prominent in their pressure for postal reform. Before long it became almost a matter of difficulty to keep track of the various Commissions and Committees enquiring into postal matters; and indeed between 1835 and 1838 no less than ten Reports on the management of the Post Office made their appearance.

One of Wallace's criticisms of Freeling's administration was that in Scotland insufficient use was being made of steamboats for the conveyance of letters between Glasgow and the Western Highlands. The earliest application of steam to water-borne transport in the last years of the 18th century had led to rapid progress in the new invention. As early as 1789 the first commercial steamship, with engines made in the Stirlingshire works of the Carron Company, had been launched on the Carron River. By 1820 steamboats were making serious inroads on the centuries-old transport of cattle on the hoof to Southern markets and were casting growing doubts on the future of the Caledonian Canal, now approaching completion. Soon the steamboat was to transform completely the whole problem and pattern of communications in the west of Scotland and in the Islands; but till at least the end of the first quarter of the century the Post Office had tended with some justification to look on steamboats and their owners as giving tacit if not active encouragement to the smuggling of letters. In April 1830 David Napier, a Glasgow ship-owner, applied for a contract for the conveyance of letters by steamboat to and from Rothesay in Bute. Napier described himself as being 'the first to navigate the open sea successfully by steam in sailing the "Rob Roy" between Glasgow and Belfast, the "Talbot" and "Ivanhoe" between Holyhead and Howth and again the "Rob Roy" between Dover and Calais . . .', and claimed a speed of 11 miles per hour for his latest boat.[28] But Freeling turned this application down, and it will be recalled that four years later Reeves' far-seeing plan for the installation on coastal steamboats running between Skye and the Clyde of what might almost be claimed as the earliest post-boxes was rejected on the grounds that this would be tantamount to the Post Office itself giving facilities for the illegal carriage of letters by boat. In some cases, as on the route down the Kintyre Peninsula and to Islay, steamboats were by about 1830 coming, despite post office prejudice arising from early abuse, to be used officially as a supplement to the land routes by horse post or foot carrier, though the land services were still regarded by the Post Office as more reliable. In the autumn of 1834 shortly after Wallace's criticism, a list prepared by Charles Reeves showed steamboats in official use for letter carriage between Glasgow and Greenock and down the Clyde Estuary to Dumbarton, Dunoon, Tarbert, Lochgilphead, Rothesay and Islay, while in the Firth of Forth letters were being regularly conveyed by steamboat from New-haven to the Fife coast at Kirkcaldy, Kinghorn and Burntisland.*

Since 1823 the nominal control of the Post Office had been in the hands of one Postmaster General instead of two. As the years passed, though Freeling remained virtually in full charge, successive Postmasters General had come to be more active in post office affairs; but in fact, instead of lessening the load on the Secretary, this added to it. Between December 1830 and May 1835 no fewer than five changes of Postmaster General took place, in one case the office being held for less than a month. Such rapidity of change at the head could not fail to add to the difficulties of the permanent staff, and it is little wonder that in July 1835 a letter from Freeling to Lord Lichfield, the newly

---

* The use of steamboats on the postal route to Fife as noted by Reeves in 1834 must have been the outcome of a recent change of policy by the Post Office, for as has been seen, a petition by the Kirkcaldy Chamber of Commerce some four years earlier asking that their mail from the South go by way of Leith and New-haven to Pettycur on the Fife coast had been turned down.

appointed Postmaster General, had almost a note of despair. Not only had there been yet another change of Postmaster General, but the calls of three separate Commissions of Enquiry entailed the constant attendance of senior officials to give evidence, while with the early expiry of Vidler's coach contract the supply of coaches for the coming year was entirely uncertain.[29]

In the last dark years before his death, while Freeling wrestled with mounting problems and a growing feeling of despondency, one small incident had taken place at the Headquarters of the Post Office in London which, though of no immediate moment, was in the years ahead to prove of much importance, both to the Post Office and to the outside world. A Minute to the Postmaster General dated 4 November 1834 reads: 'I beg to submit . . . the name of Anthony Trollope as a junior clerk in the Secretary's Office. . . . Mr Trollope has been well educated and will be subject to the usual probation as to competency.' Many years later Trollope described in his autobiography the nature of his entrance into post office service and the 'probation' as to his competency; the page of Gibbon, painfully copied for handwriting but never inspected; the arithmetic test threatened but never applied. Then the seven bleak years at Post Office Headquarters, underpaid, neglected and largely ignored, as he sank by degrees nearer and nearer to moral degradation and utter professional failure. Only the accident of a chance vacancy for a junior official in the West of Ireland – accepted by him in despair – saved Trollope from disaster and launched him on the career which was to give to the Post Office one of its most useful officers and to the English-speaking world one of its best-loved novelists.[30]

If the activities of the Member for Greenock, the exactions of the Turnpike Trustees and the insubordination of Shearer were causing Freeling to look on Scotland as a whole with jaundiced eyes, even the Scottish postal officials had come to share in his displeasure. For long the Edinburgh office had, in Freeling's view, been much too independent in their actions and too little amenable to the strict discipline which to the last he sought to enforce. As long ago as 1823 Freeling had written to the Postmaster General of those in Edinburgh, 'Perhaps there is not a single point of duty connected with that department which has not been infringed', and later in the same year, 'I trust we shall at last reform all the irregularities in our system in Scotland'.

Now in the summer of 1836, only a few weeks before his death, Freeling wrote of the Scottish Office with the despair to which Shearer too had at last reduced him, 'I grieve to see and it is a source of unfeigned lamentation that the officers in Scotland whether taking advantage of my unfortunate absence from the office or any other cause have for some months past adopted modes of writing and lines of conduct very different from what I think used to be, at least what it ought to be.'[31] Yet for all the criticisms which Freeling might level against it, evidence given before the Commission of Enquiry in 1830 appeared to show that the expenses of management of the Scottish Post Office, in marked contrast to the position in England, amounted to only about one-quarter of the gross receipts.[32]

Francis Freeling died on 10 July 1836. For many a man with far less to his credit, the end of life has been lightened by the memory of work well done and at least something achieved. To Freeling such a retrospect might well have brought comfort and no little pride. For Scotland in particular, his years at the Post Office had been marked by great advances. In 1797 when he became Secretary the mail coach service, in the introduction of which he had done so much, was still in the early stages of its growth, and no mail coaches ran north of Edinburgh or Glasgow. In the cities only Edinburgh had as yet achieved a Penny Post. Even here the new service was in its infancy though Edinburgh was fortunate in possessing one of the very few free delivery services in Britain. With this exception the arrangements for receipt and delivery of letters in Scottish cities and towns remained little different from what they had been for well over a century. Outgoing mail still required to be handed in at a central post office, where incoming letters had to be collected or were, at best, entrusted for delivery to letter-carriers who parted with them only on payment of delivery charges. In rural districts, though the total number of post offices was steadily growing, postal services over wide areas were still virtually non-existent, and throughout Scotland hundreds of villages large and small were without post offices, and many without postal services of any sort. If this was true of rural districts on the mainland, the position on the Islands was even worse. In Shetland, the arrival of letters was at little better than two-monthly intervals and even this was totally unreliable, dependent largely on mercantile traffic from Leith or Aberdeen. The post to Lewis went only once every two weeks and the continuance of even this was precarious. Postal communications between Skye and Inverness were barely maintained by a letter-carrier, ill-paid and over-burdened, who made the journey once a week, while letters from the southern half of the Long Island could reach the mainland only through Skye and that at the sole expense of the islanders themselves. In Mull, post offices had only recently been established at Tobermory and Aros, while the postal link with Islay and Jura was irregularly maintained by sailing boats conveying letters, many of them unofficially.

Now, in the summer of 1836, the postal picture was very different. Despite their liability for tolls, grudgingly conceded in 1813, mail coaches ran on all the main roads of southern Scotland, up the east coast to Aberdeen and thence, as well as through the Central Highlands, to Inverness, where other vehicles using roads and bridges built by Thomas Telford took the mail on to Thurso. Between Edinburgh and London the average speed of the mail coaches had been increased to 9 miles per hour, while even between Edinburgh and Aberdeen the 134 miles were covered in under 14½ hours. Of the cities and towns over 80 now had Penny Posts, these serving, notably in the case of Edinburgh and Glasgow, wide areas beyond the city boundaries, while the time was fast approaching when in every town and very many villages in Scotland a free delivery of all incoming letters would be given. In the country districts, too, the picture had changed out of all recognition. Letters carried by Penny Post or by ordinary mail services now reached many of the remotest parts of Kintyre and Knapdale, Morven and Ardgour, Moidart and Knoydart, while off the west coast and among the Islands the new steamboats, once the hated rivals of the Post Office, were coming to be regarded as its allies and its colleagues.

For post office servants, too, the past forty years had seen great changes for the better. Wages and salaries had been raised, albeit reluctantly, to keep pace with rising costs. The days had passed when foot-carriers were asked to walk up to 24 miles a day on 6 days a week at a speed of 4 miles per hour and for a weekly wage of under 10/−. Now an increasing number of men on the longer and more arduous routes had ponies to carry heavy mails at increased speeds. Much of this had been accomplished during years of great national stress, and if Freeling's strict economy had brought widespread criticism, its justification lay in the growing contribution which the Post Office had, under his management, been able to make to the financial needs of the nation. Within four years of Freeling's death Robert Wallace, Rowland Hill and their adherents were to bring still greater changes in nearly every sphere of post office activity, altering or sweeping away much that Freeling had come to regard as immutable and almost sacred, and incidentally involving the Post Office for many years to come in the loss of no little part of that revenue which it had been his pride to maintain. That Freeling did not live to see these changed times can only be considered as merciful, and if his last years were saddened by the knowledge of impending change, at least he could look back on forty years of hard work and notable achievement when he had played a full part in the social and economic development of his country.

REFERENCES

1. Bryant, *The Age of Elegance*, ch. XI.
2. McCombie, *Cattle and Cattle Breeders*, 57
3. Quoted by Joyce, op. cit., 428.
4. Ibid, 365.
5. Post 40/446/1822.
6. Penrose Hay, *Post Office Recollections*.
7. Post 40/118, 121 and 163/1827.
8. Dick Lauder, *The Moray Floods*, 81.
9. *Annual Register 1832*, 304.
10. Post 40/249/1832.
11. Ibid./77w/1799.
12. Ibid./675/1832.
13. Ibid./46p/1803.
14. Post 15/130/1803.
15. Post 40/434/1821.
16. Ibid./434/1821.
17. Ibid./70/1828.
18. Ibid./822/1830.
19. Ibid./872/1833.
20. Ibid./789/1834.
21. Ibid./911/1835.
22. Ibid./48/1836.
23. Post 35/22/1837.
24. Ibid./22/1837.
25. Howard Robinson, op. cit., ch. XVII.
26. Joyce, op. cit., 425 et seq.
27. Post 40/64M/1803.
28. Ibid./300/1830.
29. Ibid./406/1835.

30. Anthony Trollope, *Autobiography*.
31. Post 40/306/1836.
32. Howard Robinson, *Britain's Post Office*, 124.

Appendix I. R.P.C. 3rd ser. vol. xiv, pp. 38–41

Edinburgh, 14 August 1689. Sederunt: Hamiltone; Crafurd;
Southerland; Glencairne; Eglingtone; Cassills; Lothian;
Dundonald; Carmichell; Ruthven; Sir Jo. Dalrymple;
Revilrig; Pollwart; Blackbarrony; Ormiston; Broddie.

'The tack underwrittin past betwixt the Lords of Privy Councill
and John Blair and his cautioners of the office of post master
generall for the space of seven years for payment of the yearly
tack dutie of fyve thousand ane hundred merks read and subscryvit, which was given in to Sir Thomas Moncreiff to be recorded by him in the bookes of Exchaquer, the tenor of quhilk
commission is as followes: Att Edinburgh, etc. The Lords of his
Majesties Privy Councill, considering that his Majestie hath not
named a Lord Thesaurer or Lords of the Thesaurie for the
manadging and ordoring of his revenue, and that the office of
postmaster generall within this kingdome became vaccant by the
death of John Grame, to whom was payable the soume of one
thousand pund Scots yearly for discharging of that trust, did
therfore by their proclaimatione of the date the eghteinth day of
July j^{m}vi^c eightie nyne years appoynted (*sic*) ane roupe of the
said office and place of postmaster generall within this kingdome
formerly belonging to the said deceast John Grame, to be rouped
in the Thesaurie roume upon the twentie fourth day of the said
moneth; and by their act of the said twentie fourth day they
granted warrand to the Earle of Cassills, Lord Ross and Carmichell, Sir Heugh Campbell, Sir James Montgomrie and Sir
Archibald Murray, ane committie of ther own number, or a
greater part of them, to oversee the same, and appoynted conditiones of the roupe to be as followes: Letters from Edinburgh to
Dumfrees, Glasgow and Air, Dundie, Kelsoe and Jedburgh,
Pearth and Stirling at two shilling Scots per single letter and
four shilling the double and so proportionally, and the lyke rates
to Hamilton: *Secundo,* item betwixt Edinburgh and Carlyle,
Portpatrick, Aberdeen and Dunkeld, thrie shilling for each
single letter, six shilling the double letter and so proportionally:
Tertio, item betwixt Edinburgh and Kirkcudbright, Innernes
and all other places beyond Aberdeen, four shilling for each

single letter, eight shilling for a double letter and so proportionally: *Quarto*, item all by rodds for bringing letters from the severall townes and villadges in the countrie to the nixt adjacent post
office at on shilling per letter to the persones who shall be appoynted to carie the letters from the countrie villages to the nixt
fixed post office, and wher no posts are setled that cariers may
have freedome to bring letters: *Quinto*, all pacquets at thrie unce
weight wher ther is no letters within shall pay to such places as
the letter payes two shilling, six shilling Scots each pacquett, and
wher the letters pay thrie shilling each packet shall pay nyne
shilling: *Sixto*, when the postmasters offices fall betwixt this and
Berwick that the same shall belong to the tacksmen as John
Grame hade right thereto: *Septimo*, all other posts established by
John Grame shall be void and null unles renewed by this tacksman: *Octavo*, the tack is to continue for the space of seven years
and the tack dutie to be payable at two termes in the year, Mertimis and Whitsunday be equall portiones, beginning the first
termes payment at the terme of Whitsunday nixt: *Nono*, the
Councill is to obleidge themselves in the tack to be granted be
them to the tacksman that the same shall be ratified or renewed
by the Thesaurie how soon it shall sitt, and ordaines thir articles
of the roupe to be printed: Conforme to which warrand and
proclaimatione of the saids Lords compeired in presence of
the said Earle of Cassills, Lords Ross and Carmichell and Sir
James Montgomrie, severall persones who made offor of cer-
taine soumes of money as the yearly tack dutie for the said office,
and John Blair, apothicary in Edinburgh, haveing offored fyve
thousand one hundred merks which was the greatest offor made,
the said committie declaired him to be tacksman of the said
office of postmaster generall, he finding suficient cautione to
performe and observe the conditiones of the said roupe and for
payment of the tack dutie. Therfor the saids Lords of Privy
Councill have sett and in tack and assidatione letten and be thir
presents setts and for the said yearly tack dutie of fyve thousand
one hundred merks in tack and assidatione lettes to the said John
Blair, his airs, executors or assigneyes the said place and office
of generall postmaster and overseer of all posts, horss and foot,
within this kingdome of Scotland, and that for all the dayes,
space, years and termes of seven years nixt and immediatly
following his entrie therto, which is heirby declaired to be and
beggine at the terme of Mertimis nixt to come j^{m}vi^e eightie nyne

years, and swa furth to continue dureing the space forsad without any intervale or break of termes; with full power to ... John Blair to appoynt and setle postmasters for establishing horss and foot posts at the severall stages wher the samen may be necessary for carieing of his Majesties letters, dispatches and expeditiones alse weell as these of his subjects and other letters, pacquets and dispatches from place to place, for whom he shall be answearable, with all and sundrie priviledges, immunities, casualities, dignities, profeits and duties except sellarie belonging therto, as freely and amplie as any other post master generall possessed and enjoyed the samen at any tyme bygone within this kingdome; with full power alsoe to him and his forsaids to setle and appoynt a generall letter office within the towne of Edinburgh from which all letter pacquets and dispatches may be sent with all expeditione to any place or places within this kingdome, according to their respective directiones, and at which office all letters and their answears shall lykwayes be received; with full power also to the said John Blair and his forsaids of errecting and establishing other particular letter offices at such fitt places as shall seem to him most convenient, and that notwithstanding of any gift or grant made by any generall postmaster to any persone or persones within this kingdome, which they heirby declair voyd and null as being granted to them *a non habente potestatem;* with power also to the said John Blair and his forsaids, and his deputs ane or mae to be nominated and appoynted by him, to provyd and furnish horses for pacquets and post or jurney horses, and to ask, uplift, impose and exact for such services and for transporting of such pacquets and letters the pryces abovementioned appoynted by the saids Lords; and when the postmaster office fall betwixt this and Berwick the saids Lords declair that the samen shall belong to the said John Blair and his forsaids as John Grame, late postmaster generall, hade right therto, dureing the space of the said tack; lykas in the case forsaid they give warrand to the said John Blair and his forsaids to setle and appoynt postmasters offices betwixt this and Berwick as they shall fall dureing the space of the present tack allenarly. And the saids Lords doe heirby prohibite and discharge all persone or persones, bodie pollitick, magistrats of burghs and incorporationes from errecting or setling any letter offices, and that they presume not to act in or midle with any post office within this kingdome by establishing or sending away any posts, horss or

[277]

foot, for carieing or receiveing letters, pacquets or letters (*sic*), or doing any other thing to the hurt or prejudice of the said office of postmaster generall heirby sett to him in tack and assidatione dureing the tyme forsaid, with certificatione to these who shall transgress heirin they shall be sumarly called and punished as contemners of and incroachers upon his Majesties authoritie and prerogative royall, and to be furder punished by fyning and banishment and otherwayes as shall seem fitt to the saids Lords of Privy Councill, according to the qualitie of their guilt and offence: But it is lykwayes heirby declaired that it shall be leisome and lawfull to the noblemen and gentlmen within this kingdome to send to or from this place their own servants about their own affairs and bussines allenarly. And they heirby command and requyre all shireffs of shyres, magistrates of burghes and others to concurr with and assist the said John Blair and his forsaids in setling and establishing the said post offices, horss and foot, and in makeing the samen effectuall to the effect forsaid: And the saids Lords of Privy Councill doe heirby declair that this present tack of the office of post master generall dureing the tyme forsaid shall be ratified or renued by the Lords of Thesaurie in all the heads and articles therof whenever they shall sitt. For the which causes the said John Blair as principall, and William Menzies, present thesaurer of Edinburgh, as cautioner, souertie and full debitor with and for him, bind and obleidge themselves conjunctllie and severallie, their airs, executors and intromittors with their goods and geir, and successors whatsomever, not only to observe, keep and fullfill all and sundrie the conditiones of the forsaid roupe, but alsoe thankfully to content and pay the Lords Commissioners of his Majesties Thesaurie, Thesaurer or their depute for the tyme being, or to Sir Patrick Murray, receiver of his Majesties rents, and his successors in office, the abovementioned soume of fyve thousand on hundred merks money forsaid of tack dutie abovewrittin at two termes in the year, Whitsunday and Mertimis, be equall portiones, begining the first termes payment therof at the feast and terme of Whitsunday nixt to come in the year of God $j^m vi^c$ and nyntie years, and swa furth yearly and termly therafter dureing the years of this tack, with the soume of thrie hundred merkes of liquidate expences for ilk termes failzie by and attour the performeing of the premisses; and the said John Blair binds and obleises him and his forsaids to releive and skaithles keep the abovewrittin William Menzies, his said Cautioner, his airs and executors and all others whom it effeirs of their cautionrie above-writtin and of all damnadge and expences they shall hapen to sustain therthrow. And for the more securitie both the saids parties are content and consents thir presents be insert and registrat in the bookes of Exchaquer to have the streanth of ane decreit of the judge therof interponed therto, that letters and executorialls of horning may pass heiron on ten dayes and others neidfull in forme as effeirs, and for that effect constitutes, etc. their procurators, etc. In wittnes wherof (writtin be John Forbes, servitor to William Wilsone, writter in Edinburgh) these presents are subscryvit by the Duke of Hamiltone, President of Councill, in their name and be their warrand, and be the said John Blair and his cautioner abovenamed, day and place forsaid before thir witneses, Mr Gilbert Eliot, Clark of Privy Councill, and John Nicoll, his servitor, and the said William Wilsone. *Sic subscribitur*, Hamilton, P.; John Blair; William Menzies; Gilb. Eliot, witnes; Will. Wilson, witnes; John Nicoll, witnes.'

Appendix II. S.R.O. GD 248/25/2/8

Memorial for Sir James Grant of Grant, Baronet, in behalf of himself and the other Gentlemen, and Trading People, in and about the Village of Grantown. Offered to the Consideration of the Postmaster General for Scotland. [Dated 1780]

The Village of Grantown, near Castle Grant, is Situated in the Centre of the Country of Strathspey; one of the largest and most populous Straths in Scotland, being 24 Miles long, 12 Broad, and containing 6 Parishes.

The Village itself was begun to be Built about 15 years ago, and is in a very thriving Condition; has Several Branches of Trade and Manufacture, already Established and Flurishing, in it.*

The Business, too, not only of Strathspey but also of several Neighbouring Countries, is Generally Transacted at Grantown, it being a very Convenient and Centrical Situation for the Inhabitants of the Lower parts of Badenoch, and of Rothemurchus,

---

* Linnens, Woolens, Wood manufacturers to a great extent, Dealers in Cattle and Sheep, Grocers and tradespeople of different occupations, not to mention The Gentlemen and Half pay Officers etc., in his Majesty's Service.

Strathaven, Glenlivet, and several other smaller Countries.

In Grantown there are Four Considerable Fairs held Annually, which of Course not only Convene a great Number of people on these occasions, but have also been conducive to Render it the General place of meeting on all the business of consequence in the District.

The Gentlemen and Trading people in this Country and Village have long earnestly wished for the Establishment of a Post-office at Grantown, having deeply felt the Inconveniency and loss arising from the want of a regular communication with any Post Town.

A Post Office being Established at Grantown, would not only accommodate Strathspey, But also the Countries above-mentioned, Viz$^{t\cdot}$ the lower part of Badenoch, Rothemurchus, Strathaven, Glenlivet etc., which are very Considerable in themselves, and it would greatly tend towards facilitating and enlarging Correspondence, and preserving and enlarging that Spirit of Commerce which now happily begins to diffuse itself, and which of necessary consequence would increase the Revenue.

It is therefore humbly proposed that a Post-Office be established at Grantown, and the same connected with the great post Road to Edinburgh by a Runner to be dispatched three times a week to and from Forres, which is the nearest point, being about 12 Computed, or 20 Measured Miles distant from Grantown.

It is also proposed that a Bye Bag be Established betwixt Forres and Grantown so as to Connect it with the Intermediate Towns North of Edinburgh, and this Bye Bag to be Conveyed by the same Runner.

The Memorialists will undertake that this Establishment if gone into shall be Carried on at the following Moderate Expence, Viz$^{t\cdot}$

For Runners 2/2 each course of 24 Computed miles or 6/6 per week, making per annum	£ 16. 18. –
For office duty per annum	2. – –
Sum	£ 18. 18. –

And the Memorialists are persuaded that the Ordinary Postage of Letters would be found, even in the Infancy of the Office, to be more than sufficient to answer the Expence.

Appendix III. Post 40/80. 1/1802

Memorial for Alexander, Lord MacDonald
28 December 1789

The Island of North Uist, or which is better known to Mariners by the name of the Long Island, is the sole property of the Memorialist, and is about 24 miles in length and 10 in breadth. It is the most fertile of all the Western Isles, and in favourable seasons produces grain more than sustains the Inhabitants which are about 3,300 in number, and in these favourable seasons they export their grain to such of the neighbouring Islands as most require it.

Besides this the Inhabitants rear a considerable number of black Cattle, which are annually exported to the south, and while the men are employed in fishing, the women have now begun to spin woolen and linen yarn during the winter and spring, being employed during the Summer partly in attending to their Cattle, and the Dairy, and partly in assisting such of the men as are employed in making of Kelp which the coast both to the north and south of this Island produces of the best quality annually. All which transactions occasion a correspondence with Liverpool, New Castle, Hull and other towns on the West and East coasts of England and Scotland and every obstruction to it is a great inconvenience.

On the northeast lies the Island of Harris and on the West Benbecula, South Uist and the Island of Barra, and other small Islands connected with it, which together contain an equal number of Inhabitants if not more. There is a communication between most of those Islands by land at low water.

At present the only outlet from these Islands to Edinburgh, Glasgow, or the south, is through the extensive Island of Sky, from which they are between seven and eight leagues distant at the narrowest place and they have no other opportunity of getting to it or the mainland but in open boats, which is precarious and dangerous, and often impossible for months together in the tempestuous weather in that climate from Christmas to the middle of April; and when boats are dispatched from necessity to the next post Town in Sky which is Dunvegan, many useful lives are thereby often endangered, and some lost annually, whose families of course become a burden upon the Memorialist, and the other proprietors. Besides if it should happen that the narrow passage cannot be accomplished by the shifting of the winds, (which are extremely variable in these parts), vessels are obliged to resort to distant harbours upon the coast, which multiplies the danger and risque to open boats.

To avoid this in future, the Memorialist makes this application to the Post-master General, for the purpose of obtaining a regular packet, and having it established under his direction and authority, to sail weekly between Dunvegan and Lochmaddy in North Uist, but with liberty to go three times a week when necessary, and when freight offers, between the first of May and the first of November and to be put under such other regulations as shall be approved of by the postmaster General. This Packet to be a decked vessel of from 25 to 40 Tons burden and besides the postage to arise from letters, to receive such sum as shall be established from all passengers, and for all Cattle and goods according to the number and bulk as shall be thought adequate.

This will in time produce a very considerable revenue to Government. At the same time the Memorialist is ready to confess that it may not for the first three or four years return near so much as will defray the expence of building and maintaining this Packet, and the hands necessarily employed in managing it; but if the Memorialist is allowed the sanction of Government, and the conducting of this Packet and the establishing of the necessary regulations for a term of years, he is ready and willing to take all this expence upon himself.

To facilitate the correspondence with Sky which in Summer is only once a week or fortnight, and during the Winter and Spring perhaps not once a month the Memorialist further proposes, and which will be no additional expence to Government, but on the contrary an immediate increase of revenue, that the correspondence between Edinburgh and Sky in place of being weekly, as it is now should hereafter be three times a week, in this manner.

The Runner from Dunvegan to be dispatched every second day to Sconser.

The Runner from Sconser to be sent by Kyleachin to Loch Carron and the Lochcarron runner to Inverness. Thus three will be constantly going and three returning with the Bag from Edinburgh.

By this arrangement in place of the Sky-Runner and Loch Carron Runner, going and returning from Inverness at one and the same time the former will be prevented from going and coming by sea in a small open boat from Sky to Loch Carron (being from 8 to 12 leagues) which he does at present as often as he finds an opportunity to the great detriment of the public, in order to save himself the trouble of walking round by land, which is risquing not only his own life but the loss of all the Bills and Bank-notes which may be in the different Bags, and of which there is generally to a considerable amount remitted every week in payment of black Cattle, Kelp, fish and other articles exported, part of which is again returned in payment of timber, iron, Hemp, clothing groceries &c. &c.

The increase of revenue of late years from the Post Offices of Dunvegan and Sconser in Sky once a week as at present, is well known to be very considerable, as will appear from the books, kept at the general Post Office, but when it is considered how much it will increase by adopting this mode of opening a certain and safe communication between the Long Island by the establishment of a Packet between Loch Maddy in North Uist (which is in the centre of the Long Island, say 15 miles in circumference, the constant resort of the Baltic and all home-ward and outward bound fleets, as being the best and most capacious harbour in all the Western Islands) and Dunvegan, by which a correspondence with Edinburgh, Argyle, Inverness, and Ross Shires and the kingdom at large, thrice a week in place of once will thus be opened, the advantages are apparent.

Smuggling will thus be suppressed by this Packet in that quarter or at least become very hazardous. Intelligence of the course the herrings take in those seas will be communicated instantaneously. Fishers will thereby be brought directly into their course. Salt and provisions can be forewarded, and Insurance directly made upon Ships, and Bills be received and negociated before they are passed due. In a word there can be no substantial improvement made in these Islands without they have a free constant and ready access and intercourse with the world, nor is it to be expected that strangers will ever think of settling there or engaging in the fishing or other branches of trade unless they have this advantage and are thereby put on a footing with his Majesties other subjects.

Appendix IV. Post 40/8. 1/1796

To the Right Honble the Earl of Leicester and Earl of
    Chesterfield Postmasters general of Great Britain. The
    Petition of Mrs Helen Anderson, Deputy Postmistress of
    Dunfermline, 1795.

HUMBLY SHEWETH
That your Petitioner was appointed to that Office in the Year
Seventeen hundred and Seventy Seven, with an annual Salary
of Eighteen pounds ten shillings, and a Newspaper afforded her
by the General Postoffice of Edinburgh, which brought her
from two to three pounds yearly. That beside her personal
trouble in the management of the Office, she has been at the
expence of Five Guineas yearly as the rent of a House for the
Office, and of maintaining Coal, Candle, Wax, and Paper, without any other allowance than said Salary. And for some Years
after her Appointment to that Office, the Revenue arising from
the Office amounted only to from One Hundred and Seventy,
to Two Hundred pounds, She having then only the trouble of
One Bag from Edinburgh Six days in the Week. That from the
increase of the Population and Trade of the Country, the Postmaster General of Edinburgh in the Year 1789 thought it
advisable to order a Bye Bag for each of the following Towns in
the neighbourhood of Dunfermline; Viz^{t.} North-Queensferry,
Culross, Kincardine, Alloa and Stirling, and these with the
Edinburgh Bag she was directed to make up and Dispatch
every day. This new appointment increased her trouble considerably in the Management of the Office, while at same time
the annual revenue has since increased to about Four Hundred
pounds and appears progressively to increase, And as the Postmaster General of Edinburgh only allowed her Two pounds of
additional Salary, at the time the trouble of these bye Bags com-
menced, when at same time said Newspaper was withheld from
her, which occasioned on the whole rather a diminution than an
increase of her Salary, And as she has not above Ten Guineas in
the year for her trouble after deducting all Expences, She begs
leave thus to state her case to your Lordships humbly hoping
that your Lordships will direct such additional Salary as may

appear adequate for her trouble in the management of said Office.

May it therefore please Your Lordships to take your Petitioners case into consideration and to Appoint her such addition to her Salary as to Your Lordships shall seem proper, And it has been and still shall be her care and attention to manage the business of the Office in such a manner as shall appear to her to be most for the Interest of the Revenue, And your Petitioner shall ever Pray.

Helen Anderson

Appendix V. Post 40/80. 1/1802

Memorial for the Right Honble. Lord Macdonald, General McLeod of McLeod, Ranald George Macdonald of Clanranald and his Tutors, Alex[r.] McLeod of Herries, Colin Macdonald of Boisdale, Alex[r.] MacAlister of Strathaird, Major Alex[r.] Macdonald of Lyndale, Patrick Nicolson of Ardmore and others, heritors tacksmen and possessors of land in the Islands of Sky and Uist.

To The Post Master General for Scotland, 1798.

Very soon after the establishment of a Post from Inverness to Sconcer and Dunvegan, the districts for whose accommodation it was established discovered that it was totally impossible to support a Post and keep up two offices, for receiving and dispatching Letters at Sconcer and Dunvegan from the very limited allowance made for that purpose, But unwilling to prove a burden on the Revenue the Gentlemen of the Country by a voluntary annual subscription have hitherto kept up these Post Offices, and in Uist, which is in the delivery of Dunvegan, the proprietor and Inhabitants have at their own expence supported by a subscription a Packet Boat and Runner, the annual contribution for which now amounts to £72. 17s. Notwithstanding of these very great exertions of the Inhabitants, yet it is found that untill the Post from Inverness is put on a better footing, and the salary of the Post Masters at Sconcer and Dunvegan increased, so as to make it an object for persons fit for such a charge, the establishment can be of little or no service to the Country.

It is understood to be a general rule, and for the encouragement of the Commerce of the Country it is proper it should be so, that the Post Master General or those who have the charge of that matter, always allow for Posts, Post Offices, and Packet Boats, should it be necessary, to the extent of the revenue drawn from the district, and in some cases where there is a prospect of the correspondence increasing, they have even exceeded the returns made from the district.

In the present case the Memorialists are convinced that upon investigation it will be found that the sum drawn from the district in the delivery of the Dunvegan and Sconcer Post Offices does very far exceed the expence incurred, and they therefore with the greater confidence now apply for an allowance sufficient to put the Posts and Post Offices on such a footing as to enable them to receive their Letters with more safety and expedition than they have hitherto done. Indeed so irregular and uncertain has the correspondence from that Country been, that it very frequently happens that an express is sent to Inverness with a Letter.

The Posts from Dunvegan to Inverness, who go alternately week about, have an allowance each of 5s. for every time they go to Inverness, a journey going and returning of fully 226 miles including Six Ferries. This sum of 5s. it is evident cannot be an inducement for any man to take such a Journey, and the Post of necessity has been and is still the Carrier for the whole Country, and from being overloaded with Commissions he very frequently is detained beyond his usual time, and he generally takes a small boat at Lochcarron whereby his own life as well as the mail is in eminent danger of being lost.

Another error in the management of this Post requires (it is hoped) only to be pointed out to be remedied. The Post from Dunvegan to Inverness necessarily passes the Post Office of Lochcarron and in general accompanies the Lochcarron Post to Inverness and back again. This surely is an unnecessary trouble and expence, as the Lochcarron Post could very easily carry the Dunvegan and Sconcer mails to Lochcarron where he could be met by the Sky Post, and by thus dividing the distance the Post might go twice in the week instead of once; But it will be necessary to put the Dunvegan Post on a new footing before an alteration in this respect can take place, for by his going no further than Lochcarron his traffic with Inverness could not be carried on, which from the present small allowance of 5s. he cannot afford to give up.

It is submitted that the Salary of the Post from Dunvegan should be increased, and that he should go no further than Lochcarron, and it is thought that 12s. for each trip to Lochcarron, a journey of 120 miles and two ferries, cannot but be considered as moderate in the extreme, nor indeed can it be got done for less money; but by this means it is thought a Post might be had twice in the week from Inverness to Dunvegan. For so very inadequate is the present allowance of 5s., that the Posts declare they would rather continue to go to Inverness as they do now for that sum with the privilege of carrying goods, than go to Lochcarron (not half the distance) without that privilege, the 5s. making to Lochcarron only the very moderate sum of one half penny per mile.

The establishment of a regular Packet boat from Dunvegan to Hallin in North Uist, as well as the appointment of a person to act as Postmaster at Hallin for the regular distribution of the Letters of the Long Island, consisting of North and South Uist, Benbecula and Barra containing a population of about 12,000 Inhabitants, is also a very material and necessary arrangement without which the advantage of a regular post to Dunvegan would be entirely lost to this very populous and extensive district of Country; and if it is found that the produce of the correspondence from that Country can afford it, which it is believed it can, it is hoped this very necessary measure will also receive attention.

To form an idea of the importance and public utility of establishing these posts and Post offices on a respectable and regular footing, it may be proper to notice that the trade of that remote tho' extensive part of the Country, is already by no means inconsiderable and is daily increasing. There is annually exported from that part of the Country upwards of 3000 tons of kelp, 7000 head of Black Cattle, several hundred tons of Cod and Ling fish caught on the adjacent Banks besides the herring fishing, which never fails in these Islands. This trade alone, with the necessary articles imported by the Inhabitants for their own use such as Salt, Iron, Tar &c, must necessarily occasion a very considerable correspondence and of course a proportionable revenue.

The infant villages established by the British Society at Stein and by Lord Macdonald at Portree and Lochmaddy can never extend their commerce or be increased without the benefit of a

regular communication with other countrys. [a few words il-
legible] trade from the Baltic to the West coast of Scotland and
to Ireland as well as about 500 sail of Shipping generally employed in the fishing and kelp trade, very frequently call at the
harbours in these Islands, and write from there to their owners
for the purpose of saving the Insurance, but from the irregu-
larity of the Posts and Packet the Letters seldom or never arrive
in time to prevent the Insurance being effected.

There are now in the Isles ten Companys of Volunteers perfectly trained and disciplined for service and ready to go to any
part of the Kingdom when their services may be required.
There are also many officers on the recruiting Service who, as
well as the volunteer officers, ought to make regular and pointed
returns. The want of a regular conveyance of Letters may be
attended with disagreeable consequences to the Officers and
with the loss to the Country in any Emergency of the service of
a well affected and well disciplined Body of men.

The Memorialists beg leave to submit the above remarks to
the consideration of the Post Master General which they
humbly concieve to deserve attention, and they flatter themselves with the hope that upon an Investigation it will appear
that the revenue arising from the correspondence in the delivery of the Dunvegan and Sconcer Post Offices will enable the
Post Master General to allow a sum sufficient for the purposes
required by the Memorialists, that is for a Post twice in the week
from Inverness to Lochcarron, and from thence to Sconcer and
Dunvegan, and an aid to enable the Inhabitants of Uist to keep
a letter Packet boat from Dunvegan to Hallin and a Salary to a
person to take charge of the Letters at Hallin.

Should it not be thought advisable immediately to grant the
request of the Memorialists, they humbly submit that a sum of
£40 Stg. should in the meantime be allowed annually, £20 of
which to go towards defraying the Expence of the Post from
Dunvegan to Lochcarron and the Sky Post Offices, and the
other £20 towards the expence of the Packet boat from Dunvegan to Hallin and a Post Office there.

Appendix VI. Post 40/8 w/1799

Memorial and Representation, relative to the Post in Badenoch, dated 19 March 1799.

This large District in the central Highlands of Scotland, is perhaps the only part of His Majesty's Dominions where, without any obstacle arising from local Situation, the Letters are so late of being received and conveyed by so circuitous a Route.

The Distance from Edinburgh to Pitmain measured along the military Road is only 112 miles; and by the Coast Road round by Aberdeen and Forres, – the Course that is followed at present, – it is at least 259.

The arrival of the Post from Edin^r·, in the direct Line, would be in 26 Hours; – by the plan now adopted, it requires 3 Days.

To remedy this Inconvenience, and at the same time to afford a Similar accomodation to the adjoining District of Athole, it is suggested that a Post Office ought to be established at Blair; that the Dispatches from Edinburgh for that place and Pitmain ought to be three times a week at least; the Bag to be conveyed with the customary Expedition of a *riding Post* to Blair; and to be forwarded afterwards by *Runners* to Pitmain: as, during the winter Months, it might not be always practicable for a riding Post to cross that Branch of the Grampians by which the two Countries are intersected and separated from each other.

To complete the arrangement, it would be necessary to have a Runner dispatched with a Bye-Bag, once a week, from Pitmain to Inverness, to keep open a direct Communication with the County Town, and with the Eastern and Northern Divisions of the Kingdom; AND for the whole Expences of the Establishment in Badenoch, including the Post-master's Salary, it is believed that a Sum of Fifty five pounds a year might be sufficient.

It cannot be exactly ascertained, and of Consequence it would be improper to found on It in Argument, whether the Encrease of Correspondence reasonably to be expected from this Arrangement, would be equal to the additional Expence which the Establishment will require. The Presumption is, that the Revenue will not be diminished, but should it be otherways, in an age of liberal Improvement, an accomodation tending to the general Advantage of a State, by circulating Intelligence more rapidly through all its parts, will not, it is hoped, be weighed altogether in the Scale of Common Interest; nor refused, merely on the Ground of its not being a profitable Bargain.

Appendix VII. Post 40/66 B/1800

Letter from Francis Ronaldson, Surveyor, to the Deputy Post
  Master General, Scotland

General Post Office,
Edinburgh 31st July 1800.

Dear Sir,

The great complaints made of delay in the Conveyance of the
Mails from Dunbarton to Inveraray, from Inveraray to Camp-
belltown, and from Inveraray to Oban and Fort William in the
West of Scotland, made it necessary for me to visit that part of
the Country in order to Investigate and correct the causes of
them as far as possible. In the course of this Investigation and
Journey it appeared to me that some of the Ferries as material
causes of delay might be avoided particularly those of Portsonachan, Aw and Shien Ferries.

For the Information of their Lordships His Majesty's Postmaster General, and in order to explain such improvements as
either occurred or were recommended to me for the general
accomodation of this large tract of Country, and I trust would
be also for the advantage of the Revenue, I have subjoined a
sketch of those parts connected with this Report; and in regard
to the present course of the Post from Inveraray to Bonaw it
appeared to me both from Report and observation that the
Ferries of Portsonachan and Aw, should be altogether avoided,
the first having very bad service, and that it would be more
beneficial to take in a considerable tract of Country by going
through a part of the district of Glenorchy by Dalmaly to
Bonaw.

This improvement I found very generaly wished for, and
tho' it appears from the Sketch to be 6 miles longer I am persuaded the additional Revenue and correspondence it would
bring would more than defray the additional expence, and by
avoiding the 2 Ferries of Portsonachan and Aw, with the advantage of a better and more level road no time should be lost in the
difference of Conveyance. The expence of this Improvement
would be For a Runner from Inveraray to Dalmaly 15 miles
3 times a week

at 7/6 p week or p annum	£19.	10. "
Ditto from Dalmaly to Bonaw 12 miles		
at 6/- p week or	15.	12. "
Salary to the Postmaster at Dalmaly	5.	". "
Sum	£40.	2. "

Deduct present expence vizt

Runner from Inveraray to Bonaw

21 miles at 7/^{sh}   or £18.   5.   "

Part of this service is now very
irregularly done by the Post
from Appin who once every
week travels above 50 miles
without stopping.

Allowance for Portsonachan

Ferry 52/^{sh} & Aw 26/^{sh}   3.   18.   "

Deduct   22.   3.   "

Remains additional Expence   £17.   19.   "

By this Improvement a great Tract of Country would be accomodated, and the heavy delay occasioned once a week by the Appin Post travelling such a distance to meet the Inveraray Post avoided as well as the frequent and unavoidable delays at the two Ferries.

Another Improvement adopted upon this Branch is avoiding the Ferry of Shien betwixt Bonaw and Appin and going by Crigan Ferry 2 miles shorter at a less expence than by Shien and which can always be travelled except in great storms or very bad weather when it is equally dangerous to take the Shien. So much was this the case that I found it had been the general practice before I went there for the Post from Bonaw to Appin to lodge regularly all night at or near the house of Ardhattan and did not cross the Shien till the following mornings, losing 12 hours to the Appin, Strontian and Fort William districts of Country, and I consider it an improvement of itself to remove such private lodgings or accomodations out of the way of posts, which as I have been informed is sometimes done for the sake of perusing Newspapers as well as writing or answering letters.

I would next observe upon the different applications made by the Earl of Breadalbene and other Gentlemen in the districts of

Balquhidder Lochearnhead Killin and Tyndrum as far back as 1798 for an extension of the Post to those parts; That they labour at present under great inconvenience in regard to their Correspondence not having any regular Office within 20, 30 and in some parts 40 miles of them and which for some years past from the late improvements in the rearing of Cattle and other Agricultural concerns in that Country has occasioned much embarrassment and complaint, and from a full considera-tion of which I am humbly of opinion the Revenue would very soon gain the expence of an extension, while it would also be of very great publick benefit and accomodation, and I would re-commend a trial in which if not successfule the Revenue could not suffer much and would silence the many complaints that have been made. To obtain this desired extension I would humbly propose a Foot post 3 times a week from Callander Monteith at the entrance of the Highlands to Lochearnhead

14 miles at 6/shp week or	£15. 12. ”	
Salary to the Postmaster there	5. ”. ”	
Sum	£20. 12. ”	

A Foot post from Lochearnhead to Killin 8 miles further

3 times a week at 3/ p week or	£7. 16. ”	
Salary to a Postmaster at Killin	5. ”. ”	
Sum	12. 16.	
	£33. 8. ”	

And in order to accomodate a part of the Country to the westward of Lochearnhead and Killin towards Glendochart and Tyndrum I would propose a Receiving house at Wester Lix at an allowance of £2. ”. ”
For a foot post from Lix to Luib about 5 miles from the Junc-tion of the Killin and Tyndrum road at 1/6 p week } 3. 18. ”
that ryoe Postmaster at Luib 4. ”. ”

Sum	9. 18. ”	
Total Expence of this Extension	£43. 6. ”	

As it has been represented to you by Mr Kennedy Factor for Lord Breadalbane that a subscription had been entered into by the several gentlemen of this district to the extent of £54.4/ to defray any deficiency that might be incurred to the Revenue by this extension, but their Lordships The Postmasters General having very properly disapproved of such obligations being taken or accepted, I would humbly recommend a trial to be made for a year under the usual limitations and conditions that the whole or such parts of them as may not defray their own expence shall be discontinued. – I have reason to believe that to Lochearnhead at least if not to Killin, it will do so, because in the extension a few years since of the post upon this line to Callander, which at first did little more than defray its expence of about £20 the Revenue of it has gradually increased to above £80 p annum.

Before concluding this Report, I am under the necessity to remark upon the Foot posts from Dumbarton Westward that owing to the great weight of the Mails containing Newspapers, Magazines and latterly the Publick Acts and Army Reports &c they are become so heavy as to render it impossible to make any great progress in conveying them, and should they encrease further no man will be able to travell with them. When at Dumbarton I observed them upon the heavy days or Post days beyond Inveraray to be about 3 stone weight, and I would humbly submit to their Lordships' consideration whether any remedy against this difficulty could be adopted, either by prohibiting Magazines, which I do not understand to pay anything to the Revenue, or by sending the Publick Acts and Army Reports in such degrees as may lessen proportionally the weight of these Foot Mails. I am with much regard,

    Dear Sir

        Your most Obedient and Faithfull Servant

        'Francis Ronaldson' *Surveyor*

To William Robertson Esq ·

Dy Postm Gen[l.] Edin[r.]

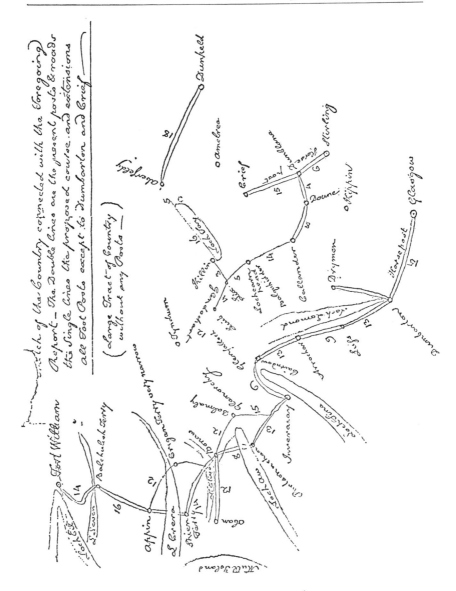

Appendix VIII. Post 40/58 P/1803

Letter from James Shearer, Surveyor, to the Deputy Post Master General, Scotland.

General Post Office
Edin^{r.} 21st Nov. 1803

Dear Sir,

I am sorry to find that Mr Freeling is not satisfied as to the necessity of an Augmentation to the Allowances of the Mail Contractors upon the line of Road from Aberdeen to Tain. He may rest assured that every exertion upon my part was used to have that part of the public service done as economically as possible, and offers were made of the employment to several persons who all refused it, before I troubled him upon the subject. It is the most unpleasant but perhaps the most necessary part of my duty, to attend to the proper conveyance of the Mails, and I have made it my constant study to have this done in the safest manner, and upon the most moderate terms – The situation of the Country, however, cannot be altered by any endeavour of ours, and in consequence of the failure of the late Crop of Hay in the Northern part of the Country, and unfortunately in those parts where the public Mails must unavoidably pass, the great scarcity of Hay, and of course the encreased price of that Article, and also of Horse Corn, renders it totally impossible for the Contractors (who in ordinary seasons have scarcely any profit from the employment) to carry on the business without an additional allowance. It is my firm belief, that unless some consideration be given, the Mails cannot be conveyed in any other way than by Expresses, at triple the expence I have proposed.

I find upon comparing my last Report to you upon the subject with a similar one in 1800, that the price of Hay is a trifle lower than it was in that year, and the price of Corn is also lower; but the season is not yet far advanced, and I only recommend one penny per mile of addition (instead of two pence which was given at that period for 123 miles) – to make 5d p. mile, under which I am convinced no man can at present undertake it with safety.

At the end of one year the former temporary addition was reduced, and I trust if Their Lordships The Postmaster General are pleased to consent to the addition now proposed, that it will not be found necessary to continue it for such a length of time.

With regard to the Comparative Value of labour both of Man and Horse in the North of Scotland and in England, I must confess myself a very inadequate judge. Few Horses are bred in the North of Scotland, and in consequence of the late augmentations of every description of the Cavalry force of the Country, Horses are become so scarce that it is impossible for a poor Mail Contractor to purchase a Horse at less than double the former value. It may be proper to observe, that Horses of the strongest kind are necessary upon the Road I have mentioned, in consequence of the great weight of the Mail, which contains the correspondence of the whole Country North of Aberdeen, with a very great number of Newspapers and the different publick Acts of the Legislature, so that this Road must be considered as very different from any of the Cross Roads, either in England or Scotland.

As to the Expence of the Riders, nothing seems to be claimed upon that score, although the Country North of Aberdeen is perhaps more than any other part of the Kingdom, drained of every description of young Men who are now serving in defence of their King and Country; which renders it extremely difficult to get either Post Riders, or farm Servants, at any wages.

I enclose some Letters which I have received from the Country, and I beg that they may be transmitted to Mr Freeling. They will give him some idea of the different prices of Horse provender, of which as yet it is very difficult to make any average, as those Articles seem to be upon the rise, and it is my opinion, that unless the present Contractors are closed with on the terms I have mentioned they will rise in their demands.

The addition proposed of one penny p. mile for 168 miles, will amount to about £63 p. Quarter, but as I stated in my last Report, other stages may be found entitled to the like addition. This is a considerable sum, but the pressure of the times renders it absolutely necessary.

I always am

Dear Sir, Your faithful and obedient servant

'James Shearer' *Surveyor*

to Robert Trotter Esq[r.]

Deputy Postmaster Gen[l.]

p.s. Neither the proposed addition in retrospect (*sic*) shall be given to any Contractor unless the absolute necessity of their situation requires it. 'j.s.'

Appendix IX. Post 40/29 m/1809

Letter from James Shearer, Surveyor, to Post Master General, Scotland.

General Post Office
Edinburgh Decr. 1808

My Lord,

I beg to return the Memorial from Mr Charles Grant Member of Parliament for Inverness to the Lords of his Majesty's Treasury, praying to have a Mail Coach Established betwixt Perth and Inverness, by Dunkeld & Blair in Athole.

After having been repeatedly on that line of Road, both in summer and winter, and after collecting every information from the Inhabitants of the District through which the Mail Coach is proposed to Travel, I am clearly of opinion, that in the present state of the Roads and Trade of that Country, a Mail Coach, however desirable such an Establishment would be, cannot be carried into effect nor be supported by any extent of Travelling to be expected betwixt Edinburgh and the North of that Route. There are other very strong obstacles to such an Establishment arising from situation and Climate, which it would be very difficult to overcome, but from the great consideration given to the Highlands of Scotland by Government, in time these difficulties may disappear.

The Road from Blair in Athole to Inverness, is extremely high and mountanous, and with the exception of that part of it betwixt the Bridge of Spey and Aviemore, a distance of about 20 miles, very barren and of course thinly Inhabited. The Roads in their present state are certainly not calculated for a Mail Coach, being both very steep and narrow; I may say it is quite impracticable to attempt a regular Mail Coach upon them even in summer, but in winter impossible, from the great quantity of snow that falls in that Country and continues untill a late period of spring, which not only puts a stop to travelling with Carriages, but for months is difficult on horseback. This, with the want of proper Inns whose possessors could afford to keep sufficient strength of horses, and the insecurity of going many miles through these mountains, out of the reach or sight of a human habitation, renders travelling upon some parts of the Road dangerous by any mode; But Carriages are entirely out of the question, nor would people venture to go at the risk of their lives by such a conveyance in the winter months.

From the unproductive state of that part of the Country, the articles of Corn, Hay and Straw are not to be had in that abundance that an Innkeeper upon that Road could from the various profits of a Mail Coach afford to lay in the quantity necessary for so many horses as he would require to carry on the business properly. A man with a stage of 13 miles would constantly require to have from 6 to 8 Horses, and on some stages 10 Horses. More Horses must be kept at each Stage of this Road than upon ordinary Roads, because if a Horse falls lame or meets with any accident, his place cannot be supplied so readily from the plough as in a cultivated Country. This of itself is a disadvantage, and when we take into the account that all these Horses will for many weeks during a deep snow in winter be constantly in the Stable eating Corn and hay without earning a sixpence, I should humbly apprehend few Contractors could be found so hardy as to undertake such a concern.

Altho' there is certainly a considerable number of Travellers upon that Road, particularly in the summer time, yet I fear they would not be much felt was there a daily Mail Coach Established betwixt Inverness and Perth. If it is practicable, however, to put a Mail Coach upon the Road, and possible to keep that Road open in winter, Travelling might encrease, and the concern prove more productive, but it will require time to bring that about.

Affording travelling accommodation of that nature to the Country must always be considered a secondry object with the Post Office. Our business in the first place is to attend to the interest and security of the public correspondence and Revenue of the Country, and when the accommodation of Travellers falls in with that object, it is most desireable. Should a Mail Coach ever be established betwixt Perth and Inverness with any security of permanency and safety to correspondence, the Touns of Inverness and the Country to the north, would save nearly a day in receiving and answering their Letters, a most desireable improvement certainly. But to get at this object we cannot command impossibilities; and to recommend a Mail Coach upon the Road in question, in its present state, or to propose sending the great Mail to Inverness and the northward by that Route, would be the last thing I should think of. I should be deceiving the public, and endangering its correspondence, if I were to propose so extravagant a measure. Altho' the northern correspondence is not so rapidly conveyed by the present Route by Aberdeen as we could wish, yet it may be counted upon to a few hours, and improvements in the mode of conveyance being now under consideration, will if adopted, still make it more expeditious and safe. I am fully persuaded that from the narrowness and inequality of the present Road from Dunkeld to Inverness, a thousand men would not keep it clear of snow in the Winter, so as to secure the regular Conveyance of a Mail by a Carriage.

With regard to the extent of the Trade and correspondence of the Toun of Inverness, together with all the Touns and Counties said to be so much benefited by such an Establishment, some idea may be formed of these, when I state, that the annual Revenue of the whole is under £6000. It is not perhaps an object to observe, that by the Establishment of a Mail Coach upon that Road, this Revenue instead of being increased would be very considerably diminished. If the measure was practicable this would I dare say be no obstacle.

From the papers I now return, having been sent by the Lords of his Majesty's Treasury for your Lordships Report, it is perhaps intended to do something in this business beyond what the strict regulations of the post office warrants me in recommending, and as Parliament has voted very considerable sums to be laid out in the Improvement of the Highlands of Scotland, by making the Caledonian Canal and various Roads in different parts of the Country, sacrificing a small sum of money in order to expedite the Conveyance of Letters by Post, seems very naturally to be connected with these Improvements, and if that should be the intention of the Lords of the Treasury, I would with much deference propose, what I consider an experiment worth trying.

To Establish a Diligence or Chaise betwixt Perth and Inverness three times a week, to carry three inside passengers and one outside, and any Bags of Letters for places upon the Road betwixt Perth and Inverness. That such a Diligence or Chaise should commence running in the beginning of April or as soon as the Snow is pretty well disolved on the Hills, and continue to run as long as the Storms of Snow in the autumn or winter permit; that as soon as the Roads are impassible for a Carriage, the Contractors should be taken bound to carry forward such Mails as it is judged safe to intrust them with, on Horseback, untill the following spring when the Diligence might be resumed. In this view of the matter It would be right to have a Contract for three years as it might happen that after dropping the Carriage in autumn they might neglect to resume it in the spring. – In order to encourage the Contractors to do the duty properly, I consider it but fair that the post office should allow them a sum of money, probably £200 p. annum, as the Revenue would save the greatest part of that sum by having some byeposts reduced in consequence of such an arrangement. And as it appears impossible in the present state of the Roads that the Diligence could run above eight months in the year with safety or certainty, I beg to suggest, the propriety of exempting it from duty. It would be no great object to Government, and would be the means of nursing the Institution into something of an Establishment that might in time, pay duty daily. The exemption I would humbly propose to continue for three years, the term of the Contract.

I consider such an arrangement as of little or no importance to the post office, but as the Gentlemen in the Northern Touns and Counties are uncommonly anxious to have such an Establishment, if the Lords of the Treasury and Their Lordships the Post Master General, are pleased to approve of the experiment, I shall have great satisfaction in carrying their intention into effect.

I have the honor to be

My Lord, Your faithful & obed[t] Servant

'James Shearer' *Surveyor*

to The Right Honb[le]

Lord Gray

Post Master General for Scotland

Appendix X. Post 40/237/1824

Letter from Charles Reeves, Surveyor, to the Secretary of the Post Office in Scotland

Edinburgh 1 May 1824.

Sir,

Connected with my report of this date on the subject of the West Highland posts I beg to state that the Postmaster of Arrochar has signified his intention of resigning.

As this office only produces £50–0–8 gross Revenue, and the amount of the Edinburgh Correspondence is only £7. 8. 10, I propose to make it a Sub Office on Luss, and reduce the Salary from £10 to £5 per Ann., thus diminishing the business along this line, precluding the necessity of a stop, and affording equal Accommodation to the Country.

As a saving of £5 per Ann. will thus be effected, I am induced to bring forward a case for the humane consideration of the Postmaster General, which has been sometime lying by, and repeatedly pressed by Mr Downie M.P. for Appin, and the other Residents of that part of the Highlands.

The Runner between Bonaw and Appin, a distance of 12 miles, has to cross two ferries, frequently dangerous, and to walk the rest of the distance through Glensalloch (or the dirty glen) the wildest path in the Highlands – so much so, that although the other road is 6 miles round and liable to great delay from the breadth of the ferries (which are crossed by the Runner at the narrowest part) I scarcely met with any Highland gentlemen who had ever been through it, the path being along a stream swelling over it on a fall of rain, which is here abundant.

(I can attest the difficulty of this path from personal inspection, having traversed it during a slight storm).

The Runner performs this stage *during the night*; and the difficulties he has to encounter during winter must be very great.

His pay is 9s. a week only, the same as is paid for a similar stage along the high road.

The present individual, his father *and Mother*, have performed this Journey with the Mails for above 25 years with zeal and astonishing regularity, and if the Postmaster General should be pleased to devote the sum of £5 to be reduced from the Salary of the Office at Arrochar to encrease the pay of this stage.

I think it would be received as a mark of recognition of long and faithful performance of a most laborious duty, and have a good effect in the Service in general.

    I am, Sir,
       Your obedient Servant,
       'Chas. F. Reeves'
to Augs. Godby, Esq.)

Appendix XI. Post 40/237/1824

Letter from Charles Reeves, Surveyor, to the Secretary of the
    Post Office in Scotland

                      Edinburgh 1   May 1824.

Sir,

The Contractor between Inverara and Arrochar having failed, after destroying all his horses, and no offer having been received for a fresh Contract, excepting at an enormous encrease of pay, I proceeded along the line to Inverara, for the purpose of making such Arrangements as might appear requisite.

    The difficulty of the mountainous road of Glencroe appears to have deterred any individual from undertaking the Ride after the failure of the late Contractor, and even those who had made offers at an encrease of £30 beyond the present Allowance of £150 drew back.

    Under these Circumstances, being unwilling to place this line at the caprice of any Individual, and not considering the difference of speed of sufficient importance to warrant a large encrease of pay, I have endeavoured to make the best possible Arrangement for the conveyance of the Mails, without entailing additional expence on the Revenue, and I beg leave to submit the details for the Consideration of the Postmaster General.

    The late Contract was for a Ride between Arrochar & Inverara 23 miles at £150 per Ann.

    I have contracted for a Ride between Inverara and Cairndow, 9 miles, at £65 per Ann. and have extended the present Ride between Luss and Arrochar nearly two miles to the head of Loch Long, at an encrease of £13 per Ann. being the greatest distance our limited time would allow – a return to Glasgow being requisite to catch the London Mail.

    This leaves the distance between Cairndow and Loch Longhead, (12 miles), to be provided for by footrunners; and includes the whole of Glencroe, & the mountain of 'Rest and be Thankful', probably the most difficult and laborious stage in the Kingdom. I have contracted for the conveyance of the Mails along this stage on foot at one guinea per week or £54. 12 p. Ann.

The loss of time may be about one hour and a half, supposing the time of the former Contract by horses had been adhered to, but in fact such were the natural obstacles, that I expect we shall neary be as regular as formerly.

The only part of the Country at which the delay will be felt, is beyond Appin: and with the view of remedying this, I propose that the pay of the Runner between Appin and Ballichulish, on which stage there are no ferries, shall be augmented from £23. 8 to £40 per Ann. on condition of his keeping a poney, and performing the stage of 13 miles in 3 instead of 4½ hours, as at present; and this will place that district, including Fort William, in the same situation as if the Ride over Glencroe could have been maintained.

A Receiving house at Loch Longhead will be requisite to exchange the Mails; and I have engaged a respectable Individual to inspect this at £1. 1. per Ann.

The late & proposed Arrangements are here contrasted.

Late		*Proposed*	
Contract between Inverara and Arrochar	}£150	Ride between Inverara & Cairndow	£65
		Foot Runner over Glencroe	£54. 12.
		Addition to Luss Ride	£13. —
		Receiving House at Loch Longhead —	£ 1. 1.
* Ballichulish		Addition to Runner between Appin &* Bonaw —	£16. 12.
			£150. 5.

being an encrease of five shillings p. Ann.

In result, very nearly the same Accommodation will be afforded to the Western Highlands as if a Ride were maintained over Glencroe at a heavy additional expence; and from the experiences of the last twelve months, during which such Ride was tried almost as an experiment, I believe that we shall secure more *regularity* over this mountain by employing runners, than by a horsepost; and I submit the foregoing as the best Arrangement the circumstances of the Country will permit.

    I have the honor to be, Sir,

        Your most obed^{t.} Servt.'

        'Chas. F. Reeves'

to Aug^s. Godby Esqr.

Important Dates in Scottish Postal History

1531/41   Various payments by Lord High Treasurer to official
          messengers recorded.

1592   Early reference to 'Post' at Dumfries.

1595   Aberdeen has a Common Post.

1603   Union of the Crowns and establishment of postal stages
          between Berwick and Edinburgh.

1616   Sir William Seton's plans for improved 'posting' system.

1635   Charles I establishes first public post for Britain.
          Withering's plan for reorganisation of English Posts.

c.1639/60   Edinburgh, Glasgow and other towns have Burgh Posts.

1642   First reference to posts to Portpatrick.

c.1650   Unofficial foot post between Edinburgh and Aberdeen.

1654   Franking started in England.

c.1662   First postal rates fixed for Scotland.

1663   Foot post between Edinburgh and Glasgow.

1669   Foot post between Edinburgh and Inverness via Aberdeen.

1674   Post between Aberdeen and Edinburgh taken over by Post
          Office.
          Ogilby's Road Survey in England.

1680   *Dockwra's Penny Post in London area.*

1695   Scots Act of Parliament fixes new postal rates.

1708   Total number of Post Offices in Scotland believed to be 34.

1711   Postal Act for United Kingdom establishes British Post
          Office.

1715   Horse Post between Edinburgh and Stirling.
          About 60 Post Offices in Scotland.
          First Postal Surveyors appointed in England.

1715/18   Temporary Horse post between Inverness and Perth
          established for Army use.

1717   Horse post established between Edinburgh and Glasgow.
          Post between Glasgow and Inveraray about this time.

1741   Post Towns in Scotland reported as over 100.

c.1750   General Introduction of horse posts and service by relays
          on main postal routes.

1756   Post Office established at Stornoway.
          First posts to Skye about this time.

1760   First Postal Surveyor (Kerr) appointed for Scotland.

c.1763   Postal arrangements for Shetland get official support.

1765   Penny Posts authorised for any Town or City.

1773   Peter Williamson's private Penny Post in Edinburgh.

1774   Court decision upholds right of free delivery in all Post
          Towns in United Kingdom.

1784   *Palmer starts Mail Coaches in England – exempt from tolls.*

1786   Mail Coach started between London and Edinburgh.

1786/1818   Francis Ronaldson Postal Surveyor in Scotland.

1788	Mail Coach between Edinburgh and Glasgow established.
	Mail Coach between London and Glasgow established.
1793	Post Office takes over Williamson's Penny Post.
	Daily Post established between Aberdeen and Inverness.
	Direct post established between Stirling and Perth.
1794	Limitation of Penny Post areas abolished.
1795	Franking privileges granted to serving soldiers.
1797	*Francis Freeling becomes Secretary to the Post Office.*
1797/1812	Progressive rise in postal rates.
1798	Mail Coach established between Edinburgh and Aberdeen.
	Daily Mail Coach between Edinburgh and Glasgow by Linlithgow.
1799/1837	James Shearer Postal Surveyor in Scotland.
1800	Penny Post established in Glasgow.
1802	Post established between Dingwall and Ullapool.
1803	Work started on Highland Roads and Bridges and Caledonian Canal.
1808	Post Office decision to use Penny Posts for villages throughout United Kingdom.
1811	Daily Mail coach between Aberdeen and Inverness.
1813	Mail Coaches in Scotland become liable for tolls.
1819	Mail Coach established between Inverness and Thurso.
1823	Over 250 Post Towns in Scotland.
1825/35	Rapid growth of free delivery in Scottish towns and villages.
1829	The Moray Floods.
1832	Cholera Epidemic in Scotland disorganizes Posts.
1836	Daily Mail Coach between Edinburgh and Inverness via Blair Athol and Dunkeld.
	Death of Francis Freeling.
1837	Mounting criticism of Post Office by Wallace, Rowland Hill and Others.
1840	Uniform Penny Postage introduced throughout the United Kingdom.

Deputy Postmasters General, Scotland

1711–1715   George Main(e)
1715–1718   James Anderson
1718–1725   Sir John Inglis
1725–1740   Archibald Douglas
1740–1742   James Colhoun (sic)
1742–1745   Sir John Inglis
1745–1764   Alexander Hamilton
1764–1795   Robert Oliphant
1795–c.1800   Thomas Elder
c.1800–1802   William Robertson
1802–1807   Robert Trotter
1807–1810   Lord Francis Gray
1811–1823   Lord Caithness
1823–1831   Sir David Wedderburn

Secretaries to the Post Office in Scotland

c.1742–c.1753   Alexander Bennet
c.1753–c.1789   William Jackson
1789–1822   William Kerr
1822–1831   Augustus Godby
1831–1842   Sir Edward Lees

Bibliography. Manuscript Sources

National Library of Scotland, Edinburgh
  Papers of James Anderson. Adv. M S 29.1.2. (vii)
  Journal of Francis Ronaldson. Acc. 3239.
Scottish Record Office, Edinburgh
  Com. Argyll Testaments. Register of Testaments, Commissariot of Argyll.
  Com. Brechin Testaments. Register of Testaments, Commissariot of Brechin.
  E.26/11. Exchequer Papers, Volume of Treasury Accounts, 1667–82.
  E.28/71. Exchequer Papers, Vouchers of Treasury Accounts, Charity.
  E.89/13. Exchequer Papers, Post Office Accounts and Papers, Copy contract
                      appointing keepers of the letter-office in
                      Aberdeen, 1690.
  E.89/15. Exchequer Papers, ditto, Extract registered contract renouncing
                      Aberdeen postmastership, 1693.
  E.208/2/1. Exchequer Papers, Pipe Office, Declared Accounts, Tacksman of
                      the letter post, 29 Sep. 1704–15 May 1707.
  G D 1/2. Gifts and Deposits, Loch Etive Trading Company Records.
  G D 46. Gifts and Deposits, Seaforth Muniments.
  G D 51. Gifts and Deposits, Melville Castle Muniments.
  G D 72. Gifts and Deposits, Hay of Park Papers.
  P S 1/75. Register of the Privy Seal, Old Series, Vol. 75.
  RH 2/8/17. Photostat Copy, Register of Protections, Sanctuary of
    Holyroodhouse, 1686–1789.
  RH 9/18. Papers of David Ross
    (formerly Register House Miscellaneous Papers, Bundle 235).
Record Office, G P O Headquarters, London
  Post 1 Financial. Treasury Letter Books 1686–1931
    Post 1/4 Indexed letter book Jan. 1706–Apr. 1712
    Post 1/6   „   „   „   Apr. 1715–July 1723
  Post 3. Financial Annual Accounts 1678–1850
    Post 3/5 Annual accounts Apr. 1710–March 1720
  Post 9 Financial. Accounts, various 1715–1874
    This class comprises a miscellaneous collection of account books
    covering a wide variety of subjects
    Post 9/7 Monthly account book, with quarterly and annual abstracts,
    1798–99
  Post 10 Inland Mails; Organisation. Road 1786–1934
    Post 10/14 Time Bills of Scottish mail coach services 1798–1835
  Post 14 Inland Mails: Organisation. Inland Offices 1757–1946
    Post 14/335 Reports from District Surveyors to Deputy Postmaster
    General, Scotland, 1795–1801
  Post 15 Inland Mails: Organisation. Letter Books 1784–1937
    Post 15/125–153 Copies of letters exchanged between Edinburgh and
    London 1789–1829
  Post 24 Inland Mails: Services, Newspaper Post 1791–1892
    Post 24/1–15 Correspondence about newspaper privilege of the Clerks of
    the Roads and the Foreign Post Office 1791–1832
  Post 30 Postmaster General's Minutes: Documents 1794–1920
    Post 30/England 474 K/1814: Toll duties in Scotland.

Post 35 Postmaster General's Minutes: Volumes 1794–1920
Post 40 Postmaster General's Reports: Documents 1791–1841
Post 42 Postmaster General's Reports: Volumes 1790–1841
Post 58 Staff: Nominations and Appointments 1756–1948
    One volume, entitled 'Orders 1737–1774' contains copies of Orders of
    the Board of the Post Office 1737–74
Post 94 Letter and Account Books of Col. Roger Whitley, Deputy PMG
    1672–77
Post 96 Papers of John Palmer, Surveyor and Comptroller of the Mails
    1786–92
    Post 96/15 Papers entitled 'Postal Matters': various, 'Part III' 1775–98

Bibliography. Official Publications

Acts of the Parliament of Scotland. 2nd revised edition. London, 1966.
Highland Roads & Bridges, Reports of the Commissioners for. 1803–60.
Post Office Revenue (Scotland) 20th Report of Commission of Enquiry 1830.
Privy Council of Scotland, Register of the: 1st, 2nd & 3rd series. 1545–1689.
    Edinburgh, 1877–1967.
Lord Treasurer of Scotland, Accounts of. 1473–1566. 11 vols. Edinburgh,
    1877–1916.
Royal Commission on Historical Manuscripts.

Bibliography. Books

Aberdeen Council Letters. Transcribed and edited by Louise B. Taylor.
    6 vols. London, 1942–61.
Argyll Estate Instructions: Mull, Morven, Tiree, 1771–1805.
    Edited by E. R. Cregeen. Edinburgh, 1964. (Scottish History Society,
    4th series, vol. 1.)
Barron, James. *The Northern Highlands in the 19th Century*. Newspaper
    index and annals. Vols. 1–3. Inverness, 1903–13.
Boswell, James. *The Ominous Years, 1774–6*. Edited by C. Ryskamp and
    F. A. Pottle. London, 1963.
Braid, F. *The Postal History of Old Glasgow, from the earliest times till the
    introduction of Penny Postage*. Glasgow, 1903.
Bryant, Sir Arthur. *The Age of Elegance, 1812–1822*. London, 1950.
Campbell, John, Baron Campbell. *Life of John, Lord Campbell, Lord High
    Chancellor of Great Britain*. Edited by his daughter. 2 vols. London, 1881.
Chambers, Robert. *Domestic Annals of Scotland*. Edinburgh, 1858–61.
Chambers, Robert. *Minor Antiquities of Edinburgh*. Edinburgh, 1833.
Chambers, Robert. *Traditions of Edinburgh*. London, 1869.
Cockburn, Henry, Lord Cockburn. *Circuit Journeys*. Edinburgh, 1889.
Cockburn, Henry, Lord Cockburn. *Memorials of his Times*. New edition.
    Edinburgh, 1909.
Corrie, John M. *The Dumfries Post Office, 1642–1910*. Dumfries, 1912.
Dickinson, W. Croft. *Two Students at St Andrews, 1711–1716*. Edited from
    the Delvine Papers. Edinburgh, 1952.

Dunbar, E.D. *Social Life in Former Days, chiefly in the province of Moray.* Edinburgh, 1865–66.

Ellis, Kenneth. *The Post Office in the Eighteenth Century*, Oxford, 1958.

Extracts from the Records of the Burgh of Edinburgh, A.D 1528–1557. Scottish Burgh Records Society: Edinburgh, 1871.

Farrugia, Jean Y. *The Letter Box. A History of Post Office Pillar and Wall Boxes.* Centaur Press, 1969.

Graham, H.G. *The Social Life of Scotland in the 18th Century.* London, 1901.

Haldane, A.R.B. *The Drove Roads of Scotland.* London, 1952.

Haldane, A.R.B. *New Ways through the Glens.* London, 1962.

Hamilton, Henry. *The Industrial Revolution in Scotland.* Oxford, 1932.

Hay, A.Penrose. *Post Office Recollections.* Inverness, 1885.

Hyde, J.W. *The Royal Mail, its curiosities and romance.* 3rd edition. London 1889.

Joyce, Herbert. *The History of the Post Office from its establishment down to 1836.* London, 1893.

Jusserand, J.A.A.J. *English Wayfaring Life in the Middle Ages.* Translated from the French by Lucy Toulmin Smith. 4th edition. London, 1950.

Kay, F.G. *The Royal Mail. The story of the posts in England from the time of Edward IVth to the present day.* London, 1951.

Kay, John. *A series of original portraits and caricature etchings.* 2 vols. Edinburgh, 1837–38.

Kennedy, William. *Annals of Aberdeen, from the reign of King William the Lion to the end of the year 1818.* 2 vols. London, 1818.

Lang, T.B. *An Historical Summary of the Post Office in Scotland.* Edinburgh, 1856.

Lauder, Sir Thomas Dick. *An Account of the great Floods of August 1829 in the province of Moray, and adjoining districts.* Edinburgh, 1830.

Lockhart, J.Gibson. *The Life of Sir Walter Scott.* Abridged. Edinburgh, 1871.

McCombie, William. *Cattle & Cattle Breeders.* Edinburgh, 1867.

Macpherson, David. *Annals of Commerce, Manufactures, Fisheries and Navigation.* 4 vols. London, 1805.

Morison, Stanley. *The History of The Times.* Edited by S.Morison. 4 vols. (in 5). London, 1935–52.

Partington, Wilfred. *Sir Walter's Post-Bag.* London, 1932.

The Post Office: an historical summary. London, 1911.

Robinson, J.Howard. *The British Post Office. A history.* Princeton N.J., 1948.

Robinson, J.Howard. *Britain's Post Office. A history.* London 1953.

Records of the Convention of the Royal Burghs of Scotland, 1295–1779. Edinburgh.

Scott, Sir Walter. *Familiar Letters.* Edinburgh, 1894.

Sinclair, Sir John. *The Statistical Account of Scotland.* 21 vols. Edinburgh, 1791–99.

The New Statistical Account of Scotland. 15 vols. Edinburgh, 1845.

Somerville, Thomas. *My Own Life & Times 1741–1814.* Edinburgh, 1861.

Trollope, Anthony. *An Autobiography.* World's Classics. Oxford University Press.

Walker, John. *Economical History of the Hebrides and Highlands of Scotland.* 2 vols. London, 1812.

Woodforde, James. *The Diary of a Country Parson, 1758–1802.* World's Classics. Oxford University Press.

Youngson, A.J. *The Making of Classical Edinburgh, 1750–1840.* Edinburgh, 1966.

Bibliography. Articles and Pamphlets

Brodlie George. *On the Fringes of Fame.* VII. Peter Williamson – adventurer and inventor. In *The Scots Magazine*, vol. 30, 1938.

Foxall & Spofford. *Monarchs of all they Surveyed.* Stationery Office, 1952.

Mercer, Sir Walter. Peter Williamson's Penny Post. In *Postal History Society Bulletin*, 1949.

Noble, John. *Miscellanea Invernessiana.* Stirling, 1902.

Smout, T.C. The Glasgow Merchant Community in the 17th Century. In *Scottish Historical Review*, vol. XLVII, 1968, pp. 53–71.

Taylor, William. The King's Mails 1603–25. In *Scottish Historical Review*, vol. XLII, 1963.

Welsh, A.N. Ayrshire Postal History. In *Postal History Society Bulletin*, no. 106.